£4.
96

1811

Using the
Social Sciences

Using the Social Sciences

Albert Cherns

Professor of Social Sciences,
University of Loughborough

Routledge & Kegan Paul
London, Boston and Henley

First published in 1979
by Routledge & Kegan Paul Ltd
39 Store Street, London WC1E 7 DD,
Broadway House, Newtown Road,
Henley-on-Thames, Oxon RG9 1EN and
9 Park Street, Boston, Mass. 02108, USA
Phototypeset in V.I.P. Times by
Western Printing Services Ltd, Bristol
and printed in Great Britain by
Lowe & Brydone Printers Ltd
Thetford, Norfolk

British Library Cataloguing in Publication Data

Cherns, Albert Bernard
Using the social sciences
1 Policy sciences – Addresses, essays, lectures
2 Social sciences – Addresses, essays, lectures
I Title
300'.8   H61   78–40917

ISBN 0 7100 0091 X

To Tommy Wilson

Contents

Acknowledgments

The author and publishers are grateful for permission to quote from the following:

'Putting psychology to work', *Occupational Psychology*, vol. 41, nos 2 and 3, 1967, pp. 77–84.

'The use of the social sciences', *Human Relations*, vol. 21, no. 4, November 1968, pp. 313–25.

'Social research and its diffusion', *Human Relations*, vol. 22, no. 3, 1969, pp. 209–18.

'Social science and policy', *The Sociological Review Monograph*, no. 16, September 1970. Also published in *Social Science and Government*, Cherns, Sinclair, Jenkins (eds), Tavistock, 1972.

'Relations between research institutions and users of research', *International Social Science Journal*, vol. 22, no. 2, 1970.

'Models for the use of research', *Human Relations*, vol. 25, no. 1, 1972, pp. 25–33.

'Negotiating the contract', in *Access Casebook*, Colin Brown, Pierre Guillet de Monthoux, and Arthur McCullough (eds), THS Co., Stockholm, 1976: Case No. 30.

'Behavioural science engagements: taxonomy and dynamics', *Human Relations*, vol. 29, no. 10, October 1976, pp. 905–10.

'The principles of sociotechnical design', *Human Relations*, vol. 29, no. 8, August 1976, pp. 783–92.

'Social science organization and policy: review for policy-makers', UNESCO, Mouton, Paris, 1974.

'Social science policy', introductory chapter to *Social Science and Government*, Cherns, Sinclair, Jenkins (eds), Tavistock, 1972.

'Organized social science research in Great Britain: parts I and II', *Social Science Information*, vol. 2 no. 1, March and July 1963, pp. 66–81 and 113–26.

'Problems facing the SSRC of Britain in its first year of existence', *Social Science Information*, vol. 6, no. 1, February, pp. 199–205.

'Social sciences in Britain', prepared for SSRC, abridged in 'The Development and Structure of Social Science Research in Britain', Cherns and Perry in *Demands for Social Knowledge*, Elisabeth Crawford and Norman Perry (eds), Sage Publications, 1976, pp. 61–89.

'On economics and social sciences in Britain', *Révue Économique*, vol. 26, no. 6, November 1975, pp. 1024–55.

'Applied sociology', chapter in *Sociology: An Outline for the Intending Student*, G. Duncan Mitchell (ed.), Routledge & Kegan Paul, 1970, pp. 160–99.

'The use of the useful', *SSRC Newsletter*, nos. 1 and 3, November 1967 and May 1968, pp. 12–17 and 24–30.

'Social science research in India', with A. Shonfield, Occasional Monograph no. 3, Indian Council of Social Science Research.

'Social science organization and policy', UNESCO, Mouton, Paris, 1974.

'The utilization of social science research in industry', chapter in *Social Science Research and Industry*, Wilson, Mitchell and Cherns (eds), Harrap, 1971.

'The social setting of ergonomic problems', *Ergonomics*, vol. 5, no. 1, January 1962, p. 175.

'Personnel management and the social sciences', *Personnel Review*, vol. 1, no. 2, 1972, pp. 4–11.

'Can behavioral scientists help managers improve their organizations?' Reprinted, by permission of the publisher, from *Organizational Dynamics*, Winter 1973, © 1973 by AMACOM, a division of American Management Associations. All rights reserved.

'Organizational behaviour', chapter in *Encyclopaedic Handbook of Medical Psychology*, Stephen Krauss (ed.), Butterworth, 1976, pp. 356–8.

'Social change and social values', *Indian Journal of Social and Economic Studies*, vol. 5, no. 1, 1977, pp. 83–100.

'Perspectives on the quality of working life', *Journal of Occupational Psychology*, vol. 48, no. 3, September, 1975, pp. 155–67.

'Work or life', Presidential Address to the British Association for the Advancement of Science (Sociology Section); and chapter in

Theories of Alienation, R. Felix Geyer and David R. Schweitzer (eds), Martinus Nijhoff, Leiden, 1976, pp. 227–44.

'Social change and work', *Personal Goals and Work Design*, P. Warr (ed.), Wiley, 1976, pp. 1–22.

'Social engineering in Britain', chapter in *Sociotechnics*, A. B. Cherns and R. Sinclair (eds) Malaby Press, 1976.

'Social psychology and development', *Bulletin* of the British Psychological Society, vol. 22, 1969, pp. 93–7.

'Political science, public administration and the problem of population', paper presented at UNESCO Workshop on Population Law, Paris, February 1974, and published in *Readings on Population for Law Students*, UNESCO, 1977.

'Traditional values and modern organizations in developing countries – the prospects of technology', *Indian Journal of Social and Economic Studies*, vol. 4, no. 2, September 1976, pp. 275–88.

'The uneasy partnership: social science and the federal government in the twentieth century', by Gene M. Lyons, Basic Books, London, 1971 – review published in *The Sociological Review*, vol. 19, no. 3, August 1971.

Preface

When in 1967 I first proposed a book on the uses of the social sciences to RKP, I had in mind something very different from what it has developed into. After experience in applied research and in research administration, I had been awarded a generous fellowship by the Nuffield Foundation to study the uses being made of the social sciences in Australia, Ghana, India, Israel and the United States. I collected an enormous amount of material in the form of published papers, pamphlets, unpublished documents and literally hundreds of interviews, which I proposed to organize, analyse and from which I intended to generalize – all against the background of my previous experience, especially my secretaryship of the government's Heyworth Committee on Social Studies.

But the more I reviewed what I had learned, the less I felt able to provide a product which matched my tidy schema. I found myself writing and publishing papers which dealt with a mass of themes all connected with the utilization of the social sciences. Some were concerned with the organization of the social sciences, some with issues of utilization and diffusion of social science research and knowledge, and some concerned with the questions of government policy towards the social sciences. In each I drew on my data, but each time from a different perspective. Sometimes I would be writing from the point of view of a director of research concerned that his work should be both scientifically respectable and usable. At other times I would be taking the perspective of a government concerned with the allocation of resources to the social sciences and faced with competing claims. As time went by the number of such papers grew but with occasional revivals my optimism shrank. Some of my papers were reviews for specific purposes at the instance of UNESCO and other bodies such as the SSRC and the Indian Council for Social Science Research, and the synoptic sometimes generates a false optimism perhaps because one does not, or at any rate I do not, enjoy the role of destructive critic or the bearer of bad news.

Also, as time passed, RKP remained so patient and I so ashamed that I winced at their letterheads. When I discovered that in one paper or another I had effectively covered virtually all the issues I originally intended my book to discuss, I suggested, and RKP agreed, that my original plan should be replaced with one based on my published papers. In fact, it is probably somewhat presumptuous of me to have used the word 'developed' in my first sentence. I find that my ideas and understanding go on developing and the long delay that has occurred since I started could easily continue indefinitely as each time I write an occasional paper I feel that what I have put in it should be included. But a stop has to be made somewhere and there are good reasons for stopping now. The ambitions and expectations for greater use of social science knowledge and research in tackling social and economic problems which helped to fuel the enormously rapid growth of the resources devoted to the social sciences have become distinctly more modest: the experience of the 1970s has caused us to re-evaluate the contribution that the social sciences make and the forms that contribution should take in the future. Now is a good time to review what I have said and written on the topic over the last decade.

How would I describe the book now? There is one linking theme: what can the social sciences usefully say about problems and policies and how is that affected by the way in which they are organized? That theme could be tackled in many ways and the examples and illustrations drawn from many fields. When I write about research in military settings (as most of what I have written on that topic remains classified there is very little in this book), or about research in industry, I write about fields in which I myself have worked; I can only discuss research into education or health or housing, for example, at secondhand, and so try to confine myself to questions of their organization and application, topics of which I have some personal knowledge. Again, when I write about the organization and use of social science in developing countries, it is as one who has discussed and researched these issues in developing countries, but I have myself engaged in no applied research of my own to speak of.

Thus I cannot treat all topics in the same way, and this created a problem of how the book should be organized. Many of the papers I have written concern both organizational issues and substantive research issues. Some concern utilization in general with reference to one or more particular areas of utilizations; others are concerned specifically with one area such as industry or development. What we have tried to do is to bring together the general questions of organization, of utilization in Part 1, devoting other parts to the more specific issues of utilizing social science in industry, military matters, development and so on. I hope that we have been able to do this without too much repetition and without fracturing the theme of each paper. It has meant surgery – bringing parts of some papers together, so that on occasion part of an original paper appears in one section and another part in another.

The task of collating and editing more than forty papers, some very long, some mercifully short, and removing the worst overlaps falls to my colleague over many years, Ruth Sinclair, with whom I had already edited two books. To her editing skills are owed the successful completion of the project and any continuity it exhibits. I cannot thank her enough. None is in precisely the form in which it was first published, but a list of them is attached with acknowledgments to their publishers. Nor can I fully express my debt to Mrs Ann Tanner, my secretary, who has typed and retyped these pages and read them, some many times, always with critical care, pointing out on many occasions the corrections required for them to make sense.

I owe thanks to the Nuffield Foundation for their generosity and to my university for allowing me to accept their award. Many of these papers were given at meetings or conferences, often abroad, which represent time away from the university. I have received nothing but support from my colleagues, despite my many absences. My thanks are also due to RKP for their extraordinary patience.

Part I

Social Science Policy: The Development, Organization and Utilization of the Social Sciences

Section I
Social Science Policy

Chapter 1
Social Science Policy

Introduction

Is it possible to give a precise meaning to the term 'social science policy'? It certainly gives rise to a good deal of confusion because it has to do duty for three separate but interrelated concepts:
(a) policy for developing the social sciences;
(b) policy for the organization of research and teaching in the social sciences; and
(c) policy for using the social sciences.

(a) *Policy for developing the social sciences*

Any policy oriented towards developing the social sciences rests upon a number of presuppositions which need to be stated. Further, the notion of a policy for the social sciences assumes that scientific endeavour can be planned and directed. This assumption rests on experience gained in the management of research in the natural sciences, and must be translated to the social sciences with care.

A policy for developing the social sciences implies the adoption of strategies: a strategy for determining how much and what kind of research is needed to develop the sciences themselves; a strategy for determining the resources available at present in terms both of finance and of manpower; what they should be in the future and how they should be allocated among disciplines or fields of interest; and a strategy for estimating the achievements of the sciences.

Whether explicit or not, claims made by social scientists for

3

resources carry implications about the potential use to which social science is to be put. Our answers to questions of 'should' inevitably rest upon our systems of values, and claims imply values of some kind. For example, suppose we take the extreme position that the social sciences *should be* supported for their own sake and not for any contribution they may have the power to make towards solving problems. Such a claim rests upon the *value* of adding to knowledge or to the education of citizens. Apart from the fact that there is no explicit basis in such a claim for preferring social science to art to sport or poetry in allocating resources, there is an appeal to a (presumably shared) value system which considers pure knowledge as desirable and worthy of receiving support at the expense of some other activity. The unvoiced utility expectation is that the study of sociology or economics develops the intellect as poetry does our sensibilities and sport does our bodies.

(b) *Policy for the organization of research and teaching in the social sciences*

Here the presuppositions are that the patterns of organization of research and the institutional mixes of research, teaching and application affect the outcome in terms of the quantity and quality of research that is produced. In order to develop such policies we require knowledge of types of organizations and their effects. For example, we need to know what are the effects of carrying out particular kinds of study in universities, independent institutes or in government establishments. Finally, such a policy requires us to have a strategy for organizational building and development, and requires a knowledge of the factors affecting these.

(c) *Policy for using the social sciences*

Social science disciplines and methods are relevant to a number of policy fields: for instance, in government for the development and evaluation of social policy, and educational policy, policy for science and technology, etc.

Policy for using the social sciences in all these fields requires that we have strategies for up-grading the capabilities of organizations for using the social sciences, and requires, furthermore, that we have strategies for building in criteria for evaluating programmes of applied social science research.

4

Pre-history

The pre-history of social science policy, like that of science policy, antedates the arbitrary divisions of these and other branches of knowledge. Bacon distinguished between 'science' and 'arts', considering the former as knowledge and the latter as the use of knowledge, warning against 'the over-ready and pre-emptory reduction of knowledge into arts and methods; from which time commonly sciences receive small or no argumentation' (Bacon, 1938).

Bacon also proposed a model for the organization of science in *The New Atlantis*. Within this organization he posited roles with regard to the collection and collation of information, the design and execution of new experiments, and the utilization of knowledge from these to design yet further experiments and to formulate comprehensive and wide-ranging theory. In addition he identified the need for specialists to carry out these tasks. But, of course, the systematic use of the natural sciences in the service of the state was not to take place for a long time, and a similar development in the social sciences is just beginning.

The first modern example of such a systematic attempt is the effort by President Hoover to mobilize the social sciences to attack the social problems (Lyons, 1969). In 1929 he set up a President's Research Committee on Social Trends with the remit

to examine and to report upon recent social trends in the United States with a view to providing such a review as might supply a basis for the formulation of large national policies looking to the next phase in the nation's development.

The 1960s saw the publication of three further American reports on how the social sciences were organized financially and how they could be better employed by the government and others (US House of Representatives, 1967; National Academy of Sciences, 1968; National Science Foundation, 1969).

The documents which best illustrate the approach Britain has made since the war to social science policy are the report of the Clapham Committee (1946), the report of the British Academy (1961) and the report of the Heyworth Committee (1965). Emphasis on the potential use of social science research has grown with each of these succeeding publications, as has the awareness of the need for some sort of policy for social sciences.

5

As a result of this latter report, the Social Science Research Council was established in 1966 with the following functions:
1 to provide support for research in the social sciences;
2 to keep under review the state of research in the social sciences;
3 to advise the government on the needs of social science research;
4 to keep under review the supply of trained research workers and to contribute resources towards this training;
5 to give special consideration to the application of research in the social sciences and to the dissemination of information about research projected and completed;
6 to give advice to the users of research (government, industry, etc.).

The question we may ask is: How far does this machinery satisfy the needs for implementing a social science policy? The powers given to the SSRC, even if exercised, do not cover all aspects of social science policy.

Universities and other research institutes are still free to develop without consideration of the paths followed by others; there is no machinery to relate the needs of industry for social science research to either the provision of researchers or practitioners.

Recent influences

The most recent developments which have raised interest in social science policy have been the simultaneous growth of two pressures upon governments. The first has been the growth of expectations about the utilization of the social sciences in dealing with social and economic problems; the second has been the growth in the budgeting and manpower demands made by the social sciences. These two strands – policy for using the social sciences and policy for developing the social sciences – have become inseparable. One cannot sensibly talk about the amount of resources which *should be* devoted to the social sciences without raising the question of what the social sciences are *for*.

Together with these two general influences are four more specific factors. First is the virtually universal adoption of some form of economic planning or regulation. Economists have been associated in some way or another and to some degree with most governments for several decades. Second is the tentative growth of 'social planning' and the discovery that economic planning may be frustrated in its absence. Associated with this discovery is the belief that sociologists, psychologists, political scientists and anthropologists may be possessed of skills which can be harnessed to the achievement of desired developments. Third is the successful use of social science methods in election forecasting, opinion polling and market research of all kinds. Governments have found themselves using social science practitioners and their methodology more and more systematically. Fourth is the growing popularity of the social sciences among students which creates problems of demands on resources and the increasing output of social science graduates from universities raises questions about employment and careers.

Relationship to science policy

Another of the major stimuli to the discussion of social science policy has been the development and growth on a national and international scale of science policy. The demands upon national resources now made by science, especially big science, are such that no government can ignore, and have made the adoption of science policy indispensable at the same time that it exposed the weakness of the framework for policy determination in scientifically the strongest countries.

Many of the sciences have associated with them highly powerful technologies. Although a policy for technology does not necessarily imply a policy for science, the increasing need to foresee future technological developments, to hasten some and to channel others emphasize for governments the advantages of a policy for the sciences themselves (for further discussion of science and technology policies, see Chapter 25). It would be pointless to deny a certain band-waggon effect. But even without this, the question of a social science policy was bound to follow in the wake of science policy. For one thing, although the claims the social sciences make on national resources are nowhere near as important as those of the natural sciences, they are no longer negligible; and although their associated technologies are puny compared with those associated with the natural sciences, their potential contribution is seductive. Also their inherent tendency to grow is obvious and the need for a planned response to these demands becomes equally obvious. To the evident parallels between science policy and social science policy-making we need to add a consideration to their interrelationship.

In the first place the organizational development of the social sciences has not only paralleled, but has also to some extent been modelled on, organizational forms devised for the natural sciences. A notable example of this is the organization of research training.

7

When it comes to application, it is not always fully appreciated that, while the application of natural sciences generally takes place through the medium of technology, the utilization of the social sciences takes place through the medium of concepts. Organizational and institutional devices appropriate to furthering the interactions between science and technology may be quite inappropriate for furthering the diffusion of concepts from science to practice and from practice to science.

An outcome has been the inclination of governments and administrators to perceive the social sciences as essentially little brothers of the natural sciences, bound to follow in their footsteps but stumbling because of their infancy. This conception may have done a good deal of damage and should again put us on our guard against assuming too readily that what is good for the natural sciences is necessarily good for the social sciences.

The second respect in which science policy is related to social science has regard to the shifting boundary between the natural and social science disciplines. The boundaries of disciplines are, of course, not immutable: part of the process of development of a discipline is, in fact, the advancing of its boundaries, sometimes at the expense of, or encroachment upon, the territory formerly claimed by other disciplines. Thus we have comparatively recently witnessed repeated crossings of the boundaries between the physical and the life sciences and the recent emergence of biophysics. The boundaries between physiology and psychology have long been hazy; psychopharmacology has grown in this borderland. Likewise, the boundaries between psychology and various engineering disciplines have become the territory of ergonomists. More recently still the development of general systems theory has been the umbrella under which shelter trading of concepts and methods has taken place among engineering, the life and the social sciences.

Closely allied to this development is the coming together of social scientists and other scientists on problems which cannot be resolved by the exercise of one expertise alone. A good example is the current concern with the environment. Biologists, sociologists, engineers, economists, psychologists, political scientists are all being brought into the attempts to assess the state of, and changes in, the environment and its effects on social life and human life chances. In one particular aspect, the built environment, psychologists, sociologists, economists and engineers and architects have been learning to work together. This not only binds social and other scientists together in a way which requires the modification of institutional forms to accommodate their joint endeavours; they are themselves critical issues in science policy.

8

Lastly, the social sciences along with the natural sciences form the most rapidly growing of all industries – the knowledge industry. The same problems of information storage and retrieval face both. Governments are bound to evolve policies for this industry and these could, without adequate analysis of the specific needs and problems of utilization of the social sciences, take the form of a maladaptive application of the principles of science policy.

We must foresee a growing interest in the social sciences on the part of organs, both national and international, whose primary mission is science policy. Our consideration of what is and what is not desirable, what is and what is not practicable will have to comprehend this development.

In this light we need to look closely at the organs of social science policy which exist or are coming into existence. We note that where research councils are the preferred method for the natural sciences, social science research councils with broadly similar remits have been, or are being, created. Where national academies of science serve as science policy-making bodies, divisions or sections of social sciences exist within them. To a considerable extent, then, social science policies are being created in the image of science policies whether this is truly appropriate or not. We must consider the question of whether the problems are truly similar, or whether the existence of a particular method has pre-empted the evolution of other methods by its very existence and in the absence of any critical examination of its aptness.

Clearly there is no single correct way of organizing and developing social science: each country must find its own way, one which matches its needs and traditions, its problems and its resources. In Section V we will look at the social sciences in a selection of other countries.

There are, however, certain minimum conditions without which a social science policy cannot be implemented. There has to be at least a recognizable degree of 'institutionalization' of social science as an activity. By institutionalization, following Ben David (1971), we mean:

1 that the social sciences are accepted in society as an important social function valued for their own sake; and
2 that social scientists' behaviour is governed by norms consistent with the aims of the social sciences and with their autonomy.

Neither of these conditions implies that there can be no unorganized social science or no social scientists who challenge the norms of autonomy of social science. But clearly if these conditions did not hold generally it would be difficult for social scientists to communi-

9

cate on a scientific basis and unlikely that social resources would be put at their disposal.

A certain degree of 'professionalization' is also required, i.e. some mechanism providing a 'licence to practise', identifying those whose activities are regarded as 'social science'.

Without this 'institutionalization', allocation of resources could only take place on a personal client basis which could hardly be seriously discussed as policy.

These prerequisites are not met in all social sciences in all countries and policy-making is clearly defective in these cases.

Characteristics of the social sciences

We would anticipate less convergence among the social science policies of different countries than among their science policies because:

(i) Social sciences are differently defined in different countries. These differences reflect real differences among societies and their cultural, historical, educational, social and political traditions.

(ii) The functions of the social sciences differ from society to society. Underlying the classification that is adopted in any particular country is a theory of an ideology about the nature of society and about the *functions* of the disciplines. The way the disciplines are defined and classified mirrors society's way of regarding itself and much can be deduced about the nature of a society from the classifications in vogue in it.

(iii) The utilization of knowledge derived from the natural sciences is mediated by technologies which also come within the scope of science policy. The utilization of the knowledge derived from the social sciences is mediated through a network of political and institutional frameworks which do not themselves come within the scope of social science policy. Thus the institutional pattern into which a social science policy has to fit is more variable than that into which a science policy has to fit.

The content of the issues which will be regarded in any particular society as sociological or political or philosophical or psychological depends to a considerable extent on the ideological presuppositions of that society. To make an easy point, the 'problem' of poverty may present itself as a theological or a sociological or an economic problem, depending both on prior beliefs about the 'meaning' of poverty and on the state of knowledge. So long as poverty was

10

believed to be divinely decreed, the problem was to determine its purpose. On the other hand, the existence in the hands of governments of comparatively sophisticated means of influencing economic activity, compared with the much cruder means available to it of producing changes in social attitudes and actions have inclined them to perceive poverty primarily in economic terms and only when economic development has still left a stubborn core of distress has the problem come to be perceived in more sociological terms. Thus the state of knowledge, the tools available and the terms in which problems are perceived are inextricably intertwined: the content of any of the social sciences cannot be sensibly regarded as having definitive meaning outside its social context.

To understand the development of the social sciences in any society we need to chart the worldwide developments within the social sciences themselves against the history of the society's educational, political and cultural institutions. In every country the principal sector within which the social sciences have their roots is the higher education sector. That is not to say that the main sector of activity in the social sciences today is necessarily that of higher education. In some countries indeed the centre of gravity of research has moved outside the universities and the higher education sector altogether. However, the state of the higher education sector by itself is an inadequate guide to the state of the social sciences. We need to know how that state has been arrived at; what are the dynamics of its development. Where, for example, the system of higher education began to expand rapidly at a time when a given social science was already established elsewhere, that social science has experienced the same kind of pattern of supply and demand as other established disciplines. Where, however, higher education expanded before that discipline was established, it may only now be experiencing growth arising from student demand without necessarily providing any corresponding career outlets for them when trained.

Other aspects may also be important. For instance, in countries where the status of women is fairly high but not equal to men's, women are more likely to enter the social sciences. And they form a substantial proportion of the available research manpower. If higher education is equally available to women as to men, this situation provides a dynamic for the expansion of social science teaching and research, which is lacking where the status of women is low and their access to higher education restricted, and also where women have equal status with men and are not inhibited by social and cultural considerations from entering the sciences and technologies.

11

The social sciences should not be treated as homogeneous. Indeed, the relative status positions of the social science disciplines is a mirror of the society in much the same way as the status of the social sciences vis-à-vis the sciences and the humanities is a reflection of a society's value system. The higher status enjoyed by economics over other social sciences is often attributed by economists to their superior success in handling the material of their discipline, to their ability to quantify and to apply mathematical treatment to their data, and hence possess a greater claim to the status of 'science'. Furthermore, they can point to greater success in predictions and in application. These claims may even be true. But the status of their discipline owes more to the fact that economic values rank above most social values in modern societies. A society which ranks psychology above sociology is likely to be one which places higher value on the individual and his problems than on social aggregates and their problems. The thesis here is that it is the perception of the need rather than proven competence which determines the prestige in which the discipline is held.

This also shows the importance of a policy for the social sciences *as a whole*, rather than separate policies for the separate social sciences. Academic organization and the dynamics of the growth and development of disciplines tend to emphasize the differences among different disciplines, but real-life social problems do not fall neatly into disciplinary divisions.

Fortunately, the realization that what appears to be 'economic' problems are not solvable in economic terms is spreading. As Gunnar Myrdal (1968) put it, economists are 'naively innocent of their own social determinants. This unawareness is reflected in their separation of economic from non-economic factors. . . .' Sir Alex Cairncross (1969), chief economic adviser to the British government, said, even more bluntly, 'There are no economic problems, only problems.'

Government policy and social science resources

One of the substantive problems for all governments is to ensure that adequate resources are available for the development of the social sciences. Governments, through their educational policy, influence, where they do not control, the supply of social scientists trained in each of the disciplines. Governments are also major users of social science, major employers of social scientists. By their own urgency, by the steps they take to see that their own needs are met, they can easily introduce distortions which may later frustrate their own purposes. The more centralized the society, the greater the danger. In a very pluralistic society it is difficult for any one source of pressure – even government – to dominate the scene. Where government exercises a virtual monopoly either of demand or of supply or both it may satisfy one need at the expense of another – often the satisfied need is the short-term one. Governments and other users have a *direct* interest in the utilization of social science and therefore an indirect interest in the development of the social sciences themselves. Only the social scientists have a *direct* interest in the development of the sciences. However, governments need to preserve a number of delicate balances. A balance in this sense is needed between one discipline and another; between supply and demand of trained practitioners and research workers; between teaching and research; between development of the disciplines and their use; between disciplinary and interdisciplinary research. The mechanisms for achieving these balances, even if in principle all could be simultaneously optimized, are lacking.

In many countries research is fleeing, or has already fled, the universities. Entry into higher education is controlled by the institutions of higher education themselves. Student demand is essentially reflected in provision for the discipline concerned. During periods of rapid growth in demand for a discipline, the teaching resources required to meet it can be found at the expense of the resources of people and time available for research. If this situation continues and if the ambitions of university professors can be met only through the expansion of their teaching departments, the outcome tends to be the flight of research from the university.

Any financial squeeze on universities squeezes research. Research needed by government now has to be done outside the universities. Government establishes research units inside government with the inevitable concomitant bureaucratic organization of research.

Another factor which affects the distribution of research effort is the fact that policy-oriented research is frequently interdisciplinary. But university teaching departments tend to be difficult environments for interdisciplinary research. Thus the major portion tends to be carried out in research institutes, either attached to universities, or independent, or government-sponsored.

Furthermore, our studies lead to the conclusion that the balance between the demands of teaching and research, disciplinary and interdisciplinary research, research and utilization is closely related to the balance of forces responsible for expansion. If the main engine of the system is the demand from a growing body of potential students, the balance will be tilted away both from research and

13

from utilization. If, however, the dynamic is provided by government's demand for social science inputs to its planning and other programmes, the balance will be struck at a different point.

Almost everywhere the social sciences have grown in attractiveness to students and grown faster than the rate at which teaching cadres could expand. The newer and weaker the discipline the worse the problem, which becomes even more acute at the postgraduate research-training level. And rapid expansion of cadres may push into university teaching appointments people who themselves have had little opportunity for acquiring a thorough training in research methods. Much training in research is conducted outside the universities or at any rate outside university teaching departments. But conducting research training in research institutes further depresses the standards of the disciplines within the universities. Moreover, it has often proved difficult, particularly in the social sciences, to arrange for experience in research institutes to be regarded as contributing towards the requirements for postgraduate degrees. A considerable defect is the requirement that the doctoral thesis or its equivalent should represent the original work of the candidate. Furthermore, he is encouraged to work within the confines of one discipline. This artificially circumscribes both the problem and the methodology the student can tackle. For many researchers the real training they receive in research takes place after their postgraduate work is over. As a substantial proportion of the research that is done in universities takes the form of doctoral theses, it tends to load the dice on the side of the single discipline. No neat solution is to be expected; the higher education sector after all serves other purposes than science or problem-solving. We should, therefore, expect the answer to these problems of balance to be in the form of a range of scientific and educational institutions providing different mixes of training, teaching, research and service, with more flexibility in careers and in the award of higher degrees.

Careers and employment of social science graduates

Graduates with qualifications in the social sciences do not all enter occupations in which these qualifications are directly used. Indeed for three reasons it is highly desirable that social science graduates should be diffused through a very wide range of occupations. First, those trained in social science can understand and criticize society from a scientific basis without the fear of losing their employment. Second, the concepts generated by social science research can only be used by those able to understand them – thus some familiarity with social science concepts should be as widely diffused as possible. Third, the alternative is dangerous: we cannot afford to surround professional social scientists with an aura of mystery and the practice of arcane arts. Thus there is no reason to be concerned with matching career opportunities precisely with training facilities.

On the other hand, as some forms of specialist advanced training are expensive and make demands on scarce resources, they are bound to be career-oriented. Further, the absence of careers for graduates is always a source of social unrest; an army of unemployed social science graduates could be the most explosive of all. While it is highly desirable that social scientists should move in and out of various posts within and outside government, universities and other sectors, all governments will feel it desirable that some careers in research should be available.

But careers appear to be most difficult to plan. If people are free to choose their occupation, to move freely from job to job, sector to sector, then some sort of market mechanism will determine their movements. The market can be influenced, and in centrally planned and controlled economies government may be virtually the sole employer; but even here a considerable degree of autonomy is possessed by the various institutions in the public sector.

A full career pattern in research is found where research is principally outside the universities. Most researchers in universities are either occupying primarily university teaching posts or are oriented towards such posts for their future careers.

The linkage between the system of higher education and the world of employment, the occupational system, differentiates among the social sciences themselves. In most countries the economics student can see a direct connection between his discipline and his future occupation. Psychology provides professional outlets in many countries. But few countries have professional careers on a large scale for sociologists. Students of sociology may be seeking an education for their own intellectual development, or perceive their future role as contributing to the growth of their society within its present framework, or else help, through their special knowledge and understanding, to change the present framework of society.

Many students of political science have a political career in mind, although comparatively few will actually make a career of politics. Many more enter journalism, the Civil Service and other occupations. Government's policies for the social sciences are bound to take into account the distinction between the professionalized

15

social sciences such as psychology, and to a lesser extent economics, and the non-professionalized sciences such as sociology and political science.

Organization and financing of research

Finance

Any attempt to establish the scale of financial support for social science research encounters serious problems:

(i) However carefully we attempt to distinguish 'research' from other activities, there is a large 'grey' area. Work done within an organization predominantly devoted to research tends to be classified as research; if conducted in another type of organization it is classified differently. Thus a great deal depends on the way in which research is organized. Every country appears, at least to some extent, to perceive expenditure on social and economic research in the context of its overall scientific R & D effort. Where the bulk of the research is carried out in universities, this context is not altogether appropriate and indeed the separation of R & D from education becomes a matter of guesswork. The distribution among fields of activity is equally imprecise.

(ii) Cost conventions differ so much from one country to another that estimates of expenditure on research provide meaningless comparisons. Concentrating on manpower as an alternative is not satisfactory either. It makes sense only if we want to compare the skilled resource input into research. But there is no virtue in increasing input unless that is the best way to increase output. And outputs of scientists in low-cost systems are not necessarily the same as those in high-cost systems. Lacking infrastructure and skilled assistance output may be lower by a substantial factor.

(iii) Underestimation of certain costs: in the last two decades there has been a general tendency for expenditures in the social sciences to rise faster than those in other sciences. Partly this is a function of their late start, partly an artefact of measurement.

Any government programme has its expenditure counted in full. Other sources are usually less fully known. Thus in any institution where government sources are overwhelmingly the most abundant the statistics are reasonably accurate. Where there is a substantial proportion of non-government funding and where, in particular, there is a large number of small such sources the figures tend to be underestimated.

Thus in most countries nobody knows what is spent on social science research, let alone whether this expenditure is rationally distributed.

Organization

Any attempt to relate social science research to policy and particularly government policy needs to do more than provide a channel whereby needs are communicated to researchers, funds are provided for the research and an arrangement is made for communicating the results of research. It needs to ensure that there is an adequate range of institutions capable of carrying out the appropriate kinds of research and that the nature of the output from such institutions should be understood.

In all countries a substantial proportion of social science research is conducted by governments in government departments and agencies. Research of this kind is the hardest to define; much of it is probably fact-collecting, a great deal consists of using well-established methods derived from the social sciences to tackle problems of economic forecasting, market research and so on. Another large proportion of government 'research' is akin to development work in the natural sciences; for example, development of methods, curricula, etc. in education. Some is evaluative – operational research aimed at evaluating the effectiveness of existing government programmes. Little of it is devoted to developing the social science disciplines themselves. This last is the area which is normally left to universities, though specialized institutes set up by governments may carry out some basic research of this kind. Thus, unless governments are prepared to share their facilities with others, the only recourse left for these sectors is to engage in short-term projects financed at universities, or to hire short-term research workers for specific projects. Sometimes governments are prepared to share the facilities of specialized institutes set up by them or under their auspices. This device could probably be made more use of. Much government research could doubtless not easily be made public, but most governments err on the side of excessive secrecy in these matters. If as much research as possible were conducted in specialized institutes of this kind, instead of within government departments, this would encourage wider publication.

Government and other users need to learn to distinguish not only the different types of research base, but also the different types of

17

research appropriate to them. The potentialities of utilization and the nature of the relationship between the organization conducting the research and the organization or system being investigated differ profoundly from one type of research to another. Some of the disappointment that 'applied' research is not applied and some of the fears that applied research implies loss of academic virginity and virtue are due to the failure to distinguish among these types of research. When it comes (a) to constructing an appropriate system of research institutions and (b) to deciding in which institution a given research should be conducted, these distinctions are vital (see Chapters 8 and 9).

Research and policy

It is clear that the problems of articulation between research and policy take different forms in different countries. For example, what happens to a research report? How do the scientists and policy-makers relate to one another? It is quite likely that one cannot see such mechanisms in action because often they do not operate as formally laid out. Most things happen behind the scenes and are then brought out and decked out on the formal structure.

Very little information is available about the ways in which what is generated by social science research and advice is put to use. While numerous organizations such as government departments have appointed advisory committees or councils of social scientists to recommend to them the social science research they should undertake or sponsor, few, if any, have asked their committee to examine their capability to use the research. Nor have such committees pressed this issue themselves either because they have not regarded it as within their province or, more culpably, because they are themselves totally unaware of the need. Too few social scientists have served on both sides of the utilization fence; if more were to do so, we could expect a higher level of sophistication and understanding of the problems.

Implications for a social science policy

It is inevitable that a social science policy must be concerned with the supply and demand of social scientists, with the scale of provision for research and with research standards, with the use as well as the generation of research. As we have discussed earlier, this implies at least a minimum degree of consensus that social science can and should be used.

Nevertheless, many social scientists seem reluctant to examine this and adopt an ambiguous attitude towards the question of the use of social science. There are several reasons for this. First, there is the proper humility of the scientist, unwilling to make claims he fears he will be unable to redeem. Second, the social scientist cannot simultaneously claim support on the grounds of the usefulness of his work to the aims of government and arrogate to himself the choice of what work he will do; thus he fears loss of his freedom to pursue his own chosen line of research. Third, he mistrusts decision-makers to make the use he would wish of his work. Fourth, his position of 'critic' of society is weakened by his acceptance of the ends to which his contribution may be put. If the social sciences are not to be 'used' to further societal aims (or if society as such can have no 'aims'), then there is no rational basis upon which a government can determine what resources should be devoted to which social sciences and in what way.

Eminence in research or teaching in a social science does not *ipso facto* equip a person with the knowledge needed to advise governments or other organizations on their social science policy. Some knowledge of a critically relevant nature is possessed by others perhaps themselves less eminent; some vital knowledge just does not exist. The former problem can be resolved by a suitable mix of experience in an advisory body; the latter cannot, and can be dealt with only by more study. Among the topics needing more research are:

  (a) the dynamics of development of the social sciences;
  (b) the effects of applying social science knowledge and research; and
  (c) the policy process itself.

(a) *The dynamics of development of the social sciences*

What are the appropriate institutional frameworks for maximizing the advance of knowledge in the social sciences? It is usually tacitly assumed that this advance is in the good hands of university departments and a few research institutes, but this is too simple a notion. The most effective activity mix for different purposes is a matter for study and planning. Institution building is an essential aspect of social science policy: we are only just beginning to learn something systematic about its nature and process.

19

(b) *The effects of applying social science knowledge and research*

As social scientists we know a good deal about social and organizational change. Certainly we know enough to warn us that these are diachronic processes and that any before/after comparison entails arbitrary divisions of time. We need to establish the necessary indicators early enough for a reliable pre-change series of readings to be obtained. But this is only conceivable where a relatively long-term engagement of social scientists with the institution concerned has been established. Just because these conditions are so infrequently met we have few reliable studies of the effects of application. Here the policy and the need for adequate knowledge on which to base the policy are intertwined. First, we must have the policy of long-term engagement; then we can have knowledge about the effects of applying social science; finally, we can use that knowledge to recommend policy.

(c) *The policy process itself*

This usefully illustrates the essentially serial nature of policy-making and brings us to the third point: knowledge about the policy process itself. The role of the social scientist in policy-making about research and its utilization is a continual one, taking different forms at different points in the process. We are still inadequately informed about the process, and without more substantive knowledge we cannot plan the most effective intervention into it. This raises fundamental questions about the points of leverage in a system. Where will intervention be likely to have the most effect?

Inevitably one finds discussion of policy focusing on the actions of governments and government agencies. The very notion of a social science policy presupposes the existence of a single decision-making body whose decisions are or can be effective – in a word that somebody is in control. We need occasionally, perhaps frequently, to be reminded that many organizations and many individuals are taking decisions about matters within their province which are, or imply, policy decisions about the social sciences. When a university senate votes to increase the enrolments of students of economics or to create a chair in sociology, or to reject a proposal for a postgraduate course in social ecology, it is taking decisions which affect the social science capability of that university and also of the wider community. When the trustees of a powerful foundation vote to commit resources to the study of race relations or to terminate its programme for the study of educationally backward children, they are taking possibly quite far-reaching decisions both about social science capability and social science utilizing capabilities. When I decide to devote some thought and effort to the question of social science policy, I am, hopefully, taking a decision which may have some eventual impact on the making of social science policy.

We are left with the question whether policy-making is possible at all. What is wrong after all with leaving the developments of disciplines to individual choices within a market framework and leaving the development of policy-oriented research completely to the market, on the assumption that the market would demand the sort of research which it would be able to use? Among the many snags with this strategy, or lack of strategy, is the fact that the efficient operation of market affairs presupposes something like a free market and that a free market is what we do not have. Second, individual choices tend to be made without adequate knowledge of the choices being made by others; the kind of information needed for rational choices, in other words, is often unavailable. This is true on the institutional scale; in Britain, the choices made by the individual universities are often made without adequate knowledge of the choices that are being made by other universities, and the choices made by the UGC are uncertain in their incidence and vary along the whole range from mandatory to merely suggestive. Furthermore, in a university the scale of research in a discipline is related to the size of the relevant department, and the size of the department is related to pressure for undergraduate teaching in that department. Thus we are faced with a situation in which the size of the research effort within the university discipline is largely determined by the preference of sixth-formers.

Nor could a policy of guidance by individual choice long survive the point at which these choices make heavy demands on real resources. Long before our little sciences became our big sciences, a pattern would begin to be imposed upon us and that pattern would tend to perpetuate the particular pattern of distribution of resources at the moment it was imposed. What this means is that you will tend to get a variant out of the range of existing policy-determining strategies of the economic 'squeeze' type; that is, existing institutional patterns are held to zero or very modest rates of increase, while new developments go to the back of the queue. All this does not argue that it is possible to develop a policy, just that it is essential to do so.

Not the least of the complications surrounding the issue of social science policy is that it is in some ways an arbitrary abstraction. There are comparatively few decisions which could be regarded as matters of social science policy and of no other kind of policy; a very considerable proportion of all social science policy issues, for example, the question of manpower, are also issues of educational policies. Similarly, decisions about the financing of social science research are part of overall government fiscal and monetary policy. When the system with which we are dealing appears so closely interrelated with other systems that we are obliged to direct our attention to a super-system embracing them, we need, as well as policies, policies about how policies should be made, what Dror (1972) has called 'meta-policies'.

The international nature of the social sciences

The most significant meta system is the international one. The knowledge industry knows no national boundaries. Policy decisions in the field of the social sciences that are made in one country very soon affect another, if only because international co-operation allows for the collection of comparative data and the exchange of information about research policy and organization in other countries. For example, we can look at the very general issue of research standards. Efforts to raise standards of research focus mainly on institutional provision. This is an area in which the sharing of experience among countries is valuable. What must be avoided is the inappropriate implantation of both problem and methodology which has been described in such terms as 'cultural colonialism'.

The supra-national character of the social science enterprise is not an attic storey superimposed on a complete building; it is a basic part of the structure and cannot be ignored in any effective national policy-making for the social sciences. In turn this places what amounts virtually to an obligation on international bodies concerned with the social sciences to evolve not only policies for their own social science activities but a meta policy for national social science policy-making. UNESCO, ISSC, and other international bodies which have concerned themselves with the social sciences, have long been interested in social science policy and have sponsored many conferences and studies to explore the many issues involved in social science policy and the problems facing its evolution. Further discussion on comparative social science policy is contained in Section V, Chapter 10.

Section II
The Organization of the Social Sciences in Britain

Chapter 2
The Organization of the Social Sciences in Britain

The origin of the disciplines: the disciplines and the universities

Our starting point is bound to be arbitrary. There is no single event which can be said to signal the beginning of social science in Britain. What we now describe as the social sciences have diverse origins and there is still a certain degree of ambiguity, on the part of many practitioners of the disciplines concerned, as to whether they are social scientists or not.

Although it is something of a simplification, it is not too far wrong to say that the social science disciplines have their intellectual origins in branches of philosophy and that their empirical research traditions derive from concern with practical administration. Philosophy in Britain (the Scottish tradition was quite different from, and often in advance of, the English) could be described as being concerned with methodological consideration – for example, meta-physics, ethics, mental philosophy or psychology, political social philosophy – although these were not discrete areas.

At different times politics and economics have both emerged from political philosophy although not uninfluenced by moral and social philosophies; psychology has struggled free of mental philo-sophy and sociology from social philosophy. But as everyone knows, sociology in Britain with its notable empirical flavour owes as much to the work of the practical reformers, Booth, Rowntree and the even earlier practical administrators such as Sir Edwin Chadwick. Anthropology, a discipline in which Britain has the longest and most robust tradition, owes its origins to the problems of administration of a worldwide empire. No philosophical origins dictated what were or were not legitimate 'problems' for anthropologists to tackle. Insofar as intellectual disciplines contributed at all these were more those of law and jurisprudence, linguistics and physical anthropology – a mixed bag which emphasized the great degree of autonomy anthropology had from older disciplinary origins.

These different 'subjects' crystallized into their contemporary disciplinary shape at different times and in different ways. To understand how they did so, we need to explore another issue. Intellectual disciplines are legitimated and sanctioned in Britain by the world of higher education. There are important exceptions to this generalization but these only marginally affect the social sciences. For example, a prestigious body such as the Royal Society, founded in the 1660s, played a greater part in the institutionalization of science than did the ancient universities. The professions, like medicine, possessed other sanctioning systems, although some or all of the training of neophytes took place in the universities. The tradition that new knowledge would be generated only within the universities or, if generated outside, would be legitimated by them, has grown more recently and is by no means inviolable in the face of prestigious government research laboratories and institutes. But the social sciences on the one hand lack this kind of professionalization and on the other came into significance when the universities were more strongly entrenched. The universities disdained the practical arts which developed into the engineering sciences; their sanctioning and the legitimation of engineering knowledge had to take place outside the universities until the attitude of the universities to them became a scandal and contributed to the founding of the civic ('provincial') universities in the last decades of the nineteenth century and the first decade of the twentieth century. These newer universities did not notably embrace the social sciences. These had neither the practical importance of engineering nor the prestige of the established disciplines. Furthermore, in so far as their subject matter was within the province of one or another variety of philosophy, they were already catered for. Had new technologies been associated with them, professional technological associations would have promoted them and the universities neglected them at the risk of losing sanctioning power over them. As it was when the Webbs, practical reforming socialists with a belief in the perfectibility of man and his system of government, wished to found an institution devoted to the sciences, which would promote the generation of new knowledge directed to these ends and which would attempt to train good government, they were obliged to do so largely outside the university framework. Hence, the London

School of Economics and Political Science, which was founded in 1895, was the first institution of higher education in Britain entirely devoted to the study of the social sciences. It has had no imitators; the British view of higher education is hostile to specialist institutions. While the LSE was somewhat more hospitable to new social science disciplines than were other universities and colleges, it is noteworthy that sociology, anthropology and psychology were all late-comers. None was among the foundation chairs. Sociology was introduced in 1904, anthropology in 1920. Social psychology was established as a subject within sociology and won its independence only in the 1960s.

The place of the social sciences in the new universities founded in the 1960s was vastly different. The ancient universities were autonomous bodies of scholars; their stipends were derived from endowments over which they exercised corporate control. They were responsible to nobody but themselves; they exercised a virtual monopoly over higher education and the schools (largely boys' grammar schools) adapted themselves to their demands. Under those circumstances the scope for new subjects was limited. Nor was the need for them greatly felt.

By the 1960s the picture had changed immeasurably. Secondary education was no longer the privilege of a minority; a whole new generation of schools had been founded, who no longer looked to the ancient foundations for their lead and expected indeed to send only the occasional pupil to them. The Victorian and post-Victorian universities accounted for some 80 per cent of the university student population in England and Wales (schools in Scotland were oriented towards the Scottish universities). The social science disciplines had become established and the interest in them by students was high and growing. New universities could make an impact most readily by fostering the social sciences, particularly sociology, the least well provided for in existing universities. It was comparatively easy for a new university quickly to establish a position in this field and to attract well qualified students. The popularity of sociology surprised almost everyone. The growth was rapid, too rapid. There are now probably as many students reading sociology in the universities as economics and far more than psychology. Social anthropology is still a very small discipline. Politics in a variety of forms is of similar size and often included in sociology or economics. Social administration has to satisfy professional as well as academic requirements and is offered at far fewer universities than the other social science disciplines.

Thus the growth and development of the social sciences in Britain has depended to a large extent on university practice and fashion.

When a period of university expansion has coincided with a growing interest in one or more of the social sciences, the disciplines concerned have expanded rapidly. The 'maturity' of the discipline at the crucial moment has not been a serious factor. Sociology was mature enough to be taught for decades before adequate university provision was made for it; psychology, with a longer history and a substantial body of knowledge, has grown far more slowly. It was ready for expansion at the wrong time – in the 1950s when favoured treatment went only to the natural sciences. Psychology departments at universities swung as far as they could into the scientific orbit, even becoming virtually branches of applied physiology in some places. But psychology was the hindmost in the natural sciences' queue. When it was the social sciences' turn a decade later, psychology was on the wrong foot and has limped behind the other social sciences. This illustrates neatly the Procrustean aspect of these groupings and definitions. For academic convenience, knowledge is divided into small chunks – disciplines – and herded together again in larger chunks – this time to suit administrative convenience. Whatever fits uneasily into one chunk or the other is handicapped.

In Britain the separation of the social sciences from their humanities' background in the universities is almost complete. Most universities now have faculties of social sciences alongside those of arts and science; and their systematic differentiation in statistics compiled by the Universities Grants Committee has accelerated this trend, as has, of course, the influence of the government's Social Science Research Council. But the status of the different disciplines is reflected in the values of the society; hence the superior status of economics as a 'science' owes more to the fact that economic values rank above most social values in modern societies. Medicine, too, owes its status less to its success in treating disease and prolonging life, great though these are, than to the high value placed upon health and longevity. It is predictable that in the United States, for example, which appears to be undergoing value changes emphasizing social problems, the status of the sociologist will rise vis-à-vis the psychologist and the economist. It is the perception of the need, rather than proven competence, which determines the prestige in which the discipline is held.

Influences outside the universities

What should by now be clear is that the 'social sciences' have not a common origin, background or history. They have come together comparatively recently in the universities, partly by accident, partly by design. Once labelled commonly they acquire a common fate and a sense of common identity. This feeling of common fate is enhanced by (a) gentle pressure from the UGC on universities to establish faculties of social science, e.g. by asking for comparable data on their social sciences' provision; and (b) the establishment of a Social Science Research Council, providing research money and acting as intermediary between social scientists and government. How far this sense of common identity goes is hard to say. Asked his occupation, a social scientist is far more likely to describe himself as an anthropologist, economist, political scientist, psychologist or sociologist than as a 'social scientist'. A British psychologist feels far more kinship with an American or even a Russian psychologist than with a British economist.

The implications of this are that the social sciences would not have been brought together by the activities of social scientists in universities; on the contrary, division by progressive differentiation is the typical response to the growth of knowledge and the special-ization and speculation of research techniques.

Why then has official action been directed towards coalescence? As soon as one wants to direct activity towards solving practical social problems one finds that they are not accessible to attack using the concepts and techniques of one discipline alone. Immediately the need for interdisciplinary or multidisciplinary research and for the training of people to undertake it is voiced. Thus mobilization for problem-solving is the engine of coalescence; growth and development of knowledge provide the motive power for differen-tiation. The stronger the leverage exercised by government, the greater the centripetal force; the more autonomous the academy, the greater the centrifugal force. Over the last few decades the control and influence exercised by government has grown, the autonomy of the universities has been weakened.

Thus far we have concentrated our attention on the universities for three reasons:

(a) because they have had a monopoly of teaching of undergraduates in the social sciences;

(b) because they have had a monopoly of postgraduate training; and

(c) because they defined what is valid knowledge.

But they have also been significant producers of research.

Their position is weakening in all these respects. The polytech-nics, directly under the control of the Department of Education and Science, have now large numbers of students reading for degrees in the social sciences awarded by the Council for National Academic

Awards (CNAA). They are also conducting, so far on a small scale, postgraduate training and the CNAA will award higher degrees. The SSRC, although its members are themselves mostly university professors, is an alternative legitimating authority; an activity supported by the SSRC does not need, but could inevitably acquire, legitimation by the universities. Moreover, the system of higher education is responsive to many pressures. For instance, employers may call for new knowledge and skills which are seen to be appropriately provided by universities, perhaps by the development of a new and partially vocationally oriented course. The traffic is two-way. The existence of people possessing a particular range of knowledge and skills influences the job market. Employers may create new jobs or demand the new qualifications for entry to jobs previously less defined in terms of a profession. Within the social sciences, personnel management is a good example.

Real world problems similarly influence the way disciplines emerge and develop. The recognition of a problem as being within the scope of the social sciences to tackle, either from within their own resources or in combination with associated disciplines, leads to the setting up of perhaps an ad hoc group of research workers. Both institutionally and through additions to knowledge this has eventual impact on the disciplines and their definition. Again the traffic is two-way: the existence of a recognized capability and the new knowledge result in problems being redefined and the new problems being recognized. Problems are formulated in terms of what is seen to be the discipline capable of tackling them.

Thus in general the universities are permeable to outside influence with the SSRC as spearhead.

Research facilities

As far as research is concerned, the amount carried out in the universities in still increasing, although far less rapidly than in the last decade. But a growing proportion is conducted outside the universities in research institutes, in the units set up by the SSRC itself, and in government and local authorities. The flight of research from the universities, such a marked feature of continental Europe, has not been paralleled in Britain. Probably the main reason for this is the 'staff–student ratio'. British universities enjoy a staffing ratio far more favourable than most countries, of the order of 8 or 9 students to 1 member of staff. They have thus been able to expand research at the same time as expanding the student intake, as a university teacher's duties include research, to which he is expected to devote one-third to one-half of his time.

Adding to this the fact that students apply to the universities to study the discipline of their choice, we arrive at the somewhat absurd conclusion that the distribution of research effort within the universities is the outcome of the fashion prevalent among school leavers. In fact, there are moderating influences, but the linkage is there. However, the attitude of government to the universities is hardening. Their combined financial demands are now large enough and salient enough to court control by their paymaster; they are no longer such elite institutions; they no longer exercise a monopoly; the staff–student ratio is threatened. It is predictable that as this ratio grows the proportion of research undertaken within the universities will decline. It may move to institutes attached to universities but separately financed and separately or jointly staffed, with some responsibility for postgraduate research training. This would keep the link with higher education while enabling government through the SSRC to exercise control over such issues as the concentration or dispersal of research effort, the avoidance or encouragement of duplication and so on. Models already exist, e.g. the SSRC's Industrial Relations Research Unit is at Warwick University and its Unit on Ethnic Relations is at Bristol University.

The research institutes

Government's own research is conducted partly by contract to universities, partly in its own in-house research units, and partly in the independent institutes, whose influence is stronger than their financial position. The foundation of these institutes is often a guide to the needs salient but unmet at the relevant time. The oldest is the National Institute for Industrial Psychology founded in 1921. At that time there were virtually no opportunities in the universities for research in that field, and between the wars it was responsible for substantial advances in selection and guidance. After World War II, with the growth of psychology departments in the universities with access to research money, it declined in attractiveness and was disbanded in 1975.

The Royal Institute of Public Administration, founded in 1922, is more interested in encouraging and promoting research than in conducting it under its own auspices. By this policy it has been highly successful in establishing the Local Government and Urban Planning Division of the Metra Consulting Group.

29

The most successful of the institutes founded between the wars were the Royal Institute of International Affairs (1926), Political and Economic Planning (1931) and the National Institute for Economic and Social Research (1938). Mass Observation, founded in 1937, failed to survive the war despite its greater popular impact. It is possible that its topics of study were essentially ephemeral. It was the first group to turn the methods of social anthropology on to the culture and subculture of its own country. At the very least it inspired countless undergraduate sociological exercises. The three surviving institutes had more stern and serious objectives. The RIIA was founded during the period of enthusiasm for the League of Nations 'to advance the sciences of international politics, economics and jurisprudence, and the study, classification and development of the literature on these subjects'. There was then no department of international relations in the universities; departments of politics and government had no research programmes and afforded no central or co-ordinating mechanism for focusing studies of international affairs. From the start it combined the roles of independent research institute and learned society, providing a forum for meetings, a library and publishing its own periodical, *International Affairs*. One is always tempted to apply the acid test to institutes which have survived from an earlier period – if it did not exist, would it need to be invented today? The RIIA would probably pass this test. There are now departments of international relations in several universities, and in others, departments of politics or centres for Asian studies and so forth, which work in the field of international organization. But most academic research is concerned more with the past than the future and is more diagnostic than predictive or prescriptive, so that the university system is inadequate for, or inappropriate to, policy-oriented research and to interprofessional activities. As policy issues are seldom resolvable through the approach of a single discipline, these two are closely related.

PEP was founded to promote and conduct research which would contribute to better planning and policy-making, particularly in government and industry and in the relations between them. In 1931 planning was the white hope for a better future and PEP was founded in the liberal reformist, practical utopian, but empirical tradition. Its mode of operation is deliberately *ad hoc*, gathering together the problem, the researchers, the finance and the steering group of interested parties for each new project, which is oriented towards publication. For the academic researcher it offers the advantage of expert assistance and a rapid substantial publication under auspices which virtually guarantee an audience of administrators and politicians as well as academics. Its flexibility of operation and its breadth of focus have ensured it a continuing though ever-changing role.

The NIESR, despite its title, has always been a predominantly economic research institute. It is less easy to see why it has survived, despite the high standing and respect in which it is held. Its work parallels closely the type of research conducted in university departments of economics and many of its research workers go on, or back, to university teaching appointments. It provides an opportunity for uninterrupted research which produces a critical mass of effort in the field of studies of the behaviour of the British economy. Its short-term forecasts have usually been more gloomy and, alas, more realistic than those of the Treasury. For this reason, if for no other, it would look bad if any government allowed the NIESR to die, but the role would probably be adopted by one of the leading university departments of economics or applied economics.

The post-war period saw the foundation of many more research institutes:

1945   National Foundation for Educational Research
1946   Tavistock Institute of Human Relations
1948   Acton Society Trust
1954   Institute of Community Studies
1958   Institute for Strategic Studies
         Institute of Race Relations
1959   Centre for Urban Studies
1960   Overseas Development Institute

NFER is the largest. While independent, its governing body includes representatives of local education authorities and government, from whom it obtains most of its finance. It is therefore less exposed than, say, the Tavistock Institute to the winds of economy that can sometimes blow fiercely around the unprotected institute. No doubt the price paid for independence is insecurity and no doubt this is accepted by those who choose independence. But the choice is not easy and the future sometimes looks rosier than it turns out to be. A lengthy period of continuous expansion, such as many organizations experienced during the early and middle 1960s, ill-prepared them for the present more stringent time, when expansion is impossible and retrenchment necessary. Institutions in whose continuance public authorities have a stake have assurance denied to the rest. Partly for this reason, more recently established institutes have tended to be founded with government support and to receive government funds on a programmatic rather than a project basis. Thus the Institute for Development Studies was set up at the University of Sussex in 1966 with funds from the Ministry of Over-

31

seas Development (now the Overseas Development Authority), the Centre for Environmental Studies began in 1967 with funds from the Ford Foundation and the Ministry of Housing and Local Government (now Department of the Environment).

The institutional scene in Britain is not, and could not be expected to be, tidy, predictable or easily comprehensible. It abounds with the unexpected, the contradictory. Institutions are established at different times under different circumstances and with different objectives. Some survive, some perish. But those which survive tend to acquire a landmark quality; their removal or demise would constitute a break with tradition, the loss of continuity as well as the scattering of an asset. In the last resort an appeal to government in one guise or another is usually successful. Today, when the threat is greater than at most times in the past, the cost of rescue is beyond the scope of most private charity. Foundations may want to help but shy from tying up their income in such a way as to reduce their ability to respond to new needs. Government, too, dislikes acquiring open-ended commitments. Some institutions possess a constituency by virtue of the programmatic or sectoral nature of their objectives. But the more broadly based the institute – for example, the Tavistock Institute – the more difficult it becomes for it to have any identifiable constituency. So in practice the Tavistock has become a clutch of institutes: some, such as the Institute of Marital Studies or the School of Family Psychiatry have identifiable (but not affluent) constituencies; others, the Centre for Applied Social Research or the Human Resources Centre for instance, have not. Where the nature of the science (as distinct from the research) provided is clear, as with the Institute for Operational Research, there may be no lack of funds. Thus there are external pressures, as well as the notorious difficulties of interdisciplinary or interprofessional activities, tending to force apart the components of the Tavistock Institute, a problem which is not shared by institutes with more closely defined territories.

Government and research

Government plays two distinct but related roles: those of sponsor and user of research. The role of sponsor can divide into initiative sponsorship and responsive sponsorship. As soon as one begins to consider the role of government one is confronted with the problem of defining 'research'. Traditionally a function of all governments, drawing upon some kind of social science knowledge and generating data of immense importance for social science research, the

32

decennial census is a good example of an activity we would nevertheless exclude from our definition of research. It is essentially a routine activity aimed at providing data for administrative purposes and using tried techniques. It provides source material for research but is not itself research. On the other hand, some of the work carried out on behalf of Royal Commissions or government committees would qualify as research, if they availed themselves of the opportunities. Wootton (1959) said:

> Traditionally the problems associated with marital
> breakdowns are presented in a legal, ethical or religious
> rather than in a sociological, or even a psychological setting;
> . . . [yet] the Commission betrayed hardly a flicker of interest
> in the sociological aspects of their problem or in the light that
> might have been thrown upon it by scientifically conducted
> social research.

More recently a whole apparatus of research has been deployed by the Royal Commission on Trade Unions and Employers' Associations (the Donovan Commission) and the Committee on Higher Education (the Robbins Committee). The statistical material collected by the latter has been a happy hunting ground for secondary analysis. But on the whole their role has been overstated. At a time when little other factual material was available, the nineteenth-century commissions were almost the sole sources until the famous studies of Booth and Rowntree. But commissions did not select their own problems to study; on the contrary, the obtrusiveness of the problem was the stimulus to the setting-up of the commission.

As far as demographic and social statistics are concerned, the government is now the main source as well as the principal user. It is instructive to enquire into the origins of these activities. The Haldane Committee on the Machinery of Government, set up in July 1917, was dissatisfied with information, research and intelligence functions of government: '. . . adequate provision has not been made in the past for the organized acquisition of facts and information, and for the systematic application of thought, as preliminary to the settlement of policy and its subsequent administration.' But the committee went on to outline the kind of activity favoured and to give examples of what already existed. It distinguished (a) Intelligence Work in Administrative Departments, (b) Research Work supervised by Administrative Departments, and (c) Intelligence and Research Work for General Use.

The Haldane Committee had been concerned to mobilize what

social science was available to assist in the task of 'Reconstruction' after World War I. The organs within government that were established by that time underwent little change in the inter-war period. There was indeed a modest expansion of the Medical Research Council (renamed from Committee) and the Department of Scientific and Industrial Research. While the MRC sponsored research in psychology, especially under the auspices of the Industrial Health Research Board (lineal descendant of the Health of Munitions Workers Committee established in 1915), DSIR had no concern with the human and social sciences. In 1918, some three years after the department's wartime birth, it joined with the Medical Research Committee to set up the Industrial Fatigue Board. The subsequent achievements of the board, later renamed the Industrial Health Research Board, are well known from the series of reports it issued until 1947, when its activities were merged into the programme of the Medical Research Council.

The effects of World War II

While the relevance of economic theory to the major issues of national life is rubbed home by the years of depression and by the controversies surrounding the views of Maynard Keynes, it was not until World War II that psychology was able to make a similar impact and it may require another convulsion, such as entry into the European Economic Community, for sociology to penetrate likewise. As we have seen, it was in World War I that the importance of applied psychology had become apparent yet the development of psychology in Britain between the wars presents a curious picture. In Cambridge the study by Bartlett of *Remembering* led to the theoretical formulations which inspired the enormously productive wartime and post-war work on human skills. At University College, London, research under Burt provided a revolution in the theory and practice of educational testing. Both these schools provided backgrounds of expertise which were badly needed when the demands of war were felt. The large numbers of men and women inducted into the services had to be categorized and allocated to a range of jobs which demanded skills found rarely in civilian life. The selection techniques and tests refined by the educational and vocational psychologists enabled the sorting process to be dealt with smoothly and efficiently, while the Cambridge studies of skill were invaluable in dealing with the new tasks required of aircrew and with the vigilance tasks of operations rooms and radar watches. These applications of experimental psychology were paralleled by the application of social psychology to the problems of selecting, and training as officers, men from social backgrounds which had previously contributed very scantily to commissioned ranks. Another major wartime advance came from the discovery that weapons and their uses formed one system; that many of the difficulties in training men to use them, in operating and in maintaining them were attributable to the fact that they were not designed with operators or maintenance men in mind. From this realization emerged enquiries which crossed the boundaries between the engineering, biological and behavioural sciences.

The war, with its attendant needs for increased control over the social and economic life of the nation, also accelerated advances in economics, social statistics and the study and practice of social administration. With total national resources, both physical and human, under scrutiny, a second flowering of statistical and factual studies and administrative reports helped to lay the foundations of the post-war 'Welfare State'. However, the problems of the utilization of one of the scarcest resources of all, social scientists, awaited scrutiny until 1946 and the Clapham Committee, of which we shall have more to say shortly.

On the main streams of development of social anthropology the war had little stimulating effect. Psychological warfare and the problems of the probable behaviour of enemies and neutrals attracted a few British anthropologists, mainly those with a leaning towards Freudian psychology which offered hypotheses about character structure of the general kind that could be applied to whole societies. This had little effect however upon the dominantly sociological orientation of British anthropologists, yet it is worth noting that, at the end of the war, there were fewer than twenty professional anthropologists in the whole of the British Commonwealth.

The Clapham Committee

During the war and even more towards its end, the series of studies we have already mentioned were set in train by the government to provide the blueprint for the kind of society Britain was to have after the war. There was an acute awareness that Britain would lack resources other than those represented by the skills of its people and of the need for a social structure that would allow these to be fully exploited. Studies were made of land use, scientific manpower and the social services. Few of these studies failed to make the case for the need for a great increase in the supply of adequate data on which political decision in the economic and social field should be based. This in turn pinpointed the scarcity of people trained in the social sciences. Therefore in 1945 the government appointed a committee under the chairmanship of Sir John Clapham to consider 'whether additional provision is necessary for research into social and economic questions'.

The committee concluded, 'There can be no doubt that progress in social and economic research has been very seriously hampered by lack of adequate finances,' and accordingly recommended:

(i) increases in the university grant, both through the provision of more chairs and other teaching posts, and through much more liberal provision for libraries, calculating machines, computing assistants, and similar facilities; and

(ii) a subcommittee to advise the University Grants Committee on social science matters.

The committee considered whether there should be an official Social and Economic Research Council and opposed the idea 'at this stage':

We believe that the parallelism which is suggested between the present needs of the social and natural sciences is ill-founded. The chief need of the social sciences at the present time is the strengthening of staff and provision for *routine* research. The existing research councils have never assisted research carried out as a normal routine function, nor are they suited to do so. Moreover the social sciences, although rich in promise, have not yet reached the stage at which such an official body could be brought into operation without danger of a premature crystallization of spurious orthodoxies. Their scope is as yet too ill-defined and the output too inadequate for a formal co-ordinating body to be appropriate. Yet another reason which has influenced us is that, the whole field being understaffed, we do not wish to see the best men – only the best would be of any use for such difficult work – diverted from doing research to co-ordinating research; already the best endowed and organised branch of the social sciences, economics, is suffering seriously from the diversion of leading workers into necessary government service.

Action taken on the Clapham Report

The suggested interdepartmental committee was set up and a substantial increase in funds was made through 'earmarked' grants from the University Grants Committee. The annual rate of expenditure rose during this period from £0·1 million in 1947 to £0·4 million in 1952. Although these sums were directed primarily to building up teaching departments, the latter, of course, provide the 'infrastructure' upon which research is based.

Post-war developments

For nearly thirty years, after its joint parenthood with the MRC of the Industrial Fatigue Research Board, the DSIR had no further direct concern with the Human Sciences. In 1950 the work started by the Schuster Panel on Human Factors was entrusted to two DSIR/MRC joint committees – one on Human Relations in Industry and the other on Industrial Efficiency in Industry.

A good American fairy was present at their christening and the money spent by the committees came from Conditional Aid Funds, totalling £175,000 over the years 1953 to 1957.

The work of the joint committees was summarized in their final reports issued in 1958. At the end of their labours they were able to express the view that industry's interest in research in the human sciences had been quickened and that a sound nucleus of fundamental research activity had been established.

At this stage there was no further need for DSIR and MRC to work in joint harness so, broadly speaking, psychology with a clinical or developmental flavour or with a strong physiological orientation was considered to be the responsibility of the MRC, as were sociological medicine and the MRC units such as the Applied Psychology Unit at Cambridge. The field of interest of DSIR was defined as 'the human sciences in relation to the needs of industry' and in 1957 the Human Sciences Committee was set up to recommend expenditure and advise on work in the human sciences. The committee was allocated £250,000 over the five years 1959–64. To service this committee and to undertake DSIR's own research, a Human Sciences Section was set up.

When we look at the work supported by the Human Sciences Committee, the practical applications, although often expressible only in qualitative terms, we find they have proved impressive. Admittedly much of the work had greater productivity as its goal and was of a very applied nature. Nevertheless, this exercise demonstrated that the techniques of psychological and sociological investigations had benefits to offer industry and that there was even more potential benefit to be reaped from advancing their methods, techniques of research, and theoretical framework. The amount allocated for expenditure on grants in the years 1961–8 was £75,000.

Additionally, some research work broadly describable as in the field of social sciences was conducted by the DSIR.

The Medical Research Council also supported research in universities and awarded a small number of studentships in psychology and in areas of the social sciences close to medicine. Among its own 'units' were the Applied Psychology Research Unit, formerly attached to the Department of Psychology at Cambridge but latterly a separate unit. By the 1960s the major MRC units in this field included the Social Psychology Research Unit at the Maudsley Hospital and the Climate and Working Efficiency Research Unit at Oxford. There were also two major MRC research 'groups' (less permanent than 'units'); one on Industrial Psychology attached to the Department of Psychology at University College London and one on Occupational Aspects of Ageing at the Department of Psychology at the University of Liverpool.

But by 1960 it was becoming plain that the country had something approaching a policy for some aspects of the social sciences but not for others. Research related to industrial problems or to medicine could be supported, and awards were available for postgraduate training in these fields. In other aspects of the social sciences there was no planned government support. Universities were able to sponsor a few research fellowships and scholarships out of their endowments. For the rest the foundations were the main source. The generosity of the Rockefeller and Ford Foundations was a great help to British social science in the years after the war. Apart from them, only the Nuffield Foundation among British trusts provided continuing and significant sponsorship.

The stimulus given to the universities by the money allocated to the UGC after the Clapham Report enabled social science departments to increase substantially in size, laying the foundations for the later increase in the teaching of these subjects. But most of the posts thus created were teaching posts; very few were for research. The UGC had no specific policy for developing the social sciences in the universities; it saw its task at that time as being far more facilitative and less directive than it has since become. At the same time more was beginning to be expected from the social sciences. The government became converted to the notion of 'planning', both economic and physical; the Civil Service began to be more initiatory and to seek information to which it had previously not had access and whose lack it had appeared to accept as inevitable. Certainly the requirement to prepare 'forward plans' drew attention to the need for better data and the Civil Service looked to the social sciences to provide them. It became fashionable for government departments to talk about the need for research although large sums were not yet available for this purpose. If large sums had indeed been available, considerable embarrassment would have resulted as there were far too few trained researchers to undertake the work.

The Social Science Research Council

This was the situation in 1963, a little over a quarter of a century after the Clapham Committee, when the Heyworth Committee (1963) was set up. Its report, published in 1965, made thirty-six recommendations of which the first, and far the most important, was for the establishment of a Social Science Research Council, to provide support for research, to keep under review the state of research, to advise government on the needs of social science research, to keep under review the supply of trained research workers, to disseminate information and to give advice on research in the social sciences and its application.

The committee estimated that the expenditure of the new council 'would rise in the fourth year to £2,250,000'. In fact, the council, which was set up in November 1965, spent in 1969–70 (its fourth full year) £2,274,892.

It should not be assumed that all social scientists were in favour of an SSRC. For one thing, there was no real community of social scientists. There were economists, sociologists, psychologists and political scientists of various persuasions, but they had little sense of community of interest. A psychologist, for example, working in Britain was, and still is, more likely to feel a sense of shared purpose with an American or a Russian psychologist working in his own field than with a British political scientist or economist, even one working in his own university. At all events there was little sense of sharing a 'common fate' before the establishment of the SSRC. As we shall describe later, one of the achievements of the SSRC has been to bring about a community of social scientists; not a tightly-knit one but one which has increasingly come to look to the SSRC as its first choice of source of support.

The setting up of the SSRC did not mean that other official sources of research funds for the social sciences were terminated. The old DSIR programme was assimilated into the SSRC, but the Medical Research Council continued its own schemes of support and, indeed, has expanded its provision. It does not give many training awards but the number of its own units in the field has increased. Besides the APRU we have already mentioned, there are MRC units:

(i) in Developmental Psychology at University College, London;

(ii) in the Study of Environmental Factors in Physical and Mental Illness at the London School of Economics;

(iii) for Epidemiological Studies in Psychiatry at Edinburgh University;

(iv) for Medical Sociology at Aberdeen University;

(v) for Social and Applied Psychology at Sheffield University;

(vi) for Social Medicine at the London School of Hygiene and Tropical Medicine;

(vii) for Social Psychology at the London University Institute of Psychiatry; and

(viii) for Speech and Communication at Edinburgh University.

Clearly the emphasis placed by the MRC on social aspects of health and disease and of medicine is increasing.

It is somewhat harder to determine the effect of the SSRC on the research programmes of other government departments. For instance, DES spends large sums on research, but an accommodation has been reached between the Council and the Department which does define in general terms what aspects of educational research each should regard as its own. Other government departments have similar, though frequently even less precise, conventions. As the SSRC's *Annual Report* for 1969–70 points out:

> Communications have been gradually built up through the system of academic liaison officers and through a variety of contacts, informal and formal, at various levels of government. The Chairman of the Council also acts as an assessor, alongside the heads of the other research councils, on the Council for Scientific Policy. Representatives of the S.S.R.C. act as assessors on certain Government committees whose work impinges on research or training in the social sciences. The opinions of official experts in the relevant Government departments are quite frequently sought by the Council on particular research applications without sacrificing any part of the independence of the research council or its exclusive responsibility for taking the ultimate decision about the content of the research which it sponsors. It is part of the Council's function to be available to give advice in its turn to the Government about research problems in the social sciences. However, the intellectual traffic on these matters, although it is a two-way flow and steadily increasing, has

40

tended to be significantly heavier in one direction, from the
S.S.R.C. towards Government, than the other. This is partly
because all of our work is in principle available for public
inspection, whereas Government departments wish to keep
some of the results of their investigations secret. Government
departments have at their disposal much information which is
of great interest to social scientists, and the conventions about
which part of its needs to be withheld, on grounds of security
or the confidentiality of personal information, and which part
can be made available without damage to the public interest,
need constantly to be updated in the light of changing
circumstances.

The most rapid growth point in Government social science
research expenditure was in commissioned research done
outside the Government machine. This was now considerably
larger in value than the research on social science undertaken
by Government departments using their own resources. And
the total volume of university research in these subjects
sponsored by Government departments is larger than that
sponsored by the S.S.R.C. Efficient communication on the
content of research would, it is clear, greatly increase the
cost-effectiveness of the total effort made by both sides.
Hence the Council Newsletter has begun to publish regularly
such partial information as is available on research grants
made by the Department of Health and Social Security, the
Department of Employment and the Home Office. There is a
strong argument for a rule which would place an obligation on
Government departments engaging in research to publicise
the nature of their activity, except where it could positively be
shown that this would be harmful to the national interest.
Unless the pre-conditions are established in this way for a
continuing dialogue among social scientists with common
research problems, the body of systematic knowledge about
society will grow at a significantly slower pace than it is
capable of achieving.

The tone of this section of the report is that of a dialogue between a
research council on the one hand, which is virtually totally financially dependent on government and while nominally independent
in its policy is yet constrained by agreements, conventions and the
power of the Secretary of State to issue directives; and, on the other
hand, government departments which are sensitive of their reputations and anxious that their tasks should not be made more difficult
by the publication of research findings from which critical attack

could be launched. On the whole, however, the SSRC has earned the restrained confidence of government.

With the advent of the SSRC and its firm establishment within the family of research councils, a *de facto* decision has been taken to locate social science policy within the framework of science policy. This was not inevitable. So long as the philosophy of the Clapham Report persisted, social science policy in so far as it existed at all was almost entirely bound up with, and part of, the policy for higher education. And until the late 1950s and, to a large extent, before the Robbins' Report in 1963, it could scarcely be claimed that there was a policy for higher education. Fragments of a social science policy were to be found in government's industrial policy, penological policy, health policy and so on. Indeed there is no self-evident reason why social science policy should not be part of social policy. Its inclusion in science policy has many profound implications for its image, its organization, its financing, its independence. Clearly, too, any aspect of the social sciences which fits most closely into the scientific mould will be regarded as the 'leading edge' and the rest expected to follow, to model themselves upon it. This kind of thinking reinforces the natural scientists' views of the social sciences as 'immature', younger brothers so to speak. 'You too can grow up and use a computer . . . .' The relationship of the Social Science Research Council to government and to the scientific establishment has, as we have indicated, been one of growing confidence. But the SSRC had also to acquire the confidence of social scientists and overcome opposition from various quarters and for various reasons. Some of the most influential economists objected. They did not wish to associate their technically advanced discipline with the backward schoolmen of sociology. They did not relish being connected in the public and governmental mind with the critical, leftish schools of social science. At neither Cambridge nor Oxford were there at that time undergraduate courses in sociology. In Cambridge social anthropology was taught to undergraduates but in Oxford only as a postgraduate subject. Eminent economists could obtain scholarships for their graduate students from foundations and private sources. They had a direct line to the councils of government and wished to see no third party intervene. Some psychologists opposed for fear of the undermining of the position they had built up as respectable natural scientists. There were prizes of new buildings, new equipment, expansion for those psychology departments which could make good their claims to be in science faculties.

At opposite ends of the political spectrum were social scientists who feared 'dirigisme', the undermining of academic freedom, and social scientists who feared the growth of an establishment view, 'the crystallization of premature orthodoxies' of the Clapham Committee, but with a different emphasis. It has been the SSRC's achievement to reconcile its opponents and to earn the confidence of its constituency. It would be idle to pretend that it has been entirely successful in that endeavour; it is suspected of favouring the large established departments, especially in regard to its distribution of postgraduate training awards. It is still suspected of harbouring designs to have a policy, to wish to direct research rather than to respond to the wishes of researchers. It would be a monument to flaccidity if no such complaints were ever heard or if none of them had substance. But it seems that the SSRC has achieved a position of balance. It is large enough, significant enough to be the leading institution, but not so large and all enhancing as to be a rigid establishment. Although the largest *single* source of funds, it accounts for much less than half of all sources. A society with a mixed economy and pluralist as regards sources of power and influence has evolved a system which, though far from perfect, is suited to its particular ethos. Whether it will prove responsive to changes in that ethos is a matter for the future.

The professional associations

The principal professional associations with which we should be concerned are:

> The British Psychological Society, founded in 1901, chartered in 1965;
> The Royal Economic Society, founded in 1890, chartered in 1902;
> The British Sociological Association, founded in 1951;
> The Royal Anthropological Institute, founded in 1843, chartered in 1907;
> The Political Studies Association of the United Kingdom, founded in 1950.

In a somewhat different category is the British Association for the Advancement of Science, founded in 1831 and Chartered in 1928.

No two of these societies are alike. The British Psychological Society requires as a minimum qualification an honours in psychology, the Association of Social Anthropologists requires a Ph.D or university teaching post in a Commonwealth University, the British Sociological Association requires that members 'work in the general field of sociology', the Royal Anthropological Institute requires simply that an applicant be proposed and seconded by

43

fellows. The BPS publishes six journals: *The British Journal of Psychology, The British Journal of Medical Psychology, The British Journal of Social and Clinical Psychology, The British Journal of Mathematical and Statistical Psychology, The British Journal of Occupational Psychology* and *The Bulletin of the BPS.* The BSA publishes *Sociology*; the Royal Economic Society publishes the *Economic Journal*; the Royal Anthropological Institute publishes *Man*; the ASA publishes no journals; the Political Studies Association publishes *Political Studies.*

While the BPS combines the roles of professional association and learned society by denying entrance to the latter to those qualified for the former, sociologists and anthropologists have developed different solutions to the same difficulty. Within the BSA there was a Sociology Teachers' Section confined to professionals, a recent victim to the growing egalitarianism of the association; the ASA is a fully professional association, the RAI solely a learned society. Of course, as a professional association, the ASA like the BPS runs scientific meetings, conferences and discussions.

Until recently only psychologists and economists were employed in a fully professional capacity, and the BPS acquired a control over entrance to professional appointments in psychology other than teaching and research. Thus the BPS occupies a role somewhat similar to that of the engineering institutions. Its internal organization reflects its dual role: it is organized into professional 'divisions' and scientific 'sections'.

The other societies have no such control over appointments. The BSA has indeed recently tried to exert its influence in a professional capacity, intervening in disputes about teaching appointments. Its authority, as a purely voluntary body, has not been acknowledged and its only other weapon, the blacklist, has proved ineffective. It is none too clear how a body whose membership does not rest upon professional qualifications can exercise the privilege of a professional body. Although sociologists are now employed professionally by local government in planning departments, they do not discharge a service to individual members of the public as do clinical and educational psychologists; the case for their full professionalization is therefore weaker.

Apart from publishing journals, available to members at a privileged price, the actual services rendered to members in their research is more problematical.

They unquestionably facilitate the communication of their members with one another through scientific meetings and play their part in the information infrastructure of research. But they play little part either in the communication of one branch of social

44

science with another or in the communication of the social scientists with the public. The British Association for the Advancement of Science is the only body in which most of the social sciences and all the natural sciences are represented. The most prominent activity of the BA, whose membership is completely open, is its Annual Meeting at which the intention is to put science on show to the public. In the days of the mass media this is no longer the unique service it formerly was.

Social sciences and the public

Broadcasting has played a large part in the communication of science, including the social sciences, to the public. Social scientists broadcast in lectures, particularly the Reith Lectures, discussion programmes and in some educational set pieces and feature programmes on television. By comparison the newspapers' coverage of social science is meagre. There is of course a vast quantity of political and economic journalism, pop sociology and pop psychology in the daily offerings of the press. Serious social science at BBC level is, however, offered only in small quantities in the 'quality' papers. One weekly journal, however, is devoted to the social sciences and since its beginnings in 1961, *New Society* has created its own loyal public. In its columns academics write for a non-academic but sophisticated public, and professional journalists with social science training know that what they write will be read by academics as well as professionals and an interested public. It is, however, hard to say what impact the journal has, but by providing a continuous flow it helps to funnel social science ideas into policy areas.

We have described most of the types of institution relevant to the research scene – the universities and other institutions of higher education, the research institutions, government research, the SSRC. Among the research institutes we noted that some were programmatic, i.e. they had a particular political or social objective, e.g. a Race Relations Institute clearly attracts people who are anxious to *improve* race relations, not only to study them. Adding to knowledge remains a vital part of the aim and motivation of the research but other aims are serviced; the role then of such an institute is partly that of pressure group, partly of research institute. More recently another kind of body has emerged, not to undertake research but to act as a pressure group using the outcome of research, either that conducted by its members in other capacities or that of others. An example is the Child Poverty Action Group;

45

another is the Council for the Advancement of State Education. Academic social scientists both enlighten other voluntary bodies with an interest in their field and act as goads to government and local government who are obliged either to accept their statements or to attempt to refute them with equally reputable studies. These groups, 'mediating institutions', play a significant and probably growing part in the relationship of research to action. They provide confrontation between academic research and government but reduce the risk of polarization of government and the academy.

Access to government data

In the relationship of government to social science research, the access provided for the latter to data generated by government is vastly important. Between the natural caution and secretiveness of government on the one hand and the desire for complete and open access by social scientists on the other, there is a gulf. But this gulf has perceptibly narrowed. The Clapham Committee, noting the vast increase in data generated by the exigencies of World War II commented:

> It is highly desirable that the government departments which collect and analyse material relevant to social and economic research should be in continuous contact with outside experts who can keep them aware of the needs which are arising in the speculative branches of the field and who can assist in assessing the value and possible uses of material which is already being collected. It is equally desirable that there should be continuous contact between the relevant divisions within the different departments, not only to avoid overlapping, but also to ensure that the potential value for research purposes of the material available is exploited from every point of view.
> We recommend therefore that there be set up an Interdepartmental Committee charged with the duty of bringing to the notice of departments the potential value for research purposes of the material which they collect and suggesting new methods and areas of collection.

The proposed Interdepartmental Committee was duly set up and issued three reports between 1947 and 1956. Although it was never officially wound up, it apparently went to sleep and the Heyworth

Committee was not notably impressed by its achievements. Nevertheless it published a series of guides to official statistics, urged greater comparability in their collection and dissemination, put researchers in touch with government sources, and persuaded some government departments to be rather more forthcoming in making records available.

More recently the SSRC set up a Standing Committee on Social Science and Government, which included at its birth, along with eight academics and the Director of the Royal Institute of Public Administration, three statisticians in government service: the Principal and Director of Studies in Statistics of the Civil Service College, and the Advisor on Survey Research of the Office of Population Censuses and Surveys.

Students of politics and government have been greatly aided by the reduction from fifty to thirty years of the embargo on Cabinet papers and similar documents. Another significant step forward is the publication of an annual survey of 'social trends' by the Central Statistical Office, bringing together informed commentary and data from otherwise widely separated sources.

Thus, while the individual researcher may encounter obstruction and obscurantism and while some data is concealed because it was acquired under seal of confidence, government takes seriously and is kept aware of its obligations to give reasonable access to data. Nor is all the obstruction irrelevant or misconceived. Real fears exist about privacy and in particular about computerized data.

Research infrastructure

1 *Libraries*

Libraries which have tried to maintain the old relationship with research must by now be failing researchers as well as students. The increase in the number of universities, the rise in the number of books and journals, and their rapidly rising costs mean that very few libraries can offer a complete service to students, to their teachers and to researchers. The most intelligent response has been for libraries to perceive their function as that of information retrieval rather than of custodian of manuscripts and book collections. Many university libraries have advanced rapidly in the use of microfilm, photo-copying and inter-library loans, greatly helped by the National Lending Library for Science and Technology at Boston Spa, Yorkshire, whose rapid photo-copying and scanning service includes the social sciences. Computer systems are being developed by libraries for cataloguing reports and papers as well as for a master retrieval system for periodical articles.

Meanwhile many researchers struggle with inadequate secretarial and clerical help, with insufficient access to photo-copying machines and without suitable library facilities. Others are even more severely handicapped by an unwary enthusiasm for computer techniques which offer the double-edged weapons of packaged statistical programmes. The danger for the enthusiast is the abdication of analytical thought in favour of a massive matrix of intercorrelations. Our capacity to cope technologically with multivariate analysis far outstrips our ability to conceptualize the substratum of relationships of which the matrix is the derived representation.

2 Data Bank

Again within the last ten years a survey data bank was established jointly by the SSRC and the University of Essex.

> The SSRC Data Bank collects data derived from social surveys sponsored by government departments, commercial organizations and academic researchers, in order that the data can be analysed by others besides the original sponsors. . . . any one directing projects or programmes involving the use of questionnaire or interview surveys is asked to get in touch with the Data Bank at an early stage in the research, so that as much assistance as possible may be obtained from this central facility for exchanging and accumulating information. The professional staff of the Data Bank carry out research into techniques of storing and retrieving social data and into secondary analysis of material. The first product of this research was the production in January 1968 of a computerised catalogue of survey questions – the first to be published and circulated by any survey archive or data bank.

3 Survey research

The SSRC also established a Survey Research Unit which acted on the SSRC's behalf in the enquiry for which this paper was originally prepared.[1] Its chief function was to give help and advice on the

---

[1] The outcome of this enquiry in which Britain shared with France, Denmark and the USA has been published under the title *Demands for Social Knowledge*, edited by Elisabeth Crawford and Norman Perry (1976).

techniques of sample survey work, particularly to academic social scientists, e.g. by organizing summer schools. The unit initiated a programme of surveys of its own and research into methods of survey research. It proved, however, to be short-lived and, in fact, closed down before the end of 1976.

A valuable service for contributors is provided by the Institute of Research Techniques, which evaluates reported findings from survey research and carries out its own trials of methods exposing errors which are commonly glossed over, ignored or unperceived.

Although there are many commercial surveys and market research organizations, their relationships with academic research are limited. The largest and most experienced of all the surveys is the government's own Social Survey (q.v.), which also is prepared under certain circumstances to undertake surveys for academic research or repayment. Social science researchers have a fairly wide range of not inexpensive choice of professional survey facilities. Many however prefer, especially for local work, their own students, for whom such work combines an educational experience with useful pocket money.

Careers in the social sciences

1 *The supply of social scientists*

There is effectively only one route whereby people become social scientists in Britain: through higher education, which in general means the universities.

In 1938–9, the last year before the war, in social science – excluding law and geography – there were 315 honours graduates, 254 men and 61 women. Even stretching the number to include ordinary degrees whose content was almost all in the social sciences, we would not reach 500.

But by 1962–3, when the Heyworth Committee was set up, the number was 1342 men, 409 women. Six years later, after a period of unprecedented expansion of the universities, a four-fold increase brought figures to 4941 men and 2531 women, about one in eight of all men graduating and one in five of all women. Thus, for every graduate in social sciences in 1938–9, just over thirty years later there were 15·4.

The social sciences are, of course, not homogeneous. If we consider them as a whole, the numbers appear to continue to grow: 5051 men and 2747 women (7798) entered the disciplines in 1971, compared with a total of 4598 in 1965.

49

However, entrants into economics barely grew during that period – from 1676 to 1729 – while entrants in psychology grew from 252 to 845 and in sociology from 724 to 1237. While men outnumbered women by 1473 to 256, women sociologists, psychologists and social anthropologists outnumbered men by 1334 to 955. The demands on the teaching of the more 'social' subjects continues to grow.

Our interest in admissions to undergraduate courses is three-fold: first because the trend represents the continually growing interest in the disciplines; second because they represent the reservoir from which future teachers and researchers can be drawn, and third because they represent the pressure on teaching which must be met.

To examine the flow of people who can actually perform research we need to turn our attention to trends in postgraduate training. The Heyworth Committee was unable to estimate the output of postgraduates, but in 1962–3 the UGC issued for the first time statistics of the recipients of higher degrees, giving three categories – economics, psychology and 'other social studies' which include sociology, politics and social anthropology.

We have extracted comparative data for 1962–3 and 1969–70. Table 1 shows a seven-fold increase.

TABLE 1

	Total				Of whom overseas students returning home			
Subject	1962–3		1969–70		1962–3		1969–70	
	Men	Women	Men	Women	Men	Women	Men	Women
Economics	86	7	388	38	36	2	91	4
Psychology	49	15	127	56	5	3	11	12
Other social studies	112	18	888	171	35	7	131	26
Total	247	40	1403	265	76	12	233	42

Looking at employment, we find that the universities' demand on higher degree graduates dropped from 35/199 (17·5 per cent) in 1962–3 to 164/1393 (11·5 per cent) in 1969–70. However, it is clear that many holders of higher degrees were available for research as well as for other forms of employment.

One further matter needs mention. There is a substantial and growing number of students reading first and higher degrees in the social sciences at the polytechnics. These degrees are of equivalent standard to those awarded by the universities and most are granted by a national body, the CNAA. While the effect on our estimates of the output of social scientists is slight, they could become more important in future if the government encourages the polytechnics to absorb a growing proportion of the annual increase in students seeking first degrees. There are indeed signs of a 'squeeze play', to borrow a term from contract bridge. Universities want to grow. But they are expensive. By threatening to sequester growth in the polytechnics the government serves warning that universities can grow only by becoming less expensive in terms of cost per student, which in effect means less time for research. As our earlier analysis has indicated, any reduction in university research would throw the research institutes into greater prominence. As we have seen, their capacity for growth is considerable but their predominant location in inner London is likely to be more a major limitation.

Nevertheless, despite their difficulties the independent institutes offer an attractive career – or perhaps more accurately an attractive stage in a career – which may be wholly devoted to research or may, if continued in a university, combine research with teaching or may even, if continued within government, combine research with administration.

It is broadly correct to say that there are few full careers in research available at universities. Those employed on full-time research at the universities are either higher degree candidates in receipt of some form of scholarship, or research assistants on temporary appointments. Some of the latter may also be reading for higher degrees and some may be of a status which earns them the title of 'Fellow' or 'Research Fellow' or 'Senior Fellow' or 'Research Associate'. But essentially they are all on fixed term appointments. Very many of them will hope to continue in the academic world and continue to do research. And this will mean obtaining teaching appointments. The exceptions to this generalization are mostly at Oxford and Cambridge colleges where some tenured fellowships do not automatically imply the holding of a university teaching appointment. The most obvious example is Nuffield College, Oxford, which has twelve 'official fellows' – full-time tenured appointments in the social sciences with no undergraduate teaching duties. These can be regarded as full-time career appointments in research.

The principal career channel is government. But it is not at all easy to review careers in social science research in government, mainly because the social sciences are not treated as a single entity.

Social scientists in established posts working full-time on research may be members of three separate classes – Psychologist Class, Economist Class, Research Officer Class – and there is a small number in the Scientific Officer Class and Statistician Class. No distinction is made between posts which are virtually entirely research and posts which are mainly advisory. Furthermore there is a comparatively high proportion of temporary appointments, especially in the Economist and Research Officer classes.

They were all set up at different times and in different ways and in response to different circumstances. The Psychologist Class was set up in 1950 after prolonged wrangling from the end of the war. Psychologists were then serving in the Admiralty, Air Ministry and the War Office, the Prison Commission and the Ministry of Labour. From the beginning there was a mélange of research, advisory and professional roles. Eventually the class was set up as a 'professional' rather than a 'scientific' class (though confusion still exists), with a four-rank structure. As a research career it has one major handicap. The Psychologist Class is virtually invisible. Because of the nature of its work – part advisory, part professional, part research, of a sensitive nature – it publishes very little either in journals or in book form. Except in the field of ergonomics its published output is minute. The National Health Service do employ 'psychologists', but their publications are greatly outnumbered by clinical psychologists in university departments of psychology and psychiatry or MRC research units. In other fields of psychology the pool is virtually scooped by the universities. While the selection policy of journal editors may account for some of this picture, it is reasonable to conclude that most research in psychology is carried out in the universities. Certainly most research that sees the light of day comes from this source.

In economics the situation is not vastly different. Economists have a far better career structure in government, there is more interchange between government and universities, but the work done by economists in government is seldom published. Economists find employment in banks, insurance companies, large industrial companies and in commercial establishments. Some are prominent in financial and economic journalism between which and research there is sometimes only a fine line drawn. Like the psychologists in the health service and in government, economists in finance, commerce and industry are mostly invisible from the research point of view, although their intelligence and advisory work may be of high quality and originality.

Sociologists' employment in government is more recent and only sporadically organized. The research officer class which contains

most of them is of recent date and has fewer senior posts. The
Fulton Committee (Fulton, 1963) was very critical of the organization of this class.

We were surprised to see how small this class is (230 in the
Service, including 50 temporaries) given the size of the
Departments concerned with social, economic and defence
policy and the technical complexities of current problems. We
would have thought that every Department and many
individual divisions in these areas of activity would have
required a research unit engaged on carrying out studies in
the evaluation of the effects of policy and reporting on any
need for change.

We thought that A.P.O.s generally, and in some cases
P.O.s, were very poorly used in the Departments where we
saw them employed. We were not surprised that most of
those we saw found their work unrewarding and frustrating.
This was because they were often confined to a 'backroom'
role too far removed from the main stream of policy decisions
and with relatively little contact with their administrative
colleagues. Some of them felt that many of the questions
referred to them by Administrators were inexpertly framed
and the answers misconstrued or misused.

The A.R.O.s we saw were largely employed on boring and
repetitive statistical tabulation. Much of this work could have
been done by Clerical Officers with 'O' level Maths.

The research groups we saw included no supporting
executive and clerical staff so that it fell to the lot of A.R.O.s
to do their own filing, stapling, collating and other simple
clerical tasks.

For those who wish to make a career in research,
encouragement to publish their findings in the learned
journals is a valuable incentive to join, and remain in, an
organization. Naturally, because of the confidential nature of
much of the work and its implications for public policy, there
cannot be complete freedom to publish but, on the other
hand, publication and open discussion are vital elements of
the world of research and are important to many research
workers. This dilemma was illustrated in one area we visited
where research had produced material which would have been
valuable to workers in related fields outside the Service. Since
this material could be construed as critical of the
Department's present policy, there was a natural reluctance to
see it published at this stage and before the Department had

been able to resolve its own attitudes towards the issues raised, though matters of security were not involved.

Since the Fulton Committee reported the number of research units has increased substantially as has the number of social scientists employed in the Research Officer Class. Negotiations to establish a Social Scientist Class have dragged on for at least two years. Meanwhile the integration of research into policy has not notably improved nor have the social scientists in permanent government employment been able to acquire advisory roles or parity of treatment with economists and statisticians.

So we see that the contribution to published research of those in careers outside the universities or research institutes is small.

The public's image of the social sciences

This section is bound to be speculative. The evidence does not exist and anyone's view of this issue is bound to be a reflection of individual experiences. What is however pretty certain is that there is no monolithic 'public'. Nor do most publics view the social sciences as a monolith. In fact, a frequent question is: what are the 'social sciences'? Although most educated people know that 'science' includes physics, chemistry, astronomy, biology and so on, they would find it less easy to mention individual social sciences except sociology, which is often treated as synonym for social science. Among the less well educated, economics is viewed with some respect, psychology with awe and sociology with derision. Long-haired revolutionary students with beards, beads and sandals have stamped their image on sociology.

On the other hand among potential consumers of social science research there is an equally irrational belief in the efficacy of sociology to solve problems. In academic circles it is still regarded by many as a soft science and a soft option lacking rigour and discipline. In some respects sociology has come to play the part occupied before the war by the psychoanalytical school. Then sex was the key concept which explained the world and ourselves to ourselves. The individual psyche was the preoccupation of inner-directed man. Post-war mass society prefers sociological concepts and class has ousted sex as *the* explanatory concept. This is particularly fitting in Britain; class guilt is evidently a strong motive especially among the young and neatly divides the generations; anyone over thirty is responsible for the class-divided world as it is; everyone under thirty is its unwilling prisoner.

54

Among senior civil servants and similar elites there is a tendency to see sociology as a potentially potent but untamed ally. It is not seen as necessarily subversive, as it appears to be in some Latin-American countries, but there is an awareness that it could be. Industry for example shows a strong preference for 'behavioural science', not merely because it is fashionable in America but more because it is safe, less likely to challenge structural assumptions, more likely to accept the perspective of senior management.

Political science for the wider public is political punditry, the indefatigable instant analysis of election night, the synthetic excitement of political forecasting and the endless journalist gossip about political figures and occasionally issues. The political parties take its market research aspects seriously; politicians defer to technical expertise and knowledge in, for example, the field of local government and planning machinery. But generally speaking political science has a somewhat blurred image.

The mass media, especially radio and television, are by no means neglectful of the social sciences. Radio and television give more space to social science than to science, probably because the latter is less amenable to presentation in talk or discussion.

The popularity of the social sciences among students is another indication of their hold on the public imagination. Increasingly, too, science fiction shows a preoccupation with topics which are less science than social science. Of course science fiction has more often been technology fiction and much social science fiction concerns uses of social science rather than new developments in theory. But the public looks to social science less for new theories than for new uses.

Summary

At the end of a review of this nature one asks oneself: what is the state of the social sciences in Britain? How well are their future growth and development provided for? Are they inheriting their rightful estate? Do they attract their fair share of young talent? Are their products useful, valuable? What is the relationship between the changes in the society and developments in social science? Is the organization of research satisfactory?

In facing these questions one is bound to acknowledge the gap between a statement, however impressionistic, of what exists, and evaluation. Between assessment and evaluation comes our own personal view of where we stand. Are the social sciences no more

55

than tenuous webs of speculative fragments as Chomsky (1972) sees them:

> Given the primitive character of the study of man and society and its general lack of intellectual substance, we can only speculate about the essential and basic factors that enter into human behaviour and it would be quite irresponsible to claim otherwise. Speculation about these matters is quite legitimate, even essential. It should be guided, where this is possible, by such limited and fragmentary knowledge as exists. But speculation should be clearly labelled as such and clearly distinguished from the achievements of scientific inquiry. This is a matter of considerable importance on a society that tends to trust in professional expertise and to rely on professional judgements. The scientist, in particular, has a responsibility to the public in this regard.

Or are they mature sciences in the making with futures modelled on those of their 'natural' cousins faced with grave tasks and with the duty to concentrate on application to current problems, as René Maheu (1970) describes?:

> To the task devolving upon the present generation, namely development, in the widest and loftiest acceptation of the term – the economic and social development of communities and the development of man himself – the contribution that can and must be made by the social and human sciences is of capital importance, provided they fulfil their twofold role: on the one hand, to contribute carefully verified data and effective operational techniques adapted to economic, social and cultural structures and duly analysed historical situations and, on the other, to help men to make their choices in the light of facts and to ensure that understanding, respect and a feeling of solidarity between men are established on a firmer foundation. This is a twofold function, for which no discipline taken in isolation can suffice but which calls for the widest co-operation between them all. It is a twofold ambition, by which they take it upon themselves to be the diverse but interrelated forms and processes of the same striving for knowledge, the same thinking and the same endeavour.

Or are they fully mature disciplines, moulding our view of ourselves and our society, with their own concepts and methods, enjoying a close, almost symbiotic relationship with the natural sciences, but not to be cast in their image as Norman McKenzie (1966) describes them:

> The parallel between the development of scientific thought and theories of society is striking. From the very beginning, the social sciences appear to have adopted concepts and methods from the natural sciences, and each new turn in science seems to have been matched by a new set of social theories. But it would be too simple an answer to a peculiarly difficult problem about the history of ideas to suggest that this is a straightforward relationship, in which the natural sciences set the pace and the social sciences follow. It may often look as though this has happened. It might be more accurate however, to conclude ... science thus provided a new way of looking at problems, and a new vocabulary for discussing them, which was bound to influence those who were trying to understand and describe the problems of human society. For our present purposes, however, it is enough to observe the way in which the natural and social sciences have grown up together.

I raise these questions because we tend, when looking at the organization and financing of research, to compare the social sciences with the natural sciences, without first enquiring whether this is the right comparison to make. When we do, our conclusions are inevitable and often expressed in terms of percentage. The USA and Britain devote 3 per cent of their GNP to research and development. In Britain the social sciences receive only 1, or 2 or 10 per cent (depending upon what basis of comparison you choose) of the resources devoted to R & D in the physical and biological sciences. Education is a multi-billion-pound enterprise, of which less than 0·1 per cent is devoted to research. These are all useful and customary debating points. But they are based on comparisons of unlikes, and on assumptions which are arbitrary as well as false.

When we look at the organization and financing of social science research we should take our minds off the natural sciences model *except* where such common factors as the requirements of access to expensive apparatus are the overriding ones.

In recording the increase in the number of organized units undertaking research we should point also to the increasing bureaucratization of research. It is no longer possible for the scholar to finance empirical research out of his own pocket. Few academic institutions have free money to allocate to research assistance and the existence of established sources of support encourage universities to reserve their funds for teaching posts, pushing academics to seek research support from external sources. These in turn develop bureaucratic mechanisms for scrutinizing and evaluating research proposals. One result is increasing professionalism in research; another is increased adherence to pattern.

The research-financing organizations like the SSRC claim that they have enough money to support almost all 'worthy' projects and similar claims have from time to time been made by foundations – the Nuffield Foundation, for example, in its evidence to the Heyworth Committee considered that it had not been obliged to reject through lack of money applications it would have wished to support. These claims should be treated with reserve. Current notions about what is 'worthy' or 'acceptable' are not independent of the resources available and, with some time lag of course, committees adjust their standards to what is practicable.[1] Nevertheless, from the point of view of the performers of research it is true to say that scarcity of good research workers has as often been the limiting factor as shortage of finance.

Research training has been greatly improved in the last decade. Where formerly there were few postgraduate-taught courses, there are now probably too many. But most offer specialist rather than research training, and although few fail to include research method among the subjects taught, probably a majority of Ph.Ds in the social sciences still have little formal training in research methodology. It is in this area that change is likely to be most rapid. The SSRC as the main source of postgraduate studentships has enormous leverage.

A working party of the council has been tackling the question of the future shape of the Ph.D in the social sciences and the council is in a strong position to influence university policy in this field.

As we have seen, the number of research centres in universities has been growing. Twenty years ago there were perhaps half a dozen, now there are more than a hundred. Some are small and little more than packets of headed writing paper; others are substantial and indeed considerably larger than many independent research institutes; all however represent some commitment to a continuing research programme, usually with some interdisciplinary element. A new feature of the landscape is the largely government-supported research institute attached to a university, or entirely separate like

---

[1] In their reports to council, 1975–6, the committees of SSRC raised for the first time as a serious problem the fact that they were prevented by lack of funds from supporting all the research they would have liked.

the centre for Environmental Studies. And within government itself there has been the growth of the statistical services and the survey services now located in the Office of Population Censuses and Surveys. The Home Office Research Unit is still the only established in-house agency of a government department with its own scientific identity and reputation, although there are units of substantial size in other government departments. The substantial number of MRC units is now being paralleled by the new SSRC units, and special services such as survey advice, data banks and lending libraries are centrally provided.

Although there is some movement between universities, institutes and government, there is not enough to constitute a plannable element in a research career. And indeed there are few full careers in research, although research forms an episode or series of episodes in other careers – teaching and administrative. Finally, most research is conducted or led by academic members of universities.

Researchers in Britain have no shortage of journals in which to publish and can, indeed, publish in American and international as well as British journals, the number of which continues to increase. There are now at least seven regular British journals in psychology, five in sociology, six in economics and four in political science. Many of the newest journals are expressly interdisciplinary or problem-orientated.

Increasingly researchers have access to computers; this is usually provided by universities to their own academic and research staffs at no fee; charges are however levied against externally sponsored research.

The infrastructure, although patchy and incomplete in some respects, is adequate and indeed beyond the imaginings of the immediate post-war generation of academic researchers. British social scientists are fond of contrasting their lot unfavourably with that of their American counterparts and British expenditure on social science research is somewhere around 3 per cent of American. But their deprivations are relative.

Section III
The Social Science Disciplines

Chapter 3
The Development of the Social Science Disciplines in Britain

To review the strengths and weaknesses of British research in the social sciences as a whole or even those of the individual disciplines is a formidable task. The strengths and weaknesses are rooted in the traditions and in the institutional frameworks of research; nor are these unrelated.

The British traditions of empiricism have been observed, appraised and criticized to the extent that it has become a shibboleth; it is now deeply rooted in the intellectual self image. British academic and research institutions are themselves at least in part the product of this self image, coming into existence to deal with a present situation in a pragmatic way rather than representing the application of a principle or a philosophy of education or research. Institutions appear to emerge, not to be planned. Thus institutional boundaries are untidy, and the institutions serve multiple purposes acquired at different stages in their life. Their present role is defensible and defended by post hoc rationalization, rather than by justification from first principles. Thus criticism is easy; there is no difficulty in pointing to gaps in the structure, to duplication of function, to defects in planning. It is harder to assess achievements except by pointing to individual pieces of work which are recognized as theoretical landmarks or methodological advances. The structure of research is such that sustained cumulative attacks on a problem area are comparatively rare, rarer in some disciplines than others as we shall see.

Furthermore the universities where the bulk of research in most of the disciplines is still done are, despite all efforts to the contrary, still mainly organized in a departmental structure which discourages work across disciplinary boundaries. This leads to a paradox. The empirical tradition favours the problem-oriented approach; the disciplinary boundaries ensure that the 'problem' is framed in terms of a single discipline. The outcome is research which contributes less than it might to theoretical advance, and less than it ought to problem-solving.

So we are obliged to assay the disciplines separately, not least because, despite their embrace by the term 'social sciences', on the whole they develop separately and with comparatively little communion.

Annual or biennial reviews of developments do not exist; occasional reviews undertaken for a particular purpose are fortunately available however. For instance, the Social Science Research Council asked its various subject committees to prepare reviews.[1] The objective was, in the words of Jeremy Mitchell (SSRC, 1968a).

To get the views of some of the leading research workers in the field about important current research developments, about likely future developments and about the research needs of the subject, in terms of men, money, other resources and research organization. As well as helping to guide the SSRC in its future policy, the research reviews will, at a time when there is increasing specialization within all social science

---

[1] The full list of SSRC reviews is as follows, published by Heinemann Educational Books:

1 *Research in Political Science*.

2 *Research on International Organization*.

3 *Research in Social Anthropology*.

4 *Social Research on Automation*.

5 *Research on Poverty*.

6 *Comparability in Social Research* (with the British Sociological Association).

7 *The Population Census*.

8 *Longitudinal Studies and the Social Sciences*.

9 *Research in Economic and Social History*.

10 *Research in Human Geography*.

Surveys in applied economics sponsored jointly with the Royal Economic Society:

11 *Regional Economics with Special Reference to the UK*, A. J. Brown.

12 *Price Behaviour of Firms*, A. Silberston.

13 *Technical Progress*, C. Kennedy and A. B. Thirlwell.

14 *Models of Consumer Behaviour*, A. J. Brown and A. Deaton.

15 *International Liquidity*, J. Williamson.

16 *Flow of Funds Analysis*, A. D. Bain.

disciplines, help social scientists and students to keep abreast of developments over a wider field. The reviews will also provide those in industry, government, the educational world and elsewhere with information about recent developments in the social sciences.

Social anthropology

Although the subject matter of social anthropology becomes increasingly hard to differentiate from the neighbouring disciplines of sociology, economics and political science, it differs from them markedly by its perspective and its methodology. In particular British social anthropology has placed great emphasis on 'participant observation' in the fieldwork, on the partial absorption of the fieldworker into the life of the community he is studying, on conforming to a considerable degree to their values. The comparative perspective of the discipline arises from the confrontation of the values of the community he is studying with those of the researcher's own society. Indeed field research of this kind is treated as an initiation rite by social anthropologists – one reason why in contrast to sociology, virtually all university teachers in this discipline are Ph.Ds.

During the last two decades or so, several powerful influences have wrought changes in the subject matter and the outlook of the discipline. The supply of unexplored remote traditional societies has dried up, the known traditional societies have been undergoing rapid change which has thrown into question the capacity of the formerly dominant structural-functional perspective to describe and explicate, and has at the same time brought home to anthropologists their need to include economic and political concepts in their theoretical framework (SSRC, 1968b).

Studies in economic anthropology and political anthropology have now become common, and joint work by social anthropologists with economists or political scientists has begun to appear. . . . Anthropological research on systems of law, especially tribal systems, drawing on the concepts and modes of analysis of Euro-American jurisprudence, has made an increasingly significant contribution to the comparative study of law and to an understanding of the basic nature of law and of processes of social control, both in instituted courts and in the ordinary affairs of life . . . this has obvious relevance to the interpretation of the economic and political future of developing nations. Both linguistics and psychology in recent years have developed a highly technical theoretical framework, much of which, like that of economics, seems to have little application to the problems of anthropology. . . . Processes of choice and decision-making, the structural complications of the language of kinship, or the principles of thought which underlie the diverse cognitive systems identified in myth, are all examples of areas where social anthropology can contribute to and draw upon the work of these other disciplines.

The questioning has gone even deeper. Many anthropologists have been returning to the philosophical foundations of the discipline, rejecting the concentration on the solution of specific problems in empirical data.

Another challenge to the dominant trends in Britain has been the work of Lévi-Strauss, opening social anthropology to influences from disciplines as diverse as linguistics, psychoanalysis and topology, focusing on the identification and construction of models and on their use in interpreting observed 'reality'. The experience of change has injected an historical perspective formerly lacking in much anthropological work. Progressively the boundaries with economics and politics are approached, as changes in traditional societies emphasize the function of the market and tend towards greater specialization of political roles. Increasingly the traditional preoccupation with kinship terms and structures appears irrelevant to the outsider. Yet these generate models which help to illumine the cognitive maps of members of other cultures. It certainly has not apparently lost its attraction for research in British anthropology.

There has of course been growing interest and concern by anthropologists with developing countries. They have studied the effects of technological innovations on social life, the relationships between planners, administrators and peasants, the effects of introduction of a monetary economy, settlement in industrialized areas, urbanization, the transformation of authority structures, the development of labour markets; the part played by voluntary associations in articulating old and new institutions with one another and with bureaucracy. The nature of development itself and the different forms which it may take are now a central concern for many anthropologists.

Progressively too anthropologists are studying aspects of advanced societies where fieldwork and participant observation are relevant techniques. The strength of British anthropology lies very

much in its standards of careful fieldwork and in the strong commitment of its teachers to research.

Very little social anthropology is conducted outside the university
framework, largely because, unlike the position in the USA, there
has not emerged an applied anthropology. 'Very few British social
anthropologists have deliberately framed a research plan to solve a
practical problem and conducted an investigation which could be
termed applied anthropology from the start' (SSRC, 1968b). Is this
a weakness in British social anthropology? Presumably the object of
a deliberately framed piece of applied research would be the potential use that could be made of it. If the potential 'user' is government
or planner or administrator this implies acceptance of the planning
or administrative perspective on the 'problem', which would surely
conflict with that of the anthropologist. Furthermore, the natural
'client' of the anthropologist is the people he studies and among
whom he lives during his fieldwork. It might well weaken anthropology more to become 'applied' than to provide analysis of situations, descriptions of behaviour and insights into motives and interests as many anthropologists do. Nevertheless, there are institutional obstacles to more effective contributions of this kind (SSRC,
1968b).

Three major studies enter into this situation. Most areas of
research in applied anthropology require a special competence
on the part of the fieldworker. He must not only be a
well-trained social anthropologist; he must also be familiar
with the basic framework of concepts relating to the particular
problem area he is investigating. If the problem is one of
changing a component in the diet of a people, he should have
a working knowledge of the main principles of nutrition. If it
concerns the introduction of a new crop he should know
something about the agricultural aspects of the problem. In
the past those anthropologists who have worked on such
problems did usually accumulate a budget of the essential
information required. But it is desirable for more effective
co-operation with the technical workers concerned that he
should receive some training in the discipline cognate to his
problem. (In some cases, and most satisfactorily, the
anthropologist has already received the appropriate medical,
agricultural or other technical training). This however, may
raise issues of timing and of financial support.

Another difficulty is of the reverse order. Experience has
shown that it is often difficult for technical experts in a
medical, agricultural or administrative field to see just where

the contribution of the social scientist lies and just what conditions he needs for his research. For effective co-operation there must be a fair measure of agreement on the definition of the objectives of research. This usually takes time to work out, and a willingness for each party to make adjustments in his conceptions of where the complexity of the problem under study lies.

A more serious difficulty in some ways is that of career structure. A medical man who takes up anthropological research, even if it bears directly on medical problems, runs the risk of getting out of line for advancement in his profession; an anthropologist who specializes in some field of applied anthropology has no clearly demarcated sphere of employment – in Britain at least – and is likely to be forced back into the ordinary academic market or take his chance in the wilderness of the international agencies.

By and large one may say that methodological advances have been more pioneered than used. The detailed field study meticulously reported, supported by genealogical data and glossaries of kinship terms has acquired the status of an advanced art form. It shows signs of yielding to studies focused especially on a particular problem, or aiming to acquire material for comparative purposes. Frequently this implies specialized methods – musicological and linguistic recordings, moving film and still photographs, standardized field notes, standardized interview schedules. These often require both expense and skilled assistance, neither of which is usually available to the fieldworker undertaking research for his Ph.D – still the principal form of research. The weaknesses in British social anthropology flow from these considerations and can be seen as a lack of contribution to multidisciplinary team research, too few collaborative and comparative studies, too few opportunities for careers in applied research.

Political science

Unlike social anthropology, whose origins were outside the universities but whose activities are now almost entirely within them, the tradition of political science in Britain developed within the universities but is now strongly represented outside them. Political science shared in the advances in the social sciences in the years before World War I, in whose wake interest was roused in international relations. University chairs were founded and the Royal Institute of International Affairs established. Teaching and research in international relations lent a new dimension to the academic study of politics. Political science shared in the further explosive growth of university social science since World War II, though less dramatically than sociology.

The 'mainstream' of political science in Britain (SSRC, 1968a) 'is related to a system of teaching which combines detailed analysis of certain classics of political thought with descriptive study of one or more polities . . . harnessing sociology and social psychology to the study of politics . . . also is part of the tradition. But 'mainstream' political scientists have been relatively slow to adopt the 'tools of social science'. . . . Their methods have been those traditional in humane scholarship, and they have in general been 'problem-oriented', not 'discipline-oriented'; that is to say, they have in general tackled issues of theory, analysis and recommendation as they arise, and have not set out to establish empirically a body of truths about politics in general.

There is also a strong vein of scepticism about any 'scientific' claim for the discipline; the belief that each political decision is special and not subject to general laws that can be illuminated by statistical enquiry. This view places the study of politics among the 'humanities' rather than the sciences – a distinction which is fortunately meaningless in French.

This emphasis is, as we shall see, partly responsible for the notable absence in British political science of grand theory, ambition, taxonomies and the formalisms of the behavioural school and the meta-theories of political analysis.

The lack of theory and the absence of the strong continental basis of legal, sociological and philosophical study have led to the raising of the question: Is politics an academic discipline? The question is really a rhetorical one; the answer is given by the growth in the number of university departments of politics and political science. What is more difficult is to separate Politics from politics or to reconcile them. 'Most practitioners of "mainstream" political science in Britain . . . their problem is to find a philosophy with which to defend a middle position: to sustain the autonomy of academic work in politics, and yet to accept the burden of responsibility for acting politically as part of a living tradition of political freedom.'

While the mainstream of political science has been concerned with government, students of politics have become increasingly aware that power relationships in smaller and more specialized units constitute a field of study which their training and conceptual equipment fits them to explore. However, while notable studies have been made of local government and the relationships between nationalized industries and government have attracted significant contributions, political scientists have only gingerly approached the study of hospitals, educational and work organizations. It would still be very difficult for someone whose work was in micro-politics to obtain a chair in political science. The existence of independent institutes such as the Royal Institute for International Affairs, Political and Economic Planning, the Institute of Strategic Studies and the Centre for Studies in Social Policy offers opportunities for research and research careers outside the universities. Political scientists interested in the 'fringe' areas of their discipline or in multidisciplinary problem-oriented research are more likely to move into these institutes for shorter or longer periods, some possibly for full careers.

While it is not yet possible to assess the effect on British political science of Britain's entry into the European Economic Community, it is clear that the study of European institutions is a growth industry, if for no other reason than the need to teach about them to students in departments of European Studies. This concern is shared with economists and is beginning to bring economists and political scientists into joint research.

Other developments external to the discipline have been affecting its methodology. These are the growth of the social sciences in general, the development of survey methodology, the development of systems theory and decision theory, the rebirth of linguistics with consequent interest in political language and content analysis, and the enormous increase in information and information-handling techniques. It is the nature of these developments that their exploitation demands greater resources than those available to the single research worker. Yet much, perhaps most research, is carried out by Ph.D students and by university members of staff working on their own. Unquestionably the foundation of the SSRC has meant a much more continuous and larger supply of grants for research than anything that went before and this has enlarged the horizons of political science departments and institutes.

One clear weakness in British political science is the lack of an adequate infrastructure to respond to the opportunities which open up with the advances in methodology and data. Just as, a generation ago, comparatively few economists were equipped to undertake studies involving a mastery of statistical and mathematical method, today there are many political scientists whose training unfits them for the use of new methods. Perhaps advances of the kind that now seem possible could be made only at the cost of a great deal more specialization. This brings us up against a feature of the British scene, which is common to most of the social sciences. There are now in Britain some forty-five universities and more than twenty polytechnics and colleges where serious degree level and post-graduate work is undertaken. Each of these institutions regards itself as incomplete without a department of politics, government or political science. Thus most are necessarily small, yet must teach the full scope of the discipline. This inhibits the specialization of groups of researchers, which can only be combined with the requirements of teaching in large departments or accommodated in institutes.

Human geography

Geography is a discipline which, like psychology, creates difficulties of classification. As organized in British universities, geography is usually a single department embracing both physical and human (social and economic) geography. The separation from geology is almost complete. The division of academic geographical activities between physical and human cannot be accurately assessed but is probably of the order of 60 per cent human, 40 per cent physical. In many of the applications of geography, such as land use studies, both aspects are involved. A substantial proportion of research is carried out overseas or in relation to countries abroad. The division of research activity between fields and between Britain and other countries is shown in Table 2.

TABLE 2 *Distribution of articles published in three leading British geographical journals, 1959–69*

	Relating to Great Britain		Relating to foreign lands		
General	Human geography	Physical geography	Human geography	Physical geography	Total
77	190	133	123	37	556

Note: The journals included are: *Transactions* of the Institute of British Geographers, *Scottish Geographical Magazine* and *Geography*.

Source: Research in Human Geography (SSRC, 1968b).

As we noted in the case of political science, the teaching of geography is spread over virtually all the universities in Britain; thus the model size of department is comparatively small – around sixteen members.

Unlike other social sciences, but like history, geography is a major school subject. Thus many of the geographers trained at university become career school teachers, which implies that the whole range of subject matter has to be covered. As with political science, the outcome is that specialization is inhibited. Again geography is seen as a synthesizing discipline relating a wide variety of phenomena into a coherent analysis of some problem in a spatial setting. The geographer has thus tended to combine a deep knowledge of some aspect of his discipline with a detailed familiarity with a geographical region. In this respect his situation is not dissimilar to that of the social anthropologists.

Research has been largely an individual activity often aimed at a Ph.D. Organized team research is a new development associated with the following factors: (i) a tendency for departments to grow; leading to (ii) increased opportunities for specialization; (iii) a tendency for geography departments to become more specialized; (iv) the appearance of new subject groupings under some such title as 'environmental' or 'ecological' sciences; (v) the provision of research grants by the SSRC for human geography and by the Natural Environment Research Council for physical geography.

Little organized geographical research contributing to the main body of knowledge takes place outside the universities. Studies, generally associated with planning, are undertaken within government and local government and studies with a geographical content are undertaken by industrial and commercial organizations. But there is no specialized geographical research institute.

There are, of course, many career outlets for people with degrees in geography but not in the form of posts especially requiring geographical expertise. This, combined with the fact that there has been a steady supply of trained geographers for many decades, has ensured that there is no manifest scarcity of trained geographers in Britain. The priority is less, then, to expand the supply of postgraduates as to assume the quality of their training and of research. Here we encounter the difficulty which has beset the SSRC from its early days in all branches of the social sciences – concentration or dispersion? All university departments want to have postgraduate work: it is stimulating to staff; it helps staff with research; it gives undergraduates a sense of what research is all about and what is happening in at least one field; it enhances the department's prestige. But if each department is to have postgraduate students, most will have very few. And if postgraduate students need the stimulus of others working on similar problems or in the same field, the dilemma becomes acute. One responsive strategy is for university departments to emphasize their differences, to offer specializations to attract postgraduate students, concentrating their research efforts in a limited number of fields instead of seeking to cater for all interests.

The strengths, then, of British geographical research have been in the wide coverage of detailed topics, all set against a general geographic background.

British work in historical geography has been concerned with the reconstruction of past landscape and the activities of the people who inhabited it and in the past distribution of industrial, agricultural and prospecting activities. In this field there has been growing use of documentary and statistical sources. Political geography has related basic spatial patterns of organization to the nature of terrain and the ethnic composition of the population.

Much work has been done on the processes of urban growth, some in co-operation with sociologists or by geographers with sociological training. Urban structure is another field which has obvious applications to present day problems of settlement, industrial development, race relations and community politics. Regional growth and development, population movements, rural development problems and communication patterns have all stimulated notable studies in some of which new techniques deriving from operational research, systems theory, graph theory and matrix algebra have been applied.

If these represent strengths, weaknesses derive from the reasons we stated earlier – the comparative level of specialization and team research. Additionally the wide scope of the subject means that some issues and problems can be undertaken only with a good knowledge of another discipline such as economics or sociology within multidisciplinary teams.

Among the weak areas identified by the SSRC's Geography Committee were the following:

'Perception' studies of the difference between the perceived and the 'real' environment, to examine the procedures people use to search and explore their environment. This involves working with techniques provided by psychologists and on applications with which sociologists and planners are concerned.

'Simulation' models of spatial systems are important aids in urban policy-making and planning. Present models are crude.

Forecasting is a hitherto neglected field for geographers.

Regional taxonomy or the effective distribution of space into operational units requires statistical techniques new to geographers.

Theoretical constructs and their empirical testing are needed to establish environmental standards.

Finally comparative studies of the spatial aspects of regional economic and social development are lacking. Their importance is clear.

Economic and social history

The economic and social development of contemporary societies is one of today's main anxieties; thus the prime focus of economic and social history is on the development of economic systems. The debate on industrialization and modernization has focused attention on the Industrial Revolution, on the process of growth, the role of agriculture, population change, and international trade.

Although economic historians tackle economic questions they usually come up with answers only partly derived from economic data and economic reasoning. The obligation to study the messy facts of history and to account for what apparently happened rather than what might or should have happened obliges them to reject or modify the abstractions of economic theory. Nevertheless in one aspect at least economic history is making progressively more use of modern economic techniques – those of mathematical economics and econometrics. Recent attempts have been made to obtain reliable measures of the growth of national income and capital formation in the early stages of industrialization, details of industrial productivity and fluctuations in the economy of the nineteenth century. The more abstrusely mathematical and statistical manipulation of series data has developed less and less rapidly in Britain than in the United States, just as statistical historical demography has developed further and faster in France than in Britain. Partly this is attributable to the inadequacies of the British source material, partly to inadequate training in the use of econometric techniques, partly to distaste and 'analytical' history: historical training strongly emphasizes synthesis. To this preference the recent recrudescence of interest in social history has been more acceptable. But even here there has been specialization around themes as well as around periods. New subdisciplines have emerged in urban history and, inspired by French influence, in the history of population. Changing social structure, the emergence of a working class, cultural and intellectual history all represent new specializations and in all of these the recognition by scholars that assistance is available for their studies from the SSRC has been surprisingly slow to dawn.

British sociology, unlike European but like its American counterpart, has been notably deficient in historical sense. In return

71

British historians have been notably leery of sociology and socio-logical method. However, with the growing emphasis on develop-ment and social change, an interest in sociological method and concepts has awakened. Some of the bridging (particularly in the field of cultural history) has been the work of those whose main discipline is English literature, and their lead has been followed by students prepared to master the concepts of sociology and the methods of history. As a consequence synthetic history has become more sociological with more emphasis on social institutions and processes, social movements, cultural developments, and compara-tive social structure.

Historical demography is the area in which most quantifications can, and have been, introduced into social history. This is an enter-prise which calls for teamwork, the specialized use of computer analysis and a commitment over a number of years. Without sub-stantial sponsorship such work could not be undertaken. There is probably scope in other fields of history for similar developments – urban and linguistic history for example. The present 'growth indus-tries' in historical research include agricultural history (for long the prime focus in economic history); urban history; population; capital formation; labour and business history.

Intellectual and cultural history, history of science and history of technology are largely cultivated outside the mainstream of histori-cal research and poorly articulated with general social and economic history. Labour history, Britain being Britain, not surpris-ingly places considerable emphasis on the emergence and problems of class, although the influence of Marx is more general than specific. Labour history has in fact formed a focus for sociologists, political scientists, students of industrial relations and historians.

The history of social policy and administration is another area where the lead has come from students of social administration, criminology and other applied studies rather than from historians. Now that the earliest social surveys are historical documents, re-peated surveys may yield growing dividends in future. There is also a growing industry in administrative histories, especially of the two world wars.

We have seen that new approaches and methods have been emerging, some still in infancy, but all affected by the data explosion caused by the reduction of the fifty-year rule to thirty, the growth of local record offices, the opening of business and family archives and the accessibility of quantitative data. The scope for the individual scholar remains but the exploitation of this rapidly growing mass of material requires another kind of approach. Only well-equipped units with physical facilities including access to computers and with

72

administrative continuity and expertise can hope to make a substantial impact. They would also help to provide a more systematic training for graduates, not only in advanced methodology, but also in the social science concepts required for this kind of research (SSRC, 1969).

> At present . . . graduate work in economic and social history is too diffused and unsystematic. In particular, the methodological difficulty of defining an acceptable range of approaches and topics, and the widespread academic problem of securing a large enough concentration of students, mean that there are considerable obstacles in the way of providing adequate course work and 'technical' training appropriate to the needs of graduate students in economic and social history.
>   . . . this indicates the need for a greater degree of selectivity in the allocation of resources (i.e. a greater concentration of effort in individual universities or in groups of universities), for it is impossible that all, or even most, university institutions can support all aspects of a broadly based postgraduate programme in economic and social history.

If, then, the weaknesses in British social and economic history are largely institutional, they also include the obverse of one of its strengths – its commonsensicality and reluctance to espouse theory too warmly.

Sociology

> In . . . the United Kingdom . . . there is criticism of what is alleged to be undue emphasis on pragmatically oriented applied research, to the detriment of endeavours which would enhance sociological theory . . . [and] there is dissension as to the proper role of quantification.

This quotation from Lazarsfeld's review of sociology in *Main Trends* (UNESCO, 1970) makes a good text on which to preach. To which we may add: 'Amateurism is design, methods and conceptualization' (Little, 1963) and 'indiscriminate use of research techniques' (*passim*) suggest that all is not well with British sociological research. But is it as bad as that?

The focus on empiricism has often been thought of as the great British sociological tradition. We all know that the major British contributions to the foundation of the discipline were the work of

73

people concerned with social problems and sponsoring reforms and interested in establishing the facts of social life rather than in elaborating theories. But since the days of Booth and Rowntree sociology has become an academic discipline, numerically among the largest of the social sciences in terms of students, staff, research grants and research publications. Yet notable contributions to theory have been few, methodology varies from highly sophisticated and mathematical to naive and inappropriate with widespread misuse of statistical method. The cumulative effect of research is bewildering rather than enlightening.

During the period of rapid growth of sociology as an academic discipline in Britain, research was heavily dominated by American influence – theory, publications and methods. The European philosophical traditions contributed weightily to the undergraduate syllabus; the reverence for Marx, Durkheim and Weber never waned, though few read them in the original. But when it came to research, the empirical strain reasserted itself and the ready availability of survey method made it the instrument of choice for quick results.

The rapid increase in university departments drew into university teaching posts graduates with Bachelor's degrees, some immediately after graduation, some with short postgraduate experience and Master's degrees. Few had any serious experience of research. The larger cohorts of graduates coming along after them produced many who wished to go on to do research and the establishment of the SSRC provided greatly expanded opportunities for research training – although the supervisors of training and research had themselves often scant experience. The weaknesses that are observable were predictable, and predicted. Nevertheless, a make haste slowly approach was neither politically possible nor in the long run academically wise. Sending large numbers of graduates for research training in the USA, for example, would have increased the influence of American sociology, accelerated the brain drain and hampered indigenous development, a pattern now rued by the Canadians. The worst is almost certainly over. New posts are coming forward more slowly and are being filled by people with greater research experience; the rediscovery of European sociology is having its influence and with luck the mounting costs of 'surveys' is having a rationing effect. Paradoxically that is the field in which methodological rigour has been most developed and taught. What is wanted far more is more rigour in problem formulation, greater development of the ability to sense what is researchable, how a problem can be phrased or rephrased in researchable terms. Greater recourse to methods other than the survey will put greater demands on these abilities. One dreadful feature of the survey method is that however poorly conceived and conceptualized the design, however slipshod the application, however inappropriate the statistical manipulation and however tendentious the conclusions, the array of tabulated matter and the existence of 'findings' have exercised a fascination for the editors of journals and their advisers. Again the worst is probably over, but it has been bad.

If the strengths of British sociological research have not been in its methodology or theoretical and conceptual sophistication, there have nevertheless been resoundingly successful areas of study and research. Borrowing from the strong anthropological tradition of intensive fieldwork supplemented by more or less judicious use of survey material, there have been substantial contributions to community studies. The rediscovery of community in urban areas, even in megapolis, has certainly influenced the outlook of social and physical planners and made a contribution to more theoretical perspectives in such fields as stratification, role theory and organizational behaviour.

There are so many fields of sociology that it is difficult even to mention all of them in the space of a single chapter let alone one purporting to cover the whole of the social sciences.

Education: More unreliable research has accumulated in this area than in any other except possibly mass communication. Among the welter of studies concerned to show the cumulative disadvantages piled on children of working-class origin by educational selection and stratification, few have adopted an analytical approach to the educational and socialization process. Most have concentrated on the shortcomings of the educational system, formulating their 'problem' in terms of an administrative perspective; very few indeed have adopted a developmental, diachronic approach to examine the way in which the child uses the educational and socialization processes in evolving a career trajectory. The approach that has been adopted has concentrated so strongly on the social consequences of the pattern of educational provision that education has been squeezed out. More imaginative has been the analysis of the sociolinguistic basis of response to the experience of formal education.

The sociology of mass communication suffered for many years from inadequate problem formulation. Insecurely linked to the sociology of knowledge on the one hand and to the sociology of organizational behaviour on the other, both of which are in fact highly relevant, the study of mass communication largely ignored sociolinguistics. By taking what was communicated as the independent variable and behaviour as the dependent variable, investigations failed to perceive mass communication as an aspect of the environment which the actor samples, extracts meaning from and uses for his own purposes. With this recognition, research on mass communication has acquired a new and hopefully more profitable lease of life.

In the field of *deviance*, again too much research was permeated with the administrative and criminological perspective accepting deviance as a dependent variable and seeking independent variables to manipulate either actually or conceptually. The identification of deviance in studies of this kind has to rely on detection and conviction of offenders. A great deal of work in this field has been of the nature of prediction studies. More recently the perspective of symbolic interactionism has inspired a newer line of research but the influences have been largely American research.

The sociology of organizations has been one field of sociology, while sociolinguistics is another, where British research has been more influential in the United States than the other way round. The analysis of organizational cultures and styles of operation and their relationship to environmental change, the relationship between technology and behaviour and the open sociotechnical systems approach (as much social psychological as sociological) have become staple material for graduate schools of management if not for departments of sociology. And these were just the lines of research which earlier received systematic continuous funding from public sources in post-war Britain. We must mention briefly *political sociology*. Naturally the favourite independent variable is 'class', usually identified by occupation, and the favourite dependent variable is voting behaviour. The search is then for intervening variables – self class identification and so on. These studies are very closely related to studies of social stratification. Although there has been growing conceptual sophistication, nearly all studies suffer from the weakness inherent in the identification of class and stratum by occupational differentiation. The worst feature of this system of categorization is its so ready availability and acceptance.

Finally, research on *social change* has received a new and interdisciplinary dimension through the concern with developing countries. Research draws upon many other disciplines and it is clear that a unidisciplinary approach provides neither solutions to problems nor contributions to theory.

Professional sociologists have virtually ignored the sociology of culture, of art and literature, leaving the most influential work in the hands of non-sociologists, straying across from university departments of English. The sociology of the military and of warfare has been neglected, and today is not considered a field in which empirical research can be undertaken from a truly 'critical' standpoint. In the sociology of sociology – the way in which sociological research is generated and used – there is a notable blank.

Until recently, the *sociology of law* was equally neglected; having been identified as a 'gap' by the SSRC it now boasts a Centre for Sociolegal Studies. Interestingly enough, three of the four units set up by the SSRC are in interdisciplinary areas – Ethnic Relations, Industrial Relations, and Sociolegal Studies; the fourth, the SSRC Survey Unit is intended to be a source and resource for the SSRC itself and for all researchers in the social sciences. The fact that all are at least partly in the domain of sociology is partly a consequence of the fact that none of the existing research institutes, apart from the Institute of Race Relations was primarily sociological – economics, politics, psychology, were all well covered with institutes in applied areas.

One consequence of the enormous range comprehended by sociology is that frequently comparability between studies is lost. Researchers in one field do not seek to ensure that the material they collect can be used for cross comparisons with material collected by workers in different fields with different objectives – for instance, the categorization of education background.

While comparability could be greatly improved, continuity is equally desirable. There are now more properly equipped research units and teams than ten or twenty years ago, although few can match the contributions of those that existed then in Edinburgh and Liverpool for example. And the continuity over five years is more frequently provided by SSRC 'programme' grants. Of course continuity of support does not imply continuity of research staff. Only in the SSRC units are research posts established and tenured. The bulk of research is still carried out by university teachers and postgraduate students. This has the advantage that most researchers have had a large part in deciding what and how to research; its disadvantage is the persistence of much amateurism.

Social psychology

The Heyworth Committee felt obliged to comment unfavourably that 'social psychology has been particularly neglected in British universities. . . . One contributing factor – has been the dispersion of social psychologists among departments of psychology, sociology and social administration' (Heyworth, 1965). This situation persists. It is still possible for students to receive honours degrees in psychology without undertaking more than a sketchy course in social psychology; there are only three universities where the student can take the equivalent of a 'major' in social psychology and a handful of postgraduate degree courses. There are four chairs in social psychology in Britain. There is of course much to be said for teaching social psychology within the mainstream of psychology, nevertheless social psychology needs to be taught from a sociological as well as a psychological perspective or rather from a perspective different from either but partaking of both. The consequence of its location merely within departments of psychology, and the overwhelming influence of American material has put a premium on experimental social psychology of the laboratory and small group type. The outcome has been the purchase of some rigour at the cost of much trivialization. To this trend the attitude of journal editors and their advisors has contributed. It is still rare but at least now possible for a theoretical article to obtain space in the *British Journal for Social and Clinical Psychology*, but the journal *Human Relations* has maintained a balance weighted in favour of empirical if not laboratory work.

The experimental approach is under severe attack at present – for artificiality, for ignoring the meanings of the experimental situation for the 'subjects', for the ethically unacceptable practices of deception of subjects, for the short-term sampling of behaviour it implies, shorn of its social context, and for the consequent dubiety of its interpretations for behaviour in the world outside the laboratory. This will no doubt weaken the addiction of British social psychologists to laboratory experiments, but it is easy to understand how it arose. In the first place it was a piece of self defence for people situated in biologically and experimentally oriented departments of psychology in which being 'scientific' was identical with conducting experiments. Second, it was one way of obtaining a clear demarcation from the sociologists. Third, it shares with the 'survey' the advantage that it always produces 'outcomes', 'results' and numerical data to support them with suitable statistical measures of their 'significance'. And of course the American influence was very strong; there was no European tradition to turn to. In response to this some British social psychologists were prime movers in the foundation of a European Association of Experimental Social Psychology with its own journal, the emphasis on experiment being maintained.

The study of human social behaviour in ordinary settings in our society lagged behind studies of behaviour in exotic societies, and studies of the behaviour of non-human species such as chimpanzees and dolphins. The outcome is that a kind of human ethology is emerging based as much on departments of zoology as psychology.

But the most impressive and most helpful signs come from the innovative work of British psychologists in the observation of the behaviour of very young children, the advances in psycholinguistics and the studies of communication patterns among 'normal' and 'abnormal' persons. A more healthy, more balanced development of research in social psychology will come when it becomes accepted that social psychology is not just a poor relation of psychology or a handmaiden to sociology, but a perspective on the world with its own validity and one which illuminates a wide range of phenomena, many of which are also within the accepted subject matter of psychology and sociology – and anthropology and economics for that matter. Anthropologists have shown a considerable interest in psychology but have been unduly influenced by psychoanalytic doctrines in the absence of any other psychology of social behaviour. As far as economics are concerned, it is clear that the assumptions made in economics about the meaning to people of inflation, for example, or the psychological factors which influence investment decisions are no longer tenable. Studies along these lines by social psychologists are beginning to have impact.

The most innovative area in social psychology in Britain has since the war been in the field of organization studies and again this is connected with the fact that continuity and focus was provided by the Tavistock Institute of Human Relations.

Economics

The advance of economics as a theoretical discipline has neatly paralleled its failure as an applied science. Nowhere is this more perfectly exemplified than in Britain. Failure in application should constitute warnings that the possibility of conducting the most intricate and sophisticated analysis too often rests on a narrowing of the focus of enquiry which removes it from the socio-political context to which it is supposed to refer. Strangely enough, this concentration on the purely economic has not been compensated by methodological navel-gazings. UNESCO's *Main Trends* (1970) comments on the

> absence of broad discussions and important writings on the general foundations and methodology of economics. There is a great contrast between the paucity of post-war publications and the famous polemics of older times and the abundant literature even between the wars. Studies on methodology are being increasingly replaced by more or less complete

79

inventories of the research techniques available to contemporary economics. . . . What is more, economists do not seem to regret the lack of methodological discussions which, on the contrary, are considered boring and futile, and regularly accorded a poor reception.

Commenting on the narrowing focus of economics, this review continues (p. 295):

Another characteristic feature has been the progressive elimination of social and meta-sociological questions. To the past belong not only the great tradition of analysing economic and social problems in their organic unity, with which such names as Karl Marx, Werner Sombart, Max Weber and Rosa Luxemburg are associated, but also the far less ambitious approach of studying economic problems at least in a limited sociohistorical context (Alfred Marshall). The very questions which made economic science a social discipline are now increasingly left to newspaper pundits and mass media experts.

The review is equally scathing of the tendency to split into narrow specializations and the contrast between the enthusiasm for empirical econometric research and refusal of all theory. The consequence of development studies has been commented upon by Streeten (1972, p. 129):

The main conclusion is to beware of the simple transfer of fairly sophisticated concepts from one setting to another, without close scrutiny of the institutional differences. . . . Scientific research and its dissemination by teachers is characterised by standard models. . . . These models are at once a crutch and a prison, since it is in their nature that they focus on some aspects of reality at the expense of others.

And by Kaldor (1972, pp. 127–8):

It is no good starting off a model with a kind of abstraction which initially excludes the influence of forces which are mainly responsible for the behaviour of the economic variables under investigation; and upon finding that the theory leads to results contrary to what we observe in reality, attributing this contrary movement to the compensation (or more than compensation) influence of residual factors that have been assumed away in the model. . . . The interpretative value of this kind of theory must of necessity be extremely small.

Economic research has a powerful base. Not only is economics a major university discipline, taught not only in departments of economics but in the form of applied micro-economics in departments of management and in the business schools, it is also taught in polytechnics and colleges. Research is conducted in a number of government departments, in commercial, financial and banking enterprises, in the nationalized industries and in independent institutes like the National Institute for Economic and Social Research and Political and Economic Planning.

A substantial proportion of research conducted in some other institutes is also economic in character – the Centre for Environmental Studies, the Institute of Development Studies are examples. Groups such as Institute of Economic Affairs, founded in 1957, serve to focus and to publish academic research as well as to carry out some of its own.

The universities provide, however, the overwhelming portion of the research base: virtually every university has a department strong enough to sustain a major commitment to research. There is however a marked advantage in size. The biggest battalions mount the heaviest guns. This is exemplified by the distribution of the SSRC's research funds of which in 1971–3 no less than 38 per cent went to Cambridge and 16 per cent to London Universities.

An analysis of SSRC grants does not necessarily match research trends; much research carried on in universities in theoretical economics requires little or no external funding, for example. Nevertheless, the trends are indicative of the balance of activities within the discipline and are neatly summarized in Table 3, recently published by the SSRC.

The increase in studies of international economics and economic growth and development represent an accommodation to the growing influence of international organization and the crises in international finance; but the most growth is in the field of economic statistics and is notable for the high proportion of successful applications (SSRC, 1974).

There has been a substantial growth of applications in international economics and land use studies, labour economics and industrial economics, most of which tend to be fairly modest amounts of finance, and to have above average success rates. Subject areas which have so far not enjoyed

81

great success have been the economics of international business, natural resources, and urban economics.

As far as methodology is concerned the most significant developments have been in the field of economic and econometric

TABLE 3 *Applications and awards by subject, 1969–71 and 1971–3*[1]

	1969–71		1971–3	
	Applications	*Awards*	*Applications*	*Awards*
000 General economics; theory; history systems[2]	7	6	9	8
100 Economic growth; development; planning; fluctuations	21	11	30	21
200 Economic statistics	5	3	14	13
300 Domestic monetary and fiscal theory and institutions	16	9	12	8
400 International economics	7	4	19	10
500 Administration; business; finance; marketing	2	2	5	3
600 Industrial organization; technological change; industry studies	24	13	25	19
700 Agriculture; natural resources	4	1	11	6
800 Manpower; labour; population	20	9	21	14
900 Welfare programmes, consumer economics; urban and regional economics	24	13	23	13
TOTAL	130	71	169	115

[1] Since 1973 the growth in grant applications has not been matched by growth in available funds. The 'success rate' by *value* had dropped to 22·4 per cent by 1976.
[2] American Economic Association classification.

Source: SSRC *Newsletter* No. 22, February 1974.

modelling and the use of computers. There are now three major models of the British economy in use – Cambridge, London and the Treasury.

Industrial relations and management research

Like education this is a field for research using the concepts, techniques and methods of the major social science disciplines – sociology, psychology, economics – rather than a discipline in its own right. All such fields suffer from the fact that the most prestigious work is in mainstream discipline rather than in 'applied fields'. Worse, these particular fields have the additional low prestige of being regarded as providing intellectually undemanding training as opposed to a higher education. The outcome is to be seen in the comments of the Educational Research Board and the Management and Industrial Relations Committee of the SSRC. The former comments (SSRC, 1974):

> Applicants have two major sources of difficulty in drawing up their proposals. The first of these is a difficulty in thinking through a piece of research to its logical conclusion, and in particular to formulate hypotheses which are firm enough to provide a framework, but yet permit flexibility in the detailed conduct of the research and the interpretation of results. Too frequently, elaborate plans for the collection of data are put forward without any indication of how the information will be dealt with and made use of.

The latter:

> One might have expected that the improved and extended resources available in recent years for management education would also help to foster a parallel developing interest in management research. In terms of satisfactory applications for research grants coming before the Committee, however, this does not seem to be borne out.

Most of the work in these areas has been in industrial relations, business economics, marketing and the behaviour, structure and operation of organizations. Comparatively little has been undertaken in the areas of small business, public sector management, managerial ideology and the decision process.

Within the British context much damage has been done by the

83

partition of industrial relations as a field for study and education from its parent disciplines of economics and labour history and its adjacent disciplines of psychology, sociology and political science. Much of the work has been conducted at a low level of conceptualization and little has been fed back into parent and adjacent disciplines. The SSRC established a unit at Warwick University largely to strengthen research in this field.

Research in applied fields such as this must presumably attempt to satisfy two criteria – their utility – the prima facie justification for entering the field – and their contribution to knowledge. It is by no means easy to satisfy both. The greatest innovation in Britain has been the work of the Tavistock Institute of Human Relations in evolving and developing the 'open sociotechnical systems' approach, drawing on psychology, sociology, systems theory and operational research, and in pioneering a research methodology to accompany it – 'action' research. Unsurprisingly their practical value has been reaped more outside than inside Britain, notably in Norway, Holland and Sweden, but growingly in other countries including France. British industry on the whole appears to prefer to import packaged 'improvements' from the United States, resting on a simpler, if simplistic, conceptual basis. The action research method makes demands difficult to satisfy from a university base; it also appeals to criteria of legitimation which are not easily assimilated to the university's scientific requirements of replicability. Most of the other researches concerned with organization are better described under the heads of psychology of organizations, sociology of organizations and industrial economics than under the rubric of management, as their contributions have been more to analysis and understanding than to practice. It makes little sense to classify studies according to their location; for example, to regard as management research those studies in business schools or university departments of management, while similar studies in social science departments are classified as psychology, sociology or economics.

A similar suspended position is occupied by statistics. 'Statistical work tends to be performed in the context of other studies. The result is that statistics suffers from a degree of invisibility.' (SSRC, 1974). Methodology or a discipline with its own substantive body of knowledge? The topics considered by the SSRC's Statistics Committee

have embraced occupational mobility, historical demography, mathematical sociology, educational cohorts, decision analysis, econometric forecasting, studies of migration, modes of voting behaviour, and the application of new mathematical

84

techniques to town planning. . . . Overall there are considerably more funds seeking good statistical research than there are statisticians (or mathematicians) interested in coming forward.

Nevertheless, the Committee perceives that a

very welcome trend is the noticeably higher proportion of applications referred to the Statistics Committee alone. We believe this genuinely reflects an important new development: the revival at last in this country of a true 'social statistics' – that is to say, of a more or less autonomous field of statistics centred on and developing in step with various social science disciplines. The increased variety of subject fields in which applications of this kind are now being received would seem to suggest that a 'critical mass' in this respect has now been reached.

The social indicators movement has so far not progressed very far in Britain but the new *Social Trends*, annually issued by the government's Central Statistical Office, represents a deliberate attempt to develop appropriate indicators to describe the quality of life in Britain.

Conclusion

Dealing in this way separately with each of the social science disciplines makes it difficult to obtain a perspective of the whole. Yet it is essential to do so; the disciplines lead separate lives, coming together only under the umbrella of the SSRC, in university faculties (as competitors for resources), in a few multidisciplinary institutes and in occasional joint research undertakings. Many economists and many historians are probably not sure whether they are social scientists or not, and most psychologists are inclined to think that they are 'life' scientists or possibly 'human' scientists. From the outside many would challenge the disciplines' right to the term science at all, an argument which is possible in English but not in French or German. Nor have they escaped the attack on 'objectivity' which has assailed the social sciences in France and Germany, although that attack appears more muted this side of the Channel.

In this account we have necessarily given full rein to doubts, disappointments and dangers, to the gaps in the record. But the sheer volume of research and publication is impressive, the expectations of utility have grown and become excessive, but nevertheless exercise a strong pull on research. Units, groups, teams, have appeared, serviced by an infrastructure of information and computing facilities quite beyond the imaginings of a mere twenty-five years ago; if the result has not been the instant solution of long-standing problems this should occasion no surprise. There are no short cuts or easy roads to knowledge in the social sciences as elsewhere.

Chapter 4
Applied Sociology

It is not the simplest thing in the world to explain what we mean by applied sociology. We understand what is meant by applied mathematics, applied physics and so on, but when we come to the social sciences the distinction between what is done in the laboratory and what is done by practitioners is less clear. After all, the world of human behaviour is the social scientist's laboratory, and it is seldom that we can get very far by thinking about social phenomena in the abstract.

Applied sociology is not just the application of sociological research findings to practical situations. The term is often used as synonymous with empirical sociology, which again is used to mean sociological research in which field data is collected. A more useful distinction is between theory-oriented and field- or problem-oriented research. Very similar empirical studies might be mounted in one case to throw light on a theoretical problem and in another case to solve a practical problem. Research undertaken with the latter motive may add significantly to the development of sociological concepts, while theory-oriented research may also develop notions or uncover facts which may throw light on a social problem.

The methods of applied sociology then are essentially the methods of sociology and a piece of work may be described as 'applied' sociology when the concepts, categories and techniques of research and study in sociology are applied to some real world problem. Hence, a good deal of present day market research can be regarded as applied sociology, although often the practitioners are not sociologists. We shall not be discussing this kind of application, but rather the application of research to new problems; once we can hand over techniques that have become routine to a layman, we can cease to think of it as applied sociological research.

The applied sociologist may need to use other methods besides those of sociology itself; for example of operational research in, say, establishing objectives and the extent to which these goals are achieved. More recently still we shall find sociologists using methods of action research with which they positively intervene so as to study the impact of changes that they have proposed.

Applied sociology is in this sense concerned with the interaction of the principles and methods of sociology with real situations leading to the development and modification of sociological ideas and methods. Robert C. Angell has said: 'When sociology is not an end in itself, but becomes a means to some other end, it is applied sociology.' We would suggest 'when sociology is not the only end in itself, but becomes, at least partly, a means to some other end, it is applied sociology'.

The application and utilization of sociological research is by no means a straightforward matter. To begin with, problems as they appear to be seen by policy-makers, managers, administrators, do not clothe themselves in sociological categories, and for the sociologist to contribute towards their solution, or even their illumination, he needs to reframe them in other terms. This may not be acceptable: for one thing, the administrator may deny the rationality of the analysis; but, even when he is prepared to accept it, the solution may be impracticable for political or administrative reasons which lay outside the sociologist's frame of reference. For him, administration is the art of the possible and what is possible may not include solutions which involve changing the relative power of different people or groups. To the sociologist it may be clear that conflicts between groups are not personality traits, but aspects of the roles that their job responsibilities require. We may see the same pattern in the mutual view of policy-maker and sociologist, and part of the process of applying sociology is indeed their mutual learning. Thus to some extent, the applied sociologist has to teach his 'clients' some of the rudiments of his science. All this helps to explain why it is difficult to pick up the results of sociological research and use them to solve problems. It is a sophisticated process and requires a degree of analysis of the problems in its setting, which cannot be left to non-sociologists and one which we discuss in more detail in Chapter 9, 'Behavioural Science Engagements'. The aim here is to show examples of the sorts of insights into practical problems in society that are provided by sociological analysis.

Urban sociology

In a sense urban sociology is the whole discipline of sociology; after all, the sociologist studies modern large-scale societies and modern large-scale societies are predominantly urban in character. So, when we talk about urban sociology we are trying to make a distinction between those aspects of modern society which derive especially from urban development and those that do not. Urban society was studied extensively in many aspects by the Chicago School of Sociologists in the 1930s and culminated in Louis Wirth's (1951) article 'Urbanism as a Way of Life'. In this he contrasted the kinds of relationship of traditional rural society with those of the dweller in the city – 'impersonal, superficial, transitory and segmental'. The city dweller tends to treat social relationships as a means to his own ends. The image of a close web of social relationships, the mutually supportive large extended family thought typical of the rural community, is replaced by the more impersonal style of relationship of urban society, in which each member is busy about his own affairs, returning to his 'nuclear' family of wife and children, in some impersonal suburb.

The modern city, typically, is multiracial, pluralistic and requires for its day-to-day survival complex essential services, which in turn requires the development of new roles for social institutions of all kinds, in particular, in the stability and function of the family. Naturally, the sociologist has an interest in the family as an institution. Sometimes the motive for the study has been a welfare one, directly inspired by the need to do something about a social problem: sometimes the study has been motivated by sociological goals, that is, to test out beliefs, hypotheses and assertions about the impact of urban living on family life. Here we see the complex interaction of pure empirical and applied sociology, because some of the applied studies have resulted in developments of theory and some of the pure empirical studies have helped to guide social action.

As an example of the first, we may take the study of Elizabeth Bott (1957) entitled *Family and Social Network*. This started from the need to develop casework methods for the family welfare associations and in the course of her studies she found that the degree of conjugal segregation (the extent to which the roles of husband and wife were different and distinct) was related to the pattern of relationship maintained by members of the family with external people, and the relationship of these external people with one another.

89

Her observations have been a contribution to our understanding of the role of the family in modern urban society, as well as helping towards the development of case work method.

Let us compare this with *Family and Kinship in East London* (1957) by M. Young and P. Willmott, who doubted the truth of the assumptions made about the impersonal urban culture. In their research they studied families in Bethnal Green (a traditional working-class suburb) and they found many of the characteristics of village society persisted. Although the environment was dismal, even seedy, from the point of view of the outsider, it provided warmth and neighbourliness for its inhabitants, with children growing up within an extended family.

Young and Willmott studied families moved to a new housing estate, a clean, new suburb which to the outsider appeared a much more favourable environment than Bethnal Green. To many of the families moved there, however, the change was seen as a bad one, as the close companionship and social networks were broken. This study was only one of several which developed these themes but was the most influential in its popular interpretation.

Other studies have demonstrated the wide variety of urban communities that exist in Britain and while Madeline Kerr's study *The People of Ship Street* (1958) showed a matriarchal society similar to that of Bethnal Green, the authors of *Coal is our Life* (1956) depicted a strongly patriarchal system in the coalfield.

These studies have proved very influential among social workers and have done much to alert planners to the defects of a good deal of post-war development of housing estates and new towns. Other studies have concentrated more on specific social problems, although in nearly every case they have pinpointed the importance of the family in modern, as in traditional society, e.g. studies of old people, testing the assumptions that the breakdown of the old extended family conduced towards the picture of lonely and deserted old people, many living on the margins of poverty, or studies of children in need of care, delinquent children, the effects on their family, especially the children, of married women taking employment, etc. In the process of urbanization, the family has undergone changes, but it would appear to be a very robust institution and one whose role even now needs more study. After all, the family is the main organ of socialization of the individual; it produces at different times and in different situations individuals who will fit into all kinds of societies – totalitarian, democratic, capitalist, socialist, etc.

Sociology of industry

Early in this century the typical worker in the most advanced sectors of industry would be a machine operator, and the variability and inefficiency of the man compared with the machine was apparent. Led by the famous F. W. Taylor, the Scientific Management School emerged: their doctrine was that of the 'one best way'. Scientific analysis of every job would lead to the design of the most efficient set of movements for achieving it. With training and adequate incentives a worker would then produce twice or three times what he did before. Of course, this did not always work and, when it did, workers were producing less than they might; this was seen as restriction of output, for which no satisfactory reason could be adduced.

The famous Hawthorne experiments of the late 1920s and early 1930s in America appeared to show that these restrictions on output were imposed by the informal groups to which workers belonged. Briefly, in the Hawthorne experiments on the working environment, the experimenters systematically altered one variable at a time and in order to observe the changes they hived off into one room a number of female operators. Many of the measurements were made on their performance; yet with each successive change in working conditions the girls' output went up. Even when they removed all the changes, output continued to rise. Among the explanations that the experimenters offered were the following: the style of supervision in the small room was more permissive and friendly than before; the girls were responding to the fact of being observed, to having interest shown in them. They developed a strong group feeling oriented towards increasing productivity, partly to please the supervisors and partly to please the experi- menters, and partly to satisfy the financial needs of their most hard-pressed colleagues. From these, and other findings, developed the human relations movement, which assumed that alongside the formal organization of an enterprise, an informal organization develops with its own goals and norms; these two sets of goals must be aligned by development of a permissive form of leadership which allowed the worker to identify with the supervisor.

At this point the sociologist first enters the picture and with him came the notion of structure and of structural conflict. The Human Relations School assumed that the basic aims of the worker and management should not be in conflict: for both, the good of the enterprise meant more security and more pay; but the worker has learned to see industrial history differently. Greater profits have not always resulted in greater security; more output per worker may mean fewer workers.

Tom Lupton showed that workers' restrictive practices were often far more rational than had been thought (Lupton, 1963). He studied factories in two different industries in Manchester: one a garment factory, the other a heavy electrical engineering concern. In the first there was little sign of the systematic restriction of output that characterized the second, where the workers developed a method of 'fiddling' which served to maintain their weekly earnings at a predictable level. They were, in fact, effectively protecting themselves against the uncertainties to which they were subjected. The structure of an industry, its market situation, its traditional practices and the way work is organized to fit in with the characteristics of the manufacturing processes and raw materials, all influence the practices workers adopt.

The effect that different kinds of technology have on management and on industrial relations was the subject of Joan Woodward's famous study (Woodward, 1965). She found the extent to which firms were successful bore no relationship to their management organization – nor did it appear that such factors as size of firm, type of ownership and so on were associated with these factors either. She then grouped firms into three categories according to their technology, unit and small-batch production; large-batch and mass production; and process production. Looking at the pattern of organization she found much larger differences between the groups than within them, that the most successful firms in each group were those whose practices were closest to the norms of their group. The group which came closest to the prescriptions of the management theorists were those in large-batch and mass production. In the typical mass-production assembly line the group of workers in the most crucial function (production) are semi-skilled machine minders. The tone of management–worker relations in such a plant takes its flavour from management control of semi-skilled production workers. The tone is quite different in unit and small-batch production, where the typical production workers are skilled craftsmen, and in process production, where the most important function for workers is process control and maintenance. Thus the tone of industrial relations in both unit and process production is pleasanter, more comradely and less conflict-ridden than in mass production.

The importance of the form which communication takes within the enterprise has been emphasized by the work of Tom Burns (Burns and Stalker, 1961). With George Stalker, he studied firms adapting after the war to a change in their market situation and where there was a premium on innovation. The crucial issue was the ability of management to obtain results from its research and development division. They found two polar types of organization: the organic and the mechanistic. The latter corresponded closely to the 'ideal bureaucratic' pattern: jobs and responsibility were clearly defined, communications flowed down and up the management hierarchy as pictured on the organization chart, people knew the extent of their responsibilities. By contrast, the organic type was far more chaotic in their appearance: typically there was more communication across the chart than up and down it; people from different divisions formed project-type groups; the boundaries of responsibilities were not sharply drawn and might change from time to time. Burns and Stalker found that the latter type of firm was far more successful in adapting to innovation than the former. Although in static conditions the mechanistic type of operation may have considerable advantages. Firms, in fact, tend to behave in a more or less mechanistic way at different times, but it does appear that those which cannot function in an organic way have not the flexibility to respond to the demands of technological advance or of market development.

What both Woodward's and Burns' studies have shown is that there is no single best form of organization. Given its primary task an enterprise is faced with a choice both of technologies and of organization. There has to be a fit between the two. The Tavistock Institute of Human Relations developed this notion into their concept of a sociotechnical system. Basically, any technical system has to be operated by people and these people have to be organized to form a social system. Any change of the technical system will produce changes affecting the social system which, in turn, will adapt to these changes in a way determined partly by the dynamics of social systems and partly by the relationships that this particular system has with others outside. Frequently, the way in which the social system responds tends to frustrate the effects intended by the devisers of the technical change. The most dramatic example reported by the Tavistock Institute was the effect of the introduction of modern machinery in coal mining (Trist, *et al.*, 1963) which produced a misfit between the social and technical systems, such that absenteeism, sickness and accident rates were higher. Then groups of miners got together to work out a system which gave more satisfaction to their needs: a form of organization emerged which re-introduced some of the aspects of the old system; morale improved and with it output.

The institute described this organizational choice as 'non-alienated work roles', and they point out how much our forms of

93

industrial organization have rested on the assumption the worker
will be 'alienated' from his work and bribed by his financial return to
endure it.

J. H. Goldthorpe and others in *The Affluent Worker* (1968) have
demonstrated how this type of role fits the trend towards family-
and house-centred living. The so-called 'affluent worker' may
choose to do a well paid manual job even though it may involve a
lower skill than he is capable of. His rewards are ownership of
house, a car and a seaside holiday for his family, with his spare time
spent more on his house and with his family than with his work-
mates. This picture is in sharp contrast to that of the traditional
working class in such industries as mining and steel.

Thus the original concept of a sociotechnical system has had to be
widened to that of an open system, in dynamic equilibrium with its
environment. Some roles occupy the boundary between the enterprise and its environment and have to manage transaction across
these boundaries, for example, dealing with customers or the
public. Workers in the Institute for Social Research at Michigan
have shown that these boundary roles are the ones which involve
greatest stress for their occupants. Similarly, much of the observable inefficiency and confusion in industrial organizations is trace-
able to attempts to control boundaries which are in the wrong place,
or to regulate processes whose discontinuities have not been
matched by adequate organizational devices.

The sociology of custodial institutions and mental health

One of the most interesting fields of work for the sociologist has
been in the way in which society deals with its temporary or permanent failures. Any society has to be protected against those who are
a danger to themselves or to others. Thus a class of institutions
grows up which seldom has much claim on the resources of society
and about which people prefer to know very little; an attitude of
isolation and denial. This area of study can be seen in two contexts:
that of total institutions and that of mental health. Total institutions
as described by Erving Goffman in his book *Asylums* (1961) are
characterized by an institutional culture so that even where membership is involuntary and where the inmates may be struggling to
get out, the maintenance of the system depends on their co-
operation and acceptance of the roles defined for them. This is
achieved by institutionalization whereby the individual's links with
the outside world are systematically cut and he is resocialized into
the culture of the institution – for example, military units by the

94

issuing of uniforms and the systematic indoctrination and initiation process, symbolically enacted on the barrack square. Modern research has focused both on the process whereby the inmate adopts his role and on the difficulties and dilemmas of the staff, leading to the demands which they make on the inmates. Staff are required to serve, at the same time, three functions: the custodial, the punitive and the rehabilitative. Organizations which serve more than one goal tend to distribute different goals among different groups of staff. Thus the conflicts between goals become conflicts between groups of individuals.

The existence of an institutional culture becomes apparent when one sees two wards in a hospital or two prisons or two army units, which apparently exist to serve the same function, but which differ in 'atmosphere'. In a similar way change in the beliefs and attitudes towards the mentally ill has led to less restraint of patients. Similarly, the inmate learns his role; he learns a set of behaviours appropriate to the role of, say, a prisoner, a set of behaviours which validate the attitudes and behaviour of the warders. It is clear that this does not have much to do with reform of the prisoner, just as restraint had little to do with curing the insane.

With changes in the treatment of the mentally ill, it has been possible for a large number to return to their families and to the community. The emphasis has therefore moved towards the problems of re-integration. Starting from studies of small groups made during the war, in the process of working out new methods of officer selection, psychologists developed theories about the influence of the primary group (the face-to-face group) and the possibilities of such groups in a therapeutic role which were explored by the Tavistock Clinic. There emerged the group therapy which is now a familiar feature of most mental hospitals. However, this tends to lead towards conflict between those members of the hospital staff who are involved in the group therapy session and those who are not, as was discussed by Robert Rapoport (1960) in his book *Community as Doctor*, which describes the experimental development of the Social Rehabilitation Unit at Belmont Hospital. He also shows how, despite their best intentions, the members of the unit found that while they created a community to which patients were able to adjust and within which they could play normal healthy roles, this did not necessarily mean that they were fully and adequately prepared for return to the world outside. The next step is towards the involvement of the outside community in therapy and this is now being explored.

The study I have just discussed is a very good example of action research; ideas were developed by research and tried out in the therapeutic situation.[1] As a result of these experiments, further hypotheses were formed and tried out and their results recorded all in the context of an on-going institution. But the experience and results have not spread rapidly to other psychiatric hospitals, although some results of the experience pass into the general stock of knowledge and have been absorbed and used, mostly without recognition of their source. In his studies, L. P. Ullman (1967) found that there is a relationship between the size of hospitals and their effectiveness, which bears out R. W. Revans's (1967) discovery that the bigger a unit becomes the lower its morale drops. Ullman shows how administrative devices may have a distorting effect: for example, if the head of a department obtained status from the size of his staff and his budget, and increased allocation is seen as a mark of approval, this does not conduce to economical practices. Further, it turns out that a hospital which discharges patients quickly, thereby, one would think, demonstrating efficiency, becomes penalized for having empty beds.

We may contrast the action research of Rapoport with this study, which is an example of the use of operational research methods in the social sciences. The steps are as follows: (i) the aims of the institution are elicited; (ii) criteria are found whereby the success or otherwise of achieving these aims may be assessed; (iii) ways are found of measuring these criteria; and (iv) these measures are then related to measures of social factors within the institution.

Sociology of education

During the past hundred years education in Britain has ceased to be the preserve of a few and has progressively become more widespread, but there is an educational pyramid with a solid majority receiving the minimum, and progressively fewer proceeding through the various stages of secondary and higher education. Although education is no longer only for an elite, entry to elite groups is through the educational channel. 'Who gets what education?' has become of great interest to sociologists. If we set on one side the private sector of education (the independent and, to some extent, the direct grant schools), the educational opportunities are

---

[1] Also in an issue of the book eight years later, Rapoport discusses the reactions to the original report, showing that the implementation of research findings and concepts is a devious process of diffusion (Rapoport, 1968).

theoretically open equally to all, but numerous sociological enquiries have demonstrated how socio-economic class origins are related to the chances of obtaining grammar school and university education.

James Douglas (1964) has conducted a longitudinal cohort study of a 5 per cent sample of all children born during one week in March 1946. At each stage the handicap suffered by those from the lowest socio-economic classes grows: fewer enter grammar schools and of those that do, year by year fewer are in 'A' streams, fewer stay beyond 'O' levels and so on. Low socio-economic status is not a once for all disadvantage but has an accumulative effect. There are, of course, many factors operating: larger families among the lower groups tending to lower IQ's; an inherited genetic advantage of higher socio-economic classes; the effect of environment. The middle-class child has a richer variety of experience, more access to books and newspapers, etc., and, most important, values of the home are more likely to be oriented towards education and congruent with those of the school. Whereas the working-class child may be faced with a set of values to which those of his home environment may be alien or even hostile.

Numerous studies have shown the effect of these factors. Professor B. B. Bernstein has shown that the linguistic equipment which the child acquires in his earliest years affects the possibilities of his conceptual development (Bernstein, 1970b). It is impossible to elaborate his findings here. What is of particular interest, however, is that this study, which originated as a pure piece of research aimed towards explaining the working classes' educational handicap, opened up prospects of remedial action, e.g. the concept of compensatory education (Bernstein, 1970b). Might it not be possible to reshape a child's linguistic equipment even after he reached nursery school age? To examine this possibility action research projects have been initiated in schools in one of the Greater London boroughs.

The question of school organization has been focused on the comprehensive/selective argument, and some sociologists have been influential in pressing the claims of the comprehensive system. The move to comprehensive schooling was undertaken with the express motive of reducing class differences; sociologists advised that the school was a crucial institution in the class structure (Jackson and Marsden, 1961), but governments and local authorities were also interested in more specifically educational goals, and here the evidence is very ambiguous (Ford, 1969).

The universities have also come in for the sociologists' attention. They, like other institutions we have described, suffer from multiplicity of goals. First, they are strongholds of learning, they add to and protect the stock of knowledge; second, they aim to educate the student in the full sense; third, they are vocational training establishments and are answerable in this respect, too, as guardians of professional standards. As prestige institutions they are expected to uphold the established order, yet they must encourage students to question that order. They are expected to implant democratic values in their students but, by their very nature as educational institutions, they encounter great difficulty in operating as democratic institutions. The discontent symbolized by student unrest and demands for relevance in their studies, and commitment from their teachers, has not only aroused concern but is a stimulus for further sociological research. Some, who cannot distinguish the role of the doctor who describes the symptoms of a disease from the role of the virus or bacterium which is its causative agent, are unfortunately inclined to blame the sociologist for the unrest.

Military sociology

Historically, the role of the military is that of organized violence in the service of the state. Yet sociologists tend to see conflict in terms of social structure and violence as a breakdown of social control, so individual violence could be treated as irrational and deviant, but violence as an instrument of social policy could not be regarded in that light. Sociologists, then, turned to certain of the obvious characteristics of professional armies. Because they have to some extent a hangover of feudal structure, their social snobberies and class bias help to preserve the social position of traditional elites. Yet the role of the military, as shown by S. E. Finer in his book *The Man on Horseback* (1962) has by no means always been to maintain existing groups in power, and military coups, representing a shift in power, are as likely to be to the left as to the right. In studying these phenomena, the sociologist has had to struggle against his biases. Not only has the military acted in traditional backward societies as a route to the emancipation of young men from low-status backgrounds, it may also function as the emancipator of peoples. But this, of course, is not its primary role. Unfortunately, studies of military revolts have been rare.

Empirical sociological studies of the military have followed in the wake of the psychologist. A major study of morale among US forces was reported in the five volumes of *The American Soldier* (1949) edited by S. A. Stouffer. Much of it was focused on leadership styles. The human relations style of leadership appeared to increase men's satisfaction and reduce the infractions of discipline, but did not necessarily lead to ready acceptance of all military regulations. The closer that soldiers get to front lines the more the trappings of authority and social rank and procedure tend to be dropped, and the feeling of kinship brought by common exposure to shared risks contributes to the mystique of combat troops.

Similarly, one study of morale in the British services during World War II showed that the pilot might even find it easier to rebel against the dictates of the RAF authorities than to act contrary to what his friends expected of him (Paterson, 1955).

It is on the face of it surprising that the pattern of organization of a military unit varies little with the type of task of the unit: the same ranks in the same proportion appear to be needed whether the task is to fight an infantry battle or to maintain a radar workshop. However, we see that the structure of military organization has its rationale in the function of maintenance of internal control, and in organizational design, despite its disfunctional characteristics, this requirement appears to have acquired overriding precedence in the services. This is an area of study that we take up in Part II, Section VI, Chapters 26 and 27.

Sociology of development

Fifty years ago the famous German sociologist Max Weber initiated one of the most influential approaches to the study of economic development. *The Protestant Ethic and the Spirit of Capitalism*, translated in 1930, remained for a long time a piece of pure theory rather than the basis for practical approaches to modern development.

Another pure approach to these problems has been represented by the development of the work of Talcott Parsons (1951). Parsons developed a framework for analysis of social systems in which he identified four functions essential to every social system: a goal attainment function; methods of adaptation; integration of the units of society and latent pattern maintenance and tension management. The social system is governed by a set of values which have to be accepted by people in the system. If the social system is not to disintegrate, there has to be some way of preserving its values and making sure that individuals accept them and conform to their requirements. This is undertaken principally by the family and other educational institutions, which provide the system with a supply of members who are socialized to its goals.

Neil Smelser, in *Social Change in the Industrial Revolution* (1959) applied this system of analysis to the development of the cotton industry in nineteenth-century Britain. The changing demands on the family made by the industry as it developed had a disorienting effect on the family, which had to adjust to a new set of functions. Smelser shows at considerable length how this took place and how auxiliary institutions, such as trade unions, emerged and focused upon themselves the functions which the family could no longer provide.

Thus, from the work of Max Weber and that of Talcott Parsons and N. J. Smelser, we are equipped with frameworks of analysis for the sociological processes involved in industrialization and development. Yet problems of development have posed themselves as economic and political, rather than as social ones and the influential texts have been those by economists such as W. W. Rostow (1960), whose five stages of economic growth are not related to stages of social organization, forcing the sociologist into the role of destructive critic. Yet it has become obvious that the impediments to economic growth have been just as much social as economic. For instance, the economic and technical problems of controlling population growth are trivial; the political, social and religious ones are enormous. Yet often information of a sociological nature may be available but is not used.

Another piece of pure research which turned out to have applications in the fields of development was David McClelland's study of the relationship of achievement motivation to economic growth (McClelland, 1961). He suggested that the seeds of achievement motivation were sown in children and has made a strong case linking the degree of achievement motivation displayed among young people and the degree of economic development in a country. These studies, pure in their original orientation, have resulted in attempts at application. If, indeed, achievement motivation is crucial in development, can it be successfully implanted in children and in adults? Numerous studies have related the quality of leadership to the successful introduction of change, e.g. the work of A. H. Niehoff (Arensberg and Niehoff, 1966). There is no further doubt about the possibilities of utilizing sociological knowledge at the micro level; at the level of central planning, however, the story is different. We know how to draw up economic plans, but so far social planning is proving a chimera. The role of sociology and the other social sciences in development is discussed in Part II, Section V.

The application of sociology is not a simple matter. It requires familiarity with the concepts and methods of social science and the ability to make use of a wide range of quantitative methods. It requires the understanding of the organizations and institutions in

What I have in mind is best illustrated by reference to the history of the emergence of organizational psychology over the last fifty odd years. I shall show that three factors determine the significance and influence of organizational researches, one of which has been the ideological climate of the time. I think it is arguable that changes in this climate have been, in turn, influenced by organizational research. In Chapter 6 of this book, 'The Use of the Social Sciences', I shall show that the effective use of social research was greatly assisted by a providential crisis to whose resolution the research was relevant. The third factor affecting the usability, durability, and influence of research is, of course, the development of the discipline itself and the consequent availability of competent research workers. These three factors – ideology, critical problems and disciplinary development – are interwoven and their interrelationship is the history of the emergence and development of organizational psychology. Pugh predicted that the future is with the inward-looking concentration on theoretical problems arising from contemplation of the discipline itself and, in particular, with his own taxonomic approach.

The last half century of organizational studies

1 Before World War I

My predictions, as we shall see, are different. Let us begin with Taylor: it is commonly supposed that the 'ideological under-pinnings' of Taylor's approach have been fully explored by simply stating that he adopted the view of 'economic man', attributing to the worker the wish to work only as much as necessary (McGregor's theory X, 1960), and to be responsive to economic motivations. What really under-pinned this belief was the individualist ideology of the late nineteenth and early twentieth century (see Hofstadter, 1955).[1] According to this ideology the unsuccessful, the indigent

---

[1] Lenin (1917) claimed that the ideology was separable from the science: The Taylor system, the last word of capitalism in this respect, like all capitalist progress, is a combination of the refined brutality of bourgeois exploitation and a number of the greatest scientific values in the field of analysing mechanical motions during work, elimination of superfluous and awkward motions, elaboration of correct methods of work, introduction of the best systems of accounting and control etc. The Soviet Republic should at all costs adopt all that is valuable in the advance of science and technology in this field.

were feckless, lazy and irresponsible; the successful were hardworking, respectable and virtuous in taking thought for the morrow. Protestant ethic or no, the individual was responsible and an individualistic attitude to work was appropriate. Clear the path for the individual workman by devising the 'best way' for him and the best workman would advance down it. Those who could not, or would not follow, would no doubt fail to benefit, and might even suffer, but profits and efficiency would show on whose side was the Right.

The individualist, laissez-faire ideology, was not explicitly embraced, accepted, defined and described by any of the research workers in the field of industrial psychology and physiology. Nor has it been the practice of more recent researchers in organization studies to state their ideological assumptions. After all, science is 'value-free'. We shall see.

2   World War I

After Taylor it is customary to discuss the events of World War I as the real beginnings of industrial psychology. We are all familiar with the crises of the time and the part played by physiology and psychological research. My first example is the ordnance factories. Pre-war, men were employed filling shells until they were sent to Flanders to fire them. The women who replaced them could not fill the shells as fast as their predecessors could fire them. Crisis. The use of the mechanistic principle: double the hours of work to double the output, failed to solve the problem. The Health of Munitions Workers Committee set on foot the studies which identified 'industrial fatigue' and its causes and from which developed the work on hours, rest pauses and environmental factors which were the first main staple of industrial psychology after World War I.

The second example is of Army alpha and beta tests which were the response to the US Army's problems of inducting, classifying and assigning to duties large numbers of untrained entrants, with minimal schooling. Selection tests became the second main staple of industrial psychology. In Britain this was possible, together with a great deal of advance in technique because of the developments in the parent discipline, psychology. The influence of statistical innovators in psychology, Pearson and Spearman, brought a great deal of sophistication into intelligence- and ability-testing generally. Theories of the 'structure of abilities' were developing. The pervading ideology of individualism received a new twist from the successes in war; 'a land fit for heroes to live in', was compatible with the opportunity for the fittest to rise, despite a humble background. The post-war educational reforms were aimed at giving the poor child of ability the opportunity to develop and use his abilities. Scientific selection was in tune with the times. The other side of the selection coin was, of course, 'guidance', again necessarily oriented to the individual and his career path.

3 *Between the wars*

The depression years made selection an easy problem. With ten men after one job, picking one who will do it reasonably well is hardly a tough job for the expert. The reaction to the Depression was not so much cut-throat competition among workers as solidarity; partly because of the common experience of comrades in arms and partly because the depths of depression produced such intense insecurity.

Thus, when the Hawthorne investigators discovered the informal group and its system of social control, the *zeitgeist* was blowing in their direction. It is too little realized that the system of social control observed by the Hawthorne and other investigators could be effective only granted certain assumptions about the motivation of the workers concerned.

Human relations training which took as its point of departure the Hawthorne findings is now severely criticized on a number of grounds, in particular the inadequacy of its theoretical foundations, its treatment of the basis of conflict, and the ideological basis, which is seen as exploitative (see Goldthorpe, 1960). While clearly managements could hardly be unaware of the advantages of a contented work force, I very much doubt whether human relations training was adopted by managements as a deliberately exploitative device. On the contrary, it appealed to just those managements who saw themselves as enlightened employers and who wanted their workers to be happy as well as good.

4 *World War II*

World War II came, then, at a time when in Britain sophisticated advances had occurred in techniques of mental testing and when in America the social psychologists had become interested in industrial organizations and in small group studies.

While experimental psychology in the US had mainly concentrated on animals, particularly rats, experimental psychologists in Britain had continued to display an interest in the human being, a far less satisfactory experimental animal, but one which provides a greater behavioural range of study. In Cambridge, in particular, Bartlett and his pupils were applying to the study of physical skill

105

some of the principles and concepts derived from his study of cognitive, particularly memory, skills.

The war then brought new problems and a new scale of urgency to old ones. Men (and women) had rapidly to be recruited into a pattern of tasks differing very greatly from civilian occupations. The first requirement then was for large-scale systems of classification of volunteer and conscripted entrants, based not so much on their existing trained capacities as on their aptitudes for specialized training. Fortunately, the methods and the practitioners were available.

The first the supply of officers: rapid expansion of the Service and the early loss of some of the young officer cadres meant that officers had to be sought from unfamiliar sources, who didn't fit in with the old methods of assessing candidates and left the COs baffled. The answer was the WOSB (War Office Selection Board), together with the OCTU (Officer Cadet Teaching Unit). What interests us here is how these answers were provided. The War Office turned to psychologists, not the lowly variety concerned with the classification of recruits, but to the more rarefied and reassuring medical psychologists. The problem was seen as one of personality, not cognitive ability! The theory of group selection testing was a mixture of social and clinical hypotheses, and was the first application of both to selection procedures. The success of this new technique was immediate; its long-term consequences we shall see later.

The supply of naval officers and the problem of pilot selection was even more acute. It was to this problem that the Cambridge group were able to turn to account their experiments in the acquisition of complex skills. They detected those likely to possess the necessary particular skills involved, first determining the precise set and balance of characteristics required, and second inventing a laboratory situation which could test them. The appropriate blend of experimental, theoretical, engineering and clinical interest, expertise and imagination existed at the time in Cambridge and probably nowhere else.

The operation and maintenance of complex equipment not only involved the problems of design and training, but also much of the radar equipment and AFVs (armoured fighting vehicles) had been designed with little consideration of the capacities of operators and even less for ease of maintenance. These last factors were crucial in the case of the AFVs and substantial redesign was required to provide manageable tasks for operators. Thus was the science (or technology, if you prefer) of ergonomics born. It was the legitimate offspring of a marriage under wartime conditions of psychologists and engineers, whose union was blessed by necessity. The war in this example, as in the others I have cited, both legitimized the application of psychology to presenting problems and also sanctioned the co-operation of psychologists and engineers.

When it came to the morale of combat troops the US Services were able to turn to psychologists to help. The Americans had available social psychologists who owed their existence, at least partly, to the multinational origins of American society and the consequent opportunities for the social curiosity of sociologists and psychologists. In Britain, indeed, the term 'social psychology' was identified with the study of 'individual differences', while in the US it was more a matter of human relations and cultural anthropology. Thus the studies brought together in *The American Soldier* (Stouffer, 1949) with their use of sociometry, attitude questionnaires and their development of the theory of small groups and leadership, represented the coming of age in the US of social psychology both as a discipline and as an analytic and diagnostic toolkit. Where the British Army had sanctioned the probing of intrapersonal capacities and the man/machine interface, the US Army had sanctioned the probing of interpersonal relationships and the man/officer interface. The social taboos of British society were effective in denying that morale problems could be structural; they must be evidence of individual failure. Thus such conditions were seen as a proper study for psychiatrists, not social psychologists.

We see, then, that the social assumptions, the ideologies which sanction the utilization of research and expertise have a good deal to do with the assumptions underlying the research and the nature of the expertise. Over and over again we find that the development of the discipline is made possible by its sanctioning as an area of enquiry, by the recognition of problems as coming within its scope.

Wars show these trends most clearly because some of the problems of shared values and ideological outlook are greatly simplified. The same factors are, however, active in peacetime. Let us go on to consider the developments since the end of the war.

5 *After World War II*

The end of the war left Britain with a modest abundance of trained practitioners and research workers in psychology and associated disciplines. The strong feeling of guilt about class distinctions, allied with the Hawthorne studies, produced human relations training for managers and supervisors, while group selection methods were used to provide a more seemly mode of replenishing managerial talent than older more overtly class-based methods.

A much stranger offspring of group selection into discoveries about group processes, was group therapy. This, in turn, had an even stranger offspring, the T-group. The success of the T-grouping, greater in the USA than in Britain, owes a great deal to the increasing other-directedness in Riesman's terms of American (and to a lesser extent British) society and the decline of belief in moral authority (Riesman, 1955).

British class guilt had a further outcome – the sanctioning of sociology. Eventually, the sociologists, with their structural modes of interpretation, breached the dykes of the human relators, while the Tavistock studies had rediscovered alienation and provided it with a new psychotechnological twist, which fused with American work on job enlargement. The earlier work on sociotechnical systems was not yet fully anchored in the sociological substructure. To open the sociotechnical system, yet another stream of sociological enquiry had to be let in – epidemiology and community studies.

With the open sociotechnical approach and the collapse of the traditional bases for authority, alienation looked suspiciously like yielding to anomie, an even more amorphous and dangerous-sounding concept. An anti-alienative, anti-anomic ideology was needed and duly arrived in the shape of 'participation'. In some of its guises participation looks suspiciously like human relations and has a similar flavour of outflanking the unions.

The future

What can we predict on the basis of my analysis? First, the ambiguities of 'participation' will save it from destruction in the short run. With 'job enrichment' (also lacking in a secure sociological base), this ideology has its natural psychological partner. But already its fudging of the issues of power and structural interests of the unions is leading to its eclipse. The concept of 'industrial democracy' is now with us. This will, in my view, be the ideology of the next 5–10 years and with it will come inputs into organizational psychology from political science and from sociolegal studies. After 'industrial democracy', the 'learning society', whatever that will mean, with another new input born of cybernetics and learning theory.

Whether this is so or not the lessons are clear: ideology, crises (or just mere problems!) and disciplines are indissolubly interwoven. A science of organizational behaviour cannot emerge or develop from its own navel!

Section IV
The Utilization of the Social Sciences

Chapter 6
The Use of the Social Sciences

In this chapter I want to consider five general questions about the use of the social sciences. These questions are, first, why study the social sciences? Second, why study them at a University of Technology?[1] Third, what is the use of all the research that is done? Fourth, why is it not more useful? And fifth, what do we intend to do about it?

When I ask, why study the social sciences, I should, perhaps, preface my answer by pointing out that this is a question that my colleagues in the so-called 'hard sciences' are mercifully not required to answer. Society is prepared to tolerate, even to encourage and certainly to venerate scientific activity, partly because of its talismanic quality, partly because it does not understand it, partly because of the enormous success of science, and partly because science came to maturity when gentlemanly, though unproductive, pursuits conferred high prestige. The social sciences, by contrast, are coming to their maturity in a more professional kind of world. They have not the successes of science behind them. Society thinks it understands them only too well, but fortunately, because you can't have too many talismans, is prepared, now and again, to cross the social scientist's palm with silver.

The first defence of the social sciences could be that they are a liberal education; with their aid we should understand better the operation of the society in which we live and no doubt be better

---

[1] This chapter is partly based on my Inaugural Lecture as Professor of Social Sciences at Loughborough University, hence the direction of this question.

people as a result. However, anyone who has had any acquaintance with social scientists may question whether they are indeed any better able to conduct their own affairs than other people. It has often been said that the study of any discipline can be liberal education, that what matters in this respect is not *what* is taught, but *how* it is taught, and even more importantly, how the student learns to learn. It is only too easy to find graduates in all subjects whose education appears to have been anything but liberal.

A stouter defence for the study of social sciences would for me lie in the ground that they are sciences, albeit soft ones, where the ideas are ahead of the mathematics, rather than the other way about. But the social sciences, or some of them, meet most of the five criteria of a science: first, that knowledge should be cumulative; second, their observations should be 'replicable' (i.e., if I tell you how I obtain my results, you should, if you are a competent worker, be able to produce similar results, providing, of course, that you can identify the relevant parameters); third, hypotheses which are proposed should be falsifiable, in principle, by empirical data and should indeed lead to the search for such data; fourth, data should be quantifiable; and fifth, that the experimental technique be followed of controlling other variables in order to estimate or measure the effect of the one under study. Now, there is a hard end of the social sciences, namely, experimental psychology, where all these criteria can be satisfied and there are soft areas where the last two criteria are less easily satisfied, but even here the adoption of the concept of the 'model' enables the discipline to progress by what is essentially an adaptation of scientific method: hypothesis–observation–hypothesis. We are already familiar with the power of the model in economics; more recently, the infiltration of methods borrowed from the operational research man's little black bag has opened new prospects for the analysis of social systems.

My third justification for the study of the social sciences would be to point to their specific utility and to the fact that they are, or can be, useful and this I shall discuss later.

I turn now then to the second question I posed, what role have the social sciences in a university of technology? I would disclaim any ambition to civilize the rude technologists, not so much because I think this is a hopeless task, as that I would expect that a university education, whatever the main subject of study, should be a civilizing experience, and also because I don't regard the social sciences as especially civilized. On the other hand, I do believe that the social sciences provide a special set of tools for the analysis of technological systems and are thus natural partners in a technological university. This is because technical systems require people to organize, install, operate and maintain them, to define their aims and criteria for successful operation and so on. These people behave not as a mere assortment of individuals, but as groups, communicating and relating to each other. Now, just as the technologist can study and analyse the flow of energy and materials, so can the social scientist study the flow of information, communication and decision. But the way in which people are organized to operate the technical system is not just a network for information flow and decision-making; it is also a career structure and political system. The effect, therefore, of a change in the technical process brought about by new technical developments, by changes in markets, or by changes in the supply of materials, may change the balance of power among different groups, affect their career prospects with consequent effects on the flow of communication and the processes of decision-making. We are dealing with a system which is not just technical and not just social, but sociotechnical and its behaviour can be described and understood, not in purely technological nor in purely sociological terms. When this is forgotten, as it usually is, we may find we have incurred massive expenditure on systems which people won't operate or won't operate economically. 'Liner' trains and freight terminals are only the latest in a long sad series. A very homely illustration comes from India. Wells were dug and villagers shown how to use them and taught the value of a clean water supply. Five months later the wells were blocked and disused and the villagers were drinking the polluted water of the river once more. Why? It doesn't take advanced technical knowledge to maintain a well, but it does take *some* technical knowledge and it requires organization and training, neither of which existed and neither of which had been considered by the experts. The water supply of a village, just as much as the latest automatic factory, is a sociotechnical system.

I should like now to turn to the question of the usefulness of research and the problems attending the process of using it.

In the first place, the progress we shall make in the next ten years in making use of our knowledge depends not on the new knowledge that will be generated in that decade, but on the stock of knowledge already in our society. Why, then, add to our stock, while so much remains unused? To this I offer no answer except the old fable about the goose that laid golden eggs, but no one can tell which goose is going to lay them. If, then, all areas of research are in this regard equi-potential, there are two activities which are more equal than the others. The first is updating the existing stock of knowledge and the other is work on the problems of making use of the existing stock; and these have been the least fashionable, the least glamorous and the least discussed. If I may quote from Dr Hornig's,

111

chairman of the US President's Scientific Advisory Committee (1967), opinion:

> To many, the output of science is a collection of facts which can be stored and made available when needed. It is assumed that it will be put to use. But anyone who has ever worked in the sciences is aware that in fact recorded information is often singularly useless, that it depends on how it is presented, whether written or oral, with what attitude the potential user approaches the information, the degree to which he is stimulated to *use* that information. And information that is not used in some ways helps no-one.

Let me give you an example. Through the generosity of the Nuffield Foundation and through the equally generous leave from this university, I was able to spend nearly six months visiting a number of countries, including Israel, India, Australia and the United States, and this first example comes from Israel.[1] It is an example of the failure to make use of existing knowledge in the social sciences. Professor Eisenstadt of the Hebrew University has studied the social structure of the various groups migrating into Israel and a good deal is now known about them (Eisenstadt, 1954, 1967). These have in the past few years been mainly Jews from the Middle East and North African countries – from Iraq, Tunisia, The Yemen and so on. Rightly, the Israel authorities have tried to avoid these migrating groups drifting to the cities, particularly Tel Aviv, where they would tend to become slum-dwelling proletariats. Immediately upon arrival, migrating groups have been taken to new village settlements where they have been provided with temporary accommodation. In one such village, on the day after arrival and settling in, a bus arrived to take able-bodied males out to the fields where they were put to work and shown how to use agricultural implements. While they were away, social workers descended on the village to instruct their wives in the arts of home-making, caring for children, and so on. Thus when the men returned, having spent a day in which, in the regions from which they had come was regarded as women's work, they found that their expectations of how they would find their homes were confounded by their wives saying, 'Oh, no, that is not the way we do things here. The ladies have come and told us how we do these things.' With these blows the axe had been laid to the foundations of the social structure, the authority of the

---

[1] A full discussion of the development and utilization of the social sciences in these countries is included in Section V of this book.

head of the family was shattered. What was said by the husbands to their wives that night is mercifully unrecorded, but when the bus arrived the following morning, the men were on strike. Now to repeat: enough was already known about the social structure of these immigrants for this trouble to have been predicted and avoided. This, indeed, is an example of failure to use research which was not undertaken specially at the behest of the organization, but which the organization could have taken out of the stock of knowledge, but didn't.

How does research get into use at all? I believe we can identify three main ways in which research results get applied: first, by changes in the climate of opinion, second, by diffusion and third, by deliberate planned application. The most obvious, the slowest and most chancy is through the change in people's belief systems. I don't mean by this the displacement of religion by sociology, to which Shils (1967) refers, when he writes:

> For those who believe neither in Christianity nor in Marxism,
> sociology is becoming a mild surrogate religion. It is replacing
> prayer as a source of guidance and those who need this
> consolation and guidance are not going to be finicky about
> the language in which it comes.

What I do mean is that there is a climate of opinion, a mythology, a way of looking at the world which is affected by new knowledge. We can think of the work of Freud. Over the last half century, whether by acceptance or through rejection of what Freud was understood or represented as having said – and he said many different things at different times – attitudes to child-rearing, delinquency, sexual deviation and whatnot have undergone widespread and profound change. But note the lag between the research and the change in attitudes. And note the uncertain, unreliable and inaccurate nature of this process. A less dramatic example is in the acceptance of changed notions about the industrial worker as a factor in production brought about by research in industrial psychology and sociology. But the new set of generally accepted ideas about, for example, the relationship of morale to productivity, contain a good deal that is false or oversimplified. And again, the current myth is about twenty-five years behind the research.

The next most common way in which knowledge arising from social science research gets into use is by the diffusion of practice, which is more rapid but scarcely less chancy. Practices adopted as an outcome of research in one organization, whether it be factory, school, hospital or whatever, are taken as a model by others or transferred to them by consultants, by managers changing jobs, or exchanging visits. Alas, what works in one setting may not in another. Everyone knows that you can't get pineapple to grow in the open in Scotland, but some people are quite happy to try to get incentive schemes and training programmes which are successful in one enterprise to take root in another. Later I shall argue that the successful translation of the essential element of a practice from one organization to another requires a sophisticated analysis of the social and power structure of the organization. Because this is not understood or, if understood, neglected, this country and others are littered with the debris of training schemes, incentive schemes, joint consultation schemes and so on which were either non-viable from the outset or could not survive changes in the host organization.

The third way in which research is utilized is by planned application of research conducted especially for the organization concerned. Few organizations as yet think in these terms, and fewer can report really satisfactory experience. I hope that by the end of this chapter the reasons for this will be clearer: partly it is because a strategy for implementation is not built into the study from the beginning; partly because the relationship between researcher and administrator ensures neither a comprehension by the research of the real choices of action that face the administrators, nor a comprehension by the administrator of the real potentialities of the research. I shall be developing all these themes as I go on.

Certainly, the social scientist and the administrator live in different worlds and neither is equipped to undertake the tasks of application and transformation of knowledge.

By 'transformation' I mean the case where knowledge is channelled into other unexpected uses. Paradoxically we now expect the unexpected and defend, for example, expenditure on aerospace and defence research on the ground of probable 'technological fall-out'. As I said the social scientist and the administrator inhabit different worlds and here I am not talking about the two cultures of Lord Snow or of the different educational experiences of the humanist and the scientist, but of the different reward structures of the academic and the administrator. To start with, the time scale, as well as the reference groups of research workers and administrators, are different. Administrators, even university administrators, want the answer to their problems yesterday or at any rate not later than twelve noon today, while a piece of university research takes three years (and six months more to write up). Furthermore, the administrator who agrees to a research being undertaken has probably moved on to another job long before the study is complete. Even if he hasn't, he is by now concerned with some new problem and has little more than an 'academic' interest in the old one.

Another problem is in the nature of the contract between the university and the organization or, to put it more accurately, the implied terms of the contract. I quote from another recent American report, this one issued by the National Academy of Sciences' Advisory Committee on Government Programs in the Behavioral Sciences (NAS/NRC, 1968):

> These [the difference between the standards of the administrator and the academic] may be made even wider by contact. The government official may misperceive the academician's role in expecting too much in the way of answers to his problems. Often, resort to social science may occur only after trouble has arisen and no action will prevent it. This tendency has been matched by some overselling of the research potential of social science. Overexpectation and overselling both reflect failure to communicate.

But communication is not enough, involvement is also needed: I have not been able to trace in practice one example of a study carried out in a university or in a research institute or anywhere else which resulted in direct application except where the researcher has become involved in following through his studies into application. As the report of the US Office of Naval Research says, 'Formulation of possible applications of research findings requires extensive knowledge in the field of application in which research is to be attempted' (Mackie and Christensen, 1967). I can substantiate this again and again from my observations and I have selected as examples of successful applications of research one each from Israel, India and Australia. In each case the conversion of knowledge to utilization has been a major piece of social science research.

The first illustration takes us back to the problems of oriental immigrants to Israel, this time to the difficulties that have arisen with the education of their children who are, in the jargon of today, 'culturally disadvantaged'. In their first grade at school they averaged 15 points of IQ behind the rest of the population and with each year the gap increased. Research at the Institute of Applied Behavioural Sciences in Jerusalem concentrated on methods of developing abstract thinking in these children and on identifying the age at which the IQ gap first appears, and the factors associated with its emergence. Enough was learned quickly for the institute to conclude that a special educational programme was possible, even as late as in the years of secondary education, and, in each of the

115

areas studied, a crash programme was proposed for the top quartile of oriental immigrant children in the primary schools. Not unnaturally, the secondary school heads were reluctant to enrol them and in order to carry out the programme the researchers had to become politically involved. I don't mean by this that they had to take a partisan position on a political question. What they did have to do was to convince the ministry and the education authorities, badger them and the school heads, whip up support in influential quarters and generally make it the path of least resistance to give way to them rather than to put further difficulties. Finally, the secondary schools were coerced into admitting the children and three groups were admitted. Their results were then compared with groups of non-immigrant children as controls. The school-leaving diploma was obtained by 86·4 per cent of the control group of non-immigrant children, while 92·3 per cent of the immigrant group were successful. Now the Ministry of Education have such centres all over the country. I am not advertising this as a magical solution or a superior conjuring trick – of course the problems are not all solved – but a demonstration of what could work was the outcome of the involvement of the researchers and would not have come about without their involvement.

The second example, from India, is not yet a complete success story but is one of hope. Attempts to develop Indian villages have foundered time and again on the phenomenon of the villagers' resistance to change. At bottom the villagers have no motivation to 'achieve'. To us, who have the achievement motive so firmly built into our society, it is difficult to comprehend that people living in the conditions of the Indian peasant should have no apparent wish to advance themselves personally or individually. These conditions have to be seen to be comprehended. In the villages, it is not the squalor but the backwardness that impressed me. Their technology is almost entirely pre-industrial and their productivity (as distinct from their re-productivity) is, of course, fantastically low. But their traditional practices and their social cohesiveness at least provide a psychological security. It has now been shown by studies carried out from the University of Allahabad (Sinha, 1969) that the responsiveness of villages to programmes of change correlates with the villagers' individual needs for achievement. The traditionalism of Indian society is almost as strong in the educated classes: managers in Indian industry, for example, lack the urge to achieve, and the consonant willingness to take risks. Now the study of achievement motivation began as a very pure study carried out by McClelland and his associates at Harvard (McClelland, 1969). The work proceeded on an academic basis for years and no one saw any practical relevance of it until they themselves became interested in the possibilities of teaching achievement motivation – for example by inducing them to compete with one another, and now programmes of this kind are being set up as models in India. Once again, however, it is the researcher himself and his associates who have to push for, and be involved in, these steps towards utilization. A programme is now under way to develop achievement motivation in village children through the very games they play and the stories told to them in school.

My third example comes from Australia and is concerned with agricultural extension. Oeser and Emery (1956) of Melbourne University showed some years ago that the only way in which the diffusion of improved agricultural practices could be obtained was through the indoctrination of farmers who were influential in the informal farming culture. This doctrine is now fully accepted in many countries where agricultural extension services are provided, but, and there is a big but, you can't use this technique unless you can successfully identify the membership of these informal groups and who among them carries influence. But Joan Tully, a former associate of Oeser and Emery in the original studies took this further and has now shown that the identification of these groups and of their influential members requires sophisticated sociological investigation (Tully, 1964). These groups have no formal existence and the farmer who has most influence is not necessarily, or even usually, the one whose practices are most advanced. In fact, by becoming identified too closely with new methods, a farmer is very likely to isolate himself. Getting his support is more likely to hinder than to help the agricultural extension worker. But Joe is the man to whom the other farmers in the neighbourhood look. If Joe thinks it is okay, then it is worth trying. Puzzle: find Joe!

These studies underlined the need for the researcher to involve himself in the process of implementation. So we can see how the utilization of social research is unsatisfactory and how we shall fail to make it effective so long as we carry around with us models of the utilization process derived from the way we read experience in the natural sciences.

At the root of this problem lies a misconception of the processes whereby research gets translated into action. Our reading of the process in the natural sciences provides us with a model in which pure research leads through applied research to development, and from development to application. Carter and Williams (1967) showed how inadequate this model was:

The misconception . . . is that research provides something

117

which is communicated to the industrial scientist who performs some applied research and communicates the research results to someone else who takes matters a step further. We have not found any cases of successful industrial research where this left-to-right movement is not accompanied by a right-to-left movement in which management and other departments suggest projects to other departments.

The Tavistock Institute (1964), in discussing the relation of the 'pure' and the 'applied' to the 'professional' model in social science says:

In the natural sciences, the fundamental data are reached by abstracting the phenomena to be studied from their natural contexts and submitting them to basic research through experimental manipulation in a laboratory. It is only some time later that possible applications may be thought of and it is only then that a second process of applied research is set under way. The social scientist can only use these methods to a limited extent. On the whole he has to reach his fundamental data (people, institutions, etc.) in their natural state and his problem is how to reach them in that state. His means of gaining access is through a professional relationship which gives him privileged conditions. The professional relationship is a first analogue of the laboratory for the social sciences. Unless he wins conditions privileged in this way, the social scientist cannot find out anything which the layman cannot find out equally well, and he can only earn these privileges by proving his competence in supplying some kind of service. In a sense, therefore, the social scientist begins in practice, however imperfect scientifically, and works back to theory and the more systematic research which may test this and then back again to improved practice. Though this is well understood in the case of medicine, it is not so well understood, even among social scientists, that this type of model applies to a very wide range of social science activities. The model may in fact be called the professional model.

The Heyworth Committee (1965) made an allied point:

In the physical sciences the translation of research findings into practical applications is the function of the specially trained development scientist or engineer, who understands both the relevant scientific discipline and the technology of

118

the establishment in which he is employed. In the social sciences, even when allowance is made for the difference in the nature of applied research, there are few people whose functions correspond to the engineering or development function in the physical sciences, and nowhere are such people trained. If anything approaching the full potential value is to be obtained from research in the social sciences, an attempt must be made to define and analyse this function and train people to perform it. This means that organisations must also be ready to employ them when trained.

Lippitt (1965), who had also faced similar problems in America of getting application of social science to those many of us have encountered here, has identified six differences between social science research utilization and the utilization of research in other areas of science:

First, most significant adoptions of new educational or social practice require significant changes in the values, attitudes and skills of the social practitioner. This requires a deeper personal involvement in adopting the new practice than is true in the adoption of new agricultural, industrial or medical practices. There will be more problems of resistance to change and of re-learning.

Second, most significant changes in mental health or educational practice really are adaptations rather than adoptions of the innovations of others. What is being passed on is not a thing (e.g. a new seed, new implement, new drug or new machine), but is a new pattern of behaviour to be used in a new social context. Therefore, there must be significant features of adaptation in each adoption. One implication of this is that the dissemination of the new practice must therefore include much more orientation of the adopter to the basic principles or conceptions involved in the practice in order to make creative adaptation possible.

A third important difference in our field of social practice is that the concept of 'social invention' really has not been developed adequately. There are no adequate procedures for identification, documentary description and validation of new practices. This means that on the one hand there is often a large volume of poorly described nonvalidated practices tempting uncritical adoption efforts by professional colleagues. On the other hand, there is a great volume of creative practice which remains invisible and inaccessible to review

119

and consideration. This means that the diffusion of significant new practice is a very retarded and chaotic situation.

A fourth characteristic of the social practice situation is that the practitioner gets very little feedback about the effectiveness of his adoption effort. The farmer can quickly see that his soil is more fertile or that the new seed produces more corn per acre. The doctor can check whether the new drug reduces infection more rapidly. The engineer can check objectively on the increased output of a new machine. But the teacher or mental health worker typically lacks the criteria and the tools to make this type of check. There is less sense of reward for the effort and very little data for quality control to provide guidance to the practitioner who is making an effort to use a new practice model.

A fifth important difference is that the ways in which mental health and educational practice are organized provide little stimulus for the practitioner to take risks in searching for and using new resources. The practitioner remains relatively invisible to colleagues and supervisors. There are neither competitive challenge nor good communication channels to stimulate sharing and improvement of practice. In addition there tends to be a high sensitivity to the potentially negative reaction of various publics to changes of practice.

A sixth critical point of difference is that our social practice fields have not developed the networks, procedures and manpower resources necessary to link basic and applied research to operating practice. We lack the in-service training and support needed to stimulate and maintain the upgrading of social practice as social science resources grow and as social technology develops.

All this mounts to a very strong case for studying the role broadly corresponding to that of development scientist in the social sciences and for the study of the processes of development. Just as the development scientist represents the science capability of his organization, so the role I am discussing here would represent the social science capability. In fact, we can look again at the Heyworth Report when they said:

In the social sciences . . . there are very few people whose functions correspond to the engineering or development functions in the physical sciences, and nowhere are such people trained. If anything approaching the full potential value is to be obtained from research in the social sciences, an attempt must be made to analyse their function and train people to perform it.

But we won't get people to study the process of development and to work on these problems unless we can make these studies academically respectable.

So it was that research into the application of the social sciences and training of applied social scientists was a major part of the work of the Centre for Utilization of Social Science Research which was set up at Loughborough in 1967 with the aid of an SSRC grant and with the following aims:

1 *Research*

To study the application of research in the social sciences in as wide a variety of organizations as practicable in order to:
(a) identify key aspects of this process;
(b) identify key components of the roles of the agents of change;
(c) describe the relationship among the agents concerned, the sponsors, users, researchers.

2 *Teaching*

To train social scientists to undertake the role of researcher-change agent.

To teach administrators in government, local government, industry and other organizations how to spot situations in which social science research may be useful and how to introduce and obtain acceptance within their own organizations for applied research.

3 *Policy*

To explore the implications for a policy for the social sciences of the methods and problems of applying social science research.

Experience with the Royal Air Force taught me that the easier and more congenial parts of my role were carrying out research, analysing results and preparing their publication. The task of selling the research proposal required a different set of skills. Even more important and difficult were the discussions with those affected

121

which preceded publication and the negotiations about implementing the recommendations afterwards; I learned that if the research was conducted without maintaining the interest of the user and without continuous awareness of the users' concerns and preoccupations, the results stood little chance of leading to substantial application.

Experience with DSIR of sponsoring research in the social sciences in relation to the needs of industry impressed me with the difference in the views of research held by users (industrial mainly) and producers (researchers mainly in universities). Their expectations from even the most 'applied' projects differed considerably and in many cases differed no less at the end than at the beginning. One of my first tasks as secretary of the Human Sciences Committee of the DSIR was to ask for a substantial increase in our budget. 'What', I was asked in return, 'have we obtained for the money we have so far spent?' In vain I protested (a) that this was not the sort of question one could ask of such an activity as research; (b) that my natural science colleagues were never asked such questions; (c) that DSIR's support for the human sciences had been of too short duration to enable a proper evaluation to be made. My pleas fell on stonily deaf ears. Either I produced appropriate 'evidence' or we would not get our money. We got the money. But the evidence I presented did not satisfy me. It listed publications, testimonials from 'users', accounts of conferences and lectures disseminating 'results' to potential 'users'. But that is where the evidence ceased. Even the most celebrated studies which threw light on recognized practical issues had not led to consequent changes attributable to research, let alone quantifiable consequences.

The Heyworth Committee (1965) asked similar questions about the use of social science research, but received no satisfactory answers. Policy-makers could state clearly why they felt the need for research, what help research would give, but could not describe how research had influenced policy in the past or what guarantee there would be in the future that research would influence policy or what procedures would be adopted to conduce to that end. To a man they appeared to share the assumption that research would be applied simply because it was carried out. After all, policy-making is a matter of weighing information from a variety of sources. What is so special about information generated by research? And just so long as you think of the outcome of research as information for administrative purposes, you do not confront the fact that new data is only one of the products of research and by no means necessarily the most relevant or the most important. It was clear that the actual processes whereby research influenced action were not well under-

122

stood either by researchers or by administrators. Nor were they aware that they did not know that there was any problem. Time and again a line of questioning by the Heyworth Committee evoked blank uncomprehension.

Despite this, expectation among users, particularly government, had grown substantially of the benefits to be expected from the social sciences. At the same time, their ideas of what research is, what it is for, and how it can be applied to policy problems, are often very hazy and sometimes false.

We have also seen a wide range of researcher–user–sponsor relationships: researchers with an internal role, researches conducted from outside an organization. A wider range of institutions combined with different attitudes towards research and researchers exists in other countries. Consideration of these different structures suggests that there is a systematic relationship between the forms of research organization and the types of research they tended to perform, a theme that we will take up in the next chapter.

Chapter 7
Relations between Research Institutions and Users of Research

In this chapter I shall try to show that users have many different kinds of needs for different kinds of research; that there exists a wide range of actual and potential institutions for carrying out research; and that selecting the appropriate institution for any particular research requires a sophisticated knowledge both of the research needs and of the existence and competences of the research institutions. Further it will be clear that in any particular country, some of the needed research institutions are simply not available, and that there are many problems inherent in the use of research to tackle administrators' problems. I shall offer some suggestions for mitigating these problems, though it is not possible to be comprehensive.

To begin with, let me indicate the range of research institutions which I know to exist; there may indeed be others, and there is no logical completeness about this list, so that Eric Trist (1970) offers a different kind of list. My list is predicated on the existence of certain kinds of institutions in society, and a society characterized by a different range of social institutions presents different types of research institutions. Each society has its own particular way of organizing education, possesses its own range and type of social, political and economic institutions; each, therefore, tends to develop its own set of institutions for research. I shall first list the kinds of research institutions which I myself have encountered:

University departments of social science disciplines – these are to be found in all the countries I have visited.
Research centres within universities – these are typically

124

based on a faculty or school rather than on a department and flourish most within the United States.

Units attached to universities – I have in mind here such units as those of the Medical Research Council (and now of the SSRC) in the UK and the Institute for Economic Growth in New Delhi and so on.

Independent research institutes (a) financed by government funds; (b) financed by non-government funds, but non-profit-making; (c) mixed government and other finance, again non-profit-making; and (d) commercial profit-making.

In-house research agencies. These may be (a) within government at a supra-departmental level; (b) in government at an interdepartmental level; (c) within government at a departmental level; (d) non-governmental, but inside statutory bodies; and (e) within industrial or commercial institutions.

There is the kind of co-operative research institution with mixed government and industrial financing – exemplified by the research association.

Government Research Institution – These may be of two kinds – the East European Academy of Science model, or the French CNRS.

This is a purely taxonomic list of institutions for carrying out research. Within each type, institutions differ in their structure and these differences relate not only to the type of institution, but also to their orientation: disciplinary or interdisciplinary, problem-oriented or not. There are also many different types of research and these again are classifiable in a number of ways. For the purpose of this article I shall use a twofold basis of classification, by duration on the one hand and objectives on the other (see Table 4).

Long-term indefinite period of research. This is most often of a disciplinary kind; it may indeed be interdisciplinary or multidisciplinary, but its aim is, generally speaking, to solve problems arising within the disciplines, or between the disciplines concerned.

Long-term research, oriented towards a problem area.

Medium-term research, directed, generally speaking, towards a range of specific problems.

Short-term research, oriented to a specific problem, often little more than fact-finding for administrative purposes.

We can also consider the ways in which this research is used with another system of classification which is discussed below, i.e. basic,

125

TABLE 4 *Relationships between different systems of classification*

	Independent long-term research	Long-term research	Medium-term research	Short-term research
Orientation				
Disciplinary	P[1]	P	M[2]	
Interdisciplinary	P	P	M	
Problem area		P	P	
Specific problem			M	P
Structure				
University department	P	P	M	
Independent institution		P	P	
Commercial institution		M	P	P
In-house			P	P
Type of research				
Basic pure	P	P		
Basic objective		P	M	
Operational			P	P
Action			M	P
Career				
Full career in research	P	P		
Preparation for teaching (Ph.D)			P	
Preparation in research		P		
Planned experience			M	P
Preparation for consultancy			P	P
Part of teaching role	P	P	M	M

1 P = probable.
2 M = marginally probable.

pure or fundamental research; basic objective research; operational research; and action research.

The other significant taxonomy is of the users of research:

Users within government: (a) planners – most often the case in developing countries; (b) administrators concerned with the day-to-day administration of government affairs.

Local government or statutory government agencies.

Industry and other private institutions.

In Table 4 I have set out the relationships between these different systems of classification. This, at least, gives a crude picture of what to expect from each type of agency. Many research bodies are not oriented solely towards undertaking research, and the mix of skills which an institution offers is crucial to the prospects for utilization of the research it undertakes. We should, therefore, take this mix into account in deciding to which institution to commit a particular piece of research. Although many more are possible (see Trist, 1970), the mixes commonly encountered are as follows:

Research only.

Research and teaching – typical of the university department.

Research and application – generally to be found in bodies which undertake research and consultancy, i.e. research institutes, in-house research facilities and co-operative research associations.

Research-teaching application – a very rare mix indeed, and only to be found in one or two special institutions.

Application only – consultancy firms, occasionally in-house research facilities.

Lastly, we need to make a distinction between teaching and training. Formal teaching or teaching combined with research is, generally speaking, to be found only within university departments. On the other hand, there is a more or less explicit training function which may be carried out by a wide range of the institutions I have mentioned. People in their first few months of research are very much in a learning role, and one of the functions research institutions carry out willy-nilly is that of producing people who have the capacity to undertake research. This is of considerable importance when we come to consider research careers.

The kind of careers available, either within research or for which research is a part, are as follows:

The (relatively rare) long-term career in research.

Research as planned experience during the individual's progress through administrative structures.

Research as a preparation for a teaching career (doctorate).

Research as a preparation for a career in consultancy (this is only too rare).

Research as part of the functions of the university teacher, which he undertakes together with his teaching.

Research as training for research (doctorate).

One of the major problems in this whole area is the misfit between these career structures and the range of existing research institutions and agencies. There has, of course, been little if any planning of research careers and of structures so as to ensure that the different kinds of research agency will each receive a supply of adequately trained people for their functions. We all know that research institutions are constantly robbing one another and com-

127

peting for scarce research talent. Because of the mismatch between the careers structures and research institutions good people are lost to research and others are misused in the wrong kinds of research. We can summarize this simply by saying that there is no planning of careers in research.

Matching problem to institution

The administrator or planner, in formulating proposals for research into his problems, needs to scan the range of research institutions to find one appropriate to the type of problem he has. For this he needs to know the research institutions that exist and their particular strengths and skills. But he also needs a very sophisticated conception of the part that research can reasonably be expected to play in the formulation of policy, or in the determination of alternative modes of action. Unfortunately, there is a very wide gulf between the way the administrator looks at research and the perceptions held by researchers. This will be our concern in the following chapter, but let us now consider the problems of research institutions.

Problems of research institutions

First, the in-house research facility. I have visited a considerable number of these in many countries now and I think I can make some generalizations about them. The role of director of research is crucial. He has not only to inspire and lead a team, he has also to manage the boundary between the research division and the rest of the organization. To act successfully in the former role he has to maintain scientific standards and scientific credibility. In his boundary-maintaining role he has to have a real concern with the organization's problems as they appear to the directors of executive and planning divisions. He is, thus, exposed to contradictory pressures: on the one hand to identify with the organization which employs him, sharing the values and priorities of its executives, and on the other to identify completely with the scientific community with its values of purity, objectivity and scientific caution. Most directors of research fail to maintain their balance on the tight-rope and fall to one side or the other. The director who has 'sold out' to the organization is the more frequently met. His lot is unhappy; the programme of research with which he began and which contained long-term, medium-term and short-term projects now has only the last. He has encountered the first law of scientific administration: the short-term always drives out the longer-term. On the other hand, he can point to the speed and relevance of his studies, which in his view contrasts with the slowness and unrealism of university research. He will, in fact, try to block relationships between his organization and the universities. The executives, while they value the facility he provides, regard it in the light of gathering facts for administrative purposes, a task they could do themselves with their own staffs if they were not so busy with other matters. The worst problem is staff: good research workers will not stay, bad ones will not leave.

The director who has maintained his scientific purity may publish in scientific journals and attend scientific meetings, have an academic reference group, but he is insulated and isolated from the organization. His executives do not know what his programme is, nor do they care. They prefer to ask for help from people they know in universities, rather than go through the bureaucratic procedures of getting a problem into the research programme. Good research workers may stay in this division, but apart from such prestige as they bring the organization they are an expensive luxury.

In neither case do we find any utilization of research, except for the routine use of statistical data.

Universities are prepared to conduct policy-oriented research, but are organized so as to make its actual use extremely unlikely. One instance is the differences in time scales of administration and research. In universities, where one of the important pay-offs for research is the research degree, there are vested interests in prolonging research projects; it may be very difficult to take on research workers for short periods and the university does not employ unattached researchers who can be put on to projects at short notice. Many organizations, especially in government, deliberately move their senior executive staff from one job to another, thus not only foreshortening their planning horizons but making it highly probable that the executive who commissions a piece of research is not the one who receives the report. Even if he is still the same man, the problems have changed. Fairweather (1967) indicts:

> . . . folkways of the university – disengaging itself from action approaches to social problems, possible chauvinism of various academic disciplines, and the difficulty any large institution has in establishing a new academic branch with somewhat different values from those traditional in that setting.

Furthermore, the academic's interest in research is very low once he has returned the corrected page proofs to the editor of an academic journal. His rewards come from the addition to the list of articles and books to his credit; it is of little consequence to him whether the results are used by the administrators or not. To quote a distinguished academic administrator (Mackie and Christensen, 1967):

> The social structure and purpose of the university accentuate the pressure toward purity. For the university's purpose is not to solve problems that are set from outside a discipline. The university is not mission-oriented. Its purpose is to create and encourage the intellectual life *per se*. . . . In the university it is improper to ask of the scientist, 'What is the relevance of what you are doing to the rest of the world or even to the rest of science?'. The acceptable question is, 'What do your scientific peers, who view your work with the same intellectual prejudices as you, think of your work?'.

This doctrine may be weakening but led many Indian graduates in the social sciences to turn their backs on the enormous social problems of their country and to prefer to ape some of the worst kind of American studies, obtaining their Ph.Ds by examining the responses of their fellow students in the universities to question-naires of no practical relevance.

Universities with their strong disciplinary departments find interdisciplinary work hard to accommodate and the researcher who wishes to work in an interdisciplinary area puts his career at risk. Many research institutes outside universities owe their origins to this (see Jenkins and Velody, 1965). The differences in percep-tions of problems between administrator and researcher are great-est when the research is located in a university department dedi-cated to a single discipline.

Application of research

This brings me to my next major problem, the problem of the availability and validity of knowledge derived from research. I need to make some general points about the conceptions that people have about applied research and the process of applying research which create an enormous difficulty for the actual application and utilization of research and knowledge in the social sciences.

Our misconceptions begin with the words 'pure', 'applied' and 'research'. The distinctions that are frequently made between pure and applied, theoretical and empirical research in the social sciences are not only unhelpful but often downright mischievous. Confusion is worse confounded by the frequent equating of 'pure' with 'theoretical', and 'applied' with 'empirical'. We shall attempt a more useful categorization of research in the social sciences and to suggest that each type of research has its associated diffusion system. Further, we aim to show that the limitations of these diffusion systems condemn much well-meaning, so-called 'applied' research to frustration.

The classification that we adopt here owes much to that proposed by the Zuckerman Committee (1961) which offered the useful distinction between 'pure basic' and 'objective basic' research. In the social sciences these two categories, together with a third, operational research, and a fourth, action research, will serve as 'pure types'. We shall expect that in practice many studies will be of mixed varieties. We also postulate that each of these four types has associated with it a typical diffusion channel.

Definition of types

1 *Pure basic research*

This arises out of perceived needs of the discipline and is generally speaking oriented towards resolving or illuminating or exemplifying a theoretical problem.

2 *Basic objective research*

This is oriented towards a problem which arises in some field of application of the discipline, but is not aimed at prescribing a solution to a practical problem.

3 *Operational research*

This aims at tackling an on-going problem within some organizational framework but does not include or involve experimental action. This kind of research is distinguished by its strategy and methods. Broadly speaking these are:
   (a) observation of the 'mission' of the organization;
   (b) identification of its goals;
   (c) establishment of criteria of goal attainment;

131

(d) devising measures for assessing performance against these criteria;

(e) carrying out these measurements and comparing them with the goals;

(f) completing the feedback loop by reporting on the discrepancy between goal and achievement.

Note: In the course of an operational research project, changes may occur as a result of the enquiries of the operational researchers, but this is not perceived as the aim of the research, although it may be a more-or-less welcome concomitant of it.

4 *Action research*

This may involve as part of its strategy a piece of operational research, but is distinguished from an ordinary piece of operational research by the addition to the strategy of the introduction and observations of planned change. The further down the list we proceed, the more appropriate becomes the Tavistock Institute's 'professional' model.

It is instructive to consider examples taken from the field of social research to illustrate these types. Goldthorpe *et al.*'s (1968) studies of *The Affluent Worker* are in this terminology pure basic research. Because they are empirical and relate to industrial sociology, they might easily appear in the popular category of 'applied' research, but this is not so. The aim of these studies was to resolve a theoretical problem arising from the analysis of the position of the highly paid manual worker. According to one hypothesis the important factor in determining the manual worker's behaviour is his class identification, arising, partly, from the realities of his work situation. On another hypothesis, the important factor in his identification is his style of life. If the latter is true, then the effect of high wages is to provide opportunities to the worker to abandon his working class affiliation. A middle class style of life would lead to middle class identifications or *enbourgeoisement.* If the class hypothesis is correct, *enbourgeoisement* would not occur. Now it may well be that some of the findings could be applied in some way or another and certainly they may have interest for audiences other than those of professional sociologists, but the goal is one of pure basic research and the preferred diffusion channel of the investigators is through the scientific channel, that is, the learned publications.

We may take as examples of the objective basic research type the studies of Burns and Stalker (1961) reported in *Management of Innovation* and those of Woodward (1965) reported in *Industrial Organizations: Theory and Practice*; indeed, these titles reveal an objective orientation. Burns and Stalker's studies sought to answer the question, 'What were the factors that enabled some firms to adapt while others didn't to changing market situations?' It is true that the outcome of these studies was to throw light on the theory of organizations, but the aim was to apply the methods and principles of the social sciences to the analysis of an objectively posed problem. Woodward's studies were aimed at investigating the practical question, 'Is there one pattern of organization structure appropriate to all industrial organizations, or are there different structures appropriate to different industrial situations?' Again the theory of organization is greatly advanced by these studies, but the orientation was, at least partly, to a problem in the field of application.

As in the case of Goldthorpe and Lockwood, publication of Burns and Woodward's work took place through the traditional routes, as books issued by academic publishing houses, but it is noteworthy that in both these cases simplified industrial versions of the studies aimed at practising managers accompanied their full scale publication – indeed in Woodward's case the simplified version preceded the book by seven years.[1]

As an example of operational research we may take the collection of studies reported under the title *Institution and Outcome* by L. P. Ullmann (1967). This book reports studies of thirty psychiatric hospitals and analyses the organization of such characteristics as size, staffing, expenditure and measure of hospital effectiveness. For this the aims of the institutions have to be made explicit, criteria set up and so on. Even before studies of this kind are reported, considerable fall out, in terms of self-understanding of the organization takes place. For example, the discovery that criteria of effectiveness used by one department could militate against the criteria of another. The channel for diffusion here is, typically, the feedback process to the hospitals concerned. But the novelty of applying these methods to this field, and the possibilities of using them in similarly intractable fields justified their wider publication, thus entering another channel of diffusion at a later date.

Action research studies may themselves include operational

---

[1] The closer identification in the United States of business with the academy and the prevalence there of the business schools means that there we can expect business to be a greater part of the public for an academic publication of this kind than in Britain.

research techniques, but their essence is the introduction of planned change and the observation of its results, perhaps by participant observation. The examples that I shall mention here are Rapoport's *Community as Doctor* (1960) and Revans's hospital internal communications project (1967).

Rapoport's work involved a great deal of participant observation; he had to become involved very closely with the experimental unit concerned in order to obtain sanction for his work. A study of this kind is likely to be seen quite differently by different participants, and any participant may have 'applied' as well as 'pure' goals. Thus we find different aspects reported in publications of different kinds. It is, at least in part, action research because planned change was thoroughly documented and conclusions drawn from it. Here again, operational research aspects obtrude and we note that treatment subgoals are found to conflict with rehabilitation subgoals. This is action research which in a sense is incomplete in that, although the interactions of the unit concerned with the hospital environment in which it was located are noted meticulously and with insight, the outcome in terms of change for the institution as a whole is not evaluated. Here the time scale of institutional change appears to have been too long for the research design. However, this deficiency was made good by the follow-up published by Rapoport on the impact of the studies some eight years later (Rapoport, 1968).

Rapoport finds that the generality of the results strongly denied at the time is much more easily admitted today. Indeed, many ideas arising from the original study have been incorporated into practice, but their origins are not recognized.

Revans's studies of hospital internal communications form a usefully clear case of action research, the aims of each of the ten projects he initiated being to introduce change and observe its effects. Precautions were taken in this case to remove the evaluation from the involvement of the change agents and this sets pretty problems for the identification of the evaluator. Wieland (1967) has described the pressures put upon him to give 'positive' support to the research teams.

Diffusion versus generality

As will be seen, the further we proceed down the list from basic pure research to action research, the more is utilization likely, but the less generality is possessed by the results. In the case of basic research the potential utility may be very great. The generality of the findings is very high. They could be applied to an analysis of many different kinds of social institutions. The question is how are they likely to be useful in an appropriate situation. The results of the research are committed to the channels of diffusion that we have called 'stock of knowledge' channels. In this way the knowledge tends to enter channels of reflection rather than channels of action. In due course, after many years, ideas or facts or myths may have obtained a hold over the minds of enough people in the channels of action for action to be influenced. Alternatively the findings may be 'translated' into field-oriented terms, thus entering the channels of diffusion for 'objective' research. The rules of academic publishing set by journal editors tend to 'place' the contribution into its scientific context. In this process it becomes divorced from its own social context and much less available to the diffusion channels in that context.

With basic objective research, broadly speaking, the same channels are relied upon, with some modification. For instance, use of specialist professional journals or journals of general interest to people in particular kinds of organizations; for example, business and managerial journals. The researchers themselves, and subsequently other teachers, may communicate them in courses for managers, administrators, professional people and the like. Thus, in addition to the 'conventional channels' to which pure research is consigned, 'selective scanning' channels are also used for objective research. Providing these are effective, we may expect that the delays and distortions encountered in diffusion through conventional channels will be reduced, but still they do not usually lead directly into the decision–action foci in the organizations concerned. If, for example, a personnel department is seen as the appropriate one for 'keeping in touch with' social science research, the use that is made of the results is likely to depend on the prestige the department has in the organization, the effectiveness of its communications with other departments and the professional competence of its members. Such competence may not include the ability and knowledge to 'develop' social research into usable form in the organization concerned.

Although the 'objective' piece of research may have been stimulated by the challenge of a practical problem, its findings may be of considerable value to the development of the scientific discipline. It is not only pure research which may provide a scientific breakthrough. However, on the whole, the results must be expected to be of significance in the particular field of discourse in which the problem arose and typically the outcome is of less generality than that from pure research.

Operational research is obviously intended to solve problems or improve administration in a specific organizational setting. The

135

preferred diffusion channel is the feedback loop without which the operational research design is incomplete. Utilization is certainly not guaranteed thereby, but failure, if it occurs, is not due to lack of information in the action channels. The fact that failure occurs at all in this situation is something of a puzzle to many operational researchers, who identify the source of their discomfiture as 'resistance to change', which may be comforting but does not help to improve the design of the research–action model. The generality of operational research studies is obviously very limited: what is most generalizable is the method, the adaptations of techniques and the development of new techniques which the successful solution of a particular problem may involve. Thus there is one additional diffusion channel, principally for the method and techniques similar to those in use for basic research, i.e. a journal specializing in discussion of the methods of operational research.

We do not mean that operational research cannot illuminate general or even theoretical problems, but the generalizable material is essentially a by-product. Miller and Rice's (1967) study of airline operations is a case in point. In many respects it is a modified form of operational research. It is planned also to throw light on the 'objective' general problem of the design of task and sentient boundaries. By considering it together with other similar projects, the authors succeed in making a contribution to the general 'pure basic' theory of organizations.

In action research the creation and use of a diffusion channel is an essential part of the research. Utilization is built into the research design. The generality of the findings is, however, very low. If the research is treated as a case study and reported in such a form that it can be discussed and evaluated along with other case studies, some generality is possible. As in the case of operational research, the methods used may have some generality and secondary diffusion channels may be used; but, far more than in operational research, these channels tend to be personal to the researcher. Action research is essentially a variety of the research-consultancy mix, and as Trist (1968) has observed, 'No-one knows what a Tannenbaum, or an Argyris; in the US, or a Bridger, or a Hutte, or a Pages, or Faucheux in Europe, in fact does, unless he works with him.'

If, then, we conclude from this that the more generality and hence *potential* utility that research possesses, the weaker the system by which it may enter action–decision channels, we must ask ourselves whether we can improve the research-action diffusion channel or construct new ones. Table 5 summarizes the relationship of type of research to its generality and its preferred diffusion channels.

It appears that the factors influencing the choice of channel and

TABLE 5 Relationship of type of research to its generality and its preferred diffusion channels

A Source of problem	B Type of research	C Generality of results	Generality of strategy	D Primary diffusion channel	E Secondary diffusion channel	F Feedback
Discipline	Pure Basic ⟨ historical theoretical or empirical	High	High	Learned publications	Possibly professional publications	Into disciplinary store of knowledge from D.
Field	Basic objective Mainly empirical	High	High	Professional publications	Learned publications	Into professional store of knowledge from D. Into disciplinary store of knowledge from E.
Section of field	Operational	Low	High	Private reports and feedbacks	(a) Professional publications (b) OR journals (c) Disciplinary journals	
Single site	Action	Low	Low	Part of research	Case study	

the rate at which different kinds of information progress through them are complex, but analysable. Over and above this, we are tackling the problem from a different angle. Diffusion channels, after all, consist of people. If there is no one in an organization with an understanding of mathematics, then information available only in mathematical terms is unavailable information. For this, among other reasons, many organizations employ mathematicians, as they employ physicists, chemists and engineers in a development role. Their effective use requires a good deal of organizational sophistication and tolerance of ambiguity.

Few organizations possess this sophistication as far as the social sciences are concerned; few, if any, social scientists exist competent and willing to act in the development role; and in any case, as we have pointed out above, the use in any organization of the results of research undertaken elsewhere nearly always requires a sophisticated analysis of the organization concerned. Even where relevant results exist and a social scientist capable of understanding the necessary analytic study is available, there is no guarantee of utilization of his efforts. But if the argument presented here is correct, we may be able to make use of the operational research and action research designs for this purpose. Experiments in this area were part of the work of the Centre for Utilization of Social Science Research at Loughborough University, a centre which also provided a Master of Science degree in Social Science Utilization to provide graduates with competence in operational and action research designs and techniques, as well as relevant social knowledge.

Mutual learning

The ideas from such work tended towards a concept of mutual learning. Our own experience, and that of many others, with the problems of working with organizations is that the main way in which social scientists can contribute is in a semi-teaching, semi-learning role. What we find we contribute to the organizations with which we work is a new way of analysing data and, indeed, a new way of looking at it which is strange to administrators at the outset. We find that gradually, as they associate with us, they are acquiring new concepts and acquiring them in a context in which they are able to put them to use. As part of this process we find ourselves importing into the organization knowledge of a general kind in the social sciences and making it available to them in a form which they can understand, manipulate and evaluate (see Warren Bennis's description of 'valid knowledge' in the following chapter). Looked at from the outside, one could say that this process is one of institutional learning on the part of the organization, but it also involves learning on the part of the research team, who are not only acquiring new data and new knowledge of the organization's functioning, but also knowledge about the processes of diffusion and application of knowledge.

The researcher needs to have some expertise by which he is identified and on the basis of which the organization is prepared to grant him legitimacy. He is expected to have a theoretical framework and a battery of techniques of inquiry. One particularly useful method of approach has proved to be the use of sociotechnical analysis which we will discuss in detail in Chapter 16. It is useful in its own right as a scheme of analysis and can be modified to meet the particular requirements and technology of the organizations with which we work. Additionally, it provides an entry point which quickly provides executives with a new frame of reference. They start with a certain degree of surprise because they expected sociologists and psychologists to begin with surveys and attitude questionnaires but very quickly they pick up a new way of looking at tasks and their interrelations.

To some extent in this mutual learning process we are, of course, making good the deficiencies which arise as a result of the fact that there are few people in administrative roles with experience of carrying out applied research.

Selection of institution

We may now look again at Table 5 to consider the type of research institution that will be most appropriate to particular kinds of research and utilization. It will become plain that different requirements are likely to be satisfied by different institutions; that in any one society some of these institutions may be lacking and may have to be created; and that the association between an administrator or an administrative machine and a research institution is one which not only has to be selected with care, but one which is likely to be frustrating unless we provide for mutual learning between the two institutions.

As a result of our attempts to study the way in which our own research has been utilized, I now consider most hopeful three inter-related approaches. First, it has proved practicable for industrial and other organizations to engage with outside institutions – such as universities and research organizations – in a mutual learning capacity of the kind I described earlier in this paper. Second, organizations which have operated in this way are, I think, likely to develop successfully in-house cells able to work with outside institutions. Third, the education in the concepts and methods of the social sciences which administrators learn on all kinds of courses, if appropriately followed up, renders them, if not immune to the engineering approach to sociotechnical and socioplanning problems, at least aware of the possibilities of other approaches.

Chapter 8
Social Sciences and Policy

In this chapter we will try to show that the social sciences have contributed to policy by:

(i)   providing the policy-maker with theories, good or bad, about man and about society which underpin his decisions;

(ii)   providing data; and

(iii)   occasionally devising technical solutions to problems.

Attempts to determine the relationship of social science knowledge to policy have proved a barren task, partly because this has been seen in terms of the application of research rather than the sociology of knowledge.

Unrecognized by both social scientists and policy-makers, ideological assumptions underlie not only the identification of research problems but also the choice of research methodology, and have influenced policy.

A fuller understanding of the relationships between policy-makers and researchers is critical to the successful identification of problems accessible to research and to identification of the process whereby research can actually aid policy. Successful use of the social sciences involves accurate knowledge of the policy-making process. Only recently has this been studied from the point of view of the social scientist.

Where policy is permeable

The policy-maker, however elevated, however humble, operates on the basis of values, theories and facts.

141

It is on the basis of values that the policy-maker prefers one goal to another, thus determining his choice of ends. On the basis of other values which he holds, the policy-maker prefers one route to his goal to another, thus determining his choice of means. But the belief that the means he adopts is likely to lead to the end he seeks is based on his theories about the nature of the system he is controlling, or which he is operating. In the case of social systems, or indeed any system in which human beings are involved, his theories must include theories about the nature of man.

On the basis of his theories about cause and effect in the system, the policy-maker has views about facts. He has views as to what facts are relevant and should be taken into account in coming to a decision, and views about the reliability of his sources of information.

Thus his values and theories will not only determine the policy-maker's choice of ends and choice of means, but also the knowledge he has about the present state of his system, the further information he will seek and his evaluation of it when acquired. They will also, in particular, determine the significance he will attach to social science as a source of relevant knowledge.

What we have described so far has the makings of a perfectly closed system. However, ends are sought, means are selected, actions taken as a result of which the state of the system is changed. This new state is almost bound to be compared with the desired state. Any discrepancy is likely to lead to a re-evaluation. The least painful re-evaluation to make is of the facts. If a re-reading of these cannot explain the discrepancy, the policy-maker may re-examine his theories. If, then, we wish to introduce new or different ideas or theories our most hopeful point of entry is at the stage of re-evaluation, following the appearance of wide discrepancies between aim and achievement.

Strategy of the gaps

The strategy of pointing to the discrepancy between aim and achievement has not escaped the social scientist. In promoting this claim to a place in the political sun, social scientists have, by and large, sought to adopt two strategies of which this is one. The other has been to point to the successful uses of social science in policy-making. The search for plausible examples of such successes has usually been abandoned in sorrow.

It is easy to show that questions of the kind: 'What *specific* use has been made of research in the social sciences?' are misconceived. As

I show below, research can only have *specific* use if it is conceived both as taking a narrow view of the problem it is tackling and has a strategy for its use designed into its methodology. Research of this kind turns out to have low generalizability, which does not necessarily mean, but often does, that it is also trivial.

Much of the trouble lies in our notions about the application of research. We tend to have sophisticated ideas about it when we discuss it in terms of 'sociology of knowledge', but to revert to simplistic models taken from the natural sciences when we are arguing about 'application' and 'applied' research. Thus we continually hear talk on the one hand of the many 'problems' which could be 'solved' by the sponsorship of appropriate social science research.

However, the search for 'uses' continues: I know of four attempts to trace out the uses made by the US Federal Government and its agencies of social science.[1] In response to congressional enquiry, agencies were unable to describe the use that had been made of previous research. This should not really be surprising. No system has been set up for evaluating the research that has been done, nor are criteria for utilization built into the designs of research projects and programmes. Under these conditions it is hard to see what answers could be expected to questions about utilization, as Lazarsfeld, Sewell and Wilensky (1968) found:

> One can understand with hindsight, but it came as a surprise, to realise how difficult it is to find out how and where sociology is being used. The Loomises . . . wrote to several hundred research sociologists about the uses of sociology; only those who were actively connected with some administrative enterprise could give concrete examples . . . a questionnaire was sent to the members of the ASA Section on Medical Sociology; the majority of the respondents had only vague ideas of what happened to their own work. Clients seemed to be more likely to know of uses than the sociologists themselves. But not only are clients difficult to sample; they are often corporations, in which the officers who may have acted on the basis of a report are not easily traced.

The preferred strategy of the social scientist is to point to prob-

---

[1] The study by Gene Lyons (1969) for the Russell Sage Foundation; the reports by the National Science Foundation (1969) and the National Academy of Sciences (1968) and by the Senate Sub-Committee on Government Operations (1967).

lems which social science knowledge would help to solve or to ameliorate, outlining the *potential* uses of social science research.

These are usually formulated in terms of *information* which would be of value to policy-makers; seldom in terms of ways in which better theories and better techniques could help policy-makers. While it is no doubt true that better information makes for better decisions, it is equally true that, however good or complete the information available, it will be evaluated in terms of the policy-maker's theories and values, and that mistaken theories and inappropriate values figure as largely in bad decisions as does inadequate information. Fortunately social science is at least as relevant to the choice of theory and value as to the provision of data.

The sociologist cannot just assume that the truths he reveals in his research will find their own way into application. He has an input he wishes to make to an action system of some kind. This action system includes decisions and people who make decisions. Different systems and different components of the same system can use different kinds of input. Without understanding and analysis of the system, our social scientist can only fire his arrows into the air. They will, of course, come to earth, he knows not where. Likewise, without an adequate scanning mechanism, the decision-maker cannot locate the appropriate sources of input for his needs; he can only expose himself to any arrows which happen to be in the air.

But all this is to assume that the social scientist wants his 'findings' to be used. Some do. Many more want to be published and preferably read; or, more to the point, cited. Many of the most prestigious social scientists operate in a system whose reward structure is oblivious to 'uses', but very permeable to lists of publications and citations by other scholars.

The social scientist, then, who wants to influence policy can look to several points in the policy process where social science knowledge can be influential. We can consider first the process of selecting options; secondly that of realizing the option selected.

Points of entry

(a) *Choice of options*

(i) System characteristics
Sociological theory and political analysis can *describe* the system in which the policy-maker is operating. His choice of descriptive terms are themselves value-laden and influenced by his views as to what the 'system' is. Some sociologists have described and analysed the

144

system of education in England as a mechanism for distributing social rewards and opportunities and thus either advancing or retarding certain aspects of social change. Others may see our system of education as a mechanism for distributing limited resources to maximize more or less traditional types of learning and knowledge. The trouble is that a 'system of education' is both these and more besides. Thus the task of completely describing and analysing the 'system' is probably impossible. However, we can obtain the policy-maker's view of the goals of the system, though even these are likely to be changed or at least modified by our attempt to elucidate them. If the policy-maker understands and accepts this description, he will then be in a better position to assess both the options that are available to him and the likely outcomes of his choice.

(ii) Theories about the nature of man
The possible states which a system can have depend on the nature of the elements of which it is composed and of their interactions. Our estimate of the attainability of any particular state depends on our theories about the nature of the elements. For example, we may conclude that a state of peace between social groups is impossible because of the aggressive nature of man. By influencing the policy-maker's view of the nature of man, social science will affect his assessment of the goals he can hope to achieve, and of their attainability.

Thus by increasing the policy-maker's knowledge and understanding of the system in which he is operating and the characteristics and potentialities of its human components, social science knowledge can clarify and increase the options available to him.

(b) *Realizing options*

In choosing the means to attain his ends, the policy-maker needs to know:
(1) the present state of the system;
(2) the economic, social and political costs of the possible means he can employ;
(3) the anticipated consequences of the means he is considering; including
(4) the possible side effects of each means, both favourable (fall-out) and unfavourable (backfirings).
Here the contributions of the social sciences are technical rather than analytical.

145

To contribute to (1) the social sciences have developed techniques of measurement – statistical sampling, questionnaire measures of attitudes, and so forth. The technique of cost–benefit analysis provides the knowledge of (2). Though continually advancing in subtlety, cost–benefit analysis has so far carried with it a concealed inference on both values and the theory of the nature of man, by maintaining an economic value system together with the theory of economic man. While we cannot attempt to do justice to methods of cost–benefit analysis, their influence and their importance in this context is greatest for (3), the anticipated consequences of means. It enables the policy-maker to anticipate certain consequences but does not alert him to others.

Cost–benefit analysis here offers a good example of the difficulties inherent in almost any attempt to analyse a total system. If it is to be intellectually coherent it must offer a scheme of analysis which brings into measurable relationship with one another all the ramifications of policy decisions. But in any large system we need to break the problem down into examinable entities or subsystems. Even if we can provide solutions which optimize the operations of all the subsystems, these will not necessarily add up to an optimum solution for the operation of the total system.

But perhaps the most promising use of cost–benefit analysis is to identify the options available. By comparing alternatives some may be brought forward for technical comparison which may have been overlooked or ruled out of court on mistaken or irrelevant grounds.

As far as (4) is concerned, careful historical analysis of the unanticipated consequences of previous decisions provides the only useful technique to date.

Thus the social sciences have, to some extent, provided the policy-maker with *techniques for realizing options* through aiding him in his selection of means.

After selecting his options and the means whereby they will be achieved, the policy-maker may now seek assistance in publicizing his intentions and obtaining a favourable public response. Here again the social sciences can provide technical solutions.

A single person may be responsible for all the choices – of goal, of means and of publicity. In an organization, however, these choices are likely to be made at different and descending levels. Indeed only the first may be regarded as truly policy. To the top level choice of goal is policy, choice of means is execution of policy. At the next level the choice of means may be a policy decision, execution to take place at a lower level still. However this may be, it is likely that advice on choice of goal will be sought if at all by the top echelon; advice on means will be sought at a lower level; advice on selling a decision at yet another level. Not only will such advice be sought by different echelons, it is likely to be sought from different sources. As we shall see later, this has large implications for the strategy of social science in engaging with organizations.

Social sciences and the mechanisms for articulating public policy

We shall now examine the extent to which existing mechanisms for articulating public policy rely on, or are underpinned by, contributions from the social sciences.

These contributions are of two kinds: (a) mechanisms for obtaining data relevant to the publics concerned; and (b) assumptions derived often from social science methods used to obtain the data.

(a) Inputs to the policy-making process include statistics and survey data as well as the publications of social scientists. These inputs are both direct and indirect. Governments and other policy-making bodies utilize and set great store upon data of a quantitative nature provided by censuses of population, production and so forth and by surveys of various kinds – in Britain the government has ready recourse to findings from its own Social Survey, now a constituent of the Office of Population Censuses and Surveys (OPCS). Political parties in or out of office are influenced in their policy-making by results of polls. Social science methods of obtaining quantitative representations of social benefits are now increasingly used in cost–benefit analysis studies preceding decisions of public investment. Moreover, skilled interpretation of the data and trends from these statistics are both required and relied upon.

(b) These data import certain assumptions often unrecognized. The first point I wish to make is that the social sciences have played the predominant part in the origin of the statistics and of methods of obtaining, evaluating and presenting them, and of turning them to economic and social indicators. Any consideration of the use of the social sciences in policy-making must take this into account.

The second point is that statistics and the methods of obtaining them are by no means value-free. They rest on theories and even on ideologies. To begin with, statistics have, until recently at any rate, been virtually confined to what could be measured or counted. (Often what can be counted or measured has been identified with the logical and rational; what could not be counted or measured was irrational or metaphysical.) Thus there has been a tendency to undervalue the immeasurable and uncountable. Second, some procedures have embodied an unstated and probably unrealized ideological assumption. The counting of heads implies the equival-

147

ence of heads, or at least the propriety of treating the individual as the unit. It is one thing to sample the opinions of all adults in a community; another to sample the opinions of heads of families, villages, tribes or whatnot. Our democratic, one person, one vote, ideology infects the choice of data and method of acquiring it. When we choose the individual as our unit we imply both that the matter is one which appropriately refers to individuals as units and that individuals are equal units for that purpose. I am not attacking democracy; I am pointing out that its ideology is implicit in many of our 'objective' methods and data. We report an interesting example of this in Chapter 11, when we look at the Volta River Resettlement project in Ghana.

Furthermore, our methods of obtaining data are overwhelmingly verbal. Questionnaires, interviews, censuses are conducted through the use of verbal symbols; some behaviour is much more accessible to verbal report than others; what is less accessible is largely ignored (cf. La Père, 1934). We prefer 'hard' methods to those more difficult to assess and replicate. We prefer questionnaire data to participant observation; surveys have prospered, 'mass observation' has become unfashionable. All this is perfectly proper provided we know what we are doing. But we don't know, or we forget.

Some measures, indicators, are available which do not rely on verbal report and which are 'non-reactive', i.e. do not influence the behaviour they are designed to assess. So far they have been little used. Some are reported in *Unobtrusive Measures* (Webb, *et al.*, 1966). These, it is true, still rely on some quantitative measures or observations.

Proposals current in the United States since the later 1920s for the development of social indicators to set alongside the more prominent economic indicators are, if adopted, likely to have the effect of drawing attention to non-economic issues, but still to the more easily measurable aspects of social issues.

The points I have been trying to make in this section are:
(a) Theories and methods derived from social sciences underlie 'objective' data used in policy-making.
(b) Unstated and unrealized ideological preferences determine both the kind of data we seek and the way in which we present and draw conclusions from them.
(c) The ready availability of so much verbal symbolic material leads to our neglecting to seek evidence of people's non-verbal behaviour.
(d) To an altogether unrecognized degree the social sciences are derived from cultural assumptions and feedback so as to strengthen these assumptions first through the effect on our

consciousness of the data derived from their use, and second through their effect on the policies formulated with the help of that data. Thus:
(e) The social sciences in providing data for use by policy-makers import with those data, and wrapped up in them, ideological assumptions which on the whole tend to reinforce egalitarian and democratic assumptions and orientations of policy-makers.

Policy-making and decision-making

At this point we make a distinction between policy-making and decision-making. This distinction is not always very clearly made. Merton (1968) for example treats policy as identical with administrative action when he discusses the 'world of practical decision'. Potentially we weaken the argument for the role of the social sciences if we let it be thought that we are claiming their relevance to all decision-making. A close reading of Merton's article and, in particular, of his taxonomy of research objectives makes it clear that he is thinking of policy objectives, not of decision-making *per se*. He classifies research problems into:

Diagnostic:	e.g. providing information on whether the situation has changed.
Prognostic:	e.g. forecasting future needs.
Differential prognosis:	e.g. selecting options.
Evaluative:	e.g. comparing performance with aim.
'Educative' research:	e.g. setting out the true facts for the public.
Strategic fact-finding:	e.g. systematic purposive assembling of descriptive data.

This classification, though logically complete, can make sense as policy research only if all policy is taken to have a programmatic referent.

However, policy may not be programmatic though it is distinguished from decision-making by being iterative. Rose (1969) points out that:

> Policy-making involves a long series of more-or-less related activities rather than a single, discrete decision. . . . It thus covers far more than the term decision-making. The study of decision-making usually involves analysing the intentions of policy makers up to and including the point at which binding . . . action is taken. . . . Outcomes may be affected less by

conscious decision to act than by conscious or unconscious preferences for inaction. . . . The sense of continuous activity and adjustment involved in policy-making is best conveyed by describing it as a process, rather than a single once-for-all act.

However, Snyder and Paige (1958) define decision-making as '. . . a sequence of activities which results in selection of one course of action intended to bring about the particular future state of affairs envisaged by the decision-makers'.

This is almost identical with our chosen definition of policy-making. We do need definitions, though they need not be too precise. We shall therefore read policy for decision in Snyder and Paige's description, stressing again the continuity involved in policy. If policy-making then is not a once-for-all affair, can the effective contribution of social science be a once-for-all affair? Rather I would maintain that the sequential nature of decision-making in policy offers a number of points where social science research can make an input. Furthermore it allows for a more developed relationship between researcher and policy-maker.

Relationship between policy-maker and social scientist

Whether the social scientist is described as one of adviser or consultant, researcher or even critic, his relationship with the policy-maker is essentially one of provider of knowledge, whether it be an analytical framework or new facts or new relationships between previously known facts. The knowledge to be usable must have validity for the client.

Niehoff (1966) discusses ways in which knowledge must be adapted to pass effectively from one culture system to another. He refers to the 'sociocultural component, which means simply that technical know how and economic patterns are embedded in cultural systems, elaborate patterns of customs and beliefs, which can either act as sanctions or barriers to technical or economic change'. It may be presumptuous to point to the difference between administrative and academic cultures in one's own country as obstacles to acceptance of the validity of social science knowledge. Nevertheless, we are not entitled to assume that all administrative organizations in our society are equally ready to accept the legitimacy of ideas. Hauser (1967) has made the point that in a complex society we have 'almost every stage of social evolution simultaneously present'. So what is seen as valid knowledge in one frame of reference will not necessarily be similarly accepted in another.

Warren Bennis (1961) has sketched what is required for knowledge generated by the social sciences to be 'valid'. His 'desiderata' include taking into consideration 'the behaviour of persons operating within their specific institutional environment', accepting that groups and organizations are 'as amenable to empirical and analytical treatment as the individual', and, above all, including 'variables the practitioner can understand, manipulate and evaluate'. But even the most heroic efforts to generate 'valid' knowledge will fail if the 'practitioner' (as Bennis calls him though sometimes referring to him generically as the 'client system'), or, in our terms, the policy-maker, fails to generate the corresponding capacity to assimilate the knowledge provided. The demands on the social scientist to make himself understood, his advice practical, are familiar. But there is equal need for a corresponding effort on the part of the policy-maker to acquire familiarity with the concepts of social science, if only to provide a conceptual framework which enables him to relate 'values' to probable action.

But above all, the client system must have, or must develop, channels for diffusion of the 'valid' knowledge. Lazarsfeld, Sewell and Wilensky (1968) describe this problem: 'Whatever study has been made, whatever fund of available knowledge has been drawn upon, then comes the moment when one has to make the *leap from knowledge* to decision.' But the concern of the social scientist cannot end at the point where he has made valid knowledge available to the policy-maker. He must also, if he is concerned with the usability of, as well as the validity of, this knowledge be concerned with the policy-maker's capability of adopting the conceptual base into which the knowledge can be absorbed so as to make the leap from a secure platform. This means among other things that the policy-maker and social scientist must have similar conceptions of the relationship of science to policy. Horowitz (1967) points out that social scientists are anxious to study the policy process so as to add to scientific knowledge, as well as providing 'intelligence' for government, whereas the policy-makers in government are more interested in social engineering than in social science. Horowitz (1967) makes two further important points:

Policy places a premium on involvement and influence; science places a premium on investigation and ideas. The issue is not so much what is studied or even the way an enquiry is conducted but the auspices and purposes of a study.

And further:

151

> We witness in . . . the social sciences . . . the break-up of the functionalist ideology with its value-free orientation.

This last point we must take up again in consideration of the ethical problems of the relationship of the social sciences to policy. It is important here because it shows that Bennis's valid knowledge is knowledge acquired from a particular stand-point and cannot in any case be regarded as value-free scientific knowledge. However this may reflect on the scientific status of the knowledge, it certainly implies that the valid knowledge provided by the social scientist is based on a system of values shared by both social scientist and policy-maker.

Churchman and Emery (1966) argue the consequences of this very cogently. They discuss the relationship between the organization to which the researcher belongs and the organization which he is studying. They consider three ideal types of this relationship: 'One approach . . . is to regard the researcher as a member of an organization completely independent of the organization being observed.'

In this type of relationship the researcher's reference group is the research community with its values of scientific objectivity and disinterestedness and purity. His goals are publication, a scientifically sound piece of work and the recognition of the scientific community. As a member of an entirely different kind of organization from that which he is studying he may not find it possible to identify the organization's problems in terms which meet its real needs. Nor can the research organization learn how to make its output more valuable to the organizations it studies: 'A second approach to the study of organizations is to regard the researcher as both a member of an independent research community and a member *pro tem.* of another organization that includes the one being observed.'

Here the researcher is faced with insoluble dilemmas. He cannot resolve conflicts in the goals of the two organizations. He has to restrict his involvement in the organization under study and therefore shies away from problems of central importance. Further, he has conflicting claims on his time. Should he end the research when the research organization is satisfied or go on until the observed organization accepts and understands his contribution?

A third approach to the study of organizations is to regard the researcher as a member *pro tem.* of a third organization under study to encompass the conflicting interests and yet sufficiently close to it to permit its values to be related to the concrete issues of conflict.

In this view we escape the problem of the social scientist's acquiring the values of the policy-maker by requiring that both share values sanctioned by a higher-level organization of which both are members. At the level of their interaction the policy-maker has acquired a capability of using knowledge whose validity is not determined by its relevance to his view as an administrator or the aim and functioning of his organization. Policy-maker and researcher are then able to engage in the mutual learning approach, which is the most effective way in which knowledge generated by social science research can be brought into the action frame of reference of the policy-maker. The basis for this mutual learning must, however, as Buckley (1967) puts it, be continually shifting.

> Social order is not simply normatively specified and
> automatically maintained but is something that must be
> 'worked at' and continually reconstituted. Shared agreements
> that underlie orderliness are not binding and shared
> indefinitely, but involve a temporal dimension implying an
> eventual review, and consequent renewal or rejection.

The question then arises: how much shift in the basis of the 'shared agreements' can take place without overstraining the tension between the policy-maker and the researcher? At what point do roles undergo so much change that the basis of negotiation has been changed requiring new roles? And if new roles are required, can they be assumed without a change of cast?

G. N. Jones (1969) has introduced the definition of three roles involved in the processes of change in policy in organizations. These roles are 'change agent', 'change catalyst' and 'pacemaker'.

The 'change agent' is a 'helping professional'. Like the 'client system', he possesses 'his own unique set of values, norms and behavioural patterns'.

The change catalyst examines widespread influence at small cost to himself. He may at one stage facilitate the interaction of change agent and client system and is at all times free to move between them.

The pacemaker, which may be an individual, group or organization, has as its primary function the maintenance of the change process 'by the proper and the systematic changes of stimuli'.

At different stages during the consideration and adoption of policy changes, using knowledge generated by social science research, the three functions of agent, catalyst and pacemaker become crucial and remain of importance for different durations. All three functions can be fulfilled by social scientists, but not by the same social scientist, as they involve different sets of relationships with the policy-maker. Difficulties arise in practice because, as the basis of the 'shared agreement' shifts, demands are made first on one then on another of these roles. Simple models relating one researcher to one policy-maker ignore the variety and complexities of these relationships and ignore, too, the fact that both policy-maker and researcher must operate within organizational contexts.

Not only are we obliged to consider different relationships between policy-maker and researcher at different stages of the policy process, we also need to consider the different relationships appropriate to different kinds of research. Moreover, as we saw in the previous chapter, not only do different types of research have associated with them different channels of diffusion, but different types of research are also linked to different diffusion channels.

The time characteristics of the policy–administrative process set many specific problems for research. It is not only a question of the policy maker's need for quick results nor his difficulties in attempting to predict what will be his future needs for research. Different kinds of information are needed at different phases of the policy process. Analytic studies classifying and possibly increasing options are required at the stage when options are being generated and considered. Technical studies are needed at the stage of realizing options. Manipulative 'research' may be called for at the stage of obtaining acceptance of the favoured option. For example, researchers may be asked to find out how a particular policy can be 'sold'. Or they may be asked to undertake research aimed to 'show the need for XYZ' or to make findings selectively available (see Rainwater and Yancy, 1967). The time characteristics of the phases of the policy-making process and of the associated researchers can be expected to match only in the case of action research (which cannot otherwise be undertaken).

Now when we put together the points we have made so far we see that:

1 Policy implies a sequence of decisions, with what is executive at one level becoming policy at the next level below.

2 In the stages of the policy-making process different social science inputs are required.

3 As a consequence of (1) and (2) multiple entries into the decision-making process are required both in terms of points in the sequence and level of intervention.

154

4 The basis for any transaction between policy-maker and social scientist requires: (a) some shared values sanctioned by their mutual relationship to a higher level, if temporary, organization; and (b) continuously renegotiated terms of reference.

5 The research may be of various types each of which is associated with a set of typical diffusion channels and is, therefore, best conducted by different types of research institution.

6 If the research is not of an 'operational' or 'action' type it may not enter the action channel unless it has built into it a strategy for implementation – in effect an operational or action research phase.

Following this analysis it would seem that the linkage between policy-making and social science can be improved by changes in the mutual perceptions of policy-maker and social scientist and their joint understanding of the potential relevances of research and the problems of diffusion of its results into channels of action and policy-making. A greater planned range of research institutions with special competences in one or other kind of research would doubtless help too. But we can get just so far with tailoring research to assist in the formulation and realization of policy. At least as much advantage could come from using the resources of social science to *improve the policy-making process.*

Social science and the policy-making process

The style and time-scale of policy-making, the quantity of research information which must be processed will vary with other significant parameters, including the reactiveness of the environment or, in Emery's (1968) terms, its 'turbulence'. Policy-makers in large systems, ranging from corporations, universities to governments, are operating more and more in turbulent fields of this kind and are faced with situations in which not only are they unable to predict the effects of different possible decisions, but also unable to relate consequences to actions. The problem is worse if the system's time characteristics are such that it responds sluggishly to his actions as successive Chancellors of the Exchequer in Britain well know! Can the social sciences help to devise improved schemata for policy-making in this type of situation? Emery points to 'systems management' as a possible schema. It involves: selecting and reselecting goals which appear to be attainable given the characteristics of the field as well as of the system; applying criteria derived from the goal

155

for comparing means; tighter assessment of results, particularly against interim goals; a 'flexible framework' of information and decision, using scientific and other specialized knowledge; control by information, prediction and persuasion; and better ways of predicting the interactions of simultaneous policy decisions. As Emery points out these techniques will lead to false conclusions if based on wrong assumptions about computers as artificial intelligences and about the omniscience of experts. Turbulent fields cannot be negotiated by traditionally hierarchically structured organizations. Organizational forms which can cope with turbulent fields must develop processes of policy-making which can take into account the social processes which arise through the 'mutual adjustment of the values and interests of the participants'.

This seems a formidable task and we are offered little guidance as to the means by which it can be achieved. Of course, conceptualizing the need is itself a step in the right direction.

Even though turbulent fields may negate the possibility of comprehensive centralized planning of decision-making, it also means that there need be a less rigid sequence of decision-making. What is ignored at one point in policy-making becomes central at another point, while those not attended to can be dealt with as they appear because of the successive and serial nature of analysis and policy-making.

What begins to emerge here is a concept recently adopted in social science of the 'learning' system – the system which is designed so that it can adjust its behaviour as it encounters reality.

We are, of course, witnessing both a backlash against centralized planning and a simultaneous provision of a cloak of respectability for a degree of laissez-faire. The concept of learning has the right sound of flexibility and growth. It also suggests an organic character to the process and replaces mechanical by biological images. Hirschman and Lindblom (1962) show that a number of lines of thought converge on to a model of policy management.

1 Some policy-making processes and modes of behaviour, ordinarily considered to be irrational and wasteful are rational and useful.

2 Some matters need 'wise and salutary neglect'.

3 One step ought often to be left to lead to another. It is unwise to specify objectives in much detail when the means of attaining them are virtually unknown.

4 Goals will change through experience with a succession of means–ends and ends–means adjustments.

5 A rational problem-solver wants what he can get and does

156

not try to get what he wants except after identifying what he wants by examining what he can get.

6 The exploration of alternative uses of resources can be overdone.

7 Decision-makers need to discern and react promptly to newly emerging problems, imbalances and difficulties. If they are too concerned with eliminating them in advance, by 'integrated planning' they lose the ability to react and to improvise readily and imaginatively.

8 Since we have limited capacities to solve problems and particularly to foresee the shape of future problems, we may do best the 'hard way' of learning by experience.

9 These amount to a theory of successive decision-making, relying on the clues that appear in the course of the sequence and concentrating on identification of these clues.

10 Processes of mutual adjustment of participants are capable of achieving a kind of co-ordination not necessarily centrally envisaged prior to its achievement, or centrally managed.

These points are adapted and condensed from Hirschman and Lindblom (1962). They do not amount to a recipe for blind incrementalism, but to a scheme for a reorientation of the policy-maker to (a) the characteristics of the system he is trying to plan or to control; (b) the characteristics of the behaviour of systems in turbulent fields; and (c) the role of policy-maker as that of arranging useful learning experiences for the organization; a continual process of reality-testing both of goals and of means. The social sciences can relate to this policy process most effectively in two ways: first by analysing the nature of the system which the policy-maker is controlling, and second by helping to devise the reality-testing procedures and by monitoring them. While basic research is clearly required for the former, operational and action research techniques will have to be developed on a wide scale to undertake the latter.

Example of policy-making process

I have tried to show that for the purposes of relating research to the policy-making process, we can think of this as having the following phases:

Phase 1 is the identification of the problem.

Phase 2 is the clarification of the existing options and, as a possible outcome, the revelation of new, previously unsuspected options.

Phase 3 is the stage of selecting among available options. The

social sciences contribution to this is essentially directed to improvement of the decision-making process itself; and
Phase 4 is the realization of the option selected.

To make this point clear, I am presenting a worked example. I have taken as my example an imaginary engagement of decision-makers and researchers concerned with problems of race relations and immigration in Britain.

Phase 1

The first phase of the decision-making process should be to determine the nature of the problem for which research of various kinds may be required. First, there is a need for basic facts about the populations concerned: for example, the numbers, their origins, their age distribution, birth rates, death rates, occupational distribution, and so on. The appropriate institution for carrying out this kind of basic objective research would appear to be an in-house agency, but there are snags. It is essential that the information so acquired should be available through publication for discussion of an informed kind for criticism and comment. But it is in the nature of things that the work of in-house agencies tends only to be released if the department or agency of government concerned is satisfied that adverse criticism as a result of the publication of the data need not be feared. This has two adverse outcomes. In the first place the department suppresses publication of data likely to lead to adverse criticism; second, what is made available for publication may err through unrecognized bias on the part of the researcher anxious to achieve publication. Indeed, what is published is likely to be viewed askance by academic researchers. Thus it is probably better to locate such research in some statistical or census bureau with a tradition of publication. Even this, if it is in-house, leaves the door open to interpretation of bias. Official population projections of Britain's coloured population have been shown to be liable to error. We are all fallible. But fallibility can appear suspicious if the errors favour government policy. Mr Powell's animadversions may display a suspicious mind, but government reliance on its own research provides the target. (And whose fault is it that government data have consistently turned out to be (systematically) wrong?)

To return to the research associated with Phase 1 of the decision-making process, the 'problem' is defined in terms which imply theories of behaviour. For example, an administrator may now pose it as how to advance 'integration' or 'assimilation'. Often the first result of posing a problem for research is a redefinition of

158

the problem in the light of increased understanding or of more sophisticated theories of human behaviour.

Phase 2

Phases 1 and 2 are closely linked from the point of view of research for policy. Decision-making in both is based on some model, explicit or implicit, of the nature of the system which the policy-maker is trying to control or influence. Research aimed at describing the system is mainly of the basic objective variety; the description in analytic terms of the operation of the system itself is best described as operational research. Thus we would in this example seek demographic data and seek to make projections on principles derived from demographic research applied to the nature of our population. Occupational backgrounds, national, tribal and district origins, attitudes towards the native population and towards the host culture and the attitudes of the native population towards the immigrants are all basic data clearly required for any policy-making. But beyond that, these variables are clearly likely to affect very considerably the demographic future: immigrants whose attitudes towards the host culture are positive are more likely to adopt the host culture's attitudes towards, and practices of, family-planning. Their occupational distribution is also likely to affect future family size and so on.

Building a model of the operation of this system and testing it is essentially operational research. In the course of collecting the basic data we may be made aware of the existence within our population of subpopulations which differ on relevant variables. New options may become apparent as it becomes possible to consider the adoption of different policies for different subpopulations. The problem may be redefined at this point.

In seeking to understand the system he is dealing with, the policy-maker may have recourse to still more basic research, providing him with theories of man, society, organizations. This 'pure basic' research will not of course be mounted especially for his purpose, but recourse to it may help him to recognize that it is in his interest that such research should be provided for by his government.

Phase 3

Here we move to the selection of options. The options should have been clarified and the advantages and disadvantages of each tabulated. Social science research cannot at this point choose for the policy-maker among the options available. His choice will have to be made in the light of other policies, his priorities and values. Where research is now of most value is in refining the *modes* of decision-making. It can provide him, for example, with ways of selecting trial settings; it might be a number of small areas in which to stage limited experiments or demonstration projects, chosen in such a way as to offer a representative pattern. As our example concerns immigrants, these would have to be in areas selected on the basis of demographic and class structure. These could take the form of action research, involving policy-maker, researched, and researcher in joint effort and evaluation. Setting up adequate criteria against which to evaluate trials and larger-scale ventures involves operational research into the way the system actually behaves.

The policy-maker may wish to know the likely response to a particular choice of policy; the researcher may advise the use of survey techniques – operational research again. Because surveys are essentially reactive and liable to help to form, as well as to register, opinion, their use may change the situation in such a way as to generate and reveal new options for decision. This emphasizes the essentially reiterative process of all step-by-step policy-making.

Phase 4

Action research now becomes a weapon of choice. Its roles are in demonstration projects, larger-scale experimental programmes and in dissemination of information. But for the purpose of monitoring we now need adequate indicators and these require both basic objective research into the dynamic characteristics of the system in general (relations between variables such as employment rates, occupational structure, country of origin, demographic variables) and operational research into the actual functioning of the particular system or subsystem.

This is set out in schematic form in Figure 1. As will by now be apparent the policy-maker is required to engage with all four types of research – pure basic, basic objective, operational and action research – at various phases of the policy-making process. As these different types of research are, as we have indicated, appropriate to different types of research organization, the policy-maker, or more accurately the policy-making system, must engage with a range of research organizations.

160

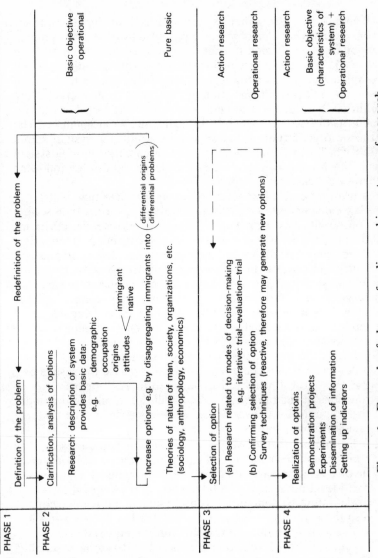

Figure 1 Example of phases of policy-making – types of research (e.g. immigrants in UK – race relations)

The utilizing organization

All this takes us yet another step forward, as it enables us now to see more clearly what kind of research provided by what kind of organization can be expected to contribute to what kind of problem at what phase of the policy-making process. But this still does not complete the necessary disaggregation. We need now to disaggregate the utilizing organization to see what characteristics are required in order for it to be able to utilize the research which it sponsors or becomes aware of through scanning mechanisms. The utilizing organization needs to acquire a utilizing system within itself which can be matched with the research generating system with which it engages. Such a system needs to have the following characteristics.

1 It must be able to operate on an appropriate time scale. Few elements of an organization can operate on a time scale appropriate to research and it therefore becomes necessary to set up a system within the organization capable of doing this, which can have the longer-term perspective necessary and which can operate on the basis of considerable anticipation.

2 It must be capable of making use of the concepts which will be generated by the research, and if it is to be concept-using, then it must be essentially a learning system and capable of entering into a teaching–learning or learning–learning relationship with the research-generating system.

3 It must be cross-functional, cross-disciplinary and multi-level. It must be cross-functional because the results of the research will need to be addressed to all principal functions of the organization or it will fail to take into account the relationships between them and, in particular, the power relationships.

Furthermore, effective use of the outcomes requires commitment to the aims and comprehension of the concepts involved on the part of all the functions involved. It must be multi-level because, not only must the top level of the organization be committed to the research and its use, but also the various operating levels will need to be related to it, both for the purpose of providing information and also because at these levels too the concepts need to be acquired if the output is to be put to effective use. This particular characteristic of the utilizing system presents a problem for the research-generating system. Most user organizations are hierarchical in structure. To provide a satisfactory 'fit' between the two systems, pressures are exerted upon the research-generating system to operate in a hierarchical fashion itself. This may often conflict with the notions about how research is carried out which require a different kind of relationship between the researchers from that which exists between the levels in a hierarchical organization.

4 It must be capable of generating values which can be shared with the research system. This in turn may lead to new values problems for the research system. We have just described the need for multi-level interaction between the systems and the tendency for people at level one in the research-generating institution to be put into relationship with people at level two and so on. The problem that this generates is that each of the different levels in the research system is now associated with what is in effect a different client and the problem of who the client is arises for the research institution.

5 It must be capable of relating with different types of research organization in order that, as shown above, it may be able to engage with the appropriate kinds of research at the appropriate stages of the policy-making process. For this, it needs to have a scanning function to keep it in touch with developments in the social sciences and to enable it to assess the capabilities and characteristics of the different research institutions.

It is clearly in the interests of social scientists to seek to develop or to assist in the development of these research-utilizing systems in the organizations with which they have relationships. Hitherto this has been a neglected role for the social sciences, but it is one that the social sciences must tackle if the utilization of social research is to be improved.

Chapter 9
Behavioural Science Engagements

Negotiating the contract

In this chapter we shall draw upon the experiences of contract research work carried out by members of the research team of the university-based Centre for Utilization of Social Science Research.

The role of negotiation of social science research contracts is rarely publicly recorded. This is partly because it is an incidental activity; the negotiator of a research contract does not perceive this role as conferring his professional identity. It is not something he engages in exclusively or, perhaps, often, yet his professional position endows him alone with the necessary authority and credibility. He may succeed in obtaining a contract which, on the face of it, offers him the opportunities for research, while offering the organization providing the contract with knowledge which will be useful to them. If subsequently expectations are disappointed, it probably will be attributed to factors arising during the conduct of the research. Mistakes and miscalculations at the contract stage are too often neglected.

The first questions we may profitably examine are How did the parties come together? What led sponsor A to researcher B? Why indeed engage with a research group at all, instead of employing consultants or trying to solve his problem within his own resources? Logically the second question is prior to the first, but I suspect that seldom are decisions taken in that order. Acquaintance with, or knowledge of, the research group and its activities may initiate the processes which lead to formulation of a problem in a form which looks accessible to research of the kind the research group appears able to provide.

In one study the employment by the sponsor of a former colleague was clearly an important factor; it was he who perceived the company's problems as having similarities to those we had tackled before. During the period of negotiation he played a most important part, not only in representing our competence to the company, but also in presenting to us the situation of the company as he saw it and the political factors inside the company which might affect our research and its outcome. It is not possible to guess how common this particular pattern is; it is likely to occur more frequently as more people with experience in research teams such as ours move into industry. Despite the obvious dangers, not least of which is the scapegoating of the go-between for any subsequent disappointments, there are tremendous advantages in there being someone who can interpret equally the values of the sponsor to the researcher and vice versa.

We experienced another variant of this model when a graduate employee of a large organization asked to register with us for a higher degree to be taken externally. This led to a discussion between the centre and the company and it became clear that the problem as it had so far been defined was beyond the competence of a trainee-postgraduate student, and also that his definition of the problem and ours differed significantly. It was in the course of the ensuing discussions between the senior management of the company and ourselves that the suggestion was mooted that the problem could be redefined and tackled by a team composed of ourselves, together with the part-time attachment of the trainee. Thus this was partly set up as an 'inside–outside' partnership.

From this it would appear that the joint inside–outside arrangement is the more successful of the joint operations. The roles of part-time pupil and collaborator can, in theory, be combined, though with some difficulty. But because of different levels of status it requires a degree of mutual knowledge and confidence which has to be built up over time. A better formula would be for a student employed by a sponsor organization to register for a Ph.D, which would be earned within the framework of a research project.

In another case a young research worker who had come to us as a student had obtained as a 'site' for her study of communication and diffusion a local pharmaceutical firm. When co-operation was agreed by the company, which was well disposed towards establishing contacts with the university, we stipulated that we would feed back the findings, which in the event were of considerable interest to them. They not only described a situation which was giving rise to anxiety within the company, but also appeared to offer a technique for probing further into the problem. We were then asked if we could propose a research project to do this.

Occasionally a sponsor may use a more or less articulated scanning process before approaching the researchers. For instance, in one company we worked with, the personnel research manager had a shopping list of projects and through his own contacts and attendance at scientific meetings drew up his own short-list of probable research centres. Indeed his long-term aim was to develop a continuing institutional relationship with one or more research centres and it was on this basis, as much as on the content of the particular research project, that he approached the CUSSR.

Another route to initial contact is through referral, either from sponsors who have first approached other centres and been referred on, or, as one of our studies began, with contacts between the company and another department of the university. Their assessment of the problem put to them was that while they could certainly make a contribution, the social scientists should also be 'brought in'. Similarly a research contract with a government department initiated from a department of engineering. Again it was thought the addition of sociological expertise to the research team would be valuable and so a joint approach was made to the ministry.

It will be noted that in almost all of these cases the contact came about before the problem was defined as one accessible to social science research, and might well never have been so defined if the contact had not previously been made. Nor in any of these cases did the initiative for the research come from the research centre in the first place.

While, then, there are many variations, there is a theme. The contact is highly personal. Potential sponsors of research have really no guidelines to follow in seeking help, nor much chance of evaluating what they are offered in the way of research. There are no research brokers, nor a research *Which?* For every case where a sponsor and a researcher 'click' there must be many where the process is blocked through the absence of contact between sponsor and researcher at the right time.

However and by whomever the contacts are first made, the point is reached where the contract negotiator – usually the director of the research centre – meets the people in the sponsoring organization who have the power to award a contract or the function of recommending it for award. The authority to grant a contract may belong to a financial or legal branch of the organization which is never in touch with the researchers, except through a formal exchange of letters. Organizations which habitually award such contracts would develop a special procedure for the purpose, but for most organizations a contract for social science research is the first ever. In these circumstances they turn to other models – a large engineering firm may try to modify the standard form of engineering or scientific research contract and the procedure for negotiating it. Other firms may turn to the management consultancy model. The researchers' model is far closer to the application for a research grant. This is written with one eye on the sponsor, and the other on one's academic peers who are likely to be approached to referee the application. What will be included is a good sprinkling of references and the new ideas with which the chosen problem is to be attacked. What is not emphasized, of course, is the detailed activity of the researchers: precisely who will be doing what and when. Nor will the nature of the 'solution' be closely outlined; the outcome of research is held to be, by its very nature, indeterminate.

But it is just this kind of precision which is reassuring to the industrial sponsor. He wants to commit the company's money to a sure thing; and if the researchers do not deliver the goods he at least wants to be able to pin the blame firmly upon them. Enough, then, must be spelled out in the research proposal to reassure the sponsor that the researcher is aiming at something he can understand, that he has a workmanlike approach to the task and that there will be some way of monitoring what is going on and some means of determining the outcome of the various phases of the research. On his side the industrialist puts emphasis on reports, recommendations and tangible objective outcomes which can be evaluated. The researcher will want to see recommendations as *joint* assessments of the possibilities for action.

Both sponsor and researcher see the merits of steering groups, committees and working parties for governing and monitoring the research. But while we perceive them as platforms for debate about the issues arising from the research and for the communication of information about other events influencing the research opportunities for mutual learning, sponsors may see them as audits to check and evaluate progress. While we say, 'Let's discuss what you and we have been doing', they say, 'Report to us what you've done and found'. Thus it is necessary to spell out before the contract is settled what we want steering groups, etc., for. Early meetings with steering groups are often battles about defining and controlling what we would do; only later, when mutual confidence is established, will they operate as intended.

The most important issue of all to be determined is the nature of the problem which the research is to tackle. Often there are considerable differences between the sponsor's first statement of the problem and the terms of reference with which the research eventually begins. A feasibility study may have the secondary function of reassessing to some degree the nature of the problem and proposing terms of reference in accordance with this reassessment.

In some respects, then, it is desirable that the period of contract negotiation should be an extended one. For one thing the researcher needs to get to know a good deal about the sponsor, his way of working and the internal and external pressures to which he is subject. Likewise the sponsor ideally needs a chance to acquaint himself with the sort of thing he is letting himself in for if he engages with the researcher. But here there are snags. Unlike consultancy organizations, which employ people on a long-term basis and deploy them from job to job to match the flow of work, the research centre is organized on totally different assumptions. Because its main aim is research, its job lengths are to be measured in years not months. Its members are in the academic career structure; many will be registered for higher degrees and will undertake some teaching or tutoring within university departments. There will not be a running tap of research capability in the centre; research people will have to be taken on with particular jobs in mind, but also with regard to their own possible careers within the centre and the balance of research interests and academic specialities within the centre. Thus on the side of the researcher there is much pressure to settle the contract. Likewise, on the sponsor's side, problems cannot wait indefinitely; at the very least something must be seen to be happening. Long-drawn-out periods of pre-contract discussion and negotiation mean rather that snags have arisen than that a planned familiarization is taking place. Furthermore, the planned familiarization is expensive in time and effort. Where the timing permits and the senior resources are available, a feasibility study is clearly an excellent device both for clarifying issues and for enabling the two parties to sample one another's behaviour.

Defining the problem

As we have indicated, the contact which is made with the sponsor is an essentially person to person affair. The first glimpse of the sponsoring organization and its 'problem' is from the perspective of the particular individual with whom contact is made. But the problem as perceived from one position in an organization may differ substantially from that perceived from another, or indeed the two perceptions may be formulated as different problems. This phenomenon of relativism may be both an advantage and a handicap. It is also a temptation. The advantage is obvious. The fact that different perspectives exist opens the possibility of a still different one – the researcher's – being considered. The handicap is that the researcher may be set off looking in the wrong direction and be unable to get to grips with the problem as it is perceived by the people in whose power is the sanctioning of research. This is part of the difficulty of being introduced to the situation by too junior or too specialist a contact. The temptation is to take advantage of this relativism. The researcher has his own disciplinary orientation, a particular congeries of problems in which he is professionally interested and he may exploit the situation to obtain a contract to study *his* problem rather than the sponsor's. Perhaps, for example, we should examine with extra care how it came about that two successive approaches made to us, one of which was on the face of it concerned with factory design, the other with the problem of keeping valuable employees when the organization moved to a new site, were both finally identified as problems of organizational design – a topic in which we had an intellectual and research interest.

Other groups might have given different advice but the sponsors were not in a position to compare what we said with what other groups might have said. Now when a client organization selects a firm of consultants, it knows by and large what it is going to get. If you are interested in management by objectives, you go to A or B; if you want an incentive scheme, go to C or D; if you want a training scheme, go to E. But when a sponsor turns to a university research group it has not preselected its acceptable range of solutions in the same way. It may even expect to be helped to identify its problem, which means that the uncertainties in the situation are much greater.

We have emphasized that a problem is perceived differently from different positions in an organization and differently again by an outsider steeped in his own discipline. Are we not reifying our concept when we speak of a problem as if it had an existence independent of the people who perceive it? Are there not as many problems as people perceiving? The observability of the event does not make it the 'real' problem. For example, 'This machine keeps breaking down', 'These people continually report faults with their machine', 'We constantly are faced with interruptions in production flow', and 'I constantly lose pay through being allocated to a duff machine', all refer to the same set of events, but each implies not only a perspective but also an implied class of solutions. It may even be possible in a case like this to obtain agreement as to what the 'real' problem is, but this consensus might by no means accommodate the perceptions of the different parties concerned. At best, then, we can obtain a working consensus on the nature or definition of the problem among those whose power or influence in the situation is relevant. But this consensus is an agreement for action rather than an abandonment of separate perspectives. And the consensus is dynamic; it will shift with time, with change in the situation, with changes in power among the parties concerned.

This is only one of the reasons why a steering group must not only be set up but written into the terms of the contract. The problem definition now becomes the property of that group and cannot be changed without the researcher knowing and indeed, as he is a member of the group whose consensus must be obtained, he plays a significant role throughout in the group's perception and definition of the problem. A researcher who sees such a steering group as a constraint or as representing an expression of lack of confidence in his ability or integrity is sadly misled. A steering group ensures the continued commitment of the sponsor to the research and also serves to monitor and check the divergence of perspective of sponsor and researcher, of representatives of different functions in the sponsoring organization. It is highly likely that other problems and preoccupations will occur during the period of the research and there will be strong pressure to assimilate these with the existing research. The researcher may be asked to 'Look into that aspect while you're at it', or he may discover that other people, mistakenly, perceive his work as directly relevant to their preoccupations. A steering group will not protect him from natural social processes nor will it suppress them; it will, however, bring them into the open so that people can see what is happening. Merton (1957) describes, as one of the techniques for resolving contradictory role expectations held by different members of the role-set, bringing together the role senders and confronting them with their divergent demands. The steering group can perform just such a function. A good deal of all this has to be spelled out when the case is made for setting up the steering group and its composition is being discussed, which means that it is part of the process of contract negotiation.

It is also a protection against encapsulation or capture, but not a foolproof one. For instance, in one contract we stipulated that a steering group be set up and that it should contain representatives of all the functions in the organization which would be affected and whose sanction would be required for implementation of any ensuing recommendations. We were assured that the personnel function possessed adequate power for these purposes and our steering group was composed exclusively of members of this function. When at a late stage it became clear and was admitted that the support of other functions would be highly desirable, if not absolutely essential, the steering group was widened by invitation. Yet we remained 'encapsulated' within the personnel function and whatever we recommended could have no more influence behind it than that which was within the power of the personnel function to provide.

Capture is the reverse side of the same medal. If, from the start, you are sponsored from a very high level, about sectional interests, the latter will seek to capture you. Deft footwork can save you, but the protection of such devices as steering groups and working parties is better.

There is, of course, a limit. You can set up so elaborate a network of committees that you can never hope adequately to service them all. Indeed in a rigidly hierarchical organization it may be difficult to avoid this.

In focusing on the process of contract negotiation and on the safeguards and vehicles which should be built into the contract, we run the risk of promoting the contract to an end in itself. Indeed the more complex the issues involved, the longer and more comprehensive the negotiation, the more important it gets to land the contract so as to justify the expenditure of thought, time, effort and money involved in the process. While it is perhaps not too difficult to avoid overselling the capacity of your centre to tackle a particular problem, it is harder to refrain from dressing up what you think you can do in terms which look more attractive to the sponsor than the reality. Moreover, a sponsor who *wants* to be convinced that you can help may be an unwitting accomplice to an unintentional oversell.

We know who is the sponsor, but who is the client? We have already referred to the phenomenon of 'capture' and its obverse 'encapsulation'. These are aspects of a wider problem which must be taken into account as far as possible at the negotiating stage. It is primarily a phenomenon associated with large hierarchical organizations with separate subordinate formations, but it exists in modified form in smaller organizations with defined levels or functions. The setting up of small joint working parties to look at the particular subproblems may lead to a paralleling of the company hierarchy with status levels in the research centre. Thus there was a tendency for each of us to have a separate client, or client group, looking for solutions to the problems as they appeared from their perspectives. Thus the researchers could be a team when alone with one another, but a status hierarchy when confronted in a committee meeting with the corresponding sponsor.

171

Behavioural science engagements

Having highlighted some of the complexities of negotiating a research contract and defining the problem to be researched, we now turn to a more general classification of the forms of engagement between social scientists and organizations.

Clark (1972) draws the conclusion, from which we would not wish to dissent, that the 'collaborative/dialogic' mode is the one which offers most potential for the constructive use of the behavioural sciences in assisting organizations to develop and to change in response to their environments.

And yet it is probable that only a minority of engagements are of this kind, although many practitioners would claim that they invariably operate in this manner. The discrepancy is part misconception, part self-delusion. The essence of the collaborative/dialogic or action research mode is joint decision-making by client and researcher/consultant. There are certain decisions which can only be implemented by one party – the decision to use a particular method of investigation or to change the content of jobs or the structure of the organization or organizational rules. In these cases the decision is perhaps more accurately described as 'consultative' rather than joint, but there seem to us to be three key areas of decisions which must be taken jointly if the requirements of collaborative dialogue are to be met. These are: the nature of the problem, the nature of the solution, and the methods of investigation.

We have already considered the process of defining the problem and suggest that if the problem definition is negotiable, the opening period of the engagement will be taken up largely with arriving at a mutually acceptable formulation, a process which has to be clearly recognized and budgeted for.

Somewhat similar considerations operate in respect of the client's perception of the type of solution he will be presented with. Indeed in his approach to the researcher the client may begin with the solution and may not even refer to the 'problem' at all. 'We need human relations training for our supervisors', or 'We need an incentive payment scheme'. Again, it is perfectly possible to do what one is bidden, but again this is to deny any diagnostic role or even a problem-solving role to the researcher.

The client may already have decided on his choice of method. 'We want an attitude survey' is one of the commonest approaches made by clients. And once again it is possible to gratify his wish. The client may even invite the practitioner to interpret the outcome for

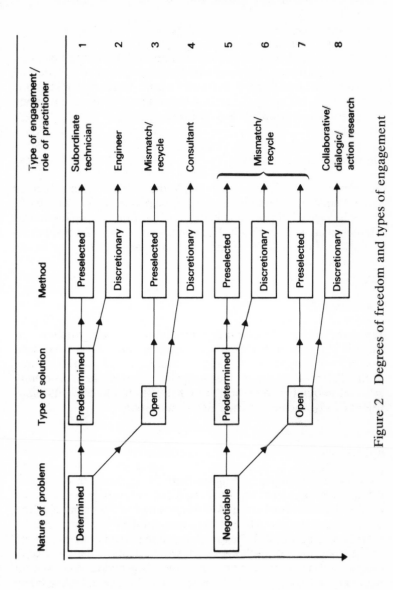

Figure 2 Degrees of freedom and types of engagement

him and perhaps even suggest what actions would be appropriate in the light of this interpretation. But the role of the practitioner is reduced to a purely technical one.

A simple figure should clarify these points and allow the introduction of a dynamic aspect.

There are eight possible combinations of the alternative positions of each of the three variables. Combinations 1, 2, 4 and 8 represent consistent combinations; 3, 5, 6 and 7 are inconsistent, which is not to say that they never occur but are unlikely to have outcomes unless the inconsistencies are removed.

Engagement 1

We have already given as an example the contract 'to conduct an attitude survey'. All that is required of the practitioner is that he use the technical skill he has in selecting the appropriate questionnaire, administering and scoring it. His role is that of a technical subordinate exercising his skills for ends determined at higher executive or political levels.

Engagement 2

When the choice of method is discretionary, our practitioner is in the role of engineer. Problem: lack of communication between one side of river and the other. Solution: build a bridge. Method: leave to the discretion of the engineer. Again, however, there is nothing especial about this role, which makes it preferable for its practitioner to be located outside the organization.

Engagement 4

Keeping the example of Engagement 2, the problem of lack of communication across the river need not necessarily be solved by the construction of a bridge. A ferry, a tunnel, are possibilities – the problem may be solved by better telecommunications. A communications consultant would be an appropriate person to advise on the appropriate mix of methods which would achieve the most cost-effective linking of people on either side of the divide. A consultant has every right to assume, if he wishes, that his client, having taken stock of his situation, knows what his problem is. Providing the nature of the solution is going to be influenced by his consulting

174

work and the method is a matter for his judgment, the consultant has an appropriate task.

Engagement 8

The distinguishing feature is the negotiability of the nature of the problem as well as the type of solution. It is negotiable, not totally open. It is unlikely that a client will ask for help or advice unless he has some problem bothering him or some change in mind. He may, as we have described already, have diagnosed his problem or he may ask for help on the basis of his symptoms – the presenting problem. If he asks for help on the basis of his own diagnosis, it is a simple matter to ask for the symptoms on which the diagnosis rests. Thus a client may put forward any of the following:
   (a) 'We have a high labour turnover' – presenting problem, symptom;
   (b) 'We have a problem of human relations' – diagnosis;
   (c) 'We need a new incentive scheme' – solution;
   or
   (A) 'We have a high number of quality rejects' – symptom;
   (B) 'We have an inspection problem' – diagnosis;
   (C) (C_1) 'We need training for our inspectors' or (C_2) 'We need a new incentive scheme' – solutions.
   If propositions (c), (C_1) or (C_2) are put to engineers (i.e. Type 2) they will doubtless be efficiently tackled whether or no they resolve the presenting problem. Propositions (b), (B) will be acceptable to a consultant (i.e. Type 4), who will expect to advise his client on the solution of his problem. If, however, the consultant is inclined to probe, to withhold a decision that he has the appropriate competence to help the client, to want to assure himself first that the presenting problem is sufficiently near the root cause not to mask something quite different, he will attempt to negotiate the nature of the problem with the client (i.e. Type 8).
   In arriving jointly at a definition of the problem, the client and the practitioner will have begun their collaboration and should have put in place some of the mechanisms for joint determination of the progress of the engagement, of data collection, analysis, solutions, implementation and evaluation.
   This will, however, be a dynamic situation, as suggested by the two vertical arrows on the left of Figure 2. The solid arrow represents the striving of the action researcher/collaborative–dialogic consultant. The hatched arrow represents the controlling urge of the organization. Uncertainty, an open system, are the conditions

175

under which inventive solutions are most likely and under which the broadening of the base of decision-making within the organization is able to come about.

Because opening everything to negotiation and challenge leads to a feeling of loss of control by organization management, they tend to enter cautiously and reluctantly into an engagement of this kind and to generate pressures towards restriction and closure, a regaining of the feeling of being in control. It should, of course, be the concern of the practitioner to keep the system open long enough to enable systemic change, where required, to take place and to aim at an end state where sufficient openness still exists for a continuing adaptive evolution. At the same time he should beware of overstraining the organization members' tolerance of uncertainty and risking a retrogressive reaction and premature termination of the engagement. The possible state of the engagement is, therefore, governed by the balance of these two opposing tendencies. The best safeguard against a disastrous attempt to hold the engagement at an inappropriate state is an understanding by both sides of the nature of the engagement and the forces operating in it.

Section V
Comparisons of Social Science Development and Use in Different Countries

This section of the book is the result of three separate studies of the way the social sciences are organized and used in various countries.

The first was a study tour, financed by the Nuffield Foundation, which took place in 1967 and 1968, during which time I visited Israel, India, Australia and Ghana. I have subsequently revisited India and Australia in 1970 and India again in 1975. The purpose of this tour was to gather information from as many sources as possible on research, administration and organization in the social sciences within each country, and in the field of applied social sciences research to look for examples of successful and unsuccessful utilization of research findings. While some of the patterns of research organization will have changed in these countries since my visits, the lessons to be learned from the illustrations of research application, or the lack of it, are still valid today.

The second exercise (and the one we shall report first) is based on a comparative study on social science organization and policy carried out on behalf of UNESCO and published in 1974. The six countries studied are Belgium, Chile, Egypt, Hungary, Nigeria and Sri Lanka.

The third section is in the form of a review essay, and looks at the social sciences in America, in particular their relations with the federal government, as seen in three major publications.

Chapter 10
Comparative Social Science Policy in Belgium, Chile, Egypt, Hungary, Nigeria, Sri Lanka

The material from the six countries was reviewed within the framework of the development of social science policy. Chapter 1 of this book has already set out our ideas on social science policy, and it is within that framework that we look at the social sciences within these countries, but beyond that we hope that this pilot study establishes comparative social science policy as a field of study worth further development.

The collection and collation of the detailed information on the social sciences within each of the six countries was carried out by social scientists working in their own countries. We have not included all this information here, but it is available in *Social Science Organization and Policy*, published by UNESCO (1974). What we do wish to include, however, is discussion of some of the procedures and problems involved in carrying out a study of comparative social science policy, using illustration from the six country studies.

The very first problem one encounters in this sort of international comparison goes right to the heart of the whole study. How do we define the social sciences? Different countries have different usages in this respect; the different usages are themselves reflections of the real differences among societies and among their cultural, educational, social and political traditions.

We should surely not try to produce a definition *per se* of the social sciences. Different definitions are required for different purposes. Nor is it possible to impose a definition on a dynamic situation. New disciplines and subdisciplines emerge and new interdisciplinary groupings come and go. The adoption of rigid definitions could not only create difficulties of interpretation, but also could, through generating corresponding administrative categories, actually hinder their emergence and development. Indeed for our own purposes here we should ideally adopt different definitions for different aspects of our study. For example, if we are assessing the manpower situation in a country, the stock and flow of people qualified to undertake social science research, we would adopt a definition which would differ from that required to assess the amount of research in the social sciences being carried out.

To avoid the difficulties arising from the varied definitions we shall try to identify a 'core' group of social sciences which should be included in all countries' analyses.

'Core' list. All definitions of social sciences will include economics, political science, social anthropology, social psychology and sociology; where social statistics and social administration are taught or treated as separate disciplines, these are also always included. This group can be regarded as the 'core' disciplines. The following disciplines or branches of them are sometimes classified as social sciences: accountancy, education, geography, history, law, management and business studies, philosophy, psychiatry, psychology (experimental, developmental, clinical, etc., but excluding animal and physiological psychology). Occasionally 'cybernetics' is included but with a restricted usage of that word.

Any such list still creates difficulties of classification, because it is clear that underlying the classification adopted in any particular country is a theory or an ideology about the nature of society and about the functions of the disciplines. Thence the way the disciplines are defined and classified mirrors a society's way of regarding itself. A complicating factor is that of deliberate imitation. When social sciences are relatively new in a country, most of its practitioners, especially with graduate degrees, will have got their training in foreign countries. Thus at the beginning they will tend to copy at home what they have experienced abroad. In so far then as societies differ radically in their self images, comparison becomes difficult and possibly forced and therefore false. Clearly comparisons will be easier where countries are reasonably homogeneous with respect to their self images. For a pilot study such as this, it would be disadvantageous to have a homogeneous grouping.

Another problem arises in considering a definition of what is research. What is research in the social sciences might in practice differ according to the disciplines or groups of disciplines involved. We can decide on a general minimum criteria of objectivity, a strict critical analysis of results, classification and orderly arrangement of facts and, whenever possible, measurement. This is compatible with the Frascati manual's distinction between R & D on the one hand

179

and scientific information and general purpose data collection on the other. The latter is an essential part of social science activities but they need to be separately recorded from other types of research expenditure.

No definition of 'research' will ever be adequate; a judgemental element will always enter. Much depends on how the data is collected – is it a primary or secondary analysis? Any of us might be able to apply reasonably reliable rules for deciding whether a particular piece of work of which we are fully cognizant did or did not meet our criteria for 'research'. But if we have to rely on what the institution concerned tells us we are on less sure ground, particularly as self interest is involved. Generally speaking 'research' has greater prestige than 'data collection' and most of us prefer to ascribe what we are doing to the more prestigious category. Is this present study research? Or is it a fact-finding exercise?

The state of the social sciences

In any country the state of higher education and its relationship with other sectors of activity is a very important factor in determining the state of the social sciences – if only because virtually all of those who can contribute to the social sciences must first pass through that system. The state of higher education is more than the number of staff and students in it. The rate at which it is developing is a potential source of strain. A rate of growth beyond the capacity of the teaching cadre to cope with not only has an adverse effect upon standards, but also, if only temporarily, reduces the capacity for research. Everywhere higher education is in flux. There is not only an unprecedented rate of growth of student numbers, but also no sign of an end to this growth. In the USA the higher education system is moving into a phase of mass higher education. All systems have travelled through an elite phase into a more broadly based meritocratic one, during which many of the assumptions underlying the whole idea of a university have had to be modified and revised. It is only as the mass phase approaches that these assumptions are in danger of having to be scrapped. The intellectual, indeed the educational, orientations of the university are brought into question. One systemic response is the differentiation of universities into elite schools and universities of lower grades. The second systemic response is the removal of all serious work to graduate professional schools, thus introducing essentially a quaternary education sector. Our six countries are all at different points along this road. Each will evolve its own characteristic response.

What can we say about the effect of all this on the state of the social sciences? For one thing, as the social sciences are in some senses international enterprises, they cannot develop from scratch in each new country. Their introduction into university systems at different stages of their development has a profound effect on their status in different systems. In Nigeria, for example, sociology does not have to struggle to free itself from the embrace of powerful schools of philosophy. Where large-scale secondary education systems are also new, social studies preparing students for university social science courses do not have to struggle with entrenched disciplines to seek a place in the sun. It is not so many years since students who were good at their school subjects were discouraged from reading, say, economics in English universities.

The linkage between the system of higher education and the world of employment, the occupational system, is another highly significant factor, and one which differentiates among the social sciences themselves. In most countries the economics student can see a direct connection between his discipline and his future occupation. But few countries have professional careers on a large scale for sociologists.

Now it is clear that in many Latin-American countries a large proportion of social scientists, particularly sociologists, perceive their role as critical rather than constructive and that in this respect there are deep divisions between one social science and another. There are, however, profound differences among societies in respect of the mechanisms and strengths of articulation of the worlds of education and employment and we can be certain that the standing of sociology, still taken as a prime example, is different in Hungary, where we are told there is a felt scarcity of sociologists, from in Chile, where we are told they face the twin problems of professional identity and fear of unemployment.

We have already alluded to the struggles that the social sciences have experienced in some countries in freeing themselves from the embrace of older, better established, more powerful disciplines. Under centralized, rigid university structures, such as those in Belgium, France, Germany, Scandinavia, their road was hard indeed. In this century Belgium may have been forced to some extent from these shackles by the need to have four of everything – permuting pairs from French and Flemish; confessional and lay.

In the United Kingdom the separation of the social sciences from their humanities background in the universities is almost complete. Most universities now have faculties of social sciences alongside those of arts and science. The degree of freedom still varies across the disciplines themselves. Psychology, which grew under the shadow of philosophy in most places, emerged from physiology in others and is now, in the United Kingdom, entirely free from its mentors, but uncertain as to whether it is a science or a social science and indeed inclined to split into its experimental and social components. Sociology is now free from philosophy and history and seen as the paradigmatic social science. Political science, however, with a long and continuous tradition in political philosophy, still has its left and right wings – a social science present living alongside its humanities past. Neither the status nor the self image of all the social science disciplines is homogeneous and the relative development of the discipline varies in these countries. Thus in Belgium psychology developed earlier than sociology. By 1961 diplomas awarded in psychology were 50 per cent more than in sociology and anthropology together. By 1971 sociology and anthropology disciplines outnumbered those in psychology by 33 per cent. Belgium serves here as an example of a country in which the mirroring of society in the social sciences is unplanned, indirect and mediated through the institutions whose administrations are unconscious of the relationship or of the processes which bring it about. We may contrast this with Hungary where the mirroring of society in the social sciences is deliberate and explicit. Thus the institute of sociology has as 'its primary task . . . exploring and analysing basic processes characteristic of Hungarian society; in constructing a theory and methodology for . . . Marxist sociology'.

It would seem that the progressive differentiation of the major social sciences from the traditional humanities and 'arts' disciplines owes much to the progressive differentiation of methodology; we may also say that it owes at least as much to the growing perception of the structural rather than the moral basis of social problems. A society aiming at a transformation of its moral basis will enlist the humanities in a similar way to the social sciences. In a society of this kind, the differentiation of humanities from social sciences will be far less marked, differentiation being based on methodology not on function.

One problem common to all these countries is that of a balanced development of the social sciences. There are many points of balance. A balance is needed between one discipline and another; between supply and demand of trained practitioners and research workers; between teaching and research; between development of the discipline and its use; between disciplinary and interdisciplinary research.

Let us first take the question of the balance of research and teaching. During periods of rapid growth in student demand for a discipline, the teaching resources required to meet it can be found

182

only by directing into teaching a greater proportion than formerly of the advanced student output of the discipline. This, combined with the increased load of teaching and administration falling upon the shoulders of those already in post, tends to reduce the resources of people and time available for research. If this situation continues the outcome tends to be a marked separation between the university and teaching, on the one hand, and research on the other. Also, severe teaching overloads leave little time for interdisciplinary projects; only individual scholarship in fundamental fields would be possible under such conditions. Among our six countries there is not one in as favourable position as the United Kingdom where the link between social science research and teaching departments persists, partly because staff and students have increased in step, and partly because research funds and support facilities have been provided by the UGC and the SSRC, as well as by government departments.

The balance of disciplinary and interdisciplinary research is bound up with the balance between teaching and research and the balance between universities and research institutes outside the university. It appears to be common experience that interdisciplinary research is more satisfactorily, or at any rate with less difficulty, established outside university teaching departments. They may remain within the university framework as university research institutes, although this does not occur very frequently. When it comes to the balance between the development of the disciplines and their use, we have less evidence. We can see, however, that this balance is closely related to the balance of forces responsible for expansion. If the demand is from a growing body of potential students the balance will be tilted away from research and from utilization. If, however, the dynamic is provided by government's demand for social science inputs to its planning and other programmes, the balance will be struck at a different point. The former is true for Chile, Egypt and Sri Lanka, the latter is the position in Hungary. Belgium and Nigeria rank between.

Social science manpower

Although on the face of it the simplest of the comparisons we have to try to make, the comparative assessment of social science manpower is full of difficulty.

Our aim was to assess the stock and flow of people with professional qualifications. We can distinguish the numbers completing a first degree in subjects belonging to, or related to, the social sciences (the raw material) and the number completing Ph.Ds (processed goods). Unfortunately the model that this implies of the educational system and its relationship to research is not universally applicable. To begin with, in many countries first degrees are typically earned on a wide range of subjects. Thus while, for example, Egypt could answer such a question as: What is the annual output of people with a first degree in economics/sociology/psychology?, other respondents such as Hungary could not. Our Hungarian respondent could provide us with detailed numbers of graduates with first degrees in 'the social sciences' but not in economics, psychology, etc. At the higher degree level this distinction could, however, be made. In Sri Lanka again, there is an enormous discrepancy between the output of 'graduates with two or more social science subjects (which) in recent years . . . averages . . . 1,700' and the output of graduates with 'special' degrees with economics, politics, or sociology as a special subject which amounted to twenty-four. A university system which produces mainly graduates as the equivalent of the English 'general' or 'ordinary' degree turns out what our Sri Lanka respondent describes as 'a large number of sub-professional social scientists which society is unable to absorb'.

We asked our respondents to provide figures for graduates in the social sciences at master's degree and Ph.D level. Here we are on firmer ground. Although there are no precise equivalents in some countries – the Candidatus Scientiarum and the Doctor Scientiarum for example do not coincide with masters and Ph.Ds – in all countries higher degrees do represent attainment in a single discipline and in all countries such degrees are regarded as the necessary, if not the sufficient, qualification for engaging in research. Indeed the qualifications may be awarded on the basis of research performance within research institutes.

In asking for data concerning the output of first-degree graduates we had in mind less the notion that they were 'finished products' to undertake research than their status as the 'raw material', the stock from which the finished products would have to be drawn and processed. Thus trends in the production of first-degree graduates would indicate the trends in the potential for production of research workers. The information we have, however, does not entirely lend itself to this treatment. So far from producing a gain to research cadres, the rapid growth in first-degree students, particularly at ordinary degree level, may represent a major diversion of effort. All available possessors of higher degrees are drawn into university teaching at low level to the detriment of their own research and of any contribution they might make to the training of research workers. At the other extreme, steps taken to hive off the best social scientists into protected research institutes exacerbate the problems of the first-degree teaching. The parameters of this system differ from country to country.

For further studies it is highly desirable to set about preparing the basis for a more sophisticated knowledge and understanding of the system of manpower flows. Manpower studies and manpower fore-casting are now well-established research areas, though as yet they have developed no easily used techniques with sufficient accuracy and reliability to make them automatically useful for this pur-pose.

Control of numbers of social science graduates (first degrees)

As we have commented earlier, entry into higher education in some countries is controlled more by the supply of intending students than by any other factor. The limits upon the capacity of the whole system of higher education are indeed set by financial provision – in most countries provided almost entirely by the State. But within that total the numbers accepted for courses in the social sciences are under comparatively weak control. 'Students vote with their feet.' Where the pattern of first-degree courses is non-specialist this con-trol is weakest. Furthermore graduates with first degrees in the social sciences are not by and large regarded as professional social scientists; their subsequent occupations may be in public or business administration or in school teaching or a wide variety of other jobs. There is therefore little meaning to the concept of 'need for social science graduates'. Nor in most countries is the output of first-degree graduates inadequate for the perceived needs for profes-sional social scientists. The bottleneck, if any exists, occurs at the level of postgraduate training.

Here, the whole system of higher education is involved. In some systems benign factors are at work. In the United Kingdom, for example, the staff–student ratio is the key leverage point. Tradi-tionally this ratio, which is maintained across departments and universities, is favourable enough to permit university staff to engage in research and in postgraduate teaching. Thus increases in undergraduate student enrolment automatically provides within a comparatively short time period a staff capacity for postgraduate training as well as an increase in the number available to receive such training. Furthermore the attractiveness of providing post-graduate courses is enhanced by (a) the satisfaction and prestige of engaging in high-level teaching and (b) the policy which allows postgraduate students to count as the equivalent of more than one

185

undergraduate student for the purpose of calculating staff–student ratios.[1]

In any system where staff–student ratios are less favourable or are allowed to deteriorate, or where postgraduate students make more demands on the time of their teachers than do undergraduate students without any compensating factor, the balancing features of the British system are absent: increased undergraduate student enrolments lead to lowered capacity for research and postgraduate teaching.

The relationship between research and postgraduate enrolments is also one which differs among systems. There are many countries, India being one, in which for the greater part research is in the form of Ph.D and master's theses. The major contribution of university teachers is their supervision of these activities. There are others in which this is a comparatively minor part of the total of social science research. Thus, although everywhere there is some linkage between postgraduate training and research, the nature of this linkage is of considerable significance. Indeed, if the main part of the research conducted in the universities consists of Ph.D theses, the need for more utilitarian forms of research or for more continuous programmes of research is likely to lead to the setting up of research institutes outside universities.

Employment and careers

This is inherently the most difficult aspect to plan or to control. Among our six countries only Hungary provides anything that approximates to a planned career system.

In Sri Lanka there is a high degree of unemployment among graduates with social science training. The vast majority of the employed are in school teaching. The principal problem here is financial. The country has made very slow progress in economic development with the result that the employment sector makes inadequate demand.

In Chile there are apparently too few social scientists with high-quality graduate training (MA and Ph.D) and relevant experience to undertake the needed research. Nevertheless, it would seem that there is a rational employment pattern. Something like half the graduate economists work in government and the public sector, over a third in the private sector – industry, banks and commerce – a tenth have their main job in the universities, and the rest are in jobs

[1] This policy has now been discontinued.

where their discipline is irrelevant. In sociology, by contrast, a third are in the universities, a quarter in the public sector and about two-fifths are in jobs irrelevant to sociology. However, a substantial proportion of those in the public sector find their work is only very superficially related to their training. In fact, the gulf between social reality and the expectations generated in university courses in sociology is a contribution to a serious problem of professional identity. The small number of graduates in social anthropology, social psychology and politics, all of which are postgraduate qualifications, work in the universities.

In Nigeria the total stock of trained social scientists is too small for any conclusions to be drawn about its employment. In Belgium it was not possible to estimate the pattern of employment of social science graduates. Nevertheless a significant comment was to the effect that many social scientists are underemployed, having regard to their presumed skills. There is probably a vicious circle here: too little responsibility given to graduates – too low degree of interest – low display of competence – consequent low degree of responsibility. It is highly unlikely that this cycle of events is confined to Belgium; only where skilled manpower is very scarce or very expensive or both is the temptation to squander it low.

Careers in research

A full career in research may be possible in all countries for the exceptional person. Jobs exist in which research and some other activity can be combined; university systems where research is an integral part of the teachers' duties provide such jobs. So do some government departments which provide tours of duty in research posts for administrators. If such combined careers are unavailable, research can be carried out only by full career research workers or by a casual arrangement such as the temporary attachment of a research student to an administrative organization or similar device. Research institutes provide research posts, but in many cases, if not most, there is little security at the lower levels. It is fair to say that only government research institutes or the few large secure non-government institutes can provide progressive careers. This need not be the case. But any other device requires a great deal of co-operation among institutes, or between institutes and universities, or between institutes and government, between universities and government research establishments. The difficulties are considerable.

Nevertheless, the system of government research establishments

187

with full careers – a scientific civil service – has its diseconomies. It makes for rigidity in scientific programmes, for routinization of research, and for reduced mobility of research workers.

Hungary possesses a system of government research establishments with full career progression. Its linkages with the universities and with teaching save it from the worst disadvantages of a closed system. Some 3,000 research workers are in government research institutes, 2,000 in university research institutes and 670 in other units. Sixty per cent of all of these research workers are economists. A graduate starts with a short-term contract (six months to two years) as trainee, leading to appointment as a research assistant. After two years in this grade he is promoted to junior researcher for a three- to five-year appointment. After ten years' experience and the award of a higher degree, he is promoted to senior researcher or principal scientific fellow. Outstanding scientists, Doctores Scientiarum, act as research advisers. The problem has been encountered of the irremovable but unsatisfactory middle-grade worker, and fixed renewable contracts for three to five years will in future be the pattern for appointment to some junior posts. The scientific civil service pattern is familiar to the United Kingdom and elsewhere but it has not applied very much to the social sciences. Recently indeed the UK Social Science Research Council has established three units on the Medical Research Council's model. Two are attached to universities and the third to the council's own headquarters. But their employees make up a small fraction of all research workers in the social sciences in the UK.

The French system is not altogether dissimilar to the Hungarian. The flight of research from the universities and the centralizing pulls of the Délégation Générale à la Recherche Scientifique et Technique (DGRST), the Centre National de la Recherche Scientifique (CNRS) and the *grands établissements* have together operated to produce a system of research centres or units, some partially linked with the universities. They have a much higher proportion of auxiliary workers to scientists than do university research institutes. They also have a system of graded posts in careers.

Research organizations and research capability

In the context of this study the question of the purpose of 'research' is most important. We are concerned both with the research-performing capability of countries and with their research-using capability. The higher the research-using capability that a country possesses, the more likely it is to demand research of the kind it wishes to 'use' (in the illumination or resolution of perceived problems). We asked our respondents to distinguish research institutions on the basis of 'mix' of services provided and on the basis of a classification of the type of research conducted as follows:

Classification of research

Research can be classified in a number of ways. The classification used here is a three-way system; first by level of research and second by discipline, subdiscipline or interdiscipline and then by field of application. The first classification is into:

1 basic pure research;
2 basic objective research;
3 operational research;
4 action research.

Research may be on more than one level.

The second classification is into discipline, e.g. economics, sociology, psychology. Type 1 is likely to be conducted in a single discipline; type 2 may be disciplinary or interdisciplinary, and types 3 and 4 are very likely to be multidisciplinary.

The third classification is into field of application, e.g. education, race relations, industry, welfare, health, crime and penology, military, international relations and so on. Research of Type 1 is less likely to have an identifiable field of application than are Types 2, 3 and 4.

Not surprisingly our respondents found this schema strange. The classifications are very approximate, some even modified the schema to suit their conditions. Thus the data, though plentiful and detailed, is not strictly comparable.

These factors will become more prominent when we come to consider the relationship between research on the one hand and planning and action on the other in a later section, 'Research and government'.

We also asked our respondents to provide information about the organization and location of research. We distinguished four types of organization within universities and four other types as follows:

1 University: (a) within disciplinary departments; (b) centres attached to disciplinary departments; (c) institutes or centres not attached to departments but completely controlled by the university; (d) institutes attached to universities but under independent or partly independent trustees.
2 Independent research institutes (non-profit).
3 Commercial research institutes.

189

4 Government-controlled research institutes (national institutes, etc.).

5 In-house research units: (a) governmental; (b) industrial, co-operative research association; (c) industrial single company; (d) other.

This is a reasonably comprehensive classification. Very few countries indeed will have representatives of all types. And some research units cannot easily be classified – for example, a research department of an independent college of management – but it is otiose to invent categories into which one or two exceptional units may fall.

We also asked for staff to be listed under the following categories: directors of institutes and programme directors; senior scientific staff (usually with higher degrees and five years' research experience); other scientific staff; ancillary staff.

We can do no more here than summarize the impressions we received from the response to these questions.

What does emerge is the wide variation in provision of research units. While we cannot be certain that our respondents all placed the same interpretation of the terms 'research centre', 'unit' and 'institute', we can assume that they were bound very largely by local usage. Our Nigerian respondent noted how difficult it was to adhere to our own definition of the term research without creating a perception gap between the social scientist and the policy-makers in this country.

Thus, in identifying social science research activities, he observes that they are directed to: (a) providing useful information to the administrators, law-makers, educators as individuals and as collectivities or to social-problem-oriented organizations; (b) utilizing research results in the formulation of economic plans; and (c) providing materials for university teaching.

The Nigerian National Institute of Social and Economic Research is the largest research centre in the country with a staff of six senior, five medium-grade and twenty-two junior research workers, together with supporting staff. Most of the research units in the country are attached to universities. Apart from the fourteen departments in universities which report some research activity, there is one research unit, the Demographic Research Unit at Ile-Ife, attached to a department, eight institutes under university control, three independent research institutes associated with universities, one totally independent (and unsatisfactory) institute, two commercial research institutes, one national institute and three in-house units (two government, one central bank). The mixes of activities and types of research are very much as would be predicted.

However, practically all devote some time to teaching, which may represent a rational response to the growing need for postgraduate training. Our respondent calculates that there are seventy-one qualified social scientists in full-time posts in research units.

For Sri Lanka we have less precise data. There do not appear to be any university research units, centres or institutes; research in Sri Lanka universities is entirely conducted by teaching staff in departments. Outside the universities there are in-house research staff in the government's Ministry of Planning and Employment, in the Department of Census and Statistics and in the Central Bank. The careers available, however, do not permit any organized research training, either in the universities or outside and most staff with higher qualifications have obtained them outside the country.

In Egypt, the main organized research activities are conducted in seven research centres of varying types. One of the largest is the National Centre for Social and Criminological Research (NCSCR) with eighty-four professional staff (fourteen senior and seventy junior). This is a fully equipped institute with nine research units and a range of training programmes. The Institute of National Planning has thirty senior staff and sixty-four research assistants. The balance of its activities leans probably more towards training than does the NCSCR and it is a government-controlled body. What we note here is the extent of concentration. These seven centres represent an impressive massing of effort. Three of them are large and two are of substantial medium size (thirty to forty professionals).

By contrast Chile reports more than thirty centres where research is conducted. A majority are in university departments or faculties and have few full-time research workers. There are such centres as the Research Department of the Central Bank of Chile, which has thirty-nine professional staff and nineteen auxiliary and administrative staff; the Planning Branch of the Ministry of Agriculture, with thirty-seven professional and nineteen other staff; the Industrial Planning Division of the CORSO with twenty-three professional staff; the institute of Economics of the University of Chile with forty teachers, who divide their time between teaching and research, and one hundred auxiliary staff; the Institute of Political Science with sixteen full-time and two half-time professional researchers; the Institute of Sociology and the Latin American Centre of Demography with thirty-four and thirty-five full-time professional staff respectively, of whom twelve and nine respectively are concerned solely with research. The picture here is one of wide dispersion.

In Belgium, there is a very considerable number of institutes attached to chairs or faculties. These combine research with post-

191

graduate teaching and in most cases undergraduate teaching. Distinguishing among these activities in any quantitative way turns out to be very difficult as their institutes are not organized around them as separate activities. Our respondents were unable to follow our guidelines in a number of respects.

A strict definition of research in the social sciences makes no sense in Belgium because fundamental research, as this is understood in the natural sciences, is virtually insignificant. A wide, very extensive definition including all scientific documentation and investigation activities would give only a distorted picture. Individual research in the social sciences in Belgium is still important as much because of lack of financial resources as personal preference, and this kind of research is done with students in institutions of learning.

Much more striking than the number of research workers is the range of research activities conducted within the university framework, with considerable research in very applied fields.

The Laboratory of Industrial Psychology and Psychopathology in the Catholic University of Louvain is one of the thirteen centres in the Faculty of Psychology and Education in the same university, covering the whole range from basic objective to action research (even undertaking some of the functions of management consultancy).

Clearly the relationships between Belgian universities and State and private industrial and commercial enterprises are potentially closer than in many, perhaps most, other countries, so there is less reason to anticipate the evolution of a substantial sector of independent research institutes. What we find, in fact, is a number (about twenty, mostly small) of such institutes or centres with strong university affiliations.

The largest, most important institute, and independent of the universities, is the Belgian Institute of Political Science, founded in 1951. The financing of this institute exemplifies a general rule. As research institutes grow and as costs simultaneously rise the institute tends to become more and more dependent upon government support provided directly or indirectly or both.

Research institutes in the public sector

Government and quasi-government bodies undertake research projects within the scope of the parent ministry or ministries. But most of their productions remain confidential to the ministries concerned. We are not told how many qualified research staff are engaged in these activities. Nor do we know their cost.

In Hungary the picture is a good deal clearer as far as the formal structure of research organization is concerned. The guiding principles are baldly stated: 'One fundamental principle of science policy . . . is that science is to serve the social, economic, cultural, etc., tasks of socialist construction.' The State undertakes to bear the financial burdens incidental to scientific activities, and government resources are to meet the ever-increasing needs of research.

Some countries can make a better job of describing the organizational structure than of providing much insight into the way research is done, while others can describe the research but weave a web of mystification over the way it is organized and financed. This is partly due to the organizational location of the respondent. If he is in a planning ministry, the description of the structure, financing and control comes naturally to him. If he is in a research institute, or even more in a university, he has a feel for the research but little grasp of the structure. But it is also a function of the type of country with which we are concerned. The first kind of picture is likely to be provided by centrally planned economies, the latter by 'free' economies. There is also an interaction between type of country and location of respondent; in the centrally planned economy your respondent will be a scientific planner; in the 'free' economy your respondent will probably be an academic. Ideally one's sources of information should be polycentred and provide a variety of perspectives.

Statistical and structural data need to be reinforced by case study treatment. In this way one can begin to understand how the system actually works and what it is like trying to operate it.

Another relevant issue is the choice of country sample. Obviously data are likely to be more closely comparable across countries of the same type. But this makes the exercise in comparison one which will tend only to reinforce the basic assumptions on which the system is built rather than open them to question, which is one of the main benefits of comparative analysis. For instance, with regard to accounting conventions, agreement on one conventional figure could only be arrived at as the result either of a meaningless compromise or of a thorough analysis leading to the revaluation of the competing set of assumptions. Now on a cross-country comparison, compromise would have even less meaning and a revaluation of assumptions could have meaning only as a result of agreement on structural change.

Then how should we proceed? We can make sensible comparisons on a statistical basis of similarity of systems and this indeed will help to refine and correct our statistical assumptions and methods of inquiry. We should proceed hesitantly to comparisons across

193

systems, taking the time and the opportunity to initiate case study analyses in depth. These will tend to show at what points and in relation to what issues one system provides better results than another, or is more suited than another to the nature of a particular kind of research. We are assuming here that the long-term benefits of comparative analyses are not to make every country adopt the same system of organizing research nor to point the road towards the convergence of systems, but to enable each system to learn from the other, to acquire an additional perspective wherewith to evaluate its own performance.

But there is a further problem. We may be misled if we concentrate too closely on the formal structure; we may in this way overlook the facts (a) that similar structures may discharge different functions and (b) that structures may sometimes be inappropriate to their functions. It is only when we can observe how they function, what goes on inside them, that we shall be able to evaluate the structures. For instance I have encountered a research institute in an Eastern European country, whose programme of research was in form determined by a committee of the Academy of Sciences. In practice, however, the scientists in the institute proposed their own research projects through an informal procedure. These were ratified and adopted as theirs by the committee, who thereupon instructed the institute to conduct the research.

Financing of research

We asked in our guidelines for data concerning the financing of research in the social sciences and for a comparison with expenditures in the natural sciences. From our data and from material from other sources it is clear that there has been in the last two decades a general tendency for expenditures in the social sciences to rise faster than those in other sciences. Partly this is a function of their late start, partly a function of the fact that the rate of growth of expenditures on R & D generally in the developed countries has tended to level off, having reached the point where exponential growth at its earlier level has become impossible. But it is also partly an artefact of measurement. There is a base level of research, which is inevitably undercalculated – e.g. research done by apparently full-time teachers, often self-financed. This base level represents a false zero in our statistics. Let us suppose its true value is 10 units. A financing programme begins very slowly – say 10 units in the first year. To begin with it will displace some of the unnoticed research so that the new 'real' total is $10 + 6 = 16$ units. In the next year another 5 units are added, so that 15 units is the official expenditure in this year. The new real total may be 10 + 5 + 5 = 20 (displacing a tiny bit more). And so on.

TABLE 6

The official figures		The 'real' figures	
Year	Expenditure	Year	Expenditure
0	0	0	10
1 of programme	10	1 of programme	16
2 of programme	15	2 of programme	20

The official figures show a 50 per cent growth between years 1 and 2; the real rate of growth is 25 per cent. Thus in the early years the rate of growth is exaggerated.

Although government expenditure may be counted in full, where there is a substantial proportion of non-government funding and where, in particular, there is a large number of small such sources the figures tend to be underestimated.

One has to handle all financial comparisons with care. For Chile we have some figures which we can use as indicators only. Universities' expenditure on all activities – teaching, research and extension work – amounted in 1970 to US $131 million, of which $83 million came from government sources, representing 5 per cent of the total government budget, a very substantial proportion indeed. Of this total university expenditure some 19 per cent is devoted to R & D, again a substantial proportion. Yet the total R & D expenditure in Chile is only of the order of 0·43 per cent of GNP (1969), which is low compared with both Western and Eastern European countries; Hungary's 1·43 per cent in 1967 is a typical example. We are also told that GNP = US $6,000 million (1969).

One implication of these figures is that one-quarter of the R & D in Chile is conducted in its university sector. Another is that the government's budget accounts for only about 10 per cent of GNP.

Turning to the expenditures on the social sciences, it appears that the University of Chile spent 12 per cent of its total R & D expenditure on the social sciences as against 7·3 per cent in the natural sciences, while for the three universities – University of Chile, University of Conception and Catholic University of Chile – the expenditure on teaching, research and extension work in the social sciences was approximately 4 per cent of all expenditure, while that on the natural sciences was just under 7 per cent.

The National Commission for Scientific and Technological Research (CONICYT) spent about 8 per cent of its budget in 1970 on the social sciences. The Research Foundation of the Catholic University of Chile devoted about $25,000 to the social sciences, while the Commission for Scientific Research of the University of Chile spent more than twice as much.

Lastly, the Ford Foundation provided $14 million for the social sciences over an eleven-year period from 1960 to 1971 (about one-sixth of its total expenditure in Chile).

From these figures we can make a very rough estimate of expenditure on social science research of all kinds in the universities of $2 million per year, which is a substantial figure. We are reduced to making estimates because of the inability of most research centres to produce figures of expenditure. For the same reason, we can say little about expenditures outside the universities, except that it must be at least equally large.

The picture of Chile is incomplete without mention here of the many organs of Latin American co-operation in which Chile participates. These are important in postgraduate training as well as in research and dispose of substantial budgets. Funds for these enterprises have come from United Nations Agencies – especially UNESCO – from the United States in many forms, including especially government sources and the Ford Foundation, and from Latin American governments themselves.

We have no such difficulty in Hungary, where we are told clearly that about US $7·5 million were spent on social science research in 1969. This corresponds to roughly 5 per cent of all R & D and to 0·09 per cent of GNP.

In Belgium, while the social sciences receive about 5 per cent of the funds spent on teaching and research, they receive about 12 per cent of the Ministry of Education's credits for basic research. The total expenditure on R & D by social science research units amounted in total in 1969 to US $14·8 million. Excluding history, this figure is reduced to $10 million. Some proportion, however, of this expenditure is probably more accurately described as postgraduate training, but it is doubtful if this would make a great deal of difference to these figures, which show that research in the social sciences is better treated in Belgium than social science teaching.

Sri Lanka provides us with a precise figure of 1969–70 of US $1·33 million, although most of this is spent by government in its own research in departments and agencies. Very little indeed is spent in the universities, although a proportion of university expenditure should be added to allow for the research conducted by university teachers and students without ear-marked research money.

It is not easy to evaluate the expenditure on social sciences in Nigeria. Although we have precise figures of income and sources of income of all social science units in Nigeria, the amounts which are devoted to research, as opposed to teaching and other activities, is not specified. We know that the Nigerian Institute of Social and Economic Research (NISER) has a budget of US $240,000; that, for example, the Nigerian Institute of International Affairs received about $240,000; that the Rural Economy Research Unit, the Institute of African Studies at Ibadan, the Economic Development Institute at Enugu and so on are all of similar size and about half as large as NISER. We know also that of the $27 million spent on the Nigerian universities in 1967, some proportion must be assessable to social science research. It would not be an unreasonable guess that the total expenditure on all research and consultancy activities in the social sciences in Nigeria would amount to some $2·5 million. This would amount to something of the order of 6–7 per cent of Nigeria's total R & D, which in turn represents about 1 per cent of its GNP.

Thus, with a good deal of heroic guesswork, it is possible to obtain some idea of the scale of research in the social sciences in different countries. But it remains only an idea. What is pretty obvious is that in most countries nobody knows what is spent on social science research, let alone whether this expenditure is rationally distributed. We shall consider later the role of a body such as a social science research council in keeping in view the distribution of funds and effort and in maintaining a perspective on the pattern of activity. Even where such a body exists, almost every specific question results in yet another questionnaire.

Professional associations

We inquired about the professional associations in each country, as these form indispensable links in the communication channels among social scientists. In Nigeria there are flourishing societies for geography and economics, a very small association for anthropology and sociology and no national organizations for political science or psychology. Our Sri Lanka respondent referred specifically to the absence of professional associations and pointed to the fact that the Sri Lanka Association for the Advancement of Science has a specifically social science section.

In Hungary the Academy of Sciences has three social science

197

sections. These are not strictly professional associations. Membership of the academy confers status and privileges but at the same time the academy and its sections are instrumentalities for the co-ordination and control of research, while the Western-type professional association continues the function of learned society with its journal and professional guild, sometimes extending as far as acting as a licensing authority for employment in professional (but not teaching) roles. In Hungary, in our field, there are the Hungarian Scientific Society of Psychology, the Hungarian Society of Economists, the Hungarian Ethnographical Society and the Hungarian Society for State Administration. But the publication of journals is the function of the academy.

We cannot form any real conclusion as to the extent to which social scientists in the countries concerned feel any such identity. Where professional societies exist, members tend to regard themselves first as practitioners of their particular branch of science. If you ask a man his profession he will reply 'physicist' or 'astronomer' or 'economist' or 'psychologist'; he is unlikely to identify himself as a 'scientist' or as a 'social scientist'. The more recent developments which have exposed 'science' to public criticism may evoke a defensive sense of common fate among scientists; the same trend is discernible among social scientists. So far the organs for the expression of this consciousness are deficient. It is at present highly probable that in a country like the United States a psychologist feels a greater identity with a psychologist in the USSR in the same field than with an American psychologist in a different field of research, let alone with an American economist or political scientist. In that situation the meaning of the 'American community of social scientists' is debatable; how much less meaningful is 'the international community of social scientists'? In a very small country with very few representatives of each social science discipline, the picture may be very different and there may be a true national community of social scientists.

Research and government

At the root of the topics with which this section deals there is an ideological question. Our Chilean respondent makes this point at the very beginning of his chapter:

> Two ideologies of science . . . not only stand in the way of
> application, but also exclude the possibility of conceiving a
> science policy. . . . One of these reflecting cultural dependence

198

in its crudest expression considers it unnecessary, if not impossible, for underdeveloped countries to have real scientific and technological research. . . . The other conceives science as an entirely autonomous phenomenon unaffected by the structure and processes of the global society. This position assigns to science internal dynamics independent of the social forces. . . . Our position differs radically from both. Our central idea . . . is that there is a strong and enduring relationship between scientific research and the political system, understanding by 'political' the processes by which power is distributed and used within the society.

The doctrine of the autonomy of science has come under attack from other sources and is now everywhere in disarray (OECD, 1971).

Ben David (1971) takes this discussion on to a more general plane. If threats to science come from within the scientific community, this problem is stronger within the social scientific community. There is a gradation of arguments which move from undermining the relationship of social scientists to a particular government, through the denial of the propriety of any relationship between social scientists and any government, through an attack on the social assumptions underlying certain kinds of research, to an attack on the basic concepts and methodologies of the social sciences. It is a gradation because each successive position includes all the previous ones. Essentially all these positions, even the first, denies the possibility of a policy for the social sciences. If the social sciences are not to be 'used' to further societal aims (or if society as such can have no 'aims'), then there is no rational basis upon which a government can determine what resources should be devoted to which social sciences and in what way. Our Chilean respondent points to the danger of our interpreting 'putting science at the service of society' as meaning 'instrumentalizing all scientific research, gradually transforming universities into consultancy enterprises in the public sector, producing technical information for the solution of immediate problems'.

The Hungarian system for control of research states the goal, which is beyond discussion: 'One fundamental principle of science policy of the Hungarian People's Republic is that science is to serve the social, economic, cultural tasks of socialist construction.'

In Sri Lanka we have a statement in similar vein: 'It is the policy of the State that scientific research and training should be oriented to economic and social development.' The methods of achieving

199

these objectives have, however, yet to be planned. But unlike in Hungary the mechanisms are not yet there.

In Belgium the situation is anarchic. Not only are politicians uninterested and public administrators too busy to take note of research, but the latter are also too protective of their bureaucratic power to put work out to universities or institutes. When it wants long-term research, beyond what it obtains through its own administrative channels, the government prefers to operate through the major associations such as the banks, the Belgian Federation of Industries, and so on, which have their own research bureaux. There is also a system linking national research centres or research institutes with government departments, either because the institute's special line of research is closely related to that department or through patronage. Thus much social research in Belgium depends on the relationships between the client researcher and the sponsoring official. If these are favourable the communication of unpublished inquiries is eased in both directions. Idea and action combine happily. If not, the worlds of administration and of research are mutually sealed.

Nigeria also lacks any kind of central co-ordinating mechanisms for relating research and policy, or for bringing the needs of one sector to the notice of the other. There is no Social Science Research Council but the National Advisory Council to the National Council of Science and Technology is able to consider and advise generally on all scientific activities, including (i) the application of research results, and (ii) scientific documentation, statistics, surveys, and general information. The absence of any provision for the establishment of a Social Science Research Council is a serious deficiency in the national science policy.

There are a number of social science bodies in the planning field and it is through them that social scientists get to know of the research needs of government departments. Social scientists serve on advisory committees, or statutory bodies, and are used by private firms.

Few social sciences are strongly established in Nigeria, and few social scientists other than economists and some political scientists concern themselves with the visible problem of Nigerian society. But even if they did it is problematic whether their studies would be usable or made use of. Our Egyptian respondent points out that government has need of research when faced with a choice of alternatives in policy, when drawing up development plans and when evaluating action programmes, but has an inadequate model of the relationships between research and policy, research and planning, research and action. Having identified these three as separate sets of problems, or at least as separate sets of needs for which research is sought, one ought to go on to note that different kinds of research, conducted under different kinds of auspices may be appropriate to them.

The policy-maker faced with a problem needs facts, but most of all he needs concepts which can help to reformulate his problem to make his choice among policies easier. However, he is most unlikely to turn to a social scientist and ask for a concept. He is more likely to ask for facts, data; and the data he requests are based on his perception of his problem. The social scientist is quite likely to accept this formulation and to provide the data required. But the data are not very useful when what is really needed is better comprehension of the system the policy-maker is trying to control.

In planning, data and concepts are both likely to be valuable. And again a knowledge of the characteristics of the system whose future state is to be foreseen or worked towards is vital and often lacking. Lastly in evaluation, indicators must be set up before they can be monitored. For a successful relationship between policy-maker or planner and researcher, these points have to be understood.

From our six reports it is clear that the problems of articulation between research and policy take different forms in different countries. One difficulty in making comparisons is that one tends either to get a picture of the machinery but not how it works, or a picture of some of the things that go on but not of the machinery. You may have a neat structure like that in Hungary. We know the functions of the various bodies described. But, for example, what happens to a research report? How do the scientists and policy-makers relate to one another? We know how they do in Belgium and Egypt, but there we do not know what the formal mechanisms for decision-making are. Perhaps they do not exist, or perhaps we can say that the formal description of the system is like the scientific paper; that is, not how it really happened, but the formula into which it must be cast afterwards.

The paucity of information about the ways in which the information generated by social science research and advice is put to use is neither unique to our studies nor unexpected. Even where our respondents do not specifically comment on the lack of utilization of research in policy, they do not point to any actual use. Countries wishing to avail themselves to the full of their own research capability must somehow develop a corresponding research-using capability. Practical advice and help in achieving this can be given only when we understand the processes involved.

One way in which countries can certainly improve their capability for using social science knowledge and research is through developing training for public administrators in the concepts of the social sciences. In this regard the framework exists in all our respondent countries.

Thus in Egypt, the Institute of Public Administration has, since 1954, provided training in social sciences for top and middle management in various government departments.

In Nigeria there are courses offered by universities at postgraduate level, aiming at three levels: (a) to increase the professional competence of young administrative officers; (b) to produce 'professional' administrators; and (c) to produce administrators with research experience. More than 200 Nigerian administrators have passed through these courses. One danger, particularly with the research degree kind of course, is that graduates tend to find senior university appointments more attractive than administration. This may not be the case in Nigeria, but internal brain drains can be as debilitating as the external variety.

We have already made mention of the situation in Belgium, where researchers have differential degrees of access to government data on a kind of client system. We must first, however, distinguish between those areas of government data which are fully and openly published and those to which only privileged access can be had. Governments are of course overwhelmingly the largest collectors of basic social science data. In any country the decennial census is a large-scale operation; in most the figures are published as often are data extracted from the census. Governments also publish extensive statistics in education, health and mortality, national income and distribution, industrial and agricultural production, employment, crime and much else. Not all statistics are of equal value or reliability; they vary in the intrinsic difficulty of obtaining accurate data, in the efficiency and care with which they are obtained and in the honesty with which they are presented. And as statistics may form the basis of political controversy, temptation faces governments to 'doctor' or to obfuscate inconvenient data. Some data are just not published, some are made available under safeguards, and to some a high degree of secrecy is given.

Our Nigerian respondent suggested that government may appear readier to disclose data to foreign than to native social scientists.

The conflict between the values of open access and of privacy exists everywhere. The point at which the values come into conflict differs from one society to another.

Thus there are two ways in which the use of government data for social science purposes can be improved. The first is, obviously, the improvement of the data themselves, not only with regard to the efficiency and ease of collection, but also with regard to the conceptual basis for their compilation. In this respect the cross-national comparability of data is of relevance. From the point of view of the social scientist, his need is for good basic data on which to erect and test theory which can in turn throw light on the process or problem concerned.

Future needs and prospects

A number of general points emerge from these studies. Let us begin with the supply of students at undergraduate level. There appears to be no scarcity here, although in the case of Sri Lanka so many graduate in general courses that there are comparatively few available for postgraduate work, and in Nigeria the teaching of some of the social sciences is so recent that substantial numbers have not yet been produced. In Egypt the press of student numbers has pushed staff–student ratios to breaking point. Few governments would wish to exercise absolute control over students' choices of discipline to study. But if they do not, they may be helpless before the waves of fashion that sweep through university populations. This problem becomes even more acute at the postgraduate research-training level. If teachers are too busy with undergraduate students – Egypt gives us figures of 60:1 in faculties of economics, politics and 234:1 in faculties of commerce – they are in no position either to give time themselves to research or to guide students in advanced training for research.

Much training in research is conducted outside the universities or at any rate outside university teaching departments. In Hungary, for instance, many research students receive their research training within a research institute. This may indeed be a solution to the problem that overcrowded universities set for research training, but has the disadvantage of separating research from teaching. The articulation between the educational sector and the science sector is however inadequate in some countries. In the UK, for example, it has often proved difficult, particularly in the social sciences, to arrange for experience in research institutes to be regarded as contributing towards the requirements for postgraduate degrees. A considerable defect is the requirement that the Ph.D, or its equivalent, should represent the original work of the candidate. This artificially circumscribes both the problem and the methodology the student can tackle, and encourages work within the confines of one discipline. The problem is exacerbated by the fact that a substantial proportion of the research that is done in universities takes the form of Ph.D theses. There is a good deal of scope for the

203

research institutes that exist to play a greater part in research training.

The uneven development of the social sciences themselves is apparent from our studies. Both in numbers of students and in institutional provision of all kinds economics is far better provided for than the other social science disciplines. Even in Belgium, where of all our countries sociology is in the most advanced state, economics heads the list in numbers of students, numbers of research units and so on. Undoubtedly the position of social psychology is very unsatisfactory and in most countries is the Cinderella of the social sciences. Our Hungarian respondent especially emphasizes the needs for the development of psychology and sociology; Sri Lanka and Nigeria have virtually no psychology; in Egypt the teaching of social psychology is very limited and even in Belgium has been unfashionable. Only Chile reports a favourable development, but there is no specialist degree of social psychology. University structures tend to be less hospitable to such bastard disciplines than to those of impeccably legitimate ancestry. This is really a good illustration of the extent to which the higher education sector dominates the development of the social sciences.

One important respect in which the higher education sector has enormous influence is in its attitude towards interdisciplinary studies. This is not the same thing as a general degree in which the student takes a number of subjects. True interdisciplinary studies involve learning to bring to bear material and concepts from different disciplines upon a single topic or problem. Indeed it is arguable that it is only when a student already possesses a first grasp of the concepts and modes of analysis provided by a discipline that he is able without confusion to subject his knowledge to the challenging and potentially contradictory inputs from other disciplines. This explains the apparent paradox that *pari passu* with deliberate attempts to introduce interdisciplinary activities at postgraduate level, we see a movement towards single-discipline courses at undergraduate level. Single-disciplinary courses are not suited to all students, and for those who will not proceed with their studies beyond the first-degree level it may be unduly limiting in perspective. Who knows sociology who only sociology knows?

Our Chilean respondent suggests that systematic and vigorous attention to interdisciplinary methods should eventually emerge as one of the most useful tools available to the social sciences for the analysis of complex phenomena. This is as yet no more than a hope.

So we see the contradiction: on the one hand his career aspirations and search for professional identity direct the student towards specialization in one discipline; on the other hand the desire and need to tackle social problems demand interdisciplinary approaches.

In some countries the higher education sector has lost what dominance it possessed in research. Where research is done predominantly in institutes operating within government or dependent upon government for support, the concentration on problem-oriented research forces at least a show of interdisciplinary activity. The brake is applied by universities' monopoly of the sanctioning system, the award of the higher degree. Only a government takeover of the award of higher degrees breaks the system completely, and this runs clearly contrary to the highly prized values of academic freedom.

Many of our respondents referred to the absence of a Social Science Research Council, or such a body responsible for the co-ordination of research and of development of the country's social science capability. It is indeed hard to see how a government can have a social science policy without some such instrument. A social science research council can review the whole field of a country's social science: the provision for teaching the postgraduate and research training; the provision of research facilities; the resources devoted to research; the publication and diffusion of research; the planning of research; and the utilization of research in policy. Such a council can be either executive or advisory – or, for that matter, executive in some fields and advisory in others. Most government departments feel the need to carry out their own research or to arrange for research to be carried out for them; few relish having to ask a council or academy or central agency of some kind to sanction these requirements. On the other hand there is a corresponding tendency for research to be duplicated or at least not adequately communicated to others working in similar fields. Thus, while a council need not be responsible for all the research carried out by government, it should be in a position to offer advice and some degree of co-ordination, if only of exchange of information. A council's activities in the field of higher education have probably to be advisory; ministries of higher education and universities have to relate the needs in, and of, the social sciences to other needs. They have to retain executive control while availing themselves of the advice the council can provide on their social science policy. In the field of postgraduate and research training a council can combine advisory and executive functions – providing the fellowships and studentships paid for out of government funds. In research a council can set up its own institutes, provide government funds for research and advise government departments and others on their research programmes. While councils of this kind work well in large and advanced countries, there is no reason why they should not work at least equally well in small and less developed countries.

While, then, each country will have to develop its own model of a council to suit its own cultural and political traditions as well as its economic and research needs, the principle is flexible enough to provide guidelines for such a model. It is probably the most effective way of mobilizing social science resources, bringing social scientists into participation in government's policy-making for the social sciences. A further function of a council is to provide the basis for international co-operation and action, whether on a regional or global level.

Should a social science research council form part of the country's science policy framework? Since research councils for the social sciences tend to be set up by countries which possess such councils for the physical and biological sciences and to be set up in their image, it tends to be taken for granted that they should belong in the same category and form part of the science policy apparatus. While this makes good sense, there is also a respect in which the social sciences are closer to social policy than to science policy and it is by no means self-evident that a social science research council should be in competition for their resources with science research councils, rather than with museums and art galleries or with parks and conservancies. In so far as research in the social sciences is organized on similar lines and in similar institutions to those of science, there is greater reason to suppose that the same principles of finance and control should apply. But the very fact of the council's being regulated by similar principles increases the likelihood that social research will be organized and institutionalized along the same lines as the sciences, whether this is truly appropriate to the nature of the activity or not.

In a small country there is an obvious case for a central social and economic research institute, closely connected with a research council if that exists. Such an institute is the government's and the council's natural first choice for research it wishes to see performed. The Danish Institute for Economic and Social Research is a model of this kind of arrangement and has been copied in Ireland and elsewhere. It need not preclude the establishment of more specialized research institutes to which in fact it may act as midwife.

It is apparent from our studies that some form of regional co-operation has considerable attraction. Chile is a country with considerable experiences of regional co-operation, participating in many institutions conceived on a scale of coverage of Latin America as a whole. These have been brought about with the aid and sponsorship of UNESCO, the Ford Foundation and others. They include Escolatina, Celade, FLACSO, Cienes and the Co-ordinating Institute of Social Research. These are not all equally successful; on the whole teaching has proved easier to develop than research on a regional basis. Nevertheless, these bodies have played a considerable part in developing the country's social science capability.

Nigeria participates in a number of African institutions, of which the most prominent in the social science field is the African Institute of Economic Development and Planning at Dakar, and to which the Nigerian contribution amounted to $50,000 in 1970–1. Hungary looks first to co-operation with the other East European countries, and second to the wider international community. Egypt is the centre for several institutes conceived on a pan-Arab scale.

Our Sri Lanka respondent makes a plea for a Regional Centre of Social Science Research for the whole of South Asia, which would provide a tremendous fillip to social development in the region. The problem of employment of resources, the development of human and material resources, educational planning and health planning are very much alike in India, Pakistan, Thailand, Philippines, Indonesia, Malaysia and Burma (as well as Sri Lanka). The pooling of the experiences, the fundamental research studies and possibly some of the human and material resources of those countries would beyond doubt be beneficial to all of them.

The case for regional co-operation, then, is based at least partly on the commonality of problems to be tackled. It probably rests partly, too, on the compatibility of infrastructure and of political aims and administrative styles. There is a possibility that it might lead to the development of different psychologies, sociologies, different economic sciences and so on, as well as different scientific ideologies, all of which could divide rather than unite the international community of social scientists and hinder the optimum development of the social sciences. So regional co-operation should preferably be part of a wider concept of interregional co-operation and should not stunt the growth of international social science co-operation in the widest sense. The other danger of regional co-operation is that new prestigious regional institutions can draw away the best scientists from their own countries, thereby weakening rather than strengthening national science effort. To mention these problems is not to deprecate regional co-operation and the setting up of regional institutions; it is to call attention to issues which must enter into their planning.

Comparative social science policy as a field of study

These international comparisons or studies often tend to open issues rather than to close them, and as such provide useful starting points, but do not offer firm guidance. Rather they expose the need for comparative social science policy and research organization as a field of study worth further development.

We are far from understanding the processes involved in the development of the social science disciplines, or those involved in the choice of careers in the social sciences, or the processes involved in the utilization of social science research. For that matter we do not know a great deal about the factors that should be taken into account in making policies for the social sciences and their organization and utilization.

If it is not immediately obvious how these interrelate and what are the systemic characteristics of the whole, that is not surprising. Of course one can plan and make policies and decisions which will be broadly efficacious without a full understanding of the system one is planning, deciding and making policy for. At present, however, decisions are almost certainly being taken with far less knowledge than need be the case and without even knowing what factors are at work, let alone how they relate to one another. The appropriate studies have not yet been conceptualized, let alone carried out.

But before we move on to developments at this level of sophistication, there are many humdrum, mundane topics needing further study. It is widely admitted that research training is inadequate. One major problem which besets it is that in all countries it lies uneasily on the borderline of, or in the no-man's-land between – the system of higher education and the system of science organization. A comparative analysis of the organization and methods of research training is perhaps a first priority.

Research organization should be the next topic. The range of institutes where research is performed is limited; there are probably fewer than ten different types. Yet we know remarkably little about them. Some types are appropriate for some kinds of research and inappropriate for other kinds. If a country has need of all types of research, it must be equipped with a range of institutions which enable it to cover them all adequately. But at the moment we could not judge whether a country is so equipped or not. Some key institution may be lacking, not necessarily in the field of research performance, but in the field of research diffusion. Or there may be inadequate channels for bringing problems needing research to the notice of social scientists. Or there may be lacking the necessary institutions for mobilizing opinion and action among social scientists. A lack of any of these may radically affect the value obtained from resources invested in the social sciences. What is required here is a comparative analysis of the institutional framework for research, research diffusion and mobilization of social science opinion.

Research utilization

Perhaps the most shadowy area of all is that of research utilization. If we, as social scientists, were asked by a national policy-maker whether he was obtaining good value from the resources devoted to social science research, we would have to use a good deal of guesswork in answering him. We could probably estimate the value of improved economic indicators and of better census data. We might even be able to estimate the value of social indicators. But for much of our work we have not developed any way of estimating. For much, perhaps most, research we rely, and probably rightly, on criteria internal to the discipline. But some resources are channelled to research which is quite specifically problem-oriented. For this we should be seeking modes of evaluation. Social scientists themselves evaluate research not by the use to which it is put, but by the esteem brought by its publication. We should need to ask: How is research diffused? What training do administrators receive in using research? What are the expectations held of research? Over what period of time would you expect to be able to see some result from research? And so on. These questions are all everywhere unanswered and seldom even discussed. Lazarsfeld has said: 'We need a theory of utilization.' We need people to believe we need a theory of utilization.

Chapter 11
Observations on the Social Sciences in India, Israel, Ghana and Australia

INDIA

Wherever you go in India there is a pervasive sense of disappointment about the contribution of the social sciences to India's development. Here is a country with a long-established and highly developed university system, with an experienced civil service and with a formidable production of theses and publications of an advanced character. As we shall see, it would be hard to sustain the view that there is a deficiency of research or a crippling lack of funds. Nor has India been short of advice and advisers of every kind; it is a country which has been intensively studied.

Of course, expectations are unrealistic; they overestimate the power of research to generate useful new knowledge and under-estimate the problems involved in using knowledge, new or old, unless the institutional framework is specially designed for its use. The residual and special disappointment in and about India is due to the fact that the institutional framework is so well developed. India possesses a rich range of institutions; indeed few economically advanced countries possess India's capacity for research in the social sciences. In this India is quite exceptional among under-developed countries.

The disciplines

The social science tradition in India is predominantly British, with the separation of all the social disciplines from one another as

210

complete in India as anywhere in the world. Economics is unquestionably the most advanced, but the particular backwardness of sociology and psychology is so noteworthy as to need explanation, or at least comment. The sociological tradition in India is predominantly anthropological, a tradition which is strongly historical, absorbing India's rich culture and history. The marriage of this tradition with predominantly American sociological methods, techniques and concepts has not been an altogether successful one.

Unlike sociology, psychology has no Indian tradition on which to build or to be grafted. There were, of course, many Indian mentalistic philosophies but modern psychology disdains relationships to them. The preoccupations and problems of the dominant American-British psychology are mostly those of an experimental biologically oriented science. 'Applied' psychology in its various forms – industrial, educational, clinical – have borne, and still bear, little relationship to the experimental behaviourist psychology which is its 'pure' correlate. It tends, therefore, to be problem-oriented and ad hoc; and the problems on which it has grown are western problems. There is thus neither an indigenous Indian psychology, nor an applied psychology providing careers – thus a lack of student demand. Until this situation changes, psychology will remain a comparatively small part of the Indian scene. There are signs that the situation is improving; the National Council of Educational Research and Training employs about fifty psychologists on educational work and the growth of the Indian institutes of management is pushing forward the development of a research-and-practice psychology of organizations appropriate to India's developing industries.

Economics is outstandingly the most active and developed branch of the social sciences in India. Economics, it is true, has a flying start everywhere. It is the most obviously useful of the social sciences to government and economists are in as much demand in India as elsewhere. Ambitious students are attracted to its study, and the discipline has very firm roots in the universities. Indian economists have contributed significantly to the discipline, particularly to development economics.

Political science is not handicapped in India by a revolutionary tradition, nor is it aided by a strong orientation towards public administration. It has a strong historical element, but studies of political sociology, election studies, etc., are growing, as are critical studies of governmental institutions. By and large, it cannot be said to have established itself in administrators' eyes as a 'useful' discipline; in fact, less is expected of it than of sociology and psychology,

211

and the disappointment and misunderstandings are correspondingly less.

The universities

The social sciences are taught in virtually all Indian universities, although departments of psychology and sociology are far fewer than departments of economics.

The universities differ enormously in their standards and in the esteem in which they are held. So varied indeed is the picture that possession of a degree has little meaning until its source is known. The most common pattern is a university with a central core and a number of constituent colleges. Most colleges are heavily burdened with undergraduate instruction and cannot be considered as significant components of India's research capability. The universities are also heavily loaded, with staff–student ratios far less favourable than their British counterparts, with recurrent student unrest, and with poor ancillary resources. By far the greatest part of the research conducted in the universities is in the form of Ph.D theses. Now it is by no means out of the question that a Ph.D thesis should be a significant contribution to a discipline: many influential books that began as a thesis appear in many countries. There are, however, obvious limitations, as we outlined in the previous chapter. Most Ph.D theses then have an 'academic' character, unconnected or only indirectly connected with the major thematic problems of Indian society. There are many reasons (see Chapter 7) why universities are usually unfavourable environments for certain kinds of research; these influences are to be seen at their most powerful in India.

Research institutes

Universities are not the most favourable institutional base for interdisciplinary, problem-oriented, commissioned research. Administrators and planners refer to this when they contemptuously dismiss the universities as ivory towers. When government departments or planning authorities feel the need for research, they have as possible choices before them the persuading or commissioning of universities to do the work, going to a non-university research institute, setting up a new specialized research institute, or carrying out the work intramurally by establishing their own research unit, or by temporary employment of research workers under their own supervision. All these variants exist in India, although it appears that government agencies are less likely to sponsor university research and that the research institutes are the beneficiaries. New institutes have emerged, largely funded by government-sponsored research: for example, the Institute of Manpower Studies, set up at the instance of the Ministry of Labour. One reason given for preferring this device to an internal research unit was the federal nature of Indian government. An internal unit would be unable to provide access to the state governments which would be the main users of the results of the research. There does, however, seem to be a growing tendency for state governments to sponsor research and support institutes within their territory. So the position of the universities appears to have weakened and that of the research institutes to have been strengthened. An aspiring researcher, anxious to participate in serious research, possibly to have a career in research and to work as a member of a team backed with adequate supporting staff and facilities, is well advised to join one of the well-established flourishing institutes. There he will also acquire a training in research method which the universities cannot provide. Hence the universities lose their most likely researchers to the institutes, which do not, in return, provide research training for the universities.

Finance

From the institutional base for carrying out research, we now need to turn to the pattern of sponsorship. In 1967 the two major sources of finance for research carried out in universities were the Research Programmes Committee of the Planning Commission (the RPC) and the United States – through US aid, US government departments such as HEW, and charitable foundations, particularly Ford. International bodies had played a significant part in helping to build up the institutional base; with help from UNESCO the Institute for Economic Growth in New Delhi had become a research centre of international repute. Domestic foundations had been at least equally influential; the Tata Institute of Social Science was initiated by the Tata Foundation, the Ghokale Institute of Economics and Politics at Poona had been founded originally by the Servants of India Society and so on.

This picture changed considerably with the inauguration in 1969 of the Indian Council for Social Science Research, a government body on the lines of the British SSRC. The pressure for setting up this council also has parallels with the prehistory of the SSRC. In both cases there was tension between the need to exploit the social sciences for practical purposes and the need to develop the social sciences themselves. The Indian council that resulted shares with the British counterpart the task of exercising leverage without having at its disposal sums which are large, either by comparison with the total social science research effort, or in relation to the total of central government expenditure on social and economic research. Its importance lies in its concern with building up the total research capability of the country and with the balance of research effort, in its role as guardian of the interests of the social science community as a whole, with its power to set standards and with its influence as spokesman for social science in the corridors of power.

The University Grants Committee, of course, continues to give grants for research universities and the volume of these appears to be increasing. But the UGC had also adopted new responsibilities with regard to some research institutes outside universities; some of these now received a form of institutional support from the UGC.

A more sinister development I noted between my visits was the growing suspicion of, and hostility to, foreign, particularly American, research funds. There was concern about the sources of some research money and about the motives of some research agencies, no doubt generated by *causes célèbres* such as Project Camelot. Certainly it was my impression that the cause of international social science had been done a disservice both by the mistakes and misguided blunders on the one side and the strength of the reaction on the other. Everyone must hope that this will pass, though one would not wish to see Indian social science as dependent, as in the past, on this source of finance.

It is notoriously difficult to estimate total expenditures on social science research, as we saw in the previous chapter. Unofficially, the ICSSR estimate that their budget accounts for 10 per cent of the total cost of social science research in India.

Research training

We have already pointed to the inadequacies of research training in India. Undoubtedly the best training is to be had by becoming a junior member of one of the good research institutes which has access to supporting facilities such as computers, survey teams and so on. Few university departments are equipped to do more than offer supervision for the traditional Ph.D student. There are very few careers in research and the Ph.D is more a licence to engage in university teaching than a preparation for a substantial period to be spent in research. Of course academic staff research as well as teach, but a very substantial portion of this research has to be the kind that can be picked up and put down in the context of a time allocation dominated by the requirements of teaching and examining. This largely precludes serious fieldwork. Furthermore, the division of responsibility between the ICSSR and UGC makes it difficult for the former to intervene directly in the field of research training. Although the administration of scholarship and studentship schemes is no light burden, it is predictable that the ICSSR will find that research training and research belong together even if the borderline between research training and advanced scholarship (a more proper concern for the UGC) proves a hard one to draw.

India, as much as anywhere, has felt the inadequacies of the approach to problems deriving from a single discipline. The technocrat, looking for answers, has a model of how the disciplines should combine, but models fail because of the drag of institutional and psychological factors which are greater than the technocrats believe or will admit. And no one has objectively studied the process of mounting interdisciplinary research and the problems involved in its utilization.

Among researchers themselves there is much scepticism. It may be expressed in the politest possible form as by the director of the Institute for Economic Growth: 'Hitherto sociologists have in India been really cultural anthropologists and since they have not been interested in empirical research economists have acted without taking notice of what sociologists might say.' That was in 1967; the sociological component of the institute's work has grown considerably.

The difficulty of organizing and undertaking interdisciplinary research in the universities, together with the growing dissatisfaction with the outcome of unidisciplinary work was one of the factors which led government departments to set up, or to assist in setting up, independent research institutes.

The distinction between team work and interdisciplinary research is fine-drawn. No two people, however alike their disciplinary orientation, share an identical view of a problem. Their learning to work together is a process of learning to build a three-dimensional model from the parallax of two flat pictures. When two or more psychologists, say, have learned to work together, they begin to see the need for an economic dimension and to have some glimmering of the process of combining psychological and economic outlooks.

The presence within the same institute of people with different disciplinary backgrounds is no guarantee of interdisciplinary research. The Institute of Community Development at Hyderabad was asked to evaluate an agricultural improvement programme carried out in villages by the Agricultural Institute. Demonstrations convinced a number of farmers, the better and more adventurous among them, to adopt new methods proposed by the Agricultural Institute. These involved investment in fertilizers and in improved seeds. The Institute of Community Development's evaluation showed that, despite their greater investment, the farmers who had co-operated in the programme achieved no better results than their less adventurous colleagues. I pressed the sociologists at the institute for their explanation. It appeared that one of the most important reasons was that the new seeds should have been sown later than the old ones, but that the rhythm of social life in the villages had put a premium on sowing the seeds at the old time, the same time as everyone else, and this was probably what had happened. When I tried to draw the moral that sociologists should be involved with the agriculturists' planning of programmes of this kind, they recoiled, 'This would mean treading on the toes of another sort of expert', and this in India is an even more horrifying thing to do than in Britain. The true comprehension of the relevance of another's discipline to your own problem was lacking.

We have already referred to the deficiencies in the organization and provision of training for research. This does not necessarily imply that there is a research bottleneck in the form of a lack of trained researchers. This is, in any case, difficult to demonstrate. An example of this was the experience of a division of ATIRA, the Associated Textile Industries' Research Association. From a flourishing Human Relations Division of some ten professional staff, it has shrunk to two or three researchers. A number of reasons could be and were advanced. First, a true understanding of the capacities and potentialities of this kind of work had never been fully acquired by the members of the governing body. Second, there was too much pressure to exploit any success, however small, leading to a thin spread of activity rather than talent-building. Third, the need to build institutions around people (a policy particularly appropriate to unusual kinds of activity or to situations of scarcity of good people) had not been understood. When eventually the head of the division left, she could not adequately be replaced. It would be wrong to conclude necessarily from this that the shortage of good research workers was proven; the story is, however, perfectly consistent with this impression.

One clear difficulty in assessing the extent to which research is handicapped by the lack of good research workers is just that the latter term is too vague and ambiguous. Research worker is not a profession like medicine, where you can tolerably hope to assess the numbers required on certain assumptions and where the stock of qualified professionals is known. Research is mostly done by people who are not making a career of it, either as preparation for an academic career or as a prelude to some other career. Nor are they interchangeable. The absence of a good mathematical statistician cannot be compensated for by employing a social anthropologist with however many years of fieldwork experience. And when research directors talk to you about research workers, they may mean junior data gatherers or senior project directors; all are 'research workers'. Nor do projects and careers fit: the director is looking for people for a project; the people he wants are looking for careers. Without proper provision of careers in research, the recruiting of researchers for projects is always going to be tricky, uncertain and to yield the appearance of scarcity.

What usually happens is that directors build projects around researchers they have and want to keep. This does not necessarily imply that the projects are inferior nor that they are fraudulent. What it does mean is that the true state of the market for research workers and for research money is obscured. Under these circumstances 'normal' market mechanisms do not operate properly, and a measure of planning becomes essential. So far as I know, no planning for research training and research careers exists in India. Nor is India any worse than most countries in this regard.

Mediating institutions

A crucial role in the relationship of research to action is played by a whole range of what I have loosely described as 'mediating institutions'.

These may be pressure groups, professional associations, voluntary or semi-voluntary welfare, educational, political or charitable organizations. They may include a specialist press, or an advisory council, a bank or an international organization such as a specialist agency of the United Nations. They enable interests to be expressed and needs kept before the eyes of governments and of researchers. Although easier to initiate than to terminate, such institutions do enable groupings to form, dissolve, and re-form as particular issues rise to significance. A good deal about the nature of a society could be gleaned from the pattern of such organizations and groupings it harbours and sustains. India is well-equipped with them and they play a notable part in the Indian social science scene.

I do not pretend to know how many social science research

institutes, councils, etc. exist in India. Some of them are registered names only, others are too recent for anything to be said about them. There is certainly a great number. Some are concerned with a specialized branch or field or application of the social sciences – for example, the Sri Ram Institute for Industrial Relations in New Delhi. Others cover a less specialized field but have a clear mission, like the Council for Social Development.

Government itself makes use of advisory committees and councils. More fettered and generally providing their advice in confidence, they are unobtrusive but serve to link research with action. It is doubtful, for example, whether the Advisory Council on Police Research has generated or stimulated much new research in criminology. It has done more to advance the use of what is already known and even such utilitarian activities as the improvement of police records and their alignment with recent knowledge is of considerable potential value.

The Indian Institute of Public Administration, another mediating institution, has a mission, a propaganda function and a research aim. Its primary function is to raise the standard of public administration at all levels. What needs improving? At the base of all administration, and research too for that matter, lie data: neither administration nor research can be better than the data on which it is based. Methods are also inadequate. Thus one of the first aims of the institute was to raise the sophistication of data collection in areas where this was low. Some of the more sophisticated research that they would like to do, or to see carried out, was dependent upon first getting better data.

State governments hardly come under the rubric of 'mediating' institutions, but in some respects they do occupy a similar role. A state government which took special interest in social research would not only be in a position to undertake or to sponsor research directly, but also to influence the actions of the central government. State governments and city administrators are pressure groups as well as centres of power. The role of state governments as sources of funds and users of research varies from state to state; the influence, however, of outstanding figures in ministries or in top administrative posts seems to be crucial.

Government planning

The importance of economic planning in India needs no underlining. Its significance for economic and social research is no less obvious. The initiation of planning in 1950–7 gave a tremendous

218

boost to research and studies of all descriptions. But as a mediating institution, the Planning Commission maintained a steady pressure on academia to accept the planners' criteria of relevance.

Whatever view one may take about the usefulness of the economic research or the failures of planning, the existence of a published plan acted as an enormous stimulus to economists. This was not the case for the other social sciences. The plan was not accompanied by a social plan – an account of the developments in Indian society that would be needed if the economic targets were to be achieved. It is true that a 'plan' of this nature would be a crude document and easy to criticize. Furthermore, the step from analysis to prescription, now an accepted part of the economist's trade, is not yet part of the sociologist's self image. Nor do sociologists have agreed goals, and even when goals can be agreed between sociologists and administrators or planners, the basic indicators that could monitor the path towards the goal are lacking. But such a 'plan' would be a challenge which social scientists could not ignore and it would present to the government and the planners the complexity of the social framework they were trying to alter. It would also stimulate the provision of the social indicators which would at least assist legislators and administrators of all kinds to know what improvements they could reasonably expect and aim for.

Utilization of research

When one asks about the application of research, of course we find examples of utilization, but these are rare compared with instances of when research was not used or of no use. If you ask questions about the help *hoped* for from research, the answers were more messianic than sceptical. I think that there is a great deal of unrealism, both about the expectations and the eventual disappointments of research. Of course, if you ask a very senior, heavily burdened official of government what he hopes for from research, he is likely to tell you that he hopes for help with his most general problem. How would you evaluate the degree to which the outcome of research could help towards the attainment of his stated goal? Let me give an instance from the Ministry of Education. India had to move from a paternalistic to a 'modern' social structure, but how was education to be shaped to assist this transition? How would you monitor the transition from paternalism to 'modernity'? And how would you evaluate the contribution of research to those changes?

At lower and lower levels you encounter people with much more

219

specific, much shorter-term problems. The kind of help they want from research is totally different.

There are areas of research where questions are not asked because they are bad form. Just as you could not carry out empirical studies of prostitution in the Soviet Union, where prostitution, having been legally proscribed, is therefore non-existent, so in India caste is no longer a research topic. For instance, in connection with rural–urban migration, because the 'backward' castes could not be integrated into traditional rural society in any new states, they drifted to towns becoming a new 'lumpenproletariat'. But this could not be a topic of study. The obverse of this is the question that must be asked even if it is meaningless. If you want your own researchers to receive a training in modern research method, you will send them to the United States. When (and if) they return, they will be agog to practise their new-found skills. And if these are most relevant to, say, problems of labour turnover, then labour turnover they will study. Labour turnover may be small, irrelevant, but it is studiable. One could instance a university which had produced five Ph.Ds in the field of industrial psychology: the topics of four of them bore little relation to any discernible Indian problems. They were a study of students using the methods of French characterology; the application of sociometry to Rorschach tests; the application of the general test battery of the US Employment Service; and the development of a scale to measure attitudes of young people. The fifth was a study of morale in a small industrial unit.

There are institutions of all types for conducting research in India; sponsors are there too, with the most important the ICSSR; mediating institutions also exist. But specifically, what institutions or institutional arrangements are there for relating research to action? The best example comes, not altogether surprisingly, from the field of education. The NCERT, which was set up in 1961, is a very substantial body indeed. The first wave of research projects were completed around 1967 and they had then to be seen into action. The response was to set up a department of field service, whose aim was to convey the results of research to the teachers 'in the field'. Encountering some resistance from the educational bureaucracy and anticipating more, they had now undertaken a study of administrative behaviour. Administrators are bound by their tradition and their code, one of whose articles is to ensure that money is actually spent for the purpose for which it was allocated. As they also determine the allocation among projects and are hostile to novelty, they can very easily, without any such intention, thwart the purposes they are faithfully serving. If administrators in this field need different attitudes, particularly towards risk-taking, the researchers are the people to attempt the task. There is nothing particularly outré about this and indeed it is no more than a realization that research results are not guaranteed utilization by their own merits. The field service teams are the engine of this realization: they can neither retreat into more research nor take refuge in rules and precedents. One illustration of administrative behaviour and of the processes involved in getting it to adjust to the findings from research may be taken from the topic of school examinations. The weaknesses and unreliability of the examination system had been demonstrated some ten years before and the researchers had been working with teachers and examiners to alter the system. Very soon they discovered that changes could not be made without the support of the administrators. The particular problem here was the role of the schools' inspector and it took ten years of negotiation to resolve this satisfactorily. These processes are slow and may be daunting, but the use of research means organizational and attitude change and these cannot be brought about by fiat nor are they rapid, spontaneous occurrences.

It becomes very difficult to get a study started with enough time before decisions and actions may need to be taken. We can see this from the following British anecdote. A certain government department approached the Social Survey, requesting it to undertake a survey which would provide data which would be helpful for drafting legislation which the department was preparing. The results were required within nine months. The Social Survey could not accept it as a nine-month assignment; fifteen months was the minimum. The legislative time table would not permit this. But we all know that legislative time tables slip. On the other hand, we may not admit this or be seen to be planning for slippage which has not been politically authorized. No project. Then the inevitable slippage occurred. Months later the ministry returned, still needing results within nine months. And so on. The project was never initiated; the time that elapsed between the first approach and the final drafting of the bill would have permitted a much more generous allocation of time than the Social Survey needed or asked for. Many possible morals could be drawn from this anecdote, including the one that important negotiations should only be conducted by people with power to negotiate. Our moral here is that timing is a much neglected but crucial aspect of the utilization of research.

To return to India, talking to people and listening to them on the topic of the institutional aspects of research utilization is an experience which has something in common with looking into a stereoscope. Two foci are presented as it were to one's two eyes; the effort of combining them into a three-dimensional picture is a strain. The two foci are the researchers and the administrators; their alignment is very hard to concentrate on. It has been suggested that in the public sector there is a particular type of administrative culture. Its members protected their aversion to anything new by making demands from it of a specific kind which it could not possibly satisfy until it became well established and no longer new. This was one among the many techniques it employed to maintain itself from potentially disrupting novelties and ideas.

The administrative reward system puts a premium on being right, or at any rate, on not being wrong. An administrator who departs from the tried methods, the familiar solutions, needs protection. If he is to do so on the grounds of the findings of some research, he feels the need at the very least for support from the researcher who will *recommend* him to do so. What is he to do when the researcher, wrapped in his role of scientific detachment, says, in effect, 'I cannot recommend; I can only present to you data or ways of looking at data. I can help perhaps to draw up for you a list of pros and cons, but I could go no further than that.' Given the administrative reward system's premium on not departing from precedent without at least better reason than sticking to it, and given the academic reward system's premium on scientific detachment and objectivity, sterile research seems bound to be the outcome of the association. Both will have to budge. Young administrators appear to be more research-minded than their predecessors. A notable proportion of recruits to the Indian administrative service comes from academic posts; one estimate puts this as high as 60 per cent. The high status of the administrative service and its ability to attract many young men away from academic careers are by no means unmixed blessings. The acceptance of new ideas or suggestions rarely comes *de haut en bas*, and while it is wholly to India's advantage to have a highly capable civil service, the country has other needs as well – for industrial managers and academic teachers and researchers. Any factor which divides these groups, rather than welding them into a single culture, hinders the early flow of communication and ideas where it is most vital.

A frequent complaint about research and equally about research utilization is 'lack of co-ordination'. The cumulative effect of many studies is lost, either because their comparability has not been given adequate thought and preparation, or because it is nobody's job to link them in an action framework. The RPC had sponsored twenty metropolitan studies. As far as I was able to ascertain, the Division of Economic and Rural Development had not undertaken a comprehensive review of these studies. The Research Programmes Committee of the Planning Commission (RPC) itself made some

222

attempts at co-ordination – for example, seventy-five studies of industrial relations were reviewed at their request. Some tentative conclusions emerged, but the reviewers were only too conscious of the fragmentary nature of the studies; their cumulative effect was not great in relation to the effort expended on the individual studies. Attempts to collate, co-ordinate and compare after the event seem to be likely to fail.

Co-ordination of research is one thing; co-ordination of research, planning and action is another thing again. We have already referred to the separation of the administrative and academic 'cultures' and to the problems of timing. To what extent are these problems of communication, understanding and of institutional framework?

By and large, administrators and researchers do not communicate except in the initiation of the research and when its report is represented. Certainly no institutional provisions exist for assuming continuous interaction throughout the process of formulation, execution and implementation of research.

Some researchers, because of their background and connections, move freely in governing circles. Their research will evoke the interest of their friends and acquaintances in government and administration, but will not necessarily be seen by them in relation to action. We can see this in the governments' reaction to studies of villages and their relationship to market towns. Governments have been very concerned about the drain of artisans from the villages to the market towns and felt that this was something that ought to be stopped – some incentives should be found for keeping artisans in the villages. But the researchers say: 'When you examine the actual movement of villagers, you will see that in fact the villagers make frequent visits to the market towns, and the government policy of trying to build up the villages is wrong. If the shoemaker moves from the village to the market town, the villagers will still be able to make use of his shoemaking and, indeed, they will have many richer experiences through their constant visits to market towns, than they would where all the services are made available in the village. Furthermore, the artisans themselves benefit both in terms of skill and opportunities from being in the market centres.' But this apparently had no discernible impact on policy, despite the fact that the administrators know the researchers well. They may say, 'I have just read your very interesting report', but that is as far as it goes.

I did find evidence of utilization, where deliberate care had been taken with the personal working relationships of administrator and researcher, where indeed a philosophy of research utilization had been hammered out. One Indian industrialist expounded his philosophy of utilization in this way. The manager must not only know of, and understand, the services available to him from the scientist, *he must feel comfortable enough to expose his own experience to conceptualization.* Equally, the scientist must learn to regard the acceptance of his concepts as a test of their validity. The arena in which these tests were best encountered was that of consultancy. I heard very little of the research-consultancy mix in India; where I did, it bore strong traces either of Tavistock influence via that institute's connections with Unilever, or of American influence through the Indian Institutes of Management. Research consultancy involved the researcher in taking risks of the kind that clashed with the tradition of academic caution and purity. This did not imply that the research consultant needs less scientific integrity; on the contrary, he needs at least as much if he is to draw the line for his client between what truly emerged from his research and what he would be inclined to say to justify the recommendations he had made.

We can see this in the following example. Mill owners had commissioned from consultants a study of jobs and loadings which had been rejected entirely by the unions. To find out why this was so, the researchers spent a long time with the union members. They found that their rejection had nothing to do with the data, though specifically they couched their rejection in terms of the quantitative material. Their real objections were, first, that they had not been consulted from the start, and second, the communications with them had been sporadic. The work was done again, with a team of people from the mill, from the research association and from the unions. That data collected, they all sat down in the evening to discuss them. There were many misunderstandings about the facts, but gradually they clarified their thinking and somehow developed norms with which to look at them. They were able to draw up a report together; there were no disagreements on data, the report was accepted and this method became institutionalized. It took one year's work.

My hundreds of interviews and notes yield many examples of research undertaken for what I can loosely describe as applied purposes; most of them tell of reports which were not implemented, or of administrative or political errors which research could have averted, or which the application of existing knowledge would have made unlikely. I have tried to pick out themes which, while they illustrate my main line of argument, are not so unrepresentative as to provide a biased picture. Does the situation in India differ in major ways from that elsewhere? The answer must be Yes. Compared with any of the other countries I have studied, except the

USA, India possesses a wider range of research facilities. Certainly there are many more research institutes than in Britain and some are of a kind not to be found there. The larger, government-supported institute, outside the government machine, with a particular remit or field of activity has few parallels elsewhere. Government institutions, such as the NCERT, are of a scale unmatched outside the United States. The emphasis within university research on the Ph.D thesis is less unfamiliar, as are disciplinary rigidities, and the cultural gap between administrator and researcher is almost a universal phenomenon.

Expectations from research are notably high in India; achievement is much harder to evaluate. The criteria are just not for the most part there. The ICSSR is in a position to exercise considerable leverage if it chooses to put its weight behind the development of institutional frameworks for research utilization.

GHANA

I visited Ghana at the end of 1967 and the beginning of 1968, after the fall of Nkrumah. I fear, therefore, that the picture that I present may represent a transitory period in the fortunes of the country and may not do adequate justice either to its longer-term resources or to the capacities and ability of its administrators.

Many Ghanaians consider that their country is a lucky one. And, as they say, you need never starve in Ghana: you have only to lie on your back, stretch out your arm and pick a banana. But a rich country Ghana certainly is not, and has to rely too much on single-crop primary products such as cocoa. Ghana does not have a long-standing tradition of learning and one is aware of the deficiency of highly qualified people and of institutions. She is not inadequately equipped with university institutions for a country of her size, nor again deficient in high-class secondary schools – at least two are modelled on the English public school system and have considerable reputations. However, she is unable to supply all the high-quality staff she needs for her universities, but this is experience she has in common with very many other developing countries. Where Ghana seemed to me to be particularly lacking in institutional framework, particularly from the point of view of the utilization of social research, is in the lack of responsible associations and pressure groups. She lacks also specialized research institutes and particularly those devoted to the attack on some social problems. Indeed, it is in this area of, as it were, mediating institutions, between government on the one hand and institutes of higher

225

learning on the other, that Ghana appeared to me to be most weak. Research is, of course, a standard activity carried on within the universities and there exist research units within departments of government. Other places where research is located are the development banks and within the administration of the Volta Resettlement Agency. To some extent replacing the mediating institution of the kind that I mentioned above are those belonging to international organizations such as the Food and Agriculture Organization and the World Health Organization.

At the time of my visit relations between the government on the one hand and the universities on the other were somewhat strained. Again and again I was told of cases where ministries claimed that they would have welcomed research, but also claimed that they were unable to interest the universities. But the counter claim by the academics was that there was never any finance to sponsor the research. As an independent observer my impression was that the Ghanaians had not solved the problem of how to make the best use of the people and facilities that exist. In one major area of the government's problems, the problem of economic development, the involvement of social scientists, other than economists, was virtually nil. The obstacles to development are clearly perceived to be non-economic, but the question of what to do about them is still posed to the economists. In fact, a true role for sociologists, social psychologists and so on had not yet been found. This results in what amounts to an overproduction of such social scientists at the university – more being turned out than could possibly obtain jobs of a professional kind under present circumstances. In fact, even where sociological research has been carried out in matters connected with economic development, the capacity to use the information thus generated is lacking. There is one outstanding example to the contrary and it is with that instance that I shall begin an account of the use of social research in Ghana.

The story concerns the resettlement section of Volta River Authority. In 1961 when the Volta Dam had been planned but not yet built, the need had become apparent to plan in advance for the resettlement of the 80,000 or so people who would be displaced by the inundations after the dam was completed. The man (Mr Amarteifio) appointed as resettlement officer to the authority had a sociological training and experience with the use of sociometric techniques in a previous resettlement project. Thus, when the Volta Dam plan was developed, Amarteifio knew what was required. The first need was for a thorough social survey of the populations affected. The survey had been designed to yield basic data at an early stage, but the researchers used their sociometric techniques to draw up a very detailed picture of the existing population and their likely resettlement patterns.

As far as the planning was concerned, a good deal of thought and effort had gone in, not only to the purely agricultural and architectural aspects, but also into attempts to make use of the social data. In fact, this whole story might well have been one of the glorious success stories of applied social research, if it were not for the first law of planning, which is that if something can go wrong, it will. In this case two things went wrong. First, the new land had, before it could be used, to be deforested and the calculations of the size of this job were incorrect. Thus the time allocated was only about one-tenth of the time really required. The second thing that went wrong was perhaps remarkable. The Russians, who were building the dam, completed it three months ahead of schedule. And the Italian engineers supplying the turbines met the same schedule; thus the whole dam was ready to go into operation before all the plans for resettlement were complete. Thus it was possible to locate only some of the villages in proximity to the villages they had selected; others had to be placed regardless of sociometric choice. The moves that were executed in accordance with sociometric choice proved to be much more durable than those executed despite such choice.

It will be noted that Amarteifio, while his appointment was administrative, had nevertheless directed, or at least partially directed, and undertaken the relevant research. In his administrative capacity, Amarteifio had three roles: the first was assessing and planning to mitigate the human and social disruption likely to result from the Volta Dam; the second role was for liaison between the people involved and the authorities; and his third role was that of helping the people to understand the programme of development in which they had been caught up.

It is very hard to know how best to generalize from this experience or indeed whether one can safely generalize at all. It seems clear that where certain kinds of administrative functions are concerned, particularly those relating to planning or those with a considerable degree of autonomy in determining what is needed, and what should be done, the appointment of someone of a sociological background and particularly with experience of applying sociological expertise in practical situations is invaluable. But how many such people would a country like Ghana possess? Indeed, how many such people would a country like Britain possess? In the absence of any concerted attempt to provide this kind of career and to develop this kind of person, the total number available must be very slight. Apart from anything else, it requires administrative and research capacities which are not always combined in one person. But even in a favourable example like this one, the problems of relating research directly to an administrative need are considerable. Let me quote from the administrators who contributed a paper to the Volta Resettlement symposium:

> From the point of view of an administrator the surveys were well done and the data relevant. The list of the villages flooding and the village grouping were ready early. But other results and analyses came too late to be used for planning; for example, if it were known that the settlers would be accompanied by 2,954 cattle, 11,600 chickens, 42,000 sheep and goats, some arrangement would have been made to cater for them. If we had known earlier that over 90 per cent of the houses were of swish, or of inferior material and that 70 per cent had thatched roofing, it might have been possible to pick out the small number with superior buildings or the households with extra large families, and to make a little better provision for their convenience. If only the sociologists involved in this type of work could try to meet some of the day to day requirements of the job, their value to the administrator would be much greater.

Thus unrealism is not a monopoly of researchers. A follow-up project was undertaken, concerned to resettle more permanently those who had been inadequately settled first time. The researcher had drawn a schedule of the activities, including research, to be carried out in the course of resettlement. He had also related the content of the research to the resources in terms of qualified people available for their conduct and had drafted the whole into a critical path analysis for the administration. If this was followed, the research results should be available when they were required, in the planning process.

It is interesting to contrast this Volta Resettlement experience in the use of social research with that of the National Investment Bank, where the sponsor, researcher and user all belong to separate organizations. The bank requires people submitting proposals for financial aid for new industrial projects to undertake relevant research before they consider supporting it. An example was a study of the habits of the fishing community to see what developments might be appropriate for the fishing industry. In considering the extension of the pig-farming industry, a survey had to be made of the percentage of Moslems in the area and of the extent to which they actually adhered to their religious dietary precepts. These studies were potentially of value far beyond their immediate objective. In a country where the amount of knowledge of a demographic and sociological character was distinctly limited, these studies could be invaluable in adding to the general picture. Some might be specifically suitable for secondary analysis. However, banks tend to be secretive organizations and information they obtain on behalf of clients is not communicable to anybody without the client's permission. In a country like Ghana the results of social and economic research are too precious to be locked up in bank vaults.

I now turn to the Ministry of Social Welfare and Community Development. The ministry operates many programmes in the regional areas: for example, an adult literacy programme; development of self-help projects; a women's work programme, teaching basic child care and home economics. The ministry thus has the task of interpreting government to rural areas and vice versa. These activities all depend for their success on a certain level of social science knowledge. Thus there is need for a problem-oriented research programme. The same is true for rehabilitation. The Rehabilitation Division had a chance of using research when it was charged with implementing a cabinet report on the handicapped. One of these recommendations was the integration of handicapped children into schools for normal children. While this had been enthusiastically accepted by the Ministry of Social Welfare, the Ministry of Education had not accepted this and had been still setting up schools of a special kind for handicapped children. Thus they were institutionalizing the children by taking them away from their homes into residential institutions. There was now a danger of their being handicapped socially, as well as physically. Divided administrative responsibilities may severely hinder the application of research; the researchers are too often easily identified with one authority. But university research workers had made no moves to undertake studies in the field of rehabilitation.

Welfare workers are trained in the ministry's School of Social Welfare. This is a lengthy training, including six years' fieldwork before they may go to the university to undertake the research certificate in social administration. This enables them to become welfare officers. Those with the necessary aptitude are encouraged to take degrees in social work or sociology. And those, again with a good degree, go on to take their MA. However, this turns out to be rather bad business for the department, as once in the university they show little enthusiasm to return. Graduates either go on to the university staff or on to England. University researchers showed no keenness to undertake research on behalf of the section, and indeed its own research division was mainly involved in collecting statistics and providing data, of which the department was not in fact making much use. Obviously the research section had very low status, was frequently forgotten and was called into activity only when data of a simple, fact-collecting type were required. This should occasion little surprise. Unless a research unit within an organization or ministry is headed by somebody of equal status with divisional directors, unless it is provided with a channel direct to the top of the organization, unless it is allowed to participate in the formulation of its own research programme, and unless it has enough professional research workers within it to make a reasonable career structure, it is highly likely that it will be confined to carrying out routine data collection and preparation of routine statistics.

I mentioned earlier the way in which international organizations tend to replace those mediating institutions which are absent in developing countries. The great American foundations like Ford operate in a similar way. The Ford Foundation had responded to a request from the government of Ghana to Harvard University for an advisory team under Mr Klopman to assist their Ministry of Economic Affairs in their day-to-day economic policy and in making an economic plan. Klopman built his strategy on two legs. The first was working with the civil servants, helping them through the process of producing a plan. The other, which Klopman considered more important, was developing an organization within the government machinery that could cope with the problems of planning. Many ministries were concerned with aspects of economic development: industry, agriculture, trade, labour, education – to mention only a few. If these were to co-operate successfully in designing and implementing a degree of economic planning, effective channels of communication among them would have to be developed. The implementation of a planning report, like the implementation of a research report, depends upon the provision of the appropriate organization. How many planners, how many researchers are experts in organizational design? How many recognize its importance? And if researchers, planners, do not concern themselves with the design of the organization needed to implement their reports, who is to do this?

Klopman was well aware of the importance of organizational structure. He pointed to the need to utilize strong structures where they exist. Ghanaian villages possessed a strong social structure. Planners had not learned how to adapt their proposals to the organizational basis this structure could provide. Unaware of what they were doing, they tended to undermine the existing structure and put nothing in its place. For example, people in towns possess a larger and looser communication network than their rural counterparts;

they recognize more ties of kinship. The villager returning from a sojourn in the town acquires greater influence. It would not be surprising to learn that the openness to change of the village structure is in large part a function of its permeation by returning members with urban experience. One can readily identify a very interesting and potentially valuable piece of operational research relating these factors to the effectiveness of attempts to work through the agency of traditional structures. But this is the one kind of research that is most obviously lacking in Ghana, except in the Volta Resettlement Authority.

The universities possess the research capability, and are not entirely averse to operational and action research. An interesting example is the course for planning assistants at the Institute of Community Planning at Kumasi. The assistants' course was originally of two years' duration. Students were taught how to carry out a range of planning services: cartography, questionnaire design, data analysis, site selection, village layout and designing, and so on. The course was designed on the assumption that as assistants they would work under the supervision of qualified planners, but there were too few planners to undertake this. Planning assistants would have to be largely independent and self-sufficient. Their course of training was extended to a third year devoted to practical work in the villages. Each student 'adopts' a village within 30 miles of Kumasi, studies it and identifies its principal problems. He conducts a planning survey for the village in the context of its region. The student picks out one of the village's needs as both urgent and manageable, prepares a plan and costs it. He then has to implement the plan for which he is provided people to work with by the Ministry of Social Welfare and Community Development. Finally the student prepares a report for his examination. It is hard to fault this design, emphasizing as it does survey, planning and implementation equally and in close relationship with each other. It could serve as a model for the research utilization process. Of course the research is of a comparatively routine, well-defined character; the momentum for implementation is provided by the programmatic nature of the activity. The student soon learns the first step towards implementation has to be the design of an organization and its establishment. For an effective organizing committee to emerge, its constitution and procedures have to be based on the social structure of the village and the personal characteristics of key individuals. Social and planning research have to be conducted together.

The universities of Ghana often receive their research funds through grants, either from the government or sources such as the American foundations. In a total research project a high proportion

231

of effort is involved in setting up, financing, organizing and staffing the research. In short-term projects, financed project by project, the proportion of effort which can be devoted to the actual research is surprisingly small. So the sporadic nature of the finance, and hence research projects, are a handicap. It struck me over and over again in Ghana that scanty resources forced many promising programmes to limp along at a pace too slow for effective purposes. Occasional injections of money would allow a start which would not be maintained, thus hampering the prospects of cumulative advance on problems.

It is in this respect that the foreign research worker is least useful. He comes with his own problem to study, his own career fish to fry. At best he will conduct a complete piece of research and leave a legacy of new data and analysis, but no one to build on it further, no preparation for continuous study of the topic. At worst he will depart with the data in whose collection he has received a substantial help from his hosts. Even where the data are finally returned, they are likely to be out of date by the time the researcher has published what he has extracted.

Despite the press of students, the research activities of departments in the social science faculties are impressive. Most of the teaching staff conduct the kind of individual research which is compatible with a heavy teaching load, and the more elaborate, longer-term team studies are conducted within the specialized institutes, such as the Demographic Research Unit and the Institute of Economic and Social Research at Legon.

Summary

It is with considerable diffidence that I would try to draw all these threads together. The background needs to be remembered. On a comparatively frail structure of primary education a few strong secondary schools and two well-established universities had been erected, together with a teachers' training college recently elevated to university status. Their graduates provided all and more than the social scientists who could be employed in the existing state of the economy. More sociologists were being trained than economists, although the professional employment of sociologists was minute. Research training capacity was small and developed effectively only within a couple of university departments. However, every aspect of Ghanaian activity suffers from shortages. The frustration is, is there anything we can tell the Ghanaians they don't already know about their problems in respect of research and research utilization? Is there anything from the Ghanaian experience which adds to or underscores our conclusions about these issues?

In some ways Ghana provides the most interesting of our case studies – a country with an underdeveloped but not a hopelessly unprosperous economy, with a young but vigorous system of higher education and with an administrative structure which, though weak in many respects, is not helpless. All three, economy, administration and higher education could grow in harmony. But hungrily growing institutions are competitors for resources. At present it takes too long for inputs into social science research to be converted into exports to other sectors, except where research is part of the action process. Social scientists in universities will not choose to work on problems of immediate relevance to, and in harness with, administrators unless administrations can afford to induce or reward them with currency as valuable as the academic prestige that represents their opportunity costs. From the point of view of short-term returns, it would look altogether sensible to exploit most academics for teaching maximum numbers of administrators, hiving off a few to man institutes linked closely with administrative problems and administrative institutions.

What would be the longer-term consequences? How far would the loss of individual personal research opportunities hinder the growth of a flourishing social science and social science community in Ghana? The priorities for Ghana could well be: first, special courses introducing administrators and planners to the concepts and methods of the social sciences; second, the establishment of centres for research and research training in association both with government and the universities; third, the stimulation of further growth in the social sciences departments of the universities. Learning how to use the potential that exists is, to my mind, oustandingly the first priority.

ISRAEL

Necessity would appear to be a powerful motive for harnessing the social sciences in Israel. The country has few basic assets other than its people. Its population possesses characteristics typical of an advanced rather than an underdeveloped country: highly educated, highly sophisticated, highly urban. Its industry is weak for a developed country, very strong for an underdeveloped one; its agriculture strong. It is in every way a-typical and unclassifiable. The pre-occupation with nation building and with defence have helped to develop strong social cohesion, validating the involvement of social scientists with government and other organizations to a degree which would lead to strong student protest in countries whose social cohension was weaker. Thus we have all the apparent basic ingredients of successful social science utilization: good social scientists, sophisticated administrators, shared value systems, pressing problems. And in some respects Israel can provide examples of successful views of the social sciences. Yet these are limited and the reasons for their limitation deserve exploring.

Research institutes

Israel possesses virtually the entire range of organizations for research in the social sciences. There are university departments in all the social science disciplines and there are university postgraduate schools of social work. In each of these, research is regarded as an activity of equal importance with training. Although a good deal of university-based research is of the 'pure' kind, the Israeli universities suffer less than many from the tradition which places a low value on applied research. Further, although teaching loads are not light, finance for research has not been impossibly short.

Independent research institutes of high quality exist too; for example, the Institute of Applied Social Research and the Institute for Behavioural Sciences in Jerusalem. The former has links with the Hebrew University though these are not institutional. All the researchers in the institute are connected in some capacity with either the Hebrew University or Tel Aviv University. Its size, although small by American standards, appears to be viable; that is, adequate to provide disciplinary support for researchers in multi-disciplinary fields, adequate to provide continuing careers in research for a few who will want to, and be fit to, devote a lifetime to research. In fact, we have here an example of an institute which is bound to go through a period of very severe reappraisal, not because it will have failed to live up to its intentions, but because of the pressure to grow.

Another problem brought by expansion is the increased scale of financing. With a small number of research workers, the chances of obtaining funds for a further project when an existing one ends are good; the chances of any new project's staffing needs being met precisely by members of the existing staff are small. With a larger working number of staff, there is greater flexibility, but the search for projects becomes a continuous process, leading the institute to look around for guaranteed sources of income.

These two institutes represent a most valuable research capability of a kind which cannot be provided within universities or within government and other large organizations. Their independence is a major resource, but forces them to live dangerously, a contingency perhaps less frightening in Israel than in most other countries. Nevertheless, institutes of this kind have a constant battle with insecurity. It is a narrow path between insolvency and complacency and its navigation inevitably takes its toll. Such institutes, however, appear to possess a capacity for survival and so long as the fight for survival does not engage too great a part of the institutes' energies, they continue to innovate for substantial periods.

Israel can boast substantial in-house research facilities in government. This is typically a somewhat smaller enterprise than the research institutes just mentioned, but operated on the basis of a nucleus of permanent staff with temporary attachments for *ad hoc* projects and with contracting-out projects to university departments. One view expressed is that the use of an external institute in close contact with the ministry, works far better than having a research department inside the ministry. Such a research department, it is believed, has a very restricted appeal to the outside community, which would be unlikely to credit the research as being unbiased.

Yet another organizational device which has few parallels is the 'shared' institute: the Settlements Study Centre, concerned with the economic and social functions of the Kibbutzim and Moshavim. The Hebrew University contributed an interest in basic research in sociology; the Jewish Agency contributed its interest in practical solutions. The centre was governed by an executive board representing various ministries and this board nominated a professional and academic committee, which in turn appointed an interdisciplinary research team. This team met weekly to discuss its programme and to formulate research projects. The programme was problem-oriented; indeed, in one view the search for 'solutions' was so strong a motive as to bias the actual research. The teams were multidisciplinary – control is a joint one between academics, sponsors and users. Under these circumstances a good deal could be said to be going for the research in terms of its potential utilization, but I have the feeling that a good deal more effort was being put into the determination of projects, their carrying out and their publication, than was going into tackling utilization.

I shall discuss the way in which the research or research performance is initiated, the relationship between researcher and user, and the degree of utilization achieved.

235

Research utilization

There are some structural features of the Israeli scene germane to
any discussion of research utilization, and it would be best to mention them here. The first is the domination of the industrial scene by
Histadrut, simultaneously the powerful trade union movement and
the largest industrial employer. Including Histadrut and the various
co-operatives (among them the Kibbutzim and Moshavim), as well
as the nationalized industries, the public sector in Israel is excep-
tionally large. Thus conventional private organizations are not
likely to be major sponsors or users of research. The second is the
structure of government. Co-ordination of government departments represents a problem everywhere; in Israel the problem is
more acute than in most places because of the coalition nature of
Israeli governments. Certain departments become traditionally the
property of particular parties. In this way, departments become
party fiefs, exacerbating the problems of interdepartmental co-
ordination. For this reason a research report which would require
for its implementation the joint action of two or more departments
is liable to more than the usual degree of frustration. A third feature
is the frequent separation of sponsor from user. The Jewish Agency,
a body with no equivalent outside Israel, agencies of the US government and charitable foundations are prominent sponsors of
research projects, the implementation of whose outcome would
require government action. These three factors are, as we shall see,
highly relevant to the question of utilization.

My first example comes from the work of Dr Rosenfeld. The
research he conducts, although applied and indeed of an operational research type, originates with himself and his colleagues. To
maintain an independent stance, he sought United States grants,
avoiding asking for money from government departments. To
obtain such access as he needed to the ministry's information files
he kept the ministry's research committee informed about his
research. He was prepared to consult it about the methods, but not
about the objectives of his researches. In his view the committee did
not really understand research. Although Dr Rosenfeld might not
himself accept the description 'operational research', this would be
the most appropriate classification of his study of the relationship
between the use people made of community services and their
degree of integration into the community. In this study he showed
that people less integrated into the community made greater use of
the health services than those better integrated, who, in turn, made
more use of the adult education services. Dr Rosenfeld did not halt

his enquiries at the point where needs are demonstrated; he pursued his activities into the area of action research.

His most successful activities from the point of view of utilization led him into problems of control. In order to obtain the necessary sanction, access and co-operation, and to stimulate interest in the user, he saw the need to work with a committee of some kind. He checked the study with the committee at every point and used this opportunity to educate the committee in the processes involved in research. He used his results to formulate and carry through practical experiments. But at this point he was obliged to relinquish control. Presumably at this point this degree of success in educating the responsible committee becomes crucial. The 'exit' problem, much discussed in connection with consultancy, has not received much attention in connection with action research. Yet it is clearly a major issue, complicated by the fact that the personality needed for successful action research may be more adapted to getting teeth in than to letting go.

Within the Ministry of Social Work initiation of research was formally at the request of divisional heads. The procedure was for them to put up proposals. If these appeared reasonable, consultants were invited to discuss them and possibly to undertake the study. In practice it appeared that ideas for research would initiate with university staff seeking projects for their graduate students.

The projects carried out, or sponsored by, the ministry are often on a very small financial scale and indeed many of the more successful projects from the point of view of utilization tend to be small. Of course, small projects mostly have to tackle small and manageable issues of policy. The needed action is likely to be within the province of the sponsor, the time scale is not too long for the policy process, and the study remains the responsibility of the sponsoring administration throughout its life.

Thus, to take a very small-scale example, a study of the ministry's practice of distributing sterilized milk to recipients of social welfare benefits showed that the conditions under which the programme was conceived and the intentions behind its initiation no longer represented the current situation. The programme could be abandoned at considerable financial saving for the ministry. This is, of course, a very simple example of operation research of a kind that ideally should be part of the routine activities of an in-house unit.

Midway in scale between mini-projects and the large long-term programme we can have a group of loosely linked projects, each requiring some organizational infrastructure. An example here is of a cross-national study of juvenile delinquency. The first phase was a study of the organization of delinquent youth, which led to an action

237

research programme, which developed into a programme for training counsellors to work with street corner youth.

These examples show that within this ministry there was no lack of interest in research, nor lack of evidence in achievement. Why was there no long-term programme, no over-arching policy for the use of research? All the researches I have described relate to the evaluation of current policies and are of use in incrementalist policy-making. The projection of larger alternative futures would require more research of the basic objective variety. Is the perspective of the ministry too narrow? Would a programme of this kind imply setting up an in-house research unit? Perhaps a comparison with the Ministry of Housing, which has a strong internal unit, will help to throw light.

The unit at the Ministry of Housing was also responsible for conducting research when required on behalf of other ministries. In view of what we said before about the independent feudalities which these ministries have become, we would expect this to be more an aspiration than an actuality. The unit, under the direction of Dr Chaim Darin, had a research programme which exceeded the resources of the permanent cadre, who are therefore reinforced by MA students hired ad hoc project by project. Experts are engaged as consultants and research is commissioned in the universities. (A bulletin of its work circulates to all scientific institutes in Israel.) Thus there is no lack of relationship with the academic world outside. In these circumstances, the relationships with the internal operating divisions are crucial to the prospects of utilization.

In the light of the budget and size of staff, the research output was formidable and the projects themselves interesting. But the evidence of utilization was weak. One study showed that only 5 per cent of the population in a particular area were satisfied with their local commercial services; there were, however, still no shops there. Studies have been carried out into the use of building space; of the incentives needed to increase the dispersion of the population; of the factors influencing land values; and into the design of new houses. This last, for example, showed that people disliked houses providing direct entrance to their dining rooms; architects also regarded this as poor design, but the houses were built in that style.

Israel's programme of new town developments raised a clutch of questions accessible to research. One debate was over the question of 'inhabited' or 'uninhabited' town centres. Should these provide just commercial services and house municipal offices, or should, for example, medical services be located there? And if doctors are to live there, who else? Can you make a centre a not too artificial residential area, or should you fall back on the uninhabited, dead, centre? In neighbourhoods, where should shops, kindergartens, elementary schools and so on be located? The enquiries into these problems used sociological methods of questionnaires and interviews.

Action arising from these studies would be the responsibility of architects and planners. However, the head of the sociological section commented that architects and planners were tending now to work better than in the past with people trained in other disciplines.

This account, selective and partial though it unavoidably is, should serve to illustrate a number of more general points. First, the studies range from basic objective, through operational to action research. Second, the former sometimes required assistance from universities or research institutes; the Institute for Applied Social Research and the Hebrew University were, for example, involved in some of the new towns' studies. The action research clearly involved co-operation with other disciplines and with administrators. Third, no one should underestimate the size of the problems facing the director of an in-house research facility. He has a number of objectives to serve:

(i)   His research programme should be relevant to the needs of the organization and must be perceived as relevant by its directors.

(ii)   The topics selected for research should be accessible to the research methods and resources available to him.

(iii)   The outcome of the research should be utilizable by the organization.

(iv)   The research should be scientifically sound.

(v)   The research projects should be of sufficient scientific, as well as practical, interest to satisfy his research staff.

(vi)   The research programme should contain an adequate variety of projects to provide activity for the skills and resources of the staff.

(vii)   The programme should contain enough publishable projects to enable staff to maintain and advance their scientific reputation.

This research unit adopted a problem-solving approach with skill, but the problems they addressed themselves to were not primarily the problems of utilization of social science knowledge and research. If, in these circumstances, evidence of utilization was lacking, it does not necessarily follow that no use was made of the information provided by the research programme. In the absence of systematic arrangements for utilization, evaluation is also absent.

We can look now at the research style of the Institute of Applied

239

Social Research. The type of research that is conducted ranges from basic objective to operational research. Arising out of research oriented towards practical problems, the institute has developed new methods and techniques, in particular that of facet analysis, which are contributions to new knowledge. The examples of successful utilization would come under the general heading of operational research. One study followed a request for advice on the location of petrol stations. The institute conducted a survey of transport patterns and the reasons for people's journeys, their average length and so on, as a result of this they were able to recommend the siting of stations at particular points following certain general principles. Here the implementation was complete, as petrol stations were sited according to the recommendations of the report. Most sponsoring organizations, and most users for that matter, are perfectly satisfied to reach a decision on the basis of recommendations and advice. Few relish the notion of further expense and further activity devoted towards following up these decisions.

Equally interesting were the examples of failure to implement research. In one such study of the settlement of immigrants, the Jewish Agency which was responsible for the settlement refused to become involved in the study at all. Thus the sponsor was not the same as the ultimate user and the recommendations were therefore neglected. Another example was from the housing field: the main burdens of the recommendations presented in the research report were that there was need of more care in the finishes of houses themselves, and their associated equipment. While the basic designs of the houses were satisfactory, they were marred by a number of trivial and not very expensive omissions. For example, the biggest complaint of all that users had was the absence of clothes lines, or a place to put them. But the ministry didn't want to know and nothing was done. Ten years later the ministry was holding a competition for the best design for the placing of clothes lines.

The director here is an outstanding apostle of the policy of involving the sponsor. In accepting sponsorship, he requires the sponsor to agree to sit in on the design of the study; they receive the first draft of the report for comment and he tries, not always successfully, to ensure that the recommendations should be made jointly by the researchers and the sponsor.

A somewhat similar approach was adopted at the Institute for Behavioural Science. The device chosen is the 'inner research committee' set up by the sponsor, whose aim is to ensure the involvement of the sponsor by providing a mechanism whereby he can be consulted, and to act as a channel for information that is needed for carrying out the research. It also seeks to involve researchers in the policy arising out of the results of the research. We see this for example in the study carried out in connection with the so-called culturally disadvantaged. In the first grade at school, children of oriental immigrants tended to score something like 15 points of IQ below their sabra colleagues and with each year at school this gap tended to increase rather than diminish. From their studies the institute reckoned that the children had adequate native ability, but that their capacity for abstract reasoning had not been developed. So, parallel with their continued studies of the intellectual development of these children, the institute's research workers developed techniques for training children in abstract thinking. They discovered that, although the earlier in the life of the child such a programme is started, the better, it is still not too late at the secondary level. They therefore recommended an action programme in secondary schools. They selected the upper quartile of children of oriental immigrants in suitable areas and asked for them to be admitted to the secondary schools. The heads of the secondary schools were unwilling to accept them on the grounds that the school's academic record would deteriorate, and that they as heads would be responsible for this deterioration. The researchers therefore had to seek to apply coercion to the heads of the secondary schools, and this they did by making a nuisance of themselves in all directions, but they also agreed to accept a considerable measure of responsibility for the outcome, which in fact was highly successful. We could see this as a model for turning small-scale experiments into major ones; indeed, it is a mixture of action research and public demonstration.

But I think the most explicit analysis of the problems of obtaining implementation of research came from the Hebrew University, which conducted a course for public administration students, including a small practical exercise. Each pair of students was charged with conducting a case study of a piece of completed research and in which there were both discernible clients and a discernible group of researchers. The students would compile a dossier, which would include how the client had first formulated his problem, what had led him to turn to the particular group of researchers, how the particular research was designed, and how the client's problems had been redefined by the researchers. Next they would attempt to reconstruct a map of the degree of contact between the clients and the researchers during the conduct of the research.

A few general findings stood out from this. First, despite the way in which the results are generally presented, the initiative much more frequently came from researchers than from clients. Second, the bargain between the client and researcher is misunderstood on both sides. The client remembers the implicit promises that the researcher's acceptance of the contract makes for the producing of something that is likely to be useful to the client. The researcher, on the other hand, remembers the caveats that he himself introduced. More than that, the client remembers the way in which the problem was originally formulated by him. The researcher remembers the reformulated problems which he had thought, or at least hoped, that he had persuaded the client to accept.

It is clear that Israel just has not copied more advanced countries unthinkingly in its designs of institutions for research. Nor has it left uncovered any of the more usual solutions to this particular problem. It has indeed been relatively successful in harnessing the energies and abilities of academic researchers to practical problems of concern to the study and its execution. It has among its administrators a reasonable proportion of research-oriented and imaginative people. But the overwhelming pragmatism which so obviously characterizes the approach of management and administration in Israel, while it opens up areas of administration to the ideas arising from research, nevertheless seems at the same time to limit their potential application. A new idea which has immediate relevance may be seized on and used, or partially so. A notion of longer-term relevance may find it very hard to obtain a footing. Yet a good deal, at any rate of medium-term relevance, would seem to have a good chance. One of the immense advantages that the country possesses, though one that it would not return many thanks for, is the cementing effect of the external and ever-present threat. As a result, it is much easier for administrators and researchers to share ultimate values than it is in many more fortunately placed countries. Israel, for example, is not yet faced with the pressing demands of students that any research which might conceivably help the government and administration to carry out their policies be abandoned on the grounds that it supports a rotten system.

AUSTRALIA

Research organization

If we are to start with a couple of gross generalizations about social sciences in Australia we can say that, with the exception of operational research in the field of education, most social science research is conducted in the universities and that a very large proportion of this is the work of Ph.D students. Among these latter is a substantial number of mature people, many of them working part-time on their degrees and financing themselves. These simple facts about organization of research are related to the financing of research, and both of course largely determine the nature of the research. This picture is not too different from that in Britain a generation ago before the days of the project, the research grant and the research contract. This means also that there are hardly any research institutes either independent of, or attached to, universities. So intermingled are the organizational base, financing arrangements and the influence of the researcher that academics exert only personal influence. Their prestige in Australian society is high, but their power is low. Individuals possess reputations and sometimes formidable ones; as they are not dependent upon public money for their research they can be very outspoken; where they are so dependent, funding authorities may try to bring pressure to bear.

The prestige of politicians and civil servants is, in general, low. Quite apart from the question of the attractiveness of those careers there are after all no fewer than seven governments serving a population of 11 millions, which, combined with a predominantly non-graduate recruitment, meant that until recently there was little sympathy between civil servants and academics. The same was true of industry. Primary industry, which was Australia's main source of wealth, tends to generate neither the complex hierarchical forms of organization nor the intellectual problems which bring managers and social scientists together. Agriculture provides plenty of interest and opportunity for social research of two kinds: studies of innovation and diffusion have typically taken agricultural practices as their focus. Closely allied to this interest has been the study of rural communities; their smallness and closeness of network have made them ideal societies for scientists interested in communities. The vast size of Australia's agricultural and pastoral holdings has not been a discouragement.

A word needs to be said too about welfare. Social scientists in Australia had the same interest in welfare problems as those elsewhere. In contrast to Britain, however, welfare is still largely a matter for the individual and for private charitable organizations operating with variable amounts of government support. The audience for welfare research is less government than private bodies with small funds available for research.

While industry is developing fast in Australia, a high proportion of the leading industrial companies are branches of international corporations with headquarters in the US or Britain and whose

243

social research tends to be seen to be a headquarters' rather than a local interest.

I have already compared the situation in research with that in early post-war Britain. There are obvious differences however. To begin with, the universities take a far higher proportion of each age group than do the British and during the last decade have undergone the same kind of rate of expansion. At the time of my visit there were fifteen universities in the Commonwealth and two more planned. Thus the university base was far stronger than was post-war Britain's. But, as in the Britain of 1950, economics and psychology are the strongest of the social sciences, with the same ambiguity about whether psychology is a social science or a biological one; social anthropology has a strong tradition. Political science is weaker in Australia than it was in Britain but sociology was very weak, although new departments were developing at four universities.

The Australian universities receive substantial proportions of their finance from the state governments, and they are not too exposed to the intervention of the Commonwealth Government.

Despite the comparative lack of platforms for organized research, the contribution of those that exist is of considerable significance. First there are institutes within universities: e.g. the Institute of Economic and Social Research at Melbourne University and the Institute of Urban Studies at Canberra.

Outside the universities two institutes are of exceptional note: the Australian Council for Educational Research and the Institute of Aboriginal Studies. The ACER is, in many ways, similar to the British National Foundation for Educational Research and operates on a similar scale. Its funds are derived from governments – state and Commonwealth – and from commercial activities – sale of tests, educational materials, reading laboratories, science kits, etc. Psychology is the social science discipline which contributes most heavily and is most strongly represented among the staff. The research covers basic objective and operational research. But I learned of no action research in the school situation or in the field of educational organization.

The Institute of Aboriginal Studies in Canberra has a pure basic research remit. It was set up by the Commonwealth Government in 1969 because rapid changes among the Aboriginals threatened the preservation of their heritage of custom. The institute was charged with studying and recording as much of this heritage as possible. Some of the research is conducted by the universities with funds from the institute.

Within government itself there are in-house research agencies, of which three types are worth mention. First, within the Common-wealth Government's Ministry of Labour and National Service there is a research division with some sixty to seventy staff. Not all of its activities are research in the strict sense, some would be better described as advice or consultancy. The second type is to be found in state departments of education. Education is the responsibility of state governments rather than of the Commonwealth. In NSW, for example, there is a strong Planning and Research Division, number-ing about sixty people. By contrast, WA Education Department employs all its psychologists in counselling and guidance work with virtually no research element. The third type of in-house agency differs from that of the NSW education research branch in being an arm of the Commonwealth Government and differs from that of the MLNS in that its audience is within the same organization, instead of being largely external to it. The clearest example of this is the Research Unit of the Army Psychology Corps. Its role appears to be principally an executive one concerned with selection and career management. The research unit is closer in formation to the psychological research branch of the Army or RAF in Britain. And, like them, its work and findings are not public.

From what I have already said about the prestige of government and public service, the chances are that university staff may perceive public servants as backwoodsmen and that the latter will regard the universities as ivory towers inhabited by impractical academics who enjoy criticizing. In the main this is true. But government does feel the need for research and for information, and universities are often anxious to be instrumental in changing or influencing government policy or merely to find a good study for a research student. As government departments infrequently have money to use on small projects or research they are inclined to ask the university if 'you could put a research student on to that'. This appears somewhat mean to the academic who, nevertheless, will try to help.

In general the state and Commonwealth governments seem to employ many more psychologists in research or quasi-research roles than any other social scientists. The rest are economists and statisti-cians and a very few anthropologists. I came across no sociologists.

Industrial consultants in Australia employ a substantial number of psychologists but not in research nor, to any great extent, in research utilization.

Financing social science research

One can classify sources of finance in any number of ways. Looking

245

at the Australian scene, however, the most useful for our purpose would be:

1 Commonwealth government – (a) direct (b) indirect.
2 State governments.
3 Universities' own funds.
4 Foundations and charities – (a) domestic (b) foreign.
5 Business and industry.

Although Australia has neither a real equivalent of the British SSRC nor the substantial departmental research programmes developed by UK government departments in the last ten years, the Commonwealth Government is the largest single source of research funds. Grants are available through the Australian Universities Commission and through its Research Grants Committee. Government departments which have financed social research include, notably, the Department of Immigration.

Other direct support is given to the Australian Council for Educational Research and the Institute for Aboriginal Studies. These direct grants account for the lion's share of Commonwealth funds for social research.

Indirect support came through four channels. Research of interest to agriculture is financed through the marketing boards. Part of these funds are provided through levies on farmers, the rest from the Commonwealth. These have supported some studies in rural sociology, diffusion of innovations, and so on.

The Commonwealth Research Bank and Development Bank have also provided funds mainly, of course, for economic research.

The third indirect route is through the CSIR, the Council for Scientific and Industrial Research, modelled on Britain's former DSIR.

The fourth route is through tax concessions. Industry and commerce contribute tax free to approved research institutes or to research institutes involved in research relevant to the contributor's business. The Ministry of Labour is charged with approving research institutes in the social science field. In time this form of tax concession could have considerable impact on the development of independent research institutes.

State governments, as is the pattern in federal constitutions, are chronically hard up and may be unable to spend on 'luxuries' like sponsored social research. Nevertheless, State governments contribute in two ways to research – directly, by way of contributions to ACER, Australian Council for Educational Research, and through departmentally sponsored work. Aboriginal welfare boards, for example, tend to finance comparatively small-scale projects, mainly anthropological.

246

Support for non-governmental sources is basically of two kinds – commercial and charitable. I came across very few examples of the first. Business firms have supported studies in departments of economics; a seed firm contributed to Joan Tully's work on diffusion of agricultural practices. But the total amount contributed in this way to research is small, even compared with other sources.

Charitable support comes from domestic foundations (Myer, Potter), charitable institutions (Rotary, Espada, etc.), and foreign foundations (Ford, Nuffield). Some of the larger research activities tend to be funded in this way; the Institute of Economic and Social Research at Melbourne University draws largely on charitable funds.

The position of the SSRC is different from the other sources described. It has itself no disposable revenue to speak of. It is a private body whose principal source of income is the subscriptions of its members. It can, however, exercise some influence and when firmly resolved has proved that it can obtain finance on what is for Australia a comparatively large scale. Its most prominent success has been the funding of the Aboriginal Research Project, which we will mention later. In one way or another it has proved possible to launch substantial schemes of research but the administrative difficulties and complexities have been great and research workers have dug into their own pockets. However, the financial burden has shifted from the individual, but there is as yet neither the planners' support for research nor the expectations on the part of researchers that the governmental tap will automatically fill deserving pitchers.

Research utilization

One aspect of Australian life which excites the comment of most observers is the tendency to 'do one's own thing'. The arrangements for support of research seem to encourage this tendency. For one thing there are few programmes sponsored by government departments, for another there is no equivalent to the British SSRC trying to fill gaps in the research spectrum, and finally there are few research institutes with their own collegial research programmes. Furthermore, as so many of the people actually carrying out research are full-time and part-time Ph.D and masters' degree students, the scene is a highly fragmented one. A search for evidence of utilization is likely to throw into high relief the work done under the auspices of such bodies as the ACER and the in-house research agencies of government departments. As it is in the field of

247

education that such facilities are most prominent, it is to education that we should look first for evidence of the use of research.

The predominant tradition in educational research in Australia has been that of psychological testing. Indispensable tools though these are, they have been more useful and more used, for maintaining the status quo than for indicating directions for change. I do not wish to suggest that all educational research has been of this kind; work has been in progress at ACER in curricular development, programmes for teaching the new mathematics, and so on. But none of this has tended to be subversive of the dominant tendencies in Australian education. Research conducted on a more freelance basis by students in university departments of education encounters certain hazards. In the first place such students tend to represent an unwelcome instrusion into the administrators' world. In the second place unwelcome findings are likely to encounter attempts to get them modified or suppressed. Again I was told of pressure brought by a state department of education to suppress public comment. The reader in the sociology of education in one university was conducting a study of the influences affecting schoolchildren's choice of jobs. In evaluating the extent of teachers' influence he noted that this was lower than it might have been because of their rapid turnover in certain schools. Graphically, and possibly gratuitously, he described their role as that of 'curriculum minders'. An overt attempt followed by the state director of education to obtain a withdrawal and guarantees that this kind of comment would not be repeated. This story is not repeated here in order to point the finger at the perpetrator of a coercive attempt, but to illustrate the attitude of some of the administrators through whose hands pass the outcome of research, whether conducted internally or outside.

I found it very difficult to obtain evidence of the utilization even of in-house research in education. That is not to say that it does not occur, but that as it is assumed that it will happen more or less automatically, there is no special watch kept on the progress of research into action. Obviously, some research *is* used automatically as it is a part of an administrative activity; for example, in setting norms for intelligence tests in specific school populations. The question is whether this is 'research', or whether it is a professional administrative activity. Indeed this example points one of the problems of an operational research department: that part of its activity which consists of rendering a professional service has a built-in system of use. It is therefore assumed that there is no problem of use, and the non-use of the more basic research is concealed. It is in fact a serious problem. What usually happens is this. The people employed in rendering professional services are in demand. But their work becomes more and more routine and less innovative or research-oriented. But it is their work that becomes the chief justification for the activity as a whole. And it tends to acquire first claim on the resources of time, money and materials at the department's disposal. Whatever else is put aside for the time being, this must continue. The longer-term, more basic problems must wait. Good, young, research-oriented staff tend to leave – if they can get out in time before they are sucked into the professional role and become gradually less attractive outside. The director may like to shed some of the more administrative professional work, but dare not.

Some encouragement is given to the universities' departments of education; students are given access to schools which the committee approves. But as one director put it, 'The pious hope is that the government will be able to use the result, but in fact they are just put in the library. Sometimes the bibliographies are useful.'

In the Educational Guidance Service, operational research and basic objective research are conducted. In the eyes of the service it is the operational research which is perceived as 'grass-roots' studies rather than the basic objective variety. Thus gathering basic data on the educational needs of the children in the area to which the researcher is assigned is perceived as 'grass-roots', while studies in the field of guidance generally (in our terms, basic objective research) is seen as more remote. The 'needs' include such factors as the requirements in particular areas for remedial reading facilities or the problems in rural areas of finding job opportunities for girls. Researchers are involved to some extent in action arising from their research. Curricular research is the most open to this. Researchers are fully involved in curricular planning in primary schools; in secondary schools, however, they run into the vested interests of 'subject' teachers.

In general, we find here that the diffusion of results into action is slow and chancy and the problems of evaluation of research are great.

Whether people teaching in schools are aware of the research being done at all depends almost entirely on whether they or their schools have been involved in a recent study. This is the case whether the research is conducted by students from the local university's department of education, or by the state's education services, or by the ACER, although news-sheets, reports, pamphlets and lists of research projects are all published. There is no doubt of the quantity and organization of educational research in Australia; assessing its impact is daunting, particularly in view of the comments about evaluation that I have described.

Returning to the Aboriginal Research Project, the outcome of that survey had significance for the policy of the State Aboriginal Welfare boards. It turns out that they had no notion of the numbers of people for whom they were in some way responsible – for example, in Brisbane, it was believed that there was a total of 400 Aboriginals; the survey disclosed 704 families.

But the willingness of the states to take note of research, particularly that of anthropologists, varies widely. In one state, anthropological research was almost totally unwelcome; the native administrator 'knew what the Abos want' and did not want evidence to prove him wrong. In others, the anthropologist's understanding of tribal practices has been valuable, and gratefully utilized. One Aboriginal tribe, recently arrived in a new area, caused anxiety through the number of children brought *in extremis* to the health centre. It appeared that they were starving. Anthropological advice was sought and investigation showed that the tribe, having moved, was for a month under a taboo which prohibited hunting. Action immediately followed to provide food for the tribe during this period of self-enforced abstinence.

Although the total problem is small, the Aboriginal question looms large in social research in Australia for three reasons: the first is its obvious attraction to anthropologists; the second is the real difficulty of coming to terms with a proportion of the population which cannot be integrated or assimilated; the third is the bad conscience of Australians for their earlier treatment of the Aboriginals.

Industry

There is little to say about Australian industry. On the whole Australian industry expects to use research that is done in other countries. Yet management consultancy firms in Australia appear to use psychologists to a greater degree than in Britain. Many have psychologists in very high posts indeed. They reflect the viewpoint of Australian industry and a shrewd commercial assessment of the acceptability to it of social science research. Yet it may be that if you rely on consultants as a diffusion channel for the results of research, you may find that it is a channel with long delays built in. Furthermore, it is by no means certain that consultants can, or persuade industry that they should, undertake the analysis needed to obtain utilization of research carried out elsewhere.

What will happen in Australia in the future? It seems a country that cannot help developing. Its natural resources are enormous and not only unrealized but unestimated. Some day, and perhaps soon, it will become an innovating country. But one cannot say that the social sciences are yet poised to play a very effective part or to lead to social innovations.

Postscript

This passage was written some years ago. Most of it could be substantiated today. But the developments at the Australian National University leading to the establishment of a Centre for Continuing Education attracted Fred Emery back from the Tavistock Institute and a strong reputation in Europe. Stimulated by a mixture of anxiety about productivity and a sense that the world was changing in unpredictable ways, firms in several cities in Australia from S. Australia to Queensland were prepared to consider introducing new forms of organization, emphasizing the 'Quality of Working Life'. Emery's response was one likely to be especially suited to the temper of Australian society. Eschewing complex experimental designs and theoretical indoctrination he introduced a 'deep slice' technique involving employees at all organizational levels in immediate diagnosis and redesign. While few substantive reports of the outcomes have yet appeared, the technique has been copied in Europe. The centre has turned its attention to the organization of service, governmental and educational institutions, some of which offer greater leverage than industry on the future of Australian society. Emery has also written scenarios for the future of Australian society intended to be guides to policy for Qantas Airways and the television networks. His approach is grounded in fundamental social science principles worked through the traditional 'arenas' of the disciplines without regard to their traditional boundaries, giving a new meaning to the word 'interdisciplinary'.

Chapter 12
Relations between the Social Sciences and the Federal Government in USA

In this third part of our international look at the social sciences we turn to America. This is in no way a survey of the facilities in the United States, but rather an attempt to draw together some of the strands of three detailed reports about the US social sciences scene. These reports are:

Gene M. Lyons, *The Uneasy Partnership: Social Science and the Federal Government in the Twentieth Century*, Russell Sage Foundation, New York, 1969.

Report of the Special Commission on the Social Sciences of the National Science Board, *Knowledge into Action: Improving the Nation's Use of the Social Sciences*, National Science Foundation, Washington, 1969.

Report by the Behavioral and Social Sciences Survey Committee, under the auspices of the National Academy of Sciences/Social Science Research Council, *The Behavioral and Social Sciences: Outlook and Needs*, National Academy of Sciences, Washington, 1969.

The discontents of American social scientists make fascinating reading, as do their hopes and aspirations. And these are paraded before us in a steady stream. During 1969 and 1970 we had *The Behavioral Sciences and the Federal Government* (the 'Young' Report), a report by the Advisory Committee on Government Programs in the Behavioral Sciences of the National Research Council, *The Behavioral and Social Sciences: Outlook and Needs* (the BASS Report), from the Behavioral and Social Sciences Survey Committee under the auspices of COSPUP (the Committee on Science and Public Policy) of the National Academy of Sciences and the Committee on Problems and Policy of the Social Science Research Council, *Knowledge into Action* (the 'Brim' Report), a report of the Special Commission on the Social Sciences of the National Science Board. We also had in 1967, Harold Orlans's four-volume staff study (US House of Representatives, 1967) for the Research and Technical Programs Subcommittee, Committee on Government Operations of the House of Representatives, not to mention the Report of the Committee on Government Operations of the Senate, *Establishment of a National Foundation for the Social Sciences*. Finally, the historical dimension is provided by Gene Lyons's account of *The Uneasy Partnership: Social Science and the Federal Government in the Twentieth Century.*

Is this all a neurotic parade of symptoms by an overfed patient? Or is it part of the restless activity which makes America look to the foreigner as if it is always pulling up its roots to see how they are growing? Or are we witnessing a climacteric in the relationship between social science and not only the federal government but society as a whole? The questions remain, but the way it looks to the social scientist is clearer. The key word of course is pluralism. Plural are the disciplines, plural are the institutions, universities, research institutes where researches are carried on, plural are the sources of support. And plural also are the points of leverage for the exercise of power and influence. These are just the conditions under which anything that could be described as a 'policy' for the social sciences looks least attractive. Without destroying the plurality of sources of money and power, having a policy could only mean having a plan for co-ordination. And co-ordination has an ominous ring. Co-ordination can lead to control; it certainly leads to the temptation to try.

How does it all look to the social scientists? They, the vocal ones at any rate, are mainly in the universities and those of the highest status occupy full-time faculty appointments. The more senior among them have seen a rapid and continuous increase in the part played by the federal government in providing funds for research and grants for graduate students. At some date in the 1950s the government became the greatest single source of funds and now account for about half of the total, which must be in the region of a billion dollars. Thus the federal dollar has become the main prop of research in the social sciences. But this means that unless the federal government can be persuaded to make available a considerable proportion of its support in the form of comparatively 'free' money for 'basic' research, the research priorities will be settled not by academics, but by customers. Thus two strategies present themselves to the social science community: the federal government

253

must be pressed to make more money available for pure research and the customers must be educated to appreciate the value to them of long-term research with a basic content. Academic values ensure that the greatest prestige comes from free, basic research, and there is an implicit continuum of 'hardness' of funds. The hardest funds of all are those from your own institution – 'free' research funds; the softest are those from some section of industry and from government agencies with an 'applied' remit. Thus NSF support is, or was, 'harder' than that from NASA or OEO or HEW or Defense.

Now that the government has become the universal provider, the importance to the social scientist of the guidance it gets is greatly increased. It must not only be helped to select the best possible advice, it must also be advised on the areas which are most likely to yield to research and the most profitable means of associating research with action. This last presents a pretty paradox. The use of research in action implies planning. Research takes time. If it is to be directed towards the solution or alleviation of problems, the problems themselves must be foreseen or at least identified before action becomes imperative. Yet the history of the utilization of social research is one of action-in-a-crisis. The great advances in the use of social research and its association with government have been in response either to war emergencies or to peacetime catastrophies, like the slump and the riots in the cities.

Indeed, one cannot help being struck in reading the reports and Lyons's book of the extent to which the successes in applying the social sciences have been in the military field. The urgency of military demand has indeed frequently pushed practice ahead of theory. If the social scientists work alongside or under the command of the defence services then the sponsor of the research is also its user and the continuity of research, utilization and follow-up can be maintained.

The institutional framework which has evolved in America for the prosecution of research is extremely effective for that purpose, and of course for obtaining the necessary resources. It has not arisen in response to pressure to implement the findings of research and it is not particularly well designed for that purpose. Underlying the realization expressed in the reports, that utilization of research is far weaker than the research itself, is an awareness less directly expressed that the institutional base is inadequate. One suggestion in the BASS Report is the development of graduate schools of applied behavioral science in the universities, but outside the established disciplines, so their research would be directed towards the solution of persistent social problems. The NAS (Young) Report (p. 4) identifies the conditions for effective use of the behavioral sciences in government as:

> (1) an understanding by top administrators of the nature of the behavioral sciences and their relevance to the policies and programs for which they are responsible; (2) a professional environment to attract behavioral scientists into government and to provide incentives and opportunities for their scientific development; and (3) a strategy for research to give cohesion and purpose to behavioral science activities carried on by a department or agency and to relate them to policy processes and program operations.

and seeks to strengthen the institutional base by co-opting professionals into government service but also suggests (p. 16) a new research institute to:

> ... serve as a center for continuing interchange between government policy-makers and scientists, and to provide a forum in the nation's capital for the full exploration of the growth and application of knowledge from all the sciences to the major issues of the society.

The National Science Board Report proposes the foundation of new 'social problem research institutes', in which social problem areas would be studied by teams of specialists from the social sciences and other sciences and professions (including engineering). Each institute would develop close relationships with the agencies of government and public and other organizations with responsibility for action. By concentrating on a relatively narrow problem area with identifiable user organizations to relate to, and by operating on a multidisciplinary basis, these institutes would both break with the traditional dominance of the disciplinary-oriented approach and with the diffuse spread of interest over many problem areas. The institutes would not however be yoked too closely to a single sponsor and would receive funds through endowments, research contracts and grants.

Lyons does not offer his own recipe but underlines (p. 309) the problem none of the committees apparently wished to call attention to.

> The quest for more effective relations between social science research and government policies and programs does not, however, begin with a strong national consensus about either

the goals of government or the predictive or analytic capacity of social science. There is often bitter disagreement over the goals of public policy, the increased reliance on 'experts' (of any kind), and the limits of objectivity in dealing with social problems: and there is an increased sense of alienation in many groups in the country from the centers of decision-making ruling their lives. In this situation, a deep desire for rationality is mixed with uneasy suspicions about the nature of science and the aims of political power.

Neither new institutions nor new value systems by themselves will turn the trick; the search for new value systems to underpin effective government–social science interaction will, however, make apparent the need for new institutions to embody them when formed.

In America social scientists have another federal partner for their dialogue – the Congress. And, indeed, government expenditure on a policy for social science owes much to the promptings of congressional committees.

But it has not been entirely over the prostrate forms of congressmen that the social sciences have been moving towards a greater involvement with government and with policy-making. And the movement has been impressive, if the results have not. PPBS, technological forecasting, social indicators are among the new techniques which have come into prominence, usually promising more than they can deliver. The machinery of government is undergoing, and has to undergo, change to accommodate itself, not only to new demands, but also to the new techniques for assessing and meeting them. The machinery for enabling the social science community to play its part is undergoing, and has to undergo, change likewise. These reports are an impressive record of the social science community communing with itself and with those who will overhear about the ways in which this can be done. So far consensus is confined to the moderately non-controversial.

What the reports do not say

There are also points and issues which no one discusses but which everyone knows. They may not be controversial, but to mention them may be tendentious. Let me instance the problem of the ideology of the social scientist.

There are surely three levels at which ideology and research interpenetrate one another; or if you prefer, three interfaces between ideology and research. The first is, perhaps, the most elusive. The received framework of knowledge and concepts binds the social scientist as the Newtonian framework of knowledge and concepts bound the prerelativistic physicist. It sets the pattern in which social facts are perceived and social data sought. It is simply true that social scientists brought up and educated in the Soviet Union see social reality through a different set of perspectives from those of their opposite number in the United States of America. In this sense an ideology-free social science for which we all truly strive is often not attainable; the social scientist like everyone else is a creature of his time and place.

The second interface is that between ideology and method. The current striving after a value-free 'scientific' social science is itself not without ideological consequence. The points I wish to stress here are, first, that the social scientist's methodology is derived from the ideology of his society and may in fact help to reinforce it; second, that his methodology of choice is also derived from a scientific value system and may produce results which look more scientific than they are, and are more easily accepted than they deserve. The ideological framework is not unaffected by the knowledge fed back by the scientist's researches. In particular, the revelations provided by the highly original thinker may considerably modify the prevailing ideology, usually after considerable delay.

The third interface is the transition from knowledge to decision, involving judgements of value. Now unfortunately it is simply not the case that the scientist takes off one hat and puts on another, making clear his action in doing so. When a social scientist approaches a 'practical' problem, he perceives the problem and reformulates it in terms of his theoretical approach. He then seeks data which are not necessarily the same as the data which would be sought by a social scientist who did not share his theoretical orientation. Thus the very selection of the kind of information the social scientist looks for is at least partly determined by his theoretical viewpoint with its ideological components. Need we be surprised that, for example, in Britain sociologists with a politically left orientation provide through their researches data which favour non-selective, non-streamed education, while those with a rightish slant tend to provide data which suggest the reverse? Neither is consciously distorting the evidence. Out of all the possible things you might look for, you choose what to you seems most important – you cannot look for everything. This is not distortion. The distortion comes in a failure to recognize that this is what you are doing.

The involvement becomes much greater when we enter the field of action research. Here the experimental action is both part of the

257

'research' and derived explicitly from some value. We know what goal we want to obtain, whether it may be more participation, higher profits or whatever. Significantly, neither *The Uneasy Partnership* nor the BASS Report has anything to say about action research. *Knowledge into Action* has one guarded passage on page 75.

The growth of action research, particularly in the context of community action, threatens to split some portions of academic society into two camps. The young, enthusiastic, ideologically committed social scientist is seen as a threat to the scientific value culture which is presented throughout these reports in measured, moderate tones. That this problem gets no mention is doubtless prudent; we must hope that the distinguished scientists were not unaware of it.

An international perspective

No people have done more to help their opposite numbers in other countries than the American social scientists. In the fashionable hullabaloo about 'cultural colonialism' fostered by the Camelot fiasco and other clumsy operations, we are in danger of forgetting what we owe to the generosity of American foundations and universities and to the far-sighted activities of agencies of the US Government, such as the Office of Naval Research, which found ways of supporting basic research in Europe when other funds were scarce. American leadership has been enormously stimulating in all the social sciences. But the traffic has not been all one way and intellectual debts are in a sense never paid.

Other countries have been experimenting with modes of sponsorship of the social sciences and with the design and creation of institutions for research and for utilization of research. Some foreign countries demonstrate how research, having fled the universities, has been gathered under the wing of government scientific institutions. Still more are experiencing the strain on applied and sponsored research in universities inspired by the hostility of students. Yet others are developing a closer partnership between government and social science than exists in the US.

The Brim Report has virtually nothing to say about foreign models for advancing the utilization of social science. The BASS Report has a chapter on worldwide development and concludes:

... international collaboration can be an effective and
acceptable way of encouraging the development of the

behavioral and social sciences outside the United States while, at the same time, securing benefits to our domestic enterprises in these fields.

No doubt the climate in the United States is not particularly favourable for a forthright internationalism, but even so I should have expected a less introverted approach. The social problems that are faced within the United States are better understood in their worldwide context; the social sciences themselves are essentially universal. To the extent that they are not, to the extent that there is an American sociology or an American economics, they lack a dimension whose absence may fault them severely, and may treat as constants, variables whose range of variation within one society, even one so large as the United States, may be small.

Why then have these reports, particularly the Brim Report, said so little about the way social science is organized and utilized in other countries? I believe this is partly because of a feeling of superiority that American social scientists have little to learn from the rest of the world; partly a fear that America in its present introspective mood is suspicious of, and resentful of, any suggestion of social scientists' foreign entanglements. There is also the divergence in world views between American social scientists in this respect, representative of the American world view, and that of social scientists in many other parts of the world as to the essentially solvable nature of problems. The basic optimism of the American social scientist is in stark contrast to the pessimism of his Latin American neighbour and to the involutional perspective of social scientists in continental Europe. American social scientists still believe that problems made by man can be solved by man, if not solved, at least greatly ameliorated. Partly again I suspect it is because of a lack of published material about the utilization of social sciences in other countries. If you set out to collect published information about organization and utilization of social research you will be hard put to find half as much from the rest of the world as from the United States itself. But social scientists should be watching with interest, and monitoring with care, the experiences of such bodies as the Social Science Research Council in Britain in holding a balance between basic and policy-oriented research, and in treading a path between detachment from government programmes and involvement in public political issues.

Suppose that all the excellent recommendations in these reports were to be implemented, what would be the outcome? There would be even more plurality in the source of funds. There would, of course, be more funds too. More people in government would be acquainted with the social sciences. More social scientists would be trained for policy-oriented research and more would be prepared for interventionist roles. More and better social indicators would be devised. More and more social scientists would spend more and more of their time helping government agencies to formulate research programmes and to allocate their research funds. More ambitious schemes would certainly emerge; hopefully there would be no Camelots among them. But the scientific value system would remain. The universities would still be places where research for the sake of 'science' had more prestige than research for use. The centre of gravity of research would possibly move towards professional schools and applied research institutes. The behavioral sciences would be geared for action certainly, but doubtfully for inspired action.

The flurry of reports which brought the 1960s to a close appeared to end the period of introspection of social science in the United States. One can only speculate as to why.

No doubt the university student riots encouraged social scientists to keep their heads down; in any case they gave them other matters to think about. Faith in the power of rationally based knowledge and the potential of the social sciences to solve social problems diminished. Reformers today are more interested in law than in sociology, an outcome of the staggering series of Supreme Court decisions in the last decade.

Sponsorship of social science research has levelled off and even declined in some areas. And social scientists acquired a new point of leverage on federal policy, the Assembly of Behavioral Sciences in the National Academy of Sciences. Symbolically this was the first of the assemblies to be established, a high-water mark in the prestige of social science in America.

Part II

The Social Sciences in Context

Section I
Industry

Chapter 13
The Utilization of Social Science Research in Industry

Social scientists have long been interested in industry as an *object* of study. Industry has been the main agent of the immense changes which have transformed society in all its aspects in the last two centuries. As the leading institution in society, it has set the pattern for the development of virtually all other institutions. Our modern family structure has emerged to meet industry's needs of people in large complexes detached from their homes, and city patterns, transport systems, governmental functions, and educational institutions have to a greater or lesser extent been tailored to industry's needs. And industry in turn has provided the capstone without which the structure is left not only incomplete but meaningless. A community whose industry declines or disappears is a sorry community indeed. In this massive change the primary interest of most social scientists has been in industry as a phenomenon, an institution, a system. And their concern is to describe, to discern relationships, and to construct descriptive and analytical theories.

The interest of industry in the social sciences is recent, and partly responds to developments in the social sciences. It is also, however, a result of industry's growing concern with the outcome of the changes which it has itself been foremost in bringing about. Its own success has provided it with less stable and more rapidly changing markets, with increasingly complex and expensive technologies, and with an accelerating speed of communication.

For industry, this has set new problems of forecasting and assessing market trends, of predicting long-term technological and social changes, of increased reliance on the interlocking skills and motivations of its employees, and of increased vulnerability to industrial action. Social scientists' interest in the problems of the company and its origins began with the recognition that 'scientific management' failed to deliver the goods when it demanded extensive change in habits, outlook, and behaviour. Selection and training of workers became more pressing with advancing technology; production-line techniques encountered unexpected organizational diseconomies; and traditional economic doctrine failed to allow for the imperfections of the markets, not least the labour market.

But gradually the work of social scientists has penetrated industry, and industry uses directly, or at one remove, many procedures, practices, and ideas, deriving from the social sciences – uses, or in some respects misuses.

For instance, much of existing personnel practice embodies the outcome of work by social scientists, ranging from the choice of colours for the walls of washrooms to schemes for management development; from the choice of wage systems to schemes for organizational development; from the use of market research to the adoption of employee-attitude surveys. But the professional role of today's personnel managers was only possible through a series of closely interrelated changes:

1 legal – placing new responsibilities on industrial management;
2 social – arousing new expectations from employees of the kind of treatment they would receive;
3 economic – making workers comparatively expensive;
4 educational – changing the skills, attainments, outlook of entrants to industry;
5 technological – changing the pattern of skills and activities for which people were needed;
6 ideological – changing social values; and
7 changes in social science knowledge, providing new theories, concepts and factual data.

The social sciences have played a significant part in providing the ideological basis on which personnel management has uneasily rested. If psychology has been more useful in putting techniques at the disposal of the personnel man, it is social psychology which has opened up the area of organizational development and organizational design, career planning and managerial assessment. Manpower planning, an even more amorphous concept than most, is appropriately interdisciplinary. But the most interdisciplinary of all, and the subject most potentially fruitful today for the personnel manager, goes by the title of 'organizational behaviour'. In its attempts to explore the interface between the organization and its environment, including the interorganizational interfaces, it is tackling problems which will become more and more salient for senior management.

Another multidisciplinary area that has contributed much useful research to industry is that of ergonomics. One of its most important contributions has been in its stressing of the importance of studying the man–machine system as a whole, although man–machine system itself is not the full story – we must also include the setting with which it is in continuous interaction. An example of the importance of this can be seen in the study of accidents. Different social groups differ not only in the subjective probability which their members will assign to a given event, but also in the degree to which they are accustomed to accepting responsibility. A further difference between social groups is in their readiness to accept risks. In particular, toleration of the danger of an accident will be high if taking care conflicts with some other value which is strongly held. Among service pilots adherence to certain safety regulations tends to conflict with other cherished values (e.g. the pilot as a 'press-on type'). The belief that 'good' flying involved showing control of their aircraft, and therefore their ability to cut the margin of safety in landing prescribed by regulations, led even average pilots to errors in landing and sometimes to accidents (Paterson, 1955).

Hence we see that in the field of safety design the ergonomist cannot afford to ignore the values of the working group.

The uses of social science research

Many mistakes in applying social science knowledge derive from unsound models or assumptions of the ways in which the social sciences can be applied. The most persuasive and pernicious is derived from models of the way in which the physical sciences are 'applied'. This depicts a straight-line process – research to development to production to marketing – which all industrialists now recognize to be false. But the notion persists that somehow social scientists make 'discoveries', and that these can be developed into packages from which a firm can select one appropriate to its needs. If we are to have successful use of social science research we need a more sophisticated approach than this.

There are at least three ways in which the social sciences are used by industry. At the most easily recognized level – it can be called 'instrumental' – the social sciences have provided *techniques* which industry can adopt for dealing with specific problems or situations. Secondly, the social sciences can provide *models* of the system which enable managers accurately to define the problem. At a third level social sciences can provide *concepts* – generalized notions with a high explanatory value. Looking first at techniques, among the most obvious of these are: sample surveys for market research, attitude surveys, selections and aptitude tests, performance assessment schemes, incentive schemes, training schemes and 'organizational development' and productivity bargaining packages. All of these techniques are in daily use and arise from the work of social scientists; nearly all of them require a minimum of social science knowledge and expertise for design, operation and interpretation. But there is no mystery about them, and if the right technique is selected and properly used the benefits can be forecast, and they will be apparent, even if not always long-lasting. The trick comes in the decision that the problem we face or the need we have is of a kind for which this particular technique is appropriate. False definition of a problem, like faulty medical diagnosis, leads to selection of the wrong technique, the wrong course of treatment, and the results may be positively harmful. Indeed, many organizations use 'packages' in the same way that many sufferers use patent medicines, and like patent medicines, they have the tendency to suppress symptoms, transferring the impact to some other problem area.

Why have so many organizations taken to 'behavioural science packages'? When scientific knowledge is made available to organizations, it is usually in the form of technology. This has led people to assume that knowledge derived from the social sciences can take the same form. And this has encouraged the premature wrapping of scientific concepts into technological packages that are not only of limited value in themselves but are regarded as alternatives to the detailed analysis that our social science knowledge can, and should, provide.

There is thus a gap between the kind of research that increases our knowledge of organizations and gives us the analytical tools for understanding what any particular organization is about and the kind of 'behavioural science' that organizations commonly use. Table 7, developed by Lawrence and Lorsch (1967) shows a list of packages developed over the past fifty years. These have derived from various perspectives: their impact on organizations needs to be thoroughly understood – as Lawrence and Lorsch point out, the odd-numbered packages are all designed to tighten organizations and the even-numbered to loosen them.

If the diagnosis or definition of a company's problem or need is to be useful, a correct, or at least an adequate model of the situation must first be adopted; and this brings us to the second level at which the social sciences are utilizable. Social science can describe the activities of a working organization, for example, in

TABLE 7 *Social science 'packages'*

1 PERT and critical path systems
2 Business gaming
3 Value analysis
4 Sensitivity or T-group laboratories
5 Long-range planning techniques
6 Decentralization, profit-centre management, unit management
7 System design techniques
8 Creativity training – brainstorming or synectics
9 Operations research, with linear programming, dynamic programming, etc.
10 Management grid training
11 Cost-effectiveness analysis
12 Scanlon plan and other profit-sharing techniques
13 Decision theory – decision trees, allocation models, etc.
14 Motivation laboratories
15 Human factors engineering

terms of roles rather than of individuals and so enable us to see beyond the apparent reasons for people's actions, including our own, and to take a less egocentric view of the situation. Or it may describe the actual operations of a company in such a way as to show that the allocation of tasks or functions to component units fails to match the changing realities of the situation and for this reason leads to conflict and delay. In short, social science can provide us with models of the system we are operating which enable us accurately to define our problem.

At a third level, the social sciences can provide concepts. Any model of the operation of a system is, in effect, a linked set of concepts whose meaning must be understood if they are to be used effectively. Concepts both liberate and enslave. They liberate by enabling us to get away from the concrete details and so to respond to an event, not as something unique but as a member of a class of events of which something is known. They enslave if they lead us to classify according to a pre-set scheme which may force us to adopt an approach, a mode of thought or analysis which is inappropriate to our situation. If we half understand we may be enslaved. Moreover, there is a complicated relationship linking facts with concepts, both with theories and all three with ideologies – see Figure 3.

Ideologies are at the top because their influence is the greatest. If

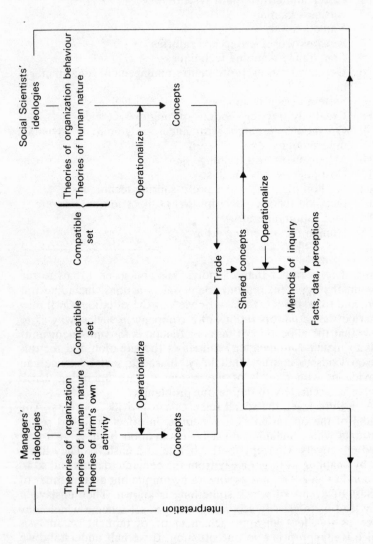

Figure 3   How managers and social scientists trade concepts

you know my ideology, you will be able to predict to a fair extent the theories I will have about a number of issues.

During recent years, our studies in organizations have made us increasingly aware of the influence of prevailing management ideologies on the possibilities of productive relationships between managers and social scientists. A change is clearly discernible: ideologies built around managerial prerogatives are yielding to ideologies that favour employee participation. The latter are much more in harmony with the current social ethos; unfortunately, they provide almost unlimited possibilities for self-deception.

It should, in principle, be no part of the task of the social scientist to alter a management's ideology, to tackle it head on, so to speak. This is not at all the same thing as claiming an 'objective', ethically neutral stance for social science. It is just the wrong level of abstraction for a confrontation.

Managers have theories of organization, theories of human nature, and theories to describe their firm's activities. Theories of this variety in most cases form a compatible set, an ideology. One such set is that immortalized by McGregor (1960) as Theory X; another, of course, is Theory Y. Thus, if you hold a theory of organization that emphasizes the functions of control, you probably also have a theory about human nature that implies that people need controlling. You probably also have a theory that your firm has a clear mandate from its shareholders. Since these theories are compatible with an ideology that exalts the managerial prerogative, I would expect you to subscribe to that, too. On the other hand, if you stressed in your theory of organization the co-operative harnessing of diverse activities and simultaneously have a theory of human nature that emphasizes man's need to enjoy joint activity with others and a theory about your firm as exercising social responsibility, I would be surprised if you failed to subscribe to an ideology of participation.

In practice, the two different managers we have been caricaturing – taking a lead from McGregor, we will call the former Manager X and the latter Manager Y – would have available different sets of concepts for interpreting reality as well as different sets of values for determining what aspects of reality were important. These concepts serve to operationalize the theories that each manager possesses and bring them to bear on experience.

It is fairly typical for the board of a large corporation to spend considerable time in producing a statement which will have undergone any number of re-writes and which purports to show the 'philosophy of management'. These are typically very different from the documents which would have been produced fifty or twenty years ago. I quote from one which has been published, concentrating in this extract (Hill, 1971) on some of the passages concerning the social responsibility and human resources:

Statement of objectives and management philosophy

1 *Primary objective*. The company is primarily concerned to maximise its contribution to the long-term profitability of the Group insofar as this arises from the efficiency with which it uses the Group's resources of men, money and material.

The resources to which it has legal rights of privileged access are nonetheless part of the total resources of society as a whole and are, in this sense, social resources; the company believes that they must be protected, developed and managed as such. It furthermore believes that its use of these resources must be such as to contribute to meeting society's requirements for products and services.

2 *Specific objectives*. Implicit in the fact that the company's resources are part of the total resources of society, are the following additional specific objectives:

(iv) Creating conditions in which employees at all levels will be encouraged and enabled to develop and to realise their potentialities while contributing towards the company's objectives.

(v) Carrying out its productive and other operations in such a way as to safeguard the health and safety of its employees and the public.

(vi) Seeking to reduce any interference that may be caused by its activities to the amenities of the community.

3 *The principle of joint-optimisation as a guide to implementation*. The company must manage both a social system, of people and their organization, and a technical system, of physical equipment and resources. Optimisation of its overall operations can be achieved only by jointly optimising the operation of these two systems; attempts to optimise the two independently of each other, or undue emphasis upon one of them at the expense or the neglect of the other, must fail to achieve optimization for the company as a whole.

The statement was evolved by a firm planning a new facility which it wanted to be designed along sociotechnical lines. It contained the usual phrases about human resources. When the facility was to open, two old plants in other locations were to be phased out. What about the employees? Would they be invited, encouraged, helped to move to the new plant if they wished? No, because they would be accustomed to old ways and might make the adoption of new ways more difficult. Then what did the phrases about human resources mean? Did they apply only to those who joined the firm after a certain date? How credible would they sound to new employees who knew what the firm had done with those who had served it for many years? The policy was recognized to be in conflict with the philosophy. The policy was altered; the philosophy had stood its first test. It had also undergone the first interpretation. As in the law, so is its meaning elucidated by case judgements.

Now let us turn to the social scientist with his ideologies, his theories of organizational behaviour and of human nature, and the concepts that he uses to interpret what he sees. Some of these concepts are familiar to managers and some tend to be less familiar. For example, the concept of system is used by the manager in a variety of contexts. A similar concept leads the social scientist to expect certain relationships among the departments or subsystems that he observes, and indeed to identify the boundaries of subsystems by observing these relationships. The notion of the 'open' system helps the social scientist to understand the organization as a system in dynamic equilibrium with its environment, responding to environmental change in predictable ways. The idea of a 'sociotechnical system' has exposed the strains on the interactions and communications of people in the firm (the social system), which result from the jobs being designed solely on technical considerations. To the manager, this concept has brought a realization that he has a choice among technological designs and that the best choice is one that jointly optimizes both the social and the technical systems of his organization.

To the social scientist the concept of an organic-mechanistic continuum has provided a way of analysing the effective organization structure from the actual patterns of communications: a predominantly vertical flow of communications (up and down the command ladder) representing a mechanistic functioning suitable for settled environments and static technologies, a predominantly horizontal flow representing an organic functioning suitable for turbulent environments and changing technologies. Too often managers perceive 'organic' as 'good', 'mechanistic' as 'bad' without regard to the context, but where they successfully understand the concept they can see whether they and their organizations are flexible enough to cope with change and with the anxieties that accompany dispersed decision-making.

Another concept that is becoming better known to managers is Goldthorpe and Lockwood's typology of calculative, bureaucratic, and solidaristic orientations to work (Goldthorpe *et al*., 1968). Again, the fact that workers bring different expectations to their working life enables the social scientist to understand some aspects of behaviour at work in terms of the family and community pressures on the worker. For the manager, the distinctions among the 'orientations' indicate that a payment system that suits a 'calculative' worker whose involvement with the firm is that of economic man may fail to motivate a 'solidaristic' worker to whom work is a way of life and may alarm the worker whose involvement is 'bureaucratic', to whom the firm represents a lifetime career.

Another example is the work of Perrow, who relates the characteristics of an organization to fundamental characteristics of its technology. He employs a simple 2 × 2 schema of 'technology variables'. Are there many 'exceptions' or few? Is the 'search' procedure for dealing with exceptions analysable or not? From this simple pattern he constructs the characterization of a firm's technology shown in Figure 4:

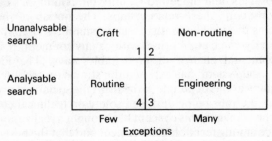

Figure 4   Types of technology

In any activity in an organization, the worker or supervisor or manager receives a great many signals, items of information, stimuli, that require him to respond. Usually he knows from experience what to do, but sometimes something occurs for which he has no ready-made or programmed response. This may be a rare event – in our figure, 'few exceptions' – or comparatively frequent – 'many exceptions'. If he is engaged in production, the source of stimuli may be his raw material. Some raw material is highly consistent (few exceptions), some very variable (many exceptions).

The other dimension, 'Search', concerns the response. When faced with the problem of how to deal with the exception, he may be able to proceed systematically through a programme. This may include consulting a manual or following a 'drill' or carrying out a carefully learned sequence of actions. His 'search' procedure is analysable and can be reduced to a drill if this has not already been done. On the other hand, the stimulus presented by the exception may be quite unfamiliar – each exception is new and different from previous ones. In that case our operator is thrown back on problem-solving skills, on his unanalysable experience, skills, knack, or intuition. His search procedure is 'unanalysable'.

Perrow offers several examples. A factory manufacturing a standard product like heating elements for electric stoves will fit into box 4. Raw material has few exceptions, and they are dealt with by standard procedure. An engineering firm building drill presses or electric motors to order (box 3) will also have standard procedure for dealing with exceptions but will encounter far more occasions when search must be instituted, constantly introducing modifications to meet customers' needs.

In a firm making fine glassware (box 1) the variety of exceptions is small, although there can be no standard procedure for dealing with them. And in a firm making nuclear fuel systems (box 2), we are faced with great variety as well as unanalysable search. These differences in turn will be reflected in the type and style of organization and in the relative powers of technical and supervisory staffs.

The concepts that I have sketchily outlined vary in generality but are all employed by social scientists in looking at organizations and they are becoming, to a greater or lesser extent, part of the managers' own ways of looking at their activities. To my mind, the most important contribution of the social scientist to management is just this provision of concepts for the manager to use. In Chapter 27 we discuss a research project undertaken within the military and here again we can see how the use of concepts by the social scientist become communicated to the client organization.

The adoption of social science concepts

How do concepts generated by advances in the social sciences become available to industry? In the first place, ideas and theories pass into the general stock of knowledge and eventually affect the climate of opinion and accepted ideas (there are obvious examples in the influence of Marx, Freud, and Keynes); second, and more directly, by executives attending lectures and seminars at management colleges or universities; more directly still, they learn from their contacts with colleagues who themselves use concepts and theories derived from the social sciences. Some learn from social scientists whom they employ or sponsor to undertake research.

273

When a social scientist is asked by management for advice on a particular problem, he must first discover which concepts are most likely to be useful to managers in their particular situation. And he finds out by learning the concepts that managers actually use to understand, explain, and control their own situation. Second, he has to devise a strategy for introducing his own concepts where they are likely to be appropriate. Thus we have a process of mutual learning; perhaps we should describe it more precisely as 'trading concepts'. Shared concepts that emerge from this trading process provide a basis for making a fruitful analysis, determining the 'facts' and influencing perceptions.

But even if he is himself knowledgeable about the social science field the industrialist is still faced with the problem of deciding what kind of assistance he needs, and who should provide it. We may assume that he will appreciate the need for help in identifying and articulating his problem. Inevitably, such identification involves casting it into terms which will be accessible to research. And here we encounter another stumbling block presented this time by the word 'research'. Its unthinking use fails to differentiate between the different kinds of research, yet different kinds are needed for different kinds of problems. Furthermore, different kinds of research are typically best performed by different kinds of institution. We have already discussed one way of classifying research in Chapter 7, but will illustrate them here with specific reference to industry. The categories we adopted are: basic pure research; basic objective research, operational research; and action research. Briefly, basic pure is concerned with tackling problems which arise within the particular discipline concerned. This is not to say that it may not throw up results of interest or value to industry, but it is unlikely that industry will itself perceive a need for this kind of research, or wish to sponsor it. Basic objective research is likely to use the same concepts, methods and techniques as pure research but is oriented towards a problem which arises 'out there', in industry or in society. Industry may well perceive the need and use of this kind of research. Since the results are likely to be of a general nature, applicable to a wide range of industrial firms with an interest in the problems concerned, it is probable that industry will look either to public bodies or to co-operative associations of firms to sponsor such research. Well-known examples of this kind of research are the studies of the Scottish electronic industry conducted by Burns and Stalker (1961) with support from the Scottish Council (Development and Industry). Another example is the work of Joan Woodward (1965), sponsored by the Department of Scientific and Industrial Research, on the effectiveness of different kinds of management organization. This work has had a considerable impact on both organizational theory and industrial practice. The translation of the findings into action by firms was through the acquisition by managers of new concepts, new ways to look at problems of organization. Research of this kind is subject to no crucial time scale, presents little difficulty over publication, and requires complete independence of outlook on the part of the researcher. It is therefore particularly appropriate to university departments and research institutes.

The third category is labelled 'operational research' and describes a particular interdisciplinary approach to practical problems, using a pattern of methods with a strong mathematical orientation. But for our present purpose, social science research can be described as operational when it is, in essence, a process by which organizational goals are identified, where criteria of attainment of these goals can be specified and their achievement measured against the criteria; and where discrepancies between the goal and the attainment can be so demonstrated that devices for diminishing the gap can be proposed. This is a description of the function and process of research on the actual operations of an ongoing organization. The problems tackled by this kind of research vary from the highly general to the extremely specific, and the industrialist, if he seeks external co-operation, will have recourse to different institutions of choice. Most organizations large enough to have sufficient problems to justify it set up departments of their own to conduct research on their operations; and more and more of them are finding it necessary to include social scientists in their teams.

Some operational problems have a very general nature, shade into basic objective research, and have outcomes which are equally influential. A well-known example of this kind of research is that undertaken by the Tavistock Institute into work organization in the mining industry (Trist *et al.*, 1963). This study, with other such Tavistock studies, led to the institute's conception of the 'open sociotechnical system'; and from this, the demonstration to managements of the reality of choice in the field of work organization (an area we shall discuss more fully in subsequent chapters). Institutes of this kind, with a multidisciplinary approach and problem-oriented missions, would be obvious choices for research of this nature. University departments would be unlikely to have the range of skills required, although some university-linked institutes might. An internal, or in-house company department would not often be appropriate: it would seldom be able to afford the required range and depth of skills and would be unlikely to have a position of sufficient independence and sufficient influence to attract support

275

for its findings and recommendations from a wide range of powerful functional departments; for the solution of problems of this kind is never a matter within the compass of one department.

Action research consists essentially of deliberate experiment, controlled as far as possible, and evaluated against pre-arranged criteria. A series of experimental changes is almost inevitably involved and this will usually have been a preliminary phase for the necessary background investigation on which – often with the operational research approach defined earlier – the relevant problems are identified, the appropriate experimental changes are designed, and the indicators for subsequent valuation are set up. The action experiment phase can take place only *after* a great deal of mutual understanding and value sharing has been accomplished. It is during the operational research phases that we in our research have most influenced the values of organizations with which we have worked. Research of this kind offers considerable difficulties to a university department, since it is based on a research-consultancy relationship by which the research workers contribute to the decision-making of the senior executives of the firm. There is always difficulty in evaluating the outcomes of research. There is seldom any doubt over the gains experienced by the firm concerned; the problem is to identify which aspects of the action research have contributed most to the gains; and for this reason the action research programme cannot be neatly packaged. In action research we are in a special field, on the borderline between research and consultancy; it requires the skills of both, and more complex institutional arrangements than either.

Research-utilizing capability

Thus far we have been discussing the research capability of various kinds of organizations. There is, of course, another side to successful application of research – the research utilizing capability of the industrial firm. This varies enormously, and it is noteworthy that the openness to social science research and knowledge is far greater in some industries than in others. At present, significant interest and activity is virtually confined to four categories of industrial company:

(a) very large firms which can afford highly specialized staff to keep in touch with social science activity;

(b) firms in science-based industries, accustomed to making use of external knowledge;

(c) firms under American control or dominance; and

(d) firms with young 'top' management, with business school or university-based management education.

For completely successful utilization, the firm concerned needs to be able to generate within itself a research-utilizing system to match the research-generating system with which it engages. Ideally, a utilizing system needs to have certain characteristics, and we have already discussed this in general terms in Chapter 6 and these needs will apply equally to industrial organizations if successful use of research is to be achieved.

We can summarize the trends in the use of the social sciences by industrial firms. There is, first, a tendency for them to seek 'behavioural science', implying a preference for an approach oriented towards social psychology, and anticipating, possibly, that 'behavioural scientists' may be more likely to share industrial values than 'social scientists'. Second, there is a tendency to move gingerly into the field, expressing a considerable preference for readily comprehensive techniques. Many firms, for example, want 'attitude surveys', whether or not this is the most appropriate answer to their problems. Third, firms seek 'packages' of social research, usually including attitude surveys and 'feedback' reports, or sensitivity-training courses, or all of these. Finally, it is often firms which have gone through these introductory or inoculatory experiences which later seek research and advice on a deeper and wider basis.

Chapter 14
Social Change and Social Values

Introduction

This paper is the result of a request from the board of a large British industrial organization for a review or background paper on the changing social environment of industrial organizations – what are the key factors in what has become a turbulent social environment and how will this affect industrial operations and strategies?

It is possible, following Parsons (1968), to identify in a society at a given time a set of dominant values ('pattern variables', as in Parsons's terminology). This does not mean that everyone, or a majority of the members of the society, adhere to these values. We can say, however, that they are the values held by those who manage, in Emery's terms, the leading institutions in the society (Emery, 1968).

Society and values are always changing but major inflections occur infrequently and are marked by succession in the role of 'leading' institution. Such an inflection occurred in early industrializing societies like Britain, when manufacturing industry became the leading institution whose values had to be served by those of other major institutions, including the former leading institutions such as the Church and the Land. Advanced Western industrial societies appear to be experiencing another period of succession; the transition to 'post industrialism' is marked by the passing of the leadership from manufacturing industry to those institutions providing 'services', both public and private. We are witnessing a corresponding shift in the 'pattern variables'.

A society is anything but homogeneous with regard to value

278

systems. Even in so homogeneous a society as Britain, regional and class differences are significant and indeed the 'dignified' (as opposed to the 'efficient') British institutions embody pre-industrial values to a high degree.

We view the future as a continuation of the trends we believe we observe today. This is a perfectly rational procedure. Of course, if the trends are short term we are less likely to be right, but with longer-term trends we have a good chance of predicting correctly. For example, political suffrage has been gradually widening in the world in general. In Britain we can trace a continuous step-wise process from the Reform Bill of 1832 to the lastest step, the reduction of the qualifying age from 21 to 18. We can reasonably predict that if there are any further changes, they will be downward in age, and that in countries where the age is set higher than 18, successful pressure will be exerted over time to reduce it to 18.

Certain changes, then, we regard as unidirectional with little chance that they will be reversed. And, indeed, changes never are reversed in the strict sense of the word. In the trivial sense, of course, time cannot be made to run backwards; in the more meaningful sense, even developments interrupted by catastrophe or war or revolution do not put us back where we were before. It is possible to be able to take a long enough view of social change to be able to treat the changes in direction brought about by even catastrophic events as perturbations, hiccoughs which were convulsive at the time but now appear as the cause of minor delays or accelerations in a continuous process.

Such a long-term view may be held over the processes associated with industrialization, the transition from an agrarian, rural, feudal type of society to an industrial, urban, capitalist society; a path that has been trodden by all of Western society and which has been occupying the last few centuries.

One can describe the nature of these long-term unidirectional changes in many ways. One of the functions of social science is to enable us to describe them in terms which not only allows us to make comparisons across countries in the course of these developments, but also with countries or societies in different situations altogether. Thus we seek categories which have some degree of universality. One such set of categories is what Parsons has called the 'pattern variables'. These describe the bases on which people in a society relate to one another; together they spell out the cultural prescription for how other people are to be treated. Each of these variables can be plotted on some sort of continuum on which the current position of any one society can be plotted. Thus each society at any time could be represented by a 'profile'. If the variables were unrelated, any kind of profile would be possible. But, in fact, they are quite closely related because a politico-socio-economic system, such as a feudal agrarian one, requires certain patterns of relationship to sustain it, while industrial capitalism requires another in its infrastructure building stage and another still in its phase of high mass consumption. Nomadic hunting societies need yet another pattern or profile. If we can, indeed, discriminate profiles characteristic of the politico-socio-economic systems of societies and of the stage of development of their systems, then we have a useful set of variables. And if the variables can be plotted on a continuum, then we may even be able to offer predictions about future patterns of development.

The particular variables selected by Parsons are these:

1 ascription   –   achievement;
2 particularism   –   universalism;
3 diffuseness   –   specificity;
4 collectivism   –   individualism;
5 affectivity   –   affective neutrality.

A word is needed to explain each of these.

1   *Ascription – achievement*

The basis on which society confers status is a fundamental characteristic of its mode of organization and is a key to a most important value – how people are valued, no less; on what basis its rewards are distributed. Kingship is usually inherited, once established. Selection on the basis either of birth or of physical characteristics such as height is 'ascriptive'. Authority and the deference due to it are ascribed to those of appropriate birth or colour or size. A feudal society in which the son of a serf is a serf, the son of a lord, a lord, is one where status is by ascription. So is a caste society where the son of a priest is a priest, the son of a grave-digger, a grave-digger, of a herdsman, a herdsman. Such a community lacks the striving dynamic, the potential for mobility and innovation without which we cannot visualize an industrializing society. We conceive achievement as the polar opposite of ascription as a basis for status. A highly mobile innovating society will reward achievement. Yet during the long process of transformation from a traditional to a modern society there is tension between these two bases of stratification, the shift from ascription to achievement being neither sudden nor complete. The degree of inequality that adheres to ascribed differences is always enough in each generation to arouse the fierce indignation of reformers.

280

2 *Particularism – universalism*

Most traditional societies are marked by a distinction between the duties owed to those who belong from what is due to those who don't. The moral community is 'us', 'they' are outside it. The moral community may be the tribe, the clan, the nation, the family, the village. Now it is true that even in the most industrialized mobile society the sense of degrees of moral community still persist, but they are not officially ethically sanctioned; our 'official' ethic stresses the same moral obligations to all, regardless of family, religion, race and place. We may accept additional voluntary obligations but the same basic ones are due to all – our ethics and morals are supposed to be universalistic not particularistic. It is clear that an advanced industrial society which needs high mobility and a certain degree of mutual trust among all citizens for goods, services and credit to flow freely, requires to be nearer the universalist than the particularist end of this continuum.

3 *Diffuseness – speciality*

A complex industrial society is built on the basis of advanced distribution of labour, high specialization and reliability of role performance. Our work roles are very specific, requiring not only that when we act as a mechanic, a teacher, a bus driver, a welder, we produce the performance expected of a mechanic, a welder, etc. but also that our other roles will not get in the way – if we are also a lay preacher or a golfer we don't preach to our bus-load or wield our spot-welding rod as a golf club. Even in traditional societies there are ritual roles which require their occupants to behave as one apart during the ritual performance but most tasks and duties fall to the individual in his ascribed statuses as husband, father, clan member. When he tills his field, plants and harvests his crops, helps out his maternal uncle with his harvest, sits with the elders under the tree to give judgement on tribal issues, teaches his son how to fish, he is simply doing all the things that are appropriate and are expected from him as occupant of his statuses; he has entered into no contracts, bartering a specific role performance for some reward or recognition. His roles are diffuse, they interpenetrate one another; his work, family, community and leisure roles are not specific and distinct. Even in our highly advanced industrial society our roles are not totally specific. We tend to relax with, and make friends of, people with whom we associate at work so that friendship intrudes

281

into our work-related role activity. But we have a choice in these matters. Some organizations have the reputation of carrying paternalism to the point where it engulfs the domestic and leisure spheres of its executives. The resentment occasioned by those demands is proof that they are no longer perceived as legitimate. The company is normally perceived as buying a pretty specific role performance when it hires help.

4 Collectivism – individualism

Traditional society placed the collective good over and above the good of the individual; collective goals above individual goals. The Church, the State commanded unquestioning loyalty. The work of the collective, the village, community, had to be done and all had an obligation to help. The individual was valued, of course, but primarily as a contribution to the collective, not on the basis of his self-development. Individualism has been an integral and vital component of the industrializing, modernizing urge. The philosophy of the general will was a pre-industrial philosophy, the philosophy of utilitarianism was an industrial philosophy – the communal good was achieved by the summation of individual goods, curbing the latter only where they infringed one another; laissez-faire economic doctrines were their counterpart. Doctrines of individual growth, development, self-actualization are examples of an advanced individualist orientation. While individualism may have been a necessary ingredient of the original industrializing urge, it is obviously not essential to a forced, or planned transformation to an industrial society as the example of the Soviet Union demonstrated and as, in its own way, China now shows.

5 Affectivity – affective neutrality

The separation of emotion from intellect is a crucial element in modern Western tradition. By this separation we are able to postpone immediate gratification in the interests of evaluating the consequences. It enabled Western man to separate the performance of work roles from self-expression. It permits the universalistic bureaucracy; your entitlement is based on your demonstration that you belong to the appropriate category, not on the emotional response your 'case' may evoke. Impersonal roles require both universalism and affective neutrality.

What we have so far shown, then, is that these five pattern

variables have each undergone a one-way movement in the course of the transformation of Western societies from agrarian to advanced industrialism. We have indicated that this development is by no means a complete one. Can we forecast, then, that the future changes in values in our society will be directed towards a completion of this process? I believe not – I believe that the changes now under way point in a new direction.

1 *Basis of Status – ascription/achievement*

We see many signs of the weakening of the value of achievement. Combined with individualism, achievement orientation favoured, indeed demanded, competitiveness. Progress was seen as the outcome of competition through a process of natural selection, the most efficient would survive and drive out the less efficient, resulting in a steady increase in efficiency. But for years now our schools have been playing down competition and advocating co-operativeness. We are even trying to curb our organizations' rewarding of achievement by insisting that they engage and even promote with a view to equalizing the treatment of 'disadvantaged' groups – women, handicapped, blacks, immigrants. And many, especially middle-class youths, have rejected for themselves the goals and demands of achievement; preferring 'growth' or self-actualization to material and intellectual achievement. There is, then, a clear movement towards a new kind of ascribed status. Unlike the traditional basis of ascription which was particularistic, the new is universalistic; your status is inferred by your membership of the human race. Of course, if we all share the same status, status disappears. In an organized society it cannot disappear completely. But there are many signs that the gradations are weakening and that many social distinctions are weakening likewise. With this weakening, the nature of authority comes under question. Authority is conferred by status in general, but in particular situations it is conferred as it were by contract.

When I purchase an airline ticket, I place myself under the authority of the captain of any airplane I enter with that ticket. This is really a very limited kind of authority, much more limited than we normally imagine operates in organizations. But it may be what we are moving rapidly towards. Simultaneously we appear to recognize all conceivable kinds of achievement rather than those which made for an economically and technologically advancing society. Pushpin is now as good as poetry.

2 Particularism – universalism

While we demand that more and more of society's institutions operate on a universalistic basis, it is less an out and out universalism than a compensatory one based on category membership. If you are a WASP, that confers upon you certain potential advantages in American society, which come to you from category membership. In order that these advantages from category membership should not be realized, you as an individual may have to be deliberately held back. This is a new twist. Universalism meant that the criteria we use for determining how people should be treated were to be the same for everyone; now they are to be the same for everyone only after certain historic injustices to the group or class from which they come have been put right. Universalism tomorrow is to come through a new particularism today. We can describe the new principle as 'compensatory particularism'.

3 Collectivism – individualism

In some ways the trend from collectivism to individualism is still continuing. Loyalty to collectives has been weakening. It is no longer considered noble to sacrifice one's own interests to those of one's country, one's company, even one's family. One's highest duty is to oneself, to the goal of 'self-actualization'. This is a very optimistic creed as it presupposes that the untrammelled self will actualize into an angel rather than a monster. There is nothing new in this philosophy; it was most clearly articulated by Rousseau, but the horrors of the French Revolution diminished its appeal to the middle classes. The even more unspeakable horrors of patriotic wars have now blackened the alternative; the face of collectivism is grim indeed. But while the force of individualism has weakened our social institutions – nation, church, family, school – the existential 'angel' it generates is too painful. And what we now see is that those for whom the old collective institutions were so oppressive as to make them wish to deny their legitimacy, to 'drop out', now seek new, or rather new-old, forms of collective institutions of which the various types of 'commune' are the most obvious example. They reject all forms of stratification, but in seeking to allow the individual freedom to 'actualize' himself, assert social control in one vital area, that of property rights. The individual is free but not to accumulate private property or to assert his rights to ownership against the community. Whether the sentiment is religious or profane, neo-christian or neo-communist, private property in things or in human relationships is seen as a constraint on true freedom. The apotheosis of individualism becomes a new communitarianism.

4   *Diffuseness – specificity*

The specificity of roles which has proved so effective in getting the work of a complex society and its institutions done, has had less desirable consequences which have been long criticized and condemned. The vogue word is 'alienation'. The separation of ownership from skill, the extreme division of labour, the segregation of work roles from community and family roles have alienated man from his work and from himself. Particularly it is claimed that in performing rigidly prescribed work roles the worker was not free to be himself. He was a screwer of a number six bolt into a number six nut, 30,000 times a day and totally interchangeable with, or replaceable by, another such – an object, not a person. That tide has already begun to recede, not only in industry, where technological change has been now seen to present us with the options of greater or less specificity, but in the growing flexibility of the concept of career and in other measures which weaken the constraints institutions exercise over their members. The roles the individual plays become less specific without becoming more diffuse. The pressure is for them to become more integral for the individual who is less concerned with role than with identity. Thus organizations are obliged to reconstruct the roles of which they are composed, so that they create more room for, and supply more opportunities for the individual to acquire an identity.

5   *Affectivity – affective neutrality*

The concomitant of the elaborate role division and specificity was the instrumental orientation that people brought to their roles. Each role is performed not for itself but for some external objective and therefore the less emotion involved in its performance, the better. Work became no place for emotion; emotion would get in the way of role performance, disinterested judgement, hard calculation – emotionality was a 'problem'. Similarly, learning was not for the sake of learning, but for vocational or professional goals; emotion hindered learning. Emotion even gets in the way of sexual 'outlet', the sexual partner becomes instrumental. The contrast is easily drawn with the primitive for whom all activities are a form of expression. There can be no doubt that our own society, while ruthlessly instrumental in many respects, has begun to rediscover expression. It is often maintained that lower class people who had no vision of self-improvement, no feeling that advance by their own efforts was a realistic possibility, had never traded expression for instrumentalism, affect for affective neutrality. Be that as it may, the value of 'doing your own thing' and tolerance for expressiveness in others has been gaining ground in many ways. Deferred gratification, never particularly popular among the young, is now less appealing than formerly to their elders; inflation plays a part as both cause and consequence.

What I have been seeking to show is that the trends which have marked the transition from traditional agrarian to modern industrial society have probably gone as far as they are likely to go. They are not being reversed – time does not run backwards – and in some respects may still continue to mop up recently invaded areas of life. But on the whole they appear to be moving in a changed direction.

We can summarize what we have been saying in Figure 5.

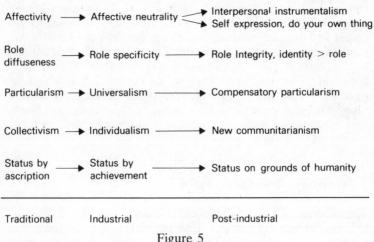

Figure 5

Social values

It is easy to see that the sets of values adhere together and that the social arrangements which promote one set of values will be quite different from those which support another. Furthermore, a situation in which the kinds of social arrangements which support certain values are in turn supported by them is a pretty stable kind of

286

system. What we generally encounter is a situation in which this is by and large true but in which there are imperfect matches which provide a continuous dynamic towards change. For example, a work organization can be constructed on the basis that its success depends upon the achievement motivation of its members and seeks, by its reward system, to encourage them. But the match is not perfect; high achievement motivation leads to the conflict of individual goals, which is dysfunctional for the organization which may moderate its reward system so as to contain conflict, thereby weakening the motivations of some for achievement. An equilibrium may be thus reached, which is stable and hard to dislodge. But even in work organizations the time that it takes to make this kind of adjustment generally means that there is a tension between what is required and what exists, between what is carried over from the old and what is new. In society as a whole the time scales are much longer; the world of work may need one set of skills, but the education system is tooled up to provide another. The friction is enough to initiate further changes which create new frictions and so on. Thus, even if we were able to see more clearly than we can the value patterns of coming society, we can be certain that before a state of stable equilibrium would be reached, further changes would be occurring, and that friction and conflict would not disappear.

Thus to say we are in a time of change is tautologous: time *is* change. Yet we persistently feel that we are witnessing large social changes, different in scale from those our grandparents experienced. What we may be witnessing now is one of many periods of inflection, marked by the fact that the present version of the generation gap is not the familiar struggle between the young and their seniors for influence, power and control, but the acceptance of, adherence to, or tolerance of, different sets of values. The difference is that between rebellion and revolution. The young always rebel, seeking to replace the wielder of authority with one closer to themselves. But revolution implies a change not just of ruler but of regime, of the legitimate basis for authority. I do not mean that the young are in revolt, hell bent for revolution, but that their image of the good society is different from that of their elders because it is *predicated on different assumptions*.

That is where I think the real difference lies between our present situation and that of immediately previous generations who witnessed changes enough in all conscience. We tend today to laugh at the Victorians for their ideas of 'progress', but this was a key concept and goal in the transformation of England to industrialism. Industrialization – more goods and cheaper – requires orientation towards the future; medieval Christianity looked to a golden past.

Industrialism needed another ethic than unworldliness; the puritans who emphasized salvation though personal effort provided it. The profile of pattern variables we have described as the industrial pole of our continuum is a snapshot of puritan values.

What has undermined this ethic, set things moving towards what has been called, for want of a better term, the post-industrial set of values? – values that are oriented more towards a world in which consumption and distribution rather than production are the problem areas. Since industry is the institution of production, it was the leading institution of a production-oriented society. A distribution-oriented society is non-industrial or post-industrial in the sense that industry ceases to be the leading institution.

And it is indeed the problem of production, the creation of plenty that for a brief interlude appeared to have been solved in the advanced industrial societies.

From the onset of industrialization, the possibility of plenty was real enough to be a goal. Malthusian nemesis appeared to be avoided by the decline in birth rates to a level comfortably outstripped by industrial-led advances in agriculture and the exploitation of new lands. But the rate of growth of wealth was slow, discontinuous and uncertain. The possibility of sustained steady economic growth at a rate which would double real incomes every 25 or 20 or even 10 years was a development of World War II and its aftermath, brought about by the experience of deliberate government stimulus to war economies and the success of the Marshall Plan in rebuilding the economies of Western Europe. The experience of the Soviet type 'planned economies' was relevant but not nearly so influential. The effect on the Western psyche was profound. It was possible to contemplate ever-increasing wealth and consumption without increased work, indeed with continually diminishing work effort in terms of days and hours at work and of physical effort in work itself. It appeared necessary no longer to defer gratification today to ensure more tomorrow, because it would always be there tomorrow. The gods of the copybook headings – work hard, save for tomorrow, never put off what you can do today – were no longer fit deities to worship. For the young growing up in this atmosphere the threat of scarcity, which meant so much to the generation of the 1930s, had no reality. Parents of post-war children can recognize the exasperation they felt with children who seemed unconcerned about the effort needed to acquire things. And nobody needs starve if he hasn't a job, nor need the lack of a job to induce feelings of guilt and shame when society can produce enough wealth for everyone with constantly diminishing work.

Other events occurred which have made the attitudes and values of young people more influential and significant than they were in previous generations. One such 'event' is commercial. The young began to possess a significant proportion of disposable income, constituting a market worth cultivating and one in which rapid changes of fashion could be induced. A 'youth culture' became a commercial proposition. The outcome was to give to youth as a whole a consciousness of self-importance and new solidarity and to set them up as trend-setters for society as a whole. The other 'event' was the culmination of the 'demographic transition', the change over 150 years of a society with few old people and families with large numbers of children to a society in which each family possessed one or two children and where most people live until after the age of retirement. Within the family, as in society in general, what is scarce is highly valued; what is abundant is not. In the past grandparents were both scarce and useful, children abundant. Today a young family is likely to have more grandparents than children. Today children are more highly valued and the old less highly valued than in previous generations. A child-centred society has emerged, investing the wishes and ideals of the young with a new importance. If the effect of these changes has been most visible in the schools and in the universities, it is because they are the institutions which first encounter them and where the concentrations of young are greatest. But industry is already encountering these changes and faces problems in assimilating them. The future demographic pattern is notoriously hard to predict. Previous forecasts have all proved false, paradoxically because demographers are concerned with the 'hard' end of the social sciences – the numerical and mathematical models and not with attitudes, values and social movements. The decisions to marry later or earlier, to have more or fewer children, wider spaced or bunched, are the engine of demographic change; and it is people's values and aspirations which drive the engine. If demographers guess these values wrongly or don't guess at all, their models, however elegant, are useless. Society's present values can be easily detected. Because so few children die, we can easily reproduce ourselves without everybody eligible getting married and without every married couple having children and without married couples staying married more than the 20 years or so needed to have and bring up a family. Consequently, if population stability is the goal, society can relax its insistence on the sanctity of marriage and the family, and tolerate sexual behaviour which is not aimed to produce children. Social morals sustain social goals; as the latter are modified, the former follow – after a time lag. The value changes and changes in moral values constitute the social environment in which industry operates.

Social environment

To talk of the social environment is to make a useful abstraction, but an abstraction nevertheless. The environment is too complex to be treated as a whole but it can be disaggregated for analytical purposes in different ways. We choose to divide into political, economic, social, technological and cultural environments but they are all interrelated. We shall discuss each of these separately and then try to bring them together in a coherent fashion so as to provide a picture of the future with which industry is faced.

Economic environment

The economic environment is the set of values placed upon the inputs and outputs of the organization. Significant changes in the economic environment occur when the values of inputs and outputs change, when what has been scarce becomes abundant or vice versa, and when what has been previously a free input or negative output ceases to be free and has, therefore, to be brought into the reckoning. These latter changes are the product of changes in social valuations and are the ones which concern us most here. That is not to disregard or underrate the importance of the economic changes brought about by technological change – new processes, new products, substitution of inputs, nor those brought about by changes in scarcity and abundance, but because the thrust of this essay is to examine the likely consequences of likely social change.

Changes in social values relating to the physical environment have put a price on formerly free goods, such as clean air and water. Similarly, some of the costs of redundancy have been pushed back onto industry by the community, and some of the costs of training have been shifted onto those who use the skills acquired at the expense of others. This is part of a continuous process, continuously revising the basis of the economic relationship between industry and community, between what should be paid for by the organization and what by other social institutions, transferring onto industry the costs of its operations to the community. On the other side of the equation we can see signs of the acceptance of the notion that industry should also be paid for the cost of services it is obliged to perform for the community whether, as in the case of nationalized industries, this obligation is to provide a service at a flat rate regardless of actual cost or, as in the case of private industry in areas of high unemployment, to provide jobs in excess of the firm's requirements. More and more the market which was expected to regulate the relationship between industry and community is being usurped. Its assumptions, which were more or less valid when industry was young and companies small, have proved inappropriate today.

Political environment

The political environment of a company is the web of legislation and regulation governing industry's transactions, the power which organized groups can exercise over it, and the power and influence which it can exert either singly or in combination with other companies and institutions. The kind of political environment with which organizations are likely to be faced is hard to predict because of the nature of our political system which poses contrasting alternatives to the electorate. What we can predict is that the political climate will tend to change so as to reflect changes in social values. It is, therefore, unlikely that we shall see a lasting shift towards more individualist, meritocratic values on the part of a major party. We can predict, then, a growing disposition for government of whatever party to intervene in industry and commerce, to use its regulatory and legislative powers, not just to curb the power of the industrial and commercial firms, but to align them with social goals now that such alignment is no longer seen to be provided by the 'hidden hand' of the market.

Whether the power of the unions will continue to grow depends upon whether they can modify their own goals to meet the changing values of their members. An indicator to watch will be the relative participation of different age groups in union affairs.

Technological environment

While it is immediately obvious that the economic and political environments are dependent on the social, we tend to treat technology as something external with its own logic. This is technological determinism, leading us to the view that what is technologically possible will inevitably occur. It is increasingly becoming apparent that our technology is an expression of our value system, that the kind of technology we create is an indication of the kind of society we are and that the technology we produce provides us with choices of many kinds, including the choice of how to use it. Thus forecasts about technology are forecasts about social choices. In the reasonably near future our social choices look like favouring certain technological goals – the reduction of pollution, the conservation of energy and, with less certainty, the enhancement of the quality of working life. We hear much about 'intermediate technology' and 'appropriate technology' in the context of discussion about developing countries. The implicit assumption is that our advanced technology is 'appropriate' to our society. In fact our technology represents the accumulated social choices of the past and is increasingly less appropriate to the values which appear to be likely to characterize our society in the future. And now that the notion is gaining ground that technology is not an external force, we may be sure that 'technological assessment', 'environmental impact statements' and other deliberate attempts to ensure that technological developments are appropriate to social goals will increase. While the thrust for some time may be on the assessment and control of new technology, pressure is bound to grow for scrutiny of existing technologies. Organizations which are concerned to survive in our changing environment will need to ensure that their research and development scientists and engineers are aware of, understand, and take account of what these mean for their own work. These are all issues that we shall consider again in Chapter 23, when we consider the prospects of technology in relation to traditional values and modern organizations in developing countries.

Social environment

We have already described the changes in social values that are taking place. They add up to a transformation which will have, indeed already is having, profound impact on all our social institutions. Rather than elaborate further on this here, I shall consider the implications of the changes in the total environment.

Cultural environment

I have tried to show a distinction between social values concerning society's goals and cultural values concerning the ways in which these goals should be achieved. It is, in fact, these cultural values which differentiate the 'feel' of one society or institution from another. Perhaps the most notable cultural change that has been affecting all our social institutions has been the increasing emphasis on their 'manifest' as against the 'latent' functions. Increasingly, for example, universities are expected to conduct their affairs with more concern for their function of preparing young people for their work roles and less on their other functions, including that of maintaining an elite culture. Similarly ceremony, whose aim is to emphasize common membership of an institution and the emotional bonds among members, which will ensure their loyalty and concern with its future, is discounted. In industrial firms we encounter similar trends – attempts to cater for these latent functions are dubbed paternalism and regarded with suspicion. This tendency hinders organizations and institutions from ensuring their future continuance.

The impact of environmental change

I do not want to overemphasize the coherence and consistency of all these changes with one another. As I said earlier, different changes occur with different speeds, a point we will take up again in some detail in Chapter 17. But we can see some clear indications for industrial companies.

First, the basis of accommodation between industry and society, the firm and the community, is changing. In the past the constraints were few. Over many decades intervention by government has grown either to correct a perceived imbalance of power between employer and employee or to safeguard national or community interests. Today government regulation or legislation affects every aspect of the relationship between employer and employee, including pay, training, contracts of employment, pensions, redundancy, dismissal.

The second type of intervention has been more variable; that is, there has not been a steady growth of restriction but over the long term we can indeed see that this is the overall trend. Industry is now subject to regulation and control over prices, dividends, location, pollution, consumer protection, permitted accounting practices, protection against fraud. Taxation belongs in this area too.

What all this amounts to is uncertain. That it represents a shift from a virtually untrammelled licence to utilize and transform the resources of the community to a very restricted one is obvious. I believe that we are experiencing a change in the basic assumptions on which industrial activity can take place. The assumptions underlying the restrictions on the 'employer's licence' are that the community possesses valuable resources, physical and human, that it has a duty to see that they are used to the best advantage of the community as a whole, and to hold them in trust for future generations. Any potential user of these resources must justify his claim that he will use them prudently and to the advantage of the community as a whole. These assumptions are a long way from being satisfied, nor have we the political, economic and social infra-structure that would enable them to be realized. Because less atten-tion is likely to be given to the capacity of our political and adminis-trative structures than to their objectives, we are likely to grossly overload them. Navigating in a system whose basic assumptions are changing faster than its capacity to realize them is likely to be a treacherous business.

The effects of these changes on industrial relations has already been experienced. The unions have successfully challenged the rights of management to dispose of resources as they think fit; they have not yet reached the pitch, as in Sweden, of challenging the manager's right to manage, although that right has been limited by all sorts of devices, not least the demarcation agreements which limit the employer's ability to assign jobs or tasks in what appears to him the most efficient manner. But it is not union pressure which appears likely to do most to alter management's approach to the basic business of managing. The changes we have referred to in the social environment have profoundly affected the expectations that people have of their lives and their attitude to authority. Very slowly the relationships between the worker and his job, the worker and his firm, the worker and his supervisor, the worker and the management are changing. They, of course, reflect the social changes we have outlined. They include the rejection of whatever can be construed as arbitrary authority and the denial of the organ-ization's right to control and influence over, or even concern with, life outside work. The organization can claim less than formerly of the individual's 'life space'; it is obliged to bargain for what it once could take for granted. Workers' expectations about the nature of work have been changing; increasing education, advancing living standards, reducing pressures to work for the means to survive, have been making workers more choosy about the kind of job they will accept. The effects of this have been masked by the presence of immigrant workers who have often been prepared to accept jobs which native white workers would not take and by the willingness of women to accept monotonous jobs of low prestige and pay. But the effects have been twofold: jobs which provide no intrinsic satisfac-tion or reward have become regarded as acceptable only as a trade-off for money and time for 'real' life, while other workers have looked for jobs which provide independence, autonomy and/or intrinsic satisfactions. There has been no enormous pressure on firms to undertake far-reaching redesign of organization and jobs. Some have, indeed, moved in that direction and some of the 'experiments' in organization and job design have been accorded a great deal of public attention. Significantly these experiments have been motivated less by humanistic considerations than by assessment that they are what will be needed to survive in an environment in which organizations will have to be capable of rapid adaptation to change and in which workers will not just be there for the hiring except at prohibitive costs in turnover and training.

Quite another set of developments, now taking shape, go into the roots of the 'contract' between employer and employee. At its most rigid the 'contract' prescribes that the individual work at a specified place for specified hours of the day. This convention has been, and still is, growing. In the docks and in the mines decasualization, or the 'lump' of the construction industry, have eroded the old system where the gang, not the individual, was the work unit. Ironically, then, organizations are now experimenting with techniques to loosen the bonds which tie the employee to his workplace at specified hours. Flexitime is the current *nouvelle vague*. Even more flexible are arrangements which allowed a single job to be covered by more than one person working part-time, with participants deciding how to share the job and pay. Schemes of this kind have been operating with married couples. Another variant makes similar arrangements with groups of women. Higher up the scale are arrangements which sever the direct relationship between employer and employee or between tasks and jobs or both: labour only subcontracting, the self-employed worker or team negotiating for a particular assignment, the autonomous work group accepting responsibility for a certain function, but dividing up the necessary task according to its own criteria.

All these devices meet some of the aspirations that social change is giving rise to: desire for greater autonomy, shared family roles, rejection of any authority which does not grow out of the needs of the situation, and so on. It is not unthinkable that organizations may bargain with community representatives for coverage of the work to be done, leaving the community to work out how this is to be done. This might bring about a new version of the cottage industry with perhaps some of the decentralization of the old, a decentralization made possible by a communications technology which hitherto has been utilized more to increase than to decrease centralization. In these projected developments the traditional concept of the job and its associated career have virtually disappeared. I very much doubt whether they or anything like them will become the dominant focus of employment in the near future. I do think that they or variants of them will prove to be creative adaptations to the environment and, where practicable, will confer benefits on both company and community, employer and employee.

295

Section II
Organizations

Chapter 15
Modern Organization Theory

When does *modern* organization theory begin? Many people are fond of tracing the origins of organization theory to Jethro's advice to Moses and this is useful if only to remind us that organizations have existed a long time and that a great deal of experience has accumulated. The systematization of this experience was most advanced in regard to military organization, concerning whose art impressive manuals date back several centuries. In the field of state organization and management, a venerable tradition is available, reaching back at least as far as Plato and concerning which many of the adumbrations of Machiavelli have a modern enough ring.

We would mark the beginnings of *classical knowledge* about organizations and their functioning with two roughly contemporary but vastly different approaches: one the scholarly researches of Max Weber; the other the pragmatic innovations of Frederick Taylor.

Bureaucracy is one of the most notable of all social inventions, substituting rules for arbitrary decision, a formally limited and defined, in place of an absolute and personal, authority, and a treatment of individuals according to universalistic rather than particularistic criteria. It is an amazingly versatile pattern and can be used to run anything from a state, an army, a church, or a police force to a steel works, a laundry or a university.

Another pervasive social invention was the division of labour beginning with those divisions ordained by our biological nature and building on these to match the contribution demanded of an individual to his capacity and experience. This social invention Taylor exploited to the limit. But these two, the systematic analysis of the phenomenon of bureaucracy and the systematic exploitation of the divisibility of labour, laid the foundations of classical organizational theory and practice. While too much organizational practice has remained based on this theoretical framework, our knowledge of people's behaviour in organizations has grown fast. Let us look at some basic characteristics of organizations.

Organizational behaviour

The concept of a social organization implies (i) a number of people, (ii) acting in common, (iii) to serve some goal or goals. Social organizations are artefacts, have a beginning in time, involve the patterned social interactions of their members and mechanisms for co-ordination and control of these interactions. They differ from such other social institutions as families, language, culture, law, which lack the formal, constructed features of organizations. They differ from groups or aggregates such as audiences or crowds in serving goals which persist, although they may change, over time.

A defining characteristic of an organization is its possession of 'structure', internal differentiation of its parts.

Because it persists over time, possesses structure and behaves in a manner directed towards the attainment of defined or implicit goals, it has frequently been compared with the biological organism. This comparison is an analogy, often fruitful, sometimes dangerously misleading. Nevertheless, the concept of 'system' invoked to understand the interrelation of the parts of the organism to the whole, and with one another, is useful in the study of organizations. The concept of system also draws attention to the organization's self-correcting capacity provided by the operation of 'feedback'. As with organisms, almost all organizations have undergone internal differentiation to the point at which special co-ordination and controlling functions have to be discharged. With increasing differentiation, additional levels of co-ordination and control are required and the organization acquires the typical hierarchical structure. One of the causes of differentiation is advancing technology; as the operations needed to attain the organizational goals become more complex and require more specialized and specially trained people, so the division of labour becomes more complex.

Theoretical development

Returning to the theoretical development, we see that one point of convergence between the theory of bureaucracy and the theory and practice of 'scientific management' has provided a very sticky point in organizational design. In bureaucracies there are 'rulers of hundreds, rulers of fifties and rulers of tens', a hierarchical pyramid based on a rationalization of the work to be done and providing simultaneously a system for delegating authority and a career ladder to be climbed. Taylorist principles, on the other hand, discriminated people clearly into levels of capacity or potential. As we shall see, one of the most pervasive pathologies of organizational functioning derives from the mismatch between the pyramidal structure of organizations and the nature of the task to be fulfilled.

Another of the bureaucratic inventions, developed especially within military formations was the distinction between 'line' and 'staff', between executive functional management and specialist advisory roles. The rigid conceptual separation of 'line' from 'staff' followed the precept 'one man, one boss'. But has anyone ever actually encountered people in organizations who receive all their instructions from one person?

Closely linked with the line–staff dichotomous distinction is the hassle about 'authority' and 'responsibility', matching the individual's authority (power over resources) to his responsibility (answerability for their use), a problem that we cannot tackle by this type of organization theory. In fact, the real problem is less that of matching authority to responsibility or vice versa; it is that of locating the power to make decisions where the information and knowledge needed to make them and the capability to use that information are.

The classical organization theory and the problems which it posed for the practical running of organizations led to, and were served by, a number of scientific specialisms. Industrial engineering, which gleefully adopted Taylor's principles of design, found as its partner industrial psychology. Taking for granted Taylor's assumptions about the role of the man vis-à-vis the machine, industrial psychology applied itself to the twin problems of selection and training (or skill development). The shape of the hole was given, the problem was to find the peg of the right shape or to find ways of whittling the peg to fit. But although what the man was to do and how he was to do it were questions outside the scope of the industrial psychologist, the conditions under which the man worked were inside it. Engineers listened to psychologists on such topics as permissible noise levels, lighting standards, heating and ventilation requirements, while managers accepted their findings about the spacing and timing of meals, and tea or coffee breaks, hours of work and so on.

In the late 1920s and early 1930s, the celebrated Hawthorne experiments raised a whole raft of questions. First they appeared to show that some of the favourable effects on productivity of improvements in working conditions might be due instead to the motivational effects on workers having notice taken of their needs. Apparently also they responded favourably to a more humane and a more permissive style of supervision. It also appeared that the workers exercised their own sets of social controls governing the amount of output considered legitimate, the acceptable degree of absenteeism and so on. This was described as an 'informal organization' paralleling the formal or official organization.

Much effort in organization theory was then devoted to the problem of 'aligning' the formal and informal organizations in the belief that if the goals of the latter could be made congruent with those of the former, the informal organization would operate so as to reinforce rather than oppose the formal organization. This was to be achieved by consultation and by a worker-oriented rather than a production-oriented supervisory style. The human relations movement and its descendant 'organization development' (OD) sprang up to achieve these aims.

The first invasion of organization theory into the field of job design colonized by Taylorism was made at the end of the last war by the new science of ergonomics. The growing sophistication of machines, especially advanced weapon systems, defied the breaking down of their operation into minute repetitive tasks. The demands made by the machine on the man appeared incompatible with man's characteristic capacities. Man is so adaptable that he usually manages somehow to compensate for his incapacities, which is why they are not generally recognized. But man is inherently bad at tasks which involve prolonged vigilance or immediate memory or controlling systems which have a sluggish response to his actions. Once these disabilities and others were recognized the message was clear. Redesign the machines. This was obviously a step in the right direction but it was focused on correcting the negative, avoiding assigning to the man tasks he could not perform. A more positive approach is to take an inventory of man's skills, social as well as technical, and design for their use. But this development has had to wait.

For twenty-five years after Max Weber the impact of sociology on a government bureaucracy but his successors were less cognizant of a government bureaucracy but his successors were less cognisant of the technology of industry. Their investigations were therefore confined to those aspects of workers' lives which were not task-determined. It was not until Joan Woodward's (1965) studies that this bias was overcome. Her studies showed that, contrary to the received theories of organization, the most adaptive structure for an organization depended on the technology it employed. The 'right' organization for a garment factory was different in shape and style from the 'right' organization for an oil refinery. But if you looked at the standard works on organization theory, the nature of the product and the process were apparently treated as irrelevant.

Another assault on classical theory arose from the analysis by Burns and Stalker (1961) of electronics firms adapting to new technologies and changed market conditions. The successful firms were those which operated during 'turbulent' periods in ways which contradicted their own formal organizational pattern and rules. Firms which persisted in functioning 'mechanistically' were less able to adapt to change than those which could operate 'organically'.

The need for an organization to respond with internal change to changes in its external environment is the first principle of open system analysis. *Modern organization theory* starts with this recognition.

The organization is an 'open' system. It receives inputs from its environment and it discharges outputs to the environment. The organizational system develops subsystems to conduct the transactions with the environment and to perform the transformations that convert input to output. A hospital has to have an admission subsystem and a discharge subsystem as well as subsystems for treating patients and monitoring their progress, for acquiring, dismissing, rewarding, punishing and promoting staff, and so on. Generally speaking these subsystems are congruent with departments or groups of departments, but certain people occupy positions in more than one subsystem, and tend to be at co-ordinating and controlling positions in the hierarchy. Sometimes, however, whole departments play a part in more than one subsystem and often they experience conflicting pressures to which the response may be some form of stress.

An organization exposed to the full impact of changes in the environment would endure insupportable stress from all but the most placid environments. Like organisms, organizations develop means of anticipating environmental change and attempt, where they can, to obtain control over the relevant aspects of their environment. As environments become less placidly predictable the need grows to replace control by anticipation. Thus commercial and manufacturing organizations acquire marketing subsystems in place of their selling subsystems – knowledge of future changes in the market and their anticipation becomes necessary for survival and growth. The subsystem on which the organization as a whole is most dependent for its survival tends to become the 'leading' subsystem; the one to which the others must give priority. This does not necessarily mean that it acquires first claim on all material resources, though often it does so, but that its values become the dominant values of the organization. Since people are both slow and reluctant to change their values, organizations in the throes of turbulent environmental change subject their members to severe stress. Occupants of roles on the 'boundary' between the organization and the environment or on the boundaries between subsystems are the most exposed to stress from this and other causes. We consider many of these characteristics of organizations again, with particular reference to the Armed Services, in Chapters 26 and 27.

Before we consider further elements in modern organization theory, it is worth pointing to some responses to change that we may consider to be pathological.

Organizational pathologies

Not all organizational change is adaptive. Organizations whose structure and mode of operation are appropriate to the relatively placid environment in which they previously operated frequently try to cope with turbulence in the environment by intensifying their efforts along traditional lines. A mixture of exhortation and greater central control is the bureaucratic nostrum which unfortunately often produces a rigid and stereotyped, instead of a flexible and imaginative, organizational response. The Ford Motor Company, having exercised control over its market environment – 'any colour so long as it's black', lost its leading position through its slowness in accepting that the market now required competitive styling. Production remained the leading subsystem long after design had replaced it in other companies.

A common organizational pathology is the proliferation of internal differentiation – a new subdepartment to deal with every new need. Each new subdepartment makes more and more demands on the organization's capacity for co-ordination and control, leading to the establishment of yet more co-ordinating, liaison and controlling roles until the organization's capacity is exercised to such a degree in internal control as to leave little to spare for external response.

People involved in subsystems serve first the goals of their subsystem and only secondly the goals of the organization. A department tends to seek to maximize its own function, whereas the optimization of the goals of the organization as a whole may require that the function be less than maximized. In hospitals, particularly mental hospitals, treatment subgoals may conflict with rehabilitation subgoals. Group therapy may fit the patient for life in the therapeutic community but not for life in the unsympathetic world outside.

Another pathological response of organizations is paradoxically their refusal to die. Organizations established for one purpose infrequently disband when that purpose is attained or is no longer attainable. Its members' role occupancy is too rewarding to be surrendered readily. The controlling members of the organization seek new goals. This is not by any means always pathological; the organization represents a large investment of people's experience, skill, time and emotions, as well as its tangible assets. On disbandment the assets may be used more economically or more effectively by a successor organization or organizations but the intangible investments may not. New goals may keep in being a valuable asset in the form of teams of people with expert skills – if only the expert skill of working effectively together.

Two other studies of hospitals as organizations illuminate general points in the theory of organizational behaviour. Management or leadership style express the 'culture' of an organization, but also affect its operation, penetrating to surprising depth. In hospitals where sisters' attitude to nurses was authoritarian, partly reflecting doctors' attitudes to them, the nurses in turn were authoritarian in their behaviour towards patients. Patients took longer to recover.

The structure of formal roles in an organization can specify only to a limited degree the way in which the roles shall be discharged. The person-in-role brings to his role performance his personality and experience. He will discharge his role differently from any other incumbent. Not only is this one part of the dynamic of organizational change, since the role will not be the same after he has left it as it was before he occupied it, but leadership roles must also satisfy the needs of the led as well as those of the organization. People in organizations need in varying degrees paternal – assertive, maternal – nurturant, and fraternal – permissive leadership. As all these cannot be provided by one leader – an intensive study of a mental hospital showed how these leadership roles were filled by the superintendent, assistant superintendent and clinical director respectively – organizations staffed with professionals, people whose professional status provides them with extra organizational moral support, encounter special difficulties particularly when professionals of different kinds have to operate in harness. The professional role places special responsibilities and claims to expertise and jurisdiction in special areas of the organization's functioning. The National Health Service suffers in its overall effectiveness through the professional interests inevitably involved.

The sociotechnical system

Let us turn again to some more positive aspects of organizational behaviour and some of the concepts inherent in modern organizational theory. Inside its boundaries an organization behaves as a sociotechnical system. The technical subsystem defines the tasks to be performed, the social subsystem prescribes the way in which they are performed. Each subsystem has its own logic. Each interacts on the other through every man–machine interface. If you attempt to design an organization solely around the logic of your technology, your social subsystem will operate waywardly. Maximizing the potentialities of the technology leads to a suboptimal sociotechnical design. The goal has to be joint optimization of the two subsystems. An injunction to pursue joint optimization would be empty advice without some technique for doing it. This technique exists – sociotechnical analysis. We shall discuss this fully in the next chapter. We can use it to scan the entire activity of an organization to locate the sources of variability in it. It is to control these that the organization is constructed. Some of the variabilities are within the capacity of a better designed technical subsystem to eliminate; others result from inadequate human functioning and can be eliminated by better allocation of tasks, better training, better communication. Yet others cannot be eliminated given the current state of technology or without unjustified expense. If the social subsystem is to cope with and control these variances, it may need to be redesigned. But the clues to what to redesign, and how, come from location of the sources of variability. Typically in the traditional classical form of organization design, sources of variability are exported from the workplace and dealt with by a supervisory structure. Layer upon layer of supervision and management, control and inspection are erected to cope with unwanted variability. Elaborate management information systems are designed so as to transmit the information about the variability to the level in this structure that is designated to hold responsibility for dealing with it. No wonder increased environmental turbulence leads to internal proliferation of management controls. Each extra layer of management devalues the currency of management; firms which have not actually increased the number of management layers have achieved a similar outcome in terms of devaluing jobs by pushing responsibility and authority upwards.

'Job enrichment' has been one of the techniques which has arisen specifically to counteract this tendency. Part of its attractiveness is in the psychological theory on which it claims to be based. Briefly

303

this theory states that there is a hierarchy of psychological needs from physiological and safety needs at the bottom to the need for 'self actualization' at the top. Until each 'lower' need is satisfied, the higher does not start to emerge and operate as a motive. If, then, people's needs for security are met – enough money to buy the necessities of life, reasonable guarantee of future income – they are free to feel the needs for meaning in their lives and particularly in their work. Job enrichment, by seeking to provide more responsibility, seeks to fulfil these needs. But because it leaves untouched the structure of the organization and its mode of responding to external change it treats the symptoms without removing the basic causes of drift. But job enrichment has contributed to modern organization theory by demonstrating the linkage between organizational structure and functioning, on the one hand, and on the other hand a plausible theory of motivation, one which clearly represents a major advance on the psychological theory underlying Taylorism.

Another advance is the attempt to meet people's needs for esteem and self-esteem which led to the recognition that people at all levels in organizations needed to be responsive to the needs and motivations of others.

Leadership has two different functions to discharge; one is to orient people towards the task to be performed; the other is to keep the group together, to prevent frictions rising to a degree which prevents co-operation. Organizational design practitioners aim to help managers achieve a balance between task leadership and interpersonal sensitivity. Generally, they assume that it is the latter which our present organizational and social structures inhibit or fail to encourage – hence the development of sensitivity training, T-group training, etc.

Again these approaches fail to remove the structural bases for conflict. Their contribution to organizational theory is to stress the fact that organizational goals can be achieved only through the actions of people and that their actions are devoted to a considerable extent towards coping with their relationships with others engaged in the same enterprise.

Many technicalities of management are now extensively catered for with new techniques: budgetary control, corporate planning, 'management by objectives', operational research, systems analysis are all powerful tools. Their use within the military is considered in Chapter 26. All alike suffer the defects of their qualities. Because they are sophisticated, because they are specialized and require the acquisition of detailed knowledge and a complex methodology, they become the province of new management specialists. Like all powerful aids they pose the question: Who is boss? Thus insecure managers either surrender their initiative to, or seal off the intrusion of, specialist advice they cannot understand or control; even secure managers are hard put to keep abreast of the developments they represent. They pose in acute form one of the key problems facing contemporary organizations: How does an organization learn? The most common response is to assign that learning function to a specialist department or departments. Corporate planners, management specialists do the learning. But the learning activity is not diffused throughout the organization. In crude anthropomorphic terms, the brain may learn how to ride a bicycle, but unless the muscles learn it too, the bicycle will go one way and the body another. And if the muscles learn but the brain does not receive the muscular messages, the bicycle and the body will go together under the nearest bus.

This requirement, that organizations *as a whole* must learn, brings us to what we may call *contemporary organization theory*. The theory of bureaucracy and scientific management represent the *classical* theory, the 'informal' organization and human relations, management systems, the hierarchy of needs, the malfunctions of leadership, the man–machine as system, the relationship of technology to structure, and the early aspects of sociotechnical system analysis represent *modern* organization theory. Contemporary theory, developing from and representing no repudiation of modern theory, is essentially a response to three processes external of organizations themselves. The first of these processes is the increased turbulence of the environment of organizations. Organizational operations have become so large in themselves, so interactive with those of other organizations and so bound up with political and social as well as economic events and developments that the environment in which they operate is not only enormously complex but is itself more than marginally affected by the organization's decisions.

The second process is really a special feature of the first. The impact of organizations on their physical and social environments has become a matter of expressed social concern. Environmental pollution, the exhaustion of natural resources, the growth of urbanization attendant upon industrialization, the power of industry to make possible a consumer society, the consequent widening of the gulf between rich and poor countries all accumulate to a pressure upon industry to accept responsibility for its social impacts. Industrial firms are obliged to accept their role as *social* institutions with *social* goals, to incorporate social goals among their institutional economic goals.

The third process is again related to the second. The firm is an employer of people. What happens to those people is a concern to the people themselves and to society as well as to the firm. And, as we saw in the previous chapter, people's expectations about their lives are increasing. They are more, if not better, educated than their predecessors. Their readiness to accept arbitrary authority has diminished. Their tendency to be critical of the social objectives of their organization is growing. Their demands from work in terms of self-fulfilment are increasing. Organizations are therefore obliged to reconsider their operations, their structure, their style, their philosophy to meet these new needs and new concerns.

Living organisms in the course of evolution have expanded their effective environment, the environmental features to which they have to respond, and are equipped to respond. In the course of this process they have sacrificed specialization to multipurposiveness, rigidity to responsiveness, redundancy of parts to redundancy of functions. Contemporary organization theory is concerned with a similar transformation of organizations. Organisms followed this path not by possessing a master plan, a blueprint, but by learning *how* to evolve. Contemporary organization theory stresses the *processual* aspects of organizational learning and organizational change. The means whereby an organization seeks to attain its objectives give it its character and culture. This is something we take up again in Chapter 22 when we consider the opportunities for organization design in developing countries. Its potential for survival and growth are determined by the mode it adopts for responding to change. Organization theory and organizational change have become inseparable. Theory can no longer lag behind practice, describing and explaining after the event. Theory is now the learning component of development and change, and hence organizational change through experiment must be our next step.

Organizational change through experiment

What are the goals of organizational change? As organizations are open systems they have to respond to change in their environment, both external and internal. Furthermore, an organization needs to do more than respond to environmental change; it also has to take initiative action to maintain control over as much of its environment as possible. So organizational change is of two kinds, responsive and initiative. But there is a third kind which we may describe as adaptive. An organization needs to equip itself for making future change. It can be very shortsighted to respond to environmental demands in such a way as to render oneself incapable of responding to future demands. Evolutionary history abounds with illustrations of living organisms which responded in ingenious ways to environmental demands, and in the process rendered themselves unable to cope with further change.

Information flow, communication, is in many organizations an open loop system. Learning in plenty takes place at the operating level but that learning never reaches the planners and designers, the co-ordinators and the controllers. Any social scientist or organization consultant entering a company knows that he will quickly learn quite vital information which is directly contrary to the beliefs of the top men.

If an organization, then, is to be adaptive as well as responsive and initiating, it must somehow close the learning loop. Decision-making must be moved to where the information is. So, in effect, the decision-making functions must be widely diffused.

The culture of a society or of an organization is characterized more by the *means* it adopts to achieve its objectives than the objectives themselves. Experiment, or more accurately, action research implies the participation in both the research and the action by all the groups concerned. It is also the mode whereby external inputs by social scientists can be made without the danger of their becoming the servants of a particular clientele. Knowledge is power, and each group concerned is aware that the knowledge acquired in the course of research can be used to strengthen the power of one group. As external researchers are brought in by management the obvious inference is that the knowledge they acquire will strengthen the hand of management. Thus sanctioning for the action research has to be given at all levels concerned. Although top management may be the sponsors of the experimental activity, all groups are equally the clients.

Experiments also need *protection*. Because they involve changes, they are threatening. Because they are novel, they evoke mistrust as well as interest. Because they are really experiments, their immediate success cannot be guaranteed. For all these reasons they need protection against premature assessment and arbitrary termination. Furthermore, they place an immense load of responsibility upon the heads of the departments or divisions within which they take place. It is quite unfair to expect a new head drafted in to such a post to accept responsibility for experimental designs to whose creation he was not a party. It is difficult, but crucial, to ensure that people in such positions should not be removed from their posts during certain agreed phases of the experiment.

It is also essential that the experiment should not be confounded or confused with other changes or research or consultancy going on at the same time. Managers sometimes do fail to let their right hand know what their left is doing, but this is not seen by their subordinates as laughable incompetence, but as deep and devious treachery. Nothing is better calculated to destroy the trust which is the essential basis for all action research and experiment.

The role of the unions

The unions are partners in design. We cannot design organizations without considering the role of the unions. They have a legitimate concern with the organization lives of their members. Likewise, we must consider the unions in any action research programme, although the principles of organization change, through experiment or action research, are essentially the same whether the organization is one with unions or not. But where the firm is unionized, special considerations are involved.

Union representatives are delegated by their constituents to deal on their behalf with management on a specified set of issues. These may vary. They always include negotiations on pay and certain conditions. In many firms there are councils and committees with elected members representing workers quite separately from their union representatives. The functions of these councils and committees are distinct from the negotiating issues between management and union.

Thus, depending upon circumstances, a union may or may not have a status by right in connection with a particular organizational change. And it may or may not have such a status by custom or courtesy and not through negotiated right. But in changes designed to increase workers' participation in decision-making about their work, unions have very complex interests.

First, this increased participation may represent a change in responsibility and skill justifying a change in job grading, a matter usually requiring negotiation with the union.

Second, changes which are perceived as favourable may lead to pressures on the union by other workers to obtain similar treatment for them.

Third, changes may involve crossing demarcation lines between trades, a serious difficulty if more than one union is involved.

Fourth, unions may be suspicious of any change which brings men into close co-operation with supervision and management. They may fear that their own mediating role will be threatened, that their members will participate in making decisions which are currently perceived as bargaining issues. If management exploit the involvement of their workers to eliminate or reduce the power of the unions, they invite their opposition.

Thus unions are likely to be ambivalent both about the experiments themselves and about participating in them. On the whole, while union sanction is essential in most cases, direct union participation is not. It may involve the union too deeply in the operation of the enterprise. But the basis on which union sanction is given must be clear. A union sanctioning an experiment does not thereby engage to co-operate in the experiment by suspending its normal activities. The degree of protection the experiment requires from the union must be negotiated and established, just as the degree of protection it requires from top management requires to be negotiated and established.

Chapter 16
The Principles of Sociotechnical Design

The art of organization design is simultaneously esoteric and poorly developed. Most existing organizations, like Topsy, were not born but 'just growed'. There is, of course, no lack of available models and no one seeking to set up an organization need invent the wheel. Engineers readily perceive that they are involved in organization design and that what they are designing is a sociotechnical system built around much knowledge and thought on the technical and little on the social side of the system. There is, of course, the danger that the term 'sociotechnical system' very rapidly becomes a shibboleth, the mere pronouncing of which distinguishes the cognoscenti from the ignorant and uninitiated. But recognizing that a production system requires a social system to relate together and integrate the activities of the people who operate, maintain and renew it, account for it and keep it fed with the resources it requires and dispose of the products, does nothing by itself to improve the design. And while discussion of the characteristics of social systems is helpful, that still leaves us with the problem that there are many ways of achieving their essential objectives.

Any social system must, if it is to survive, perform the function of Parson's four subsystems (Parsons, 1951). These functions are those of attainment of the goals of the organization; adaptation to the environment; integration of the activities of the people in the organization, including the resolution of conflict whether task-based, organization-based or interpersonally based; and providing for the continued occupation of the essential roles through recruitment and socialization. The advantage of this analysis is that it tells the designer that if he doesn't take these absolute requirements of a social system into account, he will find that they will be met in some way or other and quite probably in ways that will do as much to thwart as to facilitate the functions for which he does plan. But it still leaves wide open the question of how to design a social system or, more fundamentally, how much a social system should be designed. That there is a choice in such matters can be as much a revelation to the engineer, as the fact that there is a choice of technology to achieve production objectives is to the social scientist.

How, then, do you design a sociotechnical system? Can we communicate any principles of sociotechnical design? The first thing to be said is that a lot depends upon your objectives. As we have said, all organizations are sociotechnical systems; that is no more than a definition, a tautology. But the phrase really means that organizational objectives are best met by the joint optimization of the technical and the social aspects, exploiting the adaptability and innovativeness of people in attaining goals, instead of overdetermining technically the manner in which these goals should be attained.

It is an obvious corollary that such design requires knowledge of the way machines and technical systems behave and of the way people and groups behave, which means engineers discussing alternative technical ways of attaining objectives with social scientists. This is not easy unless social scientists will take the trouble to learn enough about technology to understand the kinds of options that are open to engineers. The design team has indeed to be a multifunctional one, as we have described in Chapter 13.

No doubt the constant interchange in the process of design of ideas between engineer, manager, social scientist, financial controller and personnel specialist and so on can do much to ensure that all aspects are considered, but the sociotechnical concepts involved need not be hammered out afresh every time. They can be collected and presented in such a way as to ensure that they are taken account of, while not straitjacketing the designer. To this end we have described nine 'Principles', but offer them as a checklist not a blueprint. They represent a distillation of experience and owe more to the writings of others (Emery and Trist, 1972; Herbst, 1974) than to our own originality. They have not, however, previously been systematized and, we hope, demystified.

The 'Principles' are:

1 *The principle of compatibility*

The process of design must be compatible with its objectives. If the objective of design is a system capable of self-modification, of adapting to change, and of making the most use of the creative capacities of the individual, then a constructively participative organization is needed. A participative social system cannot be created by fiat. A necessary condition for it to occur is that people are given the opportunity to participate in the design of the jobs they are to perform. In a redesign of an existing organization the people are already there; a new design has, however, to be undertaken before most of the people are hired; to some extent their jobs will have been designed for them in advance. But this extent can be kept to a minimum. Having defined what are the objectives to be met and the competences required to meet them, discussion of how the job is to be performed can be deferred until the individual is appointed. Clearly *some* decisions had and have to be taken in advance; there has to be a pretty firm notion of how many people will be required and of what kinds of competence to be sought, but this is governed by the second principle.

2 *The principle of minimal critical specification*

This principle has two aspects, negative and positive. The negative simply states that no more should be specified than is absolutely essential; the positive requires that we identify what *is* essential. It is of wide application and implies the minimal crucial specification of tasks, the minimal critical allocation of tasks to jobs or of jobs to roles, the specification of objectives but the minimal critical specification of methods of obtaining them. While it may be necessary to be quite precise about what has to be done, it is rarely necessary to be precise about how it is to be done. In most organizations there is far too much specificity about 'how' and indeed about 'what'. Any careful observer of people in their work situation will reveal how people contrive to get the job done in despite of the rules. As we know from the example of the railmen in Britain, the whole system can be quickly brought to a grinding halt by 'working to rule'. Many of the rules are there to provide protection when things go wrong for the man who imposed them; strictly applied, they totally inhibit adaptation or even effective action.

It is a mistake to specify more than you need, because by doing so you are closing options that could be kept open. This premature closing of options is a pervasive fault in design; it arises because of the desire to reduce uncertainty and also because it helps you to get your own way. We measure our success and effectiveness less by the quality of the ultimate design than by the quantity of our ideas and preferences that have been incorporated into it.

One way of dealing with the cavalier treatment of options is to challenge each design decision and demand that alternatives always be offered. This may result in claims that the design process is being expensively delayed. Design proposals may also be defended on the grounds that any other choice will run up against some obstacle such as a company practice, or a trade union agreement, or a manning problem. These obstacles can then be regarded and logged as constraints upon a better sociotechnical solution. When they have all been logged, each can be examined to estimate the cost of removing it. The cost may sometimes be prohibitive, but frequently turns out to be less formidable than supposed or than the engineer has presented it to be.

3 *The principle of variance control*

The principle states that 'variances', if they cannot be eliminated, must be consumed as near to their point of origin as possible. We here define 'variance' as any unprogrammed event; a 'key' variance is one which critically affects the outcome. This might be a deviation in quality of raw material, the failure to take action at a critical time, a machine failure, and so on. Much of the elaboration of supervision, inspection and management is the effort to control variance, typically by action which does less to prevent variance than to try to correct its consequences. The most obvious example is the inspection function. Inspecting a product, the outcome of any activity, does not put right what is wrong. And if this inspection is carried out in a separate department some time after the event, the correction of the variance becomes a long loop which is a poor design for learning. The principle of variance control would advise us to incorporate inspection with production, where possible allowing people to inspect their own work, thus learning from their mistakes and thus also reducing the number of communication links across departmental boundaries, an issue we take up again in our discussion of Principle 5. The fewer the variances that are exported from the place where they arise, the less the levels of supervision and control required and the more 'complete' the jobs of the people concerned – to whom it now becomes possible to allocate an objective and the resources necessary to attain it. Frequently what is required to attain this objective turns out to be the supply of the appropriate information, as discussed under the heading of Principle 6.

A detailed example of the effective use of variance analysis is given by Engelstad in his account of the Hunsfos Pulp and Paper

313

Mill (Engelstad, 1972). Briefly, variances affecting the quality of the paper arose from variances in the input material as result of their differing growing and storage conditions. Additional variances were introduced by the mixing of different woods. The various chemical processes, although conducted separately, were not independent in their effects. The requirements of the technology were not fully known or predictable. The organization, however, did not reflect the impact of these variances. The four shift foremen were responsible for the chemical and mechanical pulping, though these were not technically independent. Jobs were strictly delineated. In previous attempts to overcome difficulties, the firm had first increased the number of supervisors – the additional foreman acted as a trouble-shooter, thus increasing the segregation of the jobs of his men – second introduced a production bonus, although the operators could only influence quality, not quantity, and third introduced laboratory staff to try to improve quality, though they could only record, not influence, quality. As they reported results through the foreman, the feedback loop to the operators was both long and variable.

These arrangements provided no incentive either for sharing knowledge or learning. One boilerman, who had discovered that one of the four pulp digesters was particularly suitable for pulping a certain wood, had kept this piece of information to himself.

The critical (key) variances in the process were finally brought under control by a redesign of the organization, giving operators as a group increased access to information, responsibility for the process as a whole, a reward system based on measurement of what they *could* control, and appropriate training.

4 *The multifunctional principle:* organism versus mechanism

The traditional form of organization relies very heavily on the redundancy of parts. It requires people to perform highly specialized, fractionated tasks. There is often a rapid turnover of such people but they are comparatively easily replaced. Disadvantages arise where a range of responses is required, where the repertoire of performances required from the mechanism or the organization is large. This typically occurs where the environmental demands vary. It then becomes more adaptive and less wasteful for each element to possess more than one function. The same function can be performed in different ways using different combinations of elements. There are several routes to the same goal – the principle sometimes described as 'equifinality'. Complex organisms have all gone this route of development. The principle of minimal critical specification permits the organization to adopt this principle also. Perhaps the best example of the multiple repertoire is the military unit. It may have as its primary role a technical function, a secondary combat role and an unstated but universal requirement for representation; it must be able to represent the Army, Marines or whatever to the outside world. The three roles require different repertoires of performance, different modes of functioning. A combat unit has a formal organization for drills and internal control; in combat it functions quite differently, in more or less autonomous small teams. Multiple functioning is achieved by training the same people in a repertoire of different performances, each requiring a separate set of rules and role relationships.

5 The principle of boundary location

In any organization departmental boundaries have to be drawn somewhere. Miller (1959) has shown that such boundaries are usually drawn so as to group people and activities on the basis of one or more of three criteria – technology, territory, time. Grouping by technology is typically seen in machine shops when all the grinding machines are in one room, the grinding department, the milling machines in another, the milling department, and so on. The consequences of this for the scheduling of work has been well described by Williamson (1972). A part in construction may spend months shuffling between departments, spending 1 per cent of its time 'in progress' in contact with the machines. The consequent excessive cost of 'work in progress' has been one of the stimuli to 'group technology', the establishment of departments each containing a variety of machines so that a part can be completed within one department. This corresponds to a grouping on the basis of time – (i.e.) the contiguity in time of operations indicates that they may well be organized together. Group technology has consequences also for the operation of the department – as a team with its members taking responsibility for the scheduling of operations and possibly the rotation of jobs. Other examples of grouping on the basis of technology are, of course, the typing pool and the telephone switchboard.

The switchboard may also be an example of the criterion of *territory*. Switchboard operators are bound together by the design of the machine. But the territorial principle can operate on the basis of little other than spatial contiguity. If the engineers have for convenience located different activities in the same area, the maintenance of control over the people working there suggests that they be made answerable to the same supervision. Retail trade organization is often of this kind with a floor supervisor. Organizations of this kind give rise to 'dotted-line' relationships of functional responsibility.

All of these criteria are pragmatic and defensible up to a point. But they possess notable disadvantages. They tend to erect boundaries which interfere with the desirable sharing of knowledge and experience. A simple example may suffice. In an organization concerned with the distribution of petroleum products studied by Cherns and Taylor (unpublished report), the clerks who collected customers' orders were organized in a department separate from the drivers for whom schedules were worked out. A driver would pick up a schedule allocating him a vehicle and a route. Frequently the receipt of the routine would stimulate a string of expletives from the driver. That is because the drivers had acquired a great deal of knowledge about customers, routes, etc., but being organized in separate departments they shared very little of this knowledge with the routing clerks who, however, received the customers' complaints before the drivers. A sectoral matrix allocating a group of drivers and routes to sectors of territory was one solution to this problem.

The principle has certain corollaries. One very important one concerns the management of the boundaries between department and department, between department and the organization as a whole and between the organization and the outside world. The more that the control of activities within the department becomes the responsibilities of the members, the more the role of the supervisor/foreman/manager is concentrated on the boundary activities – assuring adequate resources to the team to carry out their functions, co-ordinating the activities with those of other departments and viewing ahead the changes likely to impart upon them. This boundary maintenance role is precisely the requirement of the supervisor in a well-designed system. A further development is to charge teams, where possible, with responsibility for managing their own boundaries, placing the responsibility for co-ordination on those whose activities require to be co-ordinated.

6   The principle of information flow

This principle states that information systems should be designed to provide information *in the first place* to the point where action on the basis of it will be needed. Information systems are not typically so designed. The capacity of computer-controlled systems to provide information about the state of the system both totally and in great detail to any organizational point has been used to supply to the top echelons of the organization information which is really useful only at lower levels and which acts as an incitement to the top management to intervene in the conduct of operations for which their subordinates are and should be responsible. The designer of the information system is naturally concerned to demonstrate its potentialities and is hard to convince that certain kinds of information can be potentially harmful when presented to high organizational levels and can lead to counter-productive behaviour. Typically, systems designers respond to such behaviour by a further turn of the screw, making the situation worse. In one hospital a computerized patients' records system sat a girl at a console VDU with a fading display (to keep her tied to her console), punching records off forms supplied to her. The computer rejected incomplete information. The girl's only contact was with her supervisor by telephone. One girl discovered that by keying five consecutive errors she could outwit the computer which gave the signal 'revert to manual', allowing the girl to leave her desk and sort out the problem with those who supplied the form. Response of the designer – 'We must tighten up the program to eliminate that possibility.' Fortunately, second thoughts have prevailed; the computer now notifies the girl of the missing data; she is to judge whether the missing information requires immediate action or can be left to a 'natural break'.

Properly directed, sophisticated information systems can, however, supply a work team with exactly the right type and amount of feedback to enable them to learn to control the variances which occur within the scope of their spheres of responsibility and competence and to anticipate events likely to have a bearing on their performance.

7   *The principle of support congruence*

The principle states that the systems of social support should be designed so as to reinforce the behaviours which the organization structure is designed to elicit. If, for example, the organization is designed on the basis of group or team operation with team responsibility, a payment system incorporating individual members would be incongruent with these objectives. Not only payment systems, but systems of selection, training, conflict resolution, work measurement, performance assessment, timekeeping, leave allocation, promotion and separation can all reinforce or contradict the behaviours which are desired. This is to say that the management philosophy should be consistent and that managements' actions should be consistent with their expressed philosophy. Not infrequently management committed to philosophies of participation simultaneously adopt systems of work measurement, for example, which are in gross contradiction. Even managements as progressive and committed to the humanization of work, as that of Volvo's Kalmar plant, have retained a commitment to a system of payment based on MTM – a technique of work measurement utilizing time and method study. This may in fact, until replaced, pose an obstacle to the further humanization of work at Kalmar to which the management is committed.

8 *The principle of design and human values*

This principle states that an objective of organizational design should be to provide a high quality of working life to its members. We recognize that quality is a subjective phenomenon, and that not everyone wants to have responsibility, variety, involvement, growth, etc. The objective is to provide these for those who do want it without subjecting those who don't to the tyranny of peer control. In this regard we are obliged to recognize that all desirable objectives may not be achievable simultaneously.

What constitutes human work is a matter again of subjective judgement based on certain psychological assumptions. Thorsrud (1972) has identified six characteristics of a 'good job' which can be striven for in the design of organizations and jobs. They are as follows:

(i)   the need for the content of a job to be reasonably demanding of the worker in terms other than sheer endurance, and yet to provide a minimum of variety (not necessarily novelty);

(ii)   the need to be able to learn on the job and to go on learning – again it is a question of neither too much nor too little;

(iii)   the need for some minimal area of decision-making that the individual can call his own;

(iv)   the need for some minimal degree of social support and recognition in the work place;

(v)   the need for the individual to be able to relate what he does and what he produces to his social life;

(vi)   the need to feel that the job leads to some sort of desirable future (not necessarily promotion).

9   *The principle of transitional organization*

This principle states that there is a changeover period from old to new which requires a transitional organization. What all introductions of new forms, design and redesign require alike is that the planning of implementation should begin with the beginning of design. It is no use producing the most perfect design if it cannot be implemented. And implementation implies a third design, besides the old and the new. During the changeover from the old to the new in redesign, the people in the organization have to run both – a requirement that must be planned, organized, *designed* and trained *for*. During the setting up and running-in period before a new design comes fully on-stream, a quite different organization is required from the on-stream one. This, too, needs planning, organizing, designing and training. On the whole these processes of implementation have received less attention from social scientists than the other aspects of design. But I believe that some unsuccessful new designs and especially redesigns fail because they have not been designed to withstand the strains of the changeover period. Essentially, what is required is a careful rehearsal of the roles to be performed during the changeover and especially the continuing training role of the supervisor.

10   *The principle of incompletion: the Forth Bridge principle*

Design is a reiterative process. The closure of options opens new ones. At the end we are back at the beginning. The Forth Bridge, in its day an outstanding example of iron technology, required painting to fend off rust. Starting at the Midlothian end a posse of painters no sooner reached the Fife end than the Midlothian end required painting again. Varying the image, Jewish tradition prescribes that one brick be omitted in the construction of a dwelling lest the jealousy of God's angels be excited. Disregarding the superstition, the message is acceptable. As soon as design is implemented, its consequences indicate the need for redesign. The multifunctional, multilevel, multidisciplinary team required for design is needed for its evaluation and review.

Need I say that these principles are guides not prescriptions? I certainly need to reiterate that the role of the social scientist is facilitatory, providing what is needed in new ways of looking at and perceiving organizations and their environments. In Chapters 23 and 24 we look at this question with particular reference to organizations, technology and their environment in developing countries, suggesting the need for a sociotechnical assessment of appropriate technology.

In this chapter I have concentrated more on design than on redesign. The design principles are no different; the processes of realizing them are. Many writers have discussed organization change; Emery has designed a system of 'deep slices', groups collected across all levels and functions of an organization to obtain rapid commitment and to release innovative ideas and suggestions. Herbst has emphasized the needs to plan for diffusion by initiating change in at least two parts of the organization. Thorsrud has pointed to the advantages of obtaining joint commitment to change by two or more organizations.

We are still learning and developing. If we are unable to provide guaranteed recipes for managers to follow, and I for one do not believe we ever could, we can help them to understand what options for design they have and how they can evaluate them.

Section III
Work

Chapter 17
Social Change and Work

Introduction – the value of work

Work is a curse. For that we have the authority of the Bible, Gen. 3
17–19:

> 'Because you have listened to your wife
> and have eaten from the tree which I forbade you
> accursed shall be the ground on your account.
> With labour you shall win your food from it
> all the days of your life.
> It will grow thorns and thistles for you,
> none but wild plants for you to eat.
> You shall gain your bread by the sweat of your brow
> until you return to the ground;
> for from it you were taken
> Dust you are, to dust you shall return.'

Marx was equally lyrical, if less contemptuous. 'The worker has
spun, and the product is his web.' However, he is apparently caught
in his own web because 'To be a productive worker is not a piece of
good luck, but a misfortune' (Marx, 1972).

The inspiration for technology, returning to Eden through
eliminating the sweat, entangled us in the web of relationships
which alienated the worker from the product of his toil. But perhaps
this is only a step on the way to automation and the conquest of
work. Aristotle had already posed this question: 'Suppose that
every tool we had could perform its function, either at our bidding

or itself perceiving the need . . . and suppose that shuttles in a loom could fly to and fro and a plucker play on a lyre all self-moved, then manufacturers would have no need of workers nor masters of slaves' (Aristotle, 1969).

If we could eliminate work we would remove the basis for oppression, the Marxian paradigm of alienation. But work has another face. By work man relates himself to the world in which he lives; to the world of people and things around him, and to his own 'self'. Fromm indeed, in his book, *Man for Himself*, uses 'productivity' as man's moral standard and aim (Fromm, 1947). In the words of Faust, 'Though not secure yet free to active toil . . . he only earns his freedom and existence, who daily conquers them anew' (Goethe, 1959). In the active use of his powers, man fulfils and constantly creates his destiny.

His work *is* the man.

Work was man's chosen route to achieve his teleology, whatever it was. He worked for the greater glory of God in the age of faith and for greater prosperity in the economic age. When salvation by faith was replaced by salvation through work, industry replaced the church as the dominant social institution. Our political, social and educational institutions had to be framed so as to enable industry to thrive and to grow, because the products of our social institutions, men and women, were needed for this above all.

Because industrial, and for that matter agricultural, work was unpleasant and hard, but had to be done, discipline was the prime virtue. And because man creates himself by his work, he had to acquire self-discipline to grow. He must learn to love his work. This brings the strange paradox that we must love our work, but if we love doing it, it is not really 'work'. Tom Sawyer, without knowing it, made the great discovery that 'work consists of whatever a body is obliged to do, and play consists of whatever a body is not obliged to do' (Twain, 1943).

Work, then, may be perceived as a burden, as a punishment for ancestral sin, as an unwelcome intrusion into the spiritual life, as the yoke and stigma of a 'working' class, or as man's true vocation, as ennobling, as the service he owes to his fellows or to his God, as his principal mode of relating to 'reality' or to his environment, as a drug to deaden the pain of thought, or a way of filling and ordering time. Most of us manage to combine some and some of us most of these concepts at different times and in different contexts. Thus it is a brave or a foolish man who would pontificate about the place of work in a whole society, or its work ethos, or of the attitudes to work of a whole people. On the other hand, we are aware of change and should seek to identify, understand and explain it, not forgetting that changes can affect differing groups in society in different ways bringing different definitions of what is to be included in 'work' to different people. We often tend to obscure issues and to confuse ourselves by talking of 'work' when we mean 'employment'. The value we attach to employment naturally tends to increase when employment becomes scarcer and to diminish when it becomes more abundant. But the value we attach to our work is not necessarily affected in the same way. When, on the other hand, the need for people to do what has been traditionally regarded as work diminishes, change may come less immediately in our beliefs about work than in our definitions of what constitutes it. Some ten years ago an editorial article in *The Economist* argued that as modernization of Britain's industrial structure required that people employed in declining industries should be forced or urged out of them to create the 'pool' from which new developing industries could create their labour force, and since they would thus be forced out of work for no fault of their own and to serve the interests of the community as a whole, they should receive an adequate wage for the job of work pool member, not unemployment pay based on subsistence considerations. Since then we have heard much more of the structural argument that the comparative affluence of the majority is built on a system of stratification which inevitably produces the exploitation of a minority whose claims are therefore for recompense not charity. These arguments, though from politically very different schools, bear more than a surface resemblance.

We should therefore be aware of the wide social and cultural influences affecting beliefs about and attitudes to work. We also need to take care to distinguish between beliefs about and attitudes to work and beliefs about and attitudes to employment. Finally, we need to remember that different groups and classes are affected unequally.

Forces making for change in society

(a) *Technology*

In trying to understand the changes in society and culture of which none of us can be unaware, we tend, because it is the most obvious and dramatic, to think of technology as the principal source and to think of it as if it were in some way exogenous to society. Now it is, of course, true that new technologies have wrought immense changes. But there has never been a time without technological innovation. What has characterized Western society since the industrial revolution has been its growing acceptance of innovation and its readiness to pay its price. This was not always so. Nor should we take for granted the uses to which technology has been put. We tend unthinkingly to subscribe to a kind of technological determinism which has two main features – first that technology is an independent exogenous factor, and second that it has its own logic. Together these make us the prisoners of a development unable to resist the inexorable logic that what can be done will inevitably *be* done – the logic of Concord. It comes as a strange idea that society has a choice of its technology and of what it will do with its technological capabilities; and, even stranger, that this is what political processes are, or should be, largely about. Indeed, one of the forces making for change in cultural attitudes to work is the revaluation of technology brought about by wider recognition of its unreckoned costs, the negative consequences of an unheeding embrace of all it offered.

The search for exogenous sources of change is in any event mistaken. Opportunities for change are always present in the environment; what is significant is what our culture predisposes us to make of them, how the structural elements of our society are differentially affected by the power shifts that would be involved in, and consequent upon, their use. We have experienced for the last 200 years the dominance in our societies of the groups whose interests were served best by the adoption of industrial technology, and who possessed the power to take the necessary decisions.

If technological policy has been widely based, the sum of many decisions taken by many people, population decisions have been so dispersed as to be unrecognizable as a policy. Yet population change has been one of the most powerful of all factors influencing attitudes of all kinds and not least those towards work and employment.

(b) *Population*

In Chapter 23 of this book we discuss in some detail the process of change in population growth, the so-called demographic transition, and do not wish to repeat it here – but will draw out some of the conclusions and their impact on 'work'.

Over the last three generations the whole shape of the population has changed, giving a population distribution in more advanced countries in which the ratio of dependent old to population of working age has greatly increased. Simultaneously the statutory school-leaving ages have tended to rise and a larger proportion of young people remain in education beyond the school-leaving age. The tendency for women to marry early by historical standards, to start their child-bearing career earlier, to have fewer children and to be free by their early 30s of caring for children under school age has provided a large reservoir of women workers. The most notable statistical change is in the ratio of men to women in work.

In Britain, for example, between 1951 and 1972 the working population grew by one and a third million, all women. In fact there were 1·4 million more working women and 45,000 fewer working men. The number of *married* women working increased by 2½ million while the number of unmarried working women dropped by 1·1 million. In 1972 women constituted 36 per cent of the working population. This proportion is expected to continue to rise strongly and to reach 38 per cent by 1986. Meanwhile the proportion of the whole population 'economically active' remained stationary at 46·5 per cent. Cultural symbols and themes based on the norm of work as the activity of the male breadwinner cannot long survive real changes of this kind. In many ways the world of work is still a man's world, as we are constantly reminded by the proponents of sex equality and women's liberation: change may be slow in coming but it is unquestionably coming and its implications are enormous. What are the changes in our view of work that have come about through its increasing feminization? A central feature of working-class culture was the acquisition of masculinity through work. Much work was physically heavy and demanding, holding your own in a man's world was the school-leaver's aim and to attain it he often had to endure a *rite de passage.* His position in the family as a contribution to its economic welfare with its concomitant due of deference and special treatment was established. Today his sister may earn as much as a typist, his work is usually less physically demanding and the work milieu less aggressively male.

We can only sketch here the consequences for work of population changes and the value changes associated with them. Changing attitudes to women's work, to adolescents at work and to retirement are obvious. The effect of migrations is equally obvious – the 6 or 7 million foreign workers in Europe, the Commonwealth immigrants in Britain make clear the association between developments in the world of work and social, political, especially international, and economic policies. As demographic change affects work, so does change in work affect population. With movements across frontiers partly open we have all the uncertainties of a partly managed open system.

(c) *Education*

A society with fewer dependent children can afford to keep them dependent longer. This is not the sole reason why children are kept longer in school and why more stay beyond the legal minimum. Our technological society has become more complex, requires more and higher-level skills to manage it. The opportunities of all kinds that society offers are open principally to the skilled and the functionally literate and numerate. The opportunities for those who have only youth and strength to offer have diminished and those that remain carry low prestige. Longer and higher education engender higher expectations from life and from work in particular. As in life in general, reality seldom or never meets rising expectations. Much of the dissatisfaction with work reported among young people owes its origin to this fact.

Popular education, even mass literacy and higher education for ever growing proportions of the population do not necessarily inevitably lead to an ever-broadening democratic basis of political mobilization; they do lead, however, to a broader base of recruitment of political elites. Meritocracy is as possible as participatory democracy.

Educational changes both follow and lead technology. The present vogue for 'continuing education', 'recyclage', and so on, recognizes that the rate of technological change renders specific skills quickly obsolete. And technology is coded knowledge, the product of education; a high level of material technology is the product of materialist values in education, as a high level of religious technology was the product of spiritual values in education.

(d) *Media*

While we should never ignore or underestimate the capacity of the political system to set work goals and place political valuations on work, other influences are as powerful. No technological innovations have affected our lives more than the strides in the technology of communications and none has had more influence on attitudes and values. In particular, the immediacy of the mass media enhances and amplifies variance and deviation. It is the unexpected, the outrageous, the new, the protesting, the law-breaking, the custom-breaking, the norm-transgressing that feed the media; what they transmit back is the interest, the excitement, the attention that far more often acts as positive than as negative feedback. Through

326

that agency the pace of cultural change, which could formerly be measured in generations, has accelerated towards instability. Superficially they may appear to be agents for cultural homogeneity, presenting similar fare similarly packaged to all. But the fare itself is far from homogeneous, one endless mindless soap opera. So far from a soft bland pap the media offer a selection of experiences presented from the instantaneous seat in the grandstand denied even to those geographically close to the event. Many competing interpretations of events, styles of life, questions, answers, opinions are all available, however improbable, however provocative, bigoted, ignorant or malicious, all given the weight of television 'coverage', fragmenting rather than binding the audience. Television pundits, commentators and interviewers reap the benefits of familiarity and, wittingly or not, promote their interpretations in place of those or in preference to those who occupy representative, elective or official posts. These tendencies accelerate but by no stretch of imagination could they be said to have initiated the decline in authority in our societies; that has a far longer history than the mass media. One of the most powerful sources of this decline is to be found in the demographic changes we have already discussed. As families have fewer children they become more valued, the child-oriented culture that results emphasizes the freedom to develop as against the duty of obedience; as the ever-present possibility of death recedes, the consolations of the church lose their salience.

Decline in authority means decline in the acceptance of authority. In modern societies this has been especially marked by changes in the basis of such authority as receives acceptance. Ascribed authority has everywhere weakened in favour of achieved authority.

The directions of change

Scholars have generally perceived change as a one-way street. Societies become more complex and more highly differentiated. Maine (1905) traced the trend for societies as they develop over time to shift the basis of rights and obligations from 'status' to 'contract'. Tönnies (1955) detected a similar shift in the nature of personal relationships from *Gemeinschaft* to *Gesellschaft*, from community to association. Durkheim (1960) traced the shift of the basis of solidarity from 'mechanical' to 'organic'. Parsons (1968), although disclaiming any inevitability in development, describes five polar 'pattern variables' along which societies differ. These we have discussed in detail in Chapter 14, 'Social Change and Social Values'.

Modern societies display the tendency for people's activities, especially their work, to be instrumental rather than expressive, for the basis of status to be achievement rather than ascription, for universalistic norms – certain kinds of behaviour are right regardless of the class of person to whom it is directed – for specificity of expertness and for personal goals as the object of endeavour rather than, say, national prestige or glory. The force of these distinctions is seen if we contrast this with the notion of an English Gentleman, the amateur who without shedding his coat could effortlessly defeat the professional. The cult of the amateur, scorned by the Fulton Committee on the Civil Service, represented a set of values congruent with the pattern variables of an earlier society.

We readily assume that the values of present-day society are more appropriate to the attainment of present-day goals. No doubt this should be the case on the basis of structural functional analysis and if we could with advantage treat societies as wholes. In fact, we are obliged to recognize that different groups in society have different and conflicting goals and that values which conduce to the attainment of one goal may hinder the attainment of another.

While, then, we can detect changes which appear to affect all societies we note first that these trends do not proceed at the same pace or in the same way or in concert in any society, and that they appear to be the outcome of the capacity for differentiation and choice brought about by technological advance, not least in the field of population. They are also outcomes of other forms of knowledge than the purely technological. We constantly need to remind ourselves that technology is not an independent exogenous variable, that it is a form of knowledge and like other forms of knowledge is used in different ways. Other ideas have power, that is to say, we can use them to change things. If we decide to use them in education we stimulate value changes which in turn initiate political change, change in the basis on which organizations rest, shifting the pattern variables and thus the point of balance between the options in every society. Eisenstadt (1973) identifies these as Liberty versus Authority; Stability and Continuity versus Change; Rationality, e.g. technology, versus Cultural Orientations, e.g. religion. But we should be naive to believe that 'modernizing' inevitably means a shift towards liberty, change and rationality. None of these is necessarily implied in the adoption of modern technology; the cultural capacity for choice and for combining the incompatible is greater than we often assume.

The unevenness of change

(a) *Within societies*

Because education and modern technology both impact unevenly on developing societies, they may exacerbate the divisions between their modern and their traditional sectors.

Change, we need constantly to remind ourselves, is not all one way and, as Goldthorpe (1971) has pointed out, we are prone to introduce historicism through the back door, replacing a crude Marxism with another brand of technological determinism. Especially when discussing the post-industrial society, this leads to a theory of the inevitability of the convergence of politico-economic systems. In the case of the underdeveloped countries we may indeed observe the weakening of tradition in the advanced sectors of the economy and its simultaneous strengthening in the traditional sectors. Change and expansion are most probable when:

1 societies become more specialized;
2 symbolic systems develop away from the primordial symbols which give identity to the society;
3 different units begin to use different symbols;
4 in both centre and periphery socio-economic differentiation produces strata or classes;
5 the functions of the centre become more differentiated than those of the periphery (Eisenstadt, 1973).

(b) *Change between societies*

This emphasizes the point I am trying to make – that change, if you like, drives a wedge between economic sectors, political centres, social foci and then affects them *unequally*. Change encourages diversity, which may or may not be divisive. What is certain is that we should not assume that change of whatever origin will have similar effects on orientations and attitudes to work of different groups and classes or in different industries and organizations. Even when change appears unambiguously to point in a single direction, further analysis may reveal substantial differences under the surface. For example, smaller families, more wealth, more economic freedom for the young contribute to the development of a youth culture familiar in all developed countries and emerging in the developing ones. But although youth cultures in different countries share a number of symbols – hair, rock music, drugs, gear, opposition to adult authority, the content may range all the way from a patriotic nationalism to a pacifist internationalism, from a militant new left to a quietist oriental mysticism. It is easy to misread as free-floating a phenomenon deeply embedded in its cultural contexts. It is impossible to understand developments within the United States without reference to the civil rights movements and Vietnam or developments in Britain or Holland except with reference to the end of empire. But whether we look across countries or within them we see how technological developments have created new discontinuities which are specific to cultures and whose consequences are equally specific.

What differs is less the technology than the adaptation to it. In all developed societies the nature of work has been changing. Fewer are employed in primary industry and their productivity has been raised by the progressive application of machine power; nor is this any longer balanced by an increase in employment in secondary (manufacturing) industry. More and more are, however, employed in service (tertiary) industries and in government, education and welfare services (the new 'quaternary' sector). With mechanization, the economics of scale previously experienced in manufacture become available in some aspects of service industry, making standardized performance readily available and comparatively cheap, while rendering more specialized custom-built service to the expensive luxuries. Thus societies have come to be more homogeneous in many respects; local flavour is harder to detect and local differences are further reduced by the mass media. Paradoxically the range of individual choice has been increased; mass markets and cheap processes make available a wide range of products. One outcome is that while major lines of social cleavage have continued, the gradations on either side of the line are less obvious. Thus in some respects we can see social stratification as consisting of a multi-dimensional space in which an individual's location on one dimension may be a poor indication of his location on others, while in other respects there appears to be a clear dividing line between classes.

If societies use the opportunities provided by technology in different ways which relate to their social and political character, can we discern the convergences and divergences, can we forecast those effects which will be the same and those which will be different? Especially in regard to work, where after all technologies are rapidly transferred across national boundaries, is there not an inevitably high degree of convergence in the outcomes? It has long been noted that a technologically advanced plant in Britain may employ anything from 50 per cent to 200 per cent more workers than a similar plant in the United States. Decisions in French firms are typically more highly centralized than in their British equivalents, despite their technological similarity. Union postures in these three and in other countries differ widely, as do the ideological assumptions underlying those postures.

Is culture then the determiner?

We are not saying, then, that technological change is used by societies only to reinforce their existing ways of doing this and that. That view, though seductive, is too 'closed system' in its implications; you have not a completely free choice of technology nor of how to use it. Because the technology itself is a cultural artefact it embodies cultural assumptions about the people who are going to operate it.

The agenda of issues facing developing countries is so formidable that questions of quality of working life may appear very small indeed, if not hopelessly idealistic. Poor countries desperately need to create employment. For their people to have work at all – any kind of working life – is the overriding aim; the quality of working life appears no more than a frill, to be introduced when luxuries can be afforded, if that happy day ever arrives.

This generally held notion is, however, a misreading based on false historicism. Because industrialization was accompanied in the past by a widespread decline in the quality of working life, it has become accepted that the price of industrialization is alienation, as well as dense urbanization. Yet neither of these consequences is an inevitable concomitant of industrialization. Furthermore, the currently present symptoms of dissatisfaction in advanced countries appear to be largely associated with, and more than partially the outcome of, steps taken to advance the efficiency of work organizations. Again the ills are seen as part of the cost of efficient operation. Costs they are, but paradoxically uncosted; necessary costs they are not. Newly industrializing countries need no more follow the road of 'scientific management' than they need begin their industrialization with the James Watt steam engine.

Indeed, the principles of scientific management and organizations based upon them stand in the way of rational industrial development, demanding a labour force trained in alienation, imposing social costs on a social infrastructure unadapted to provide them. Such organizations imply a particular kind of family structure, organized around the daily absent wage-earner whose schooling provided by a particular kind of educational system equipped him with the skills of compartmentalizing work from non-work, work from play, work from social life, work skills from social skills. Industrial countries are paying the price for this in the problems which beset virtually every social institution.

Many of these problems have been self-inflicted by the choice of industrial technology. In the case of the Western industrialized countries, choice was available, but this was not recognized; we did not realize that what was brilliantly successful and profitable in the short run might pile up enormous costs and diseconomies in the not-so-long run. Have developing countries, then, a choice in the matter? In principle, certainly: there may indeed by only one way open, once the technological decisions have been made, but there is not just one way of industrializing, one way of organizing work, one way of achieving a technological objective. There are many options open, before the technological decisions have been made, a theme we take up again in the section on development in Chapters 23 and 24.

Most planners at national or regional levels are not themselves technologists; for their technological decisions they depend on specialists, most of whom have been trained in a cultural context which has evolved together with the technology it embodies. Their solutions to technological problems are based on the unvoiced assumptions of a society already geared to the use of advanced technologies with their attendant values, their advantages, and their dysfunctional aspects. But most of these features are not problematic for the planner; his options are limited in advance in ways he is at best only dimly aware of. The technologist trained in an advanced country – this includes most technologists in policy-making roles – applying in developing countries the scientific values and technological solutions of the advanced countries is, of course, made daily aware of the limitations hindering his work. He adapts so far as he can to the social and political climate; he learns new ways of doing things; he may enlist the aid of anthropologists and sociologists to assess the acceptability of his proposals or even examine their likely effects on the life of the people concerned. And in small-scale projects he may indeed be influenced in the choice of technology by their advice. While anthropologists' advice about small-scale community projects may be precise and relevant, social science recommendations on large-scale matters tend to be vague and general and of very little use to the planner or technological adviser who needs something tangible to put into even the crudest cost-benefit analysis. On the other side, the sociologist has little or no grasp of technological considerations to be able to propose alternative solutions or indeed to realize that there are technologically feasible alternatives.

Is there a way out? We believe there is and that it lies along the lines we outlined in the previous chapter and what we may call 'sociotechnical assessment'. Every objective needs to be seen in sociotechnical terms, to become sociotechnical objectives. In most of Western society, premature fragmenting into social and technical objectives is encouraged by the separation of political systems from technical organization, so that the social objectives are set by the political system; the means of attaining them is handed over to the technocrats. If we choose technically dominated modes of solving social problems or social objectives, we inevitably acquire a society in which the machine dominates the man. Paradoxically, by subordinating the technical to the political, we subordinate man to the machine.

If, on the other hand, we take technical considerations into account in determining social objectives, we are still importing with the technical considerations a whole raft of assumptions and valuations that go with the technology. We must begin by rigorously analysing the social assumptions underlying the structure of societies and the images we have of these structures. We will then perceive that our societies are sociotechnical systems with sociotechnical objectives. Fully to recognize the costs and benefits of sociotechnical options requires a new form of sociotechnical assessment, based on the skills of people who have acquired the capacities to understand both the social and the technical characteristics of these systems.

Without this sociotechnical assessment, the developing countries are importing the quality of working life of their people along with imported technology. When a country imports a steel mill or a textile factory or an oil refinery, it imports a number of jobs designed by the engineers of steel mill, textile factory or oil refinery. One of the problems arising from this has long been recognized: the industrial skills needed to cope with these jobs may be lacking. Solutions have included the temporary appointment of expatriate staff, more minute division of labour, or the proposal to utilize 'intermediate technologies' based on the availability of existing skills and on the assumptions of a plentiful and cheap but lowly skilled supply of labour.

Problems of prediction

(a) *See-saws*

There are three kinds of prophet – optimists, pessimists and cynics.

333

For the optimist the best is yet to come, that of today which will survive is the progressive. Liberty, equality and fraternity, the liberal, social, democratic values will triumph. For the pessimist the best was in a past golden age from which we have sadly declined. We have become soft and weak – and undeserving. For that we shall be punished and the instruments of our punishment will be our own children. To the cynic there is nothing new under the sun. *Plus ça change, plus c'est la même chose.* You can't change human nature. Change is a see-saw or perhaps a cycle.

The trouble with prophets is that their unit of analysis is too big. Mankind, Civilization, History, the Dialectic, are just not manageable. From them it is easy to abstract progress, decline, inevitability, repetition. From far enough away tides are a twice daily repetition. Over a year they fluctuate from spring to neap and back again. Over the centuries the mean level rises then falls again. But the man in the surf feels the pull away from the shore *and* the rush towards it. So it is with social change. Changes of different magnitude and in different directions affect the same people at different times and different people at the same time. The same force for change may make the young more free and the middle-aged less; the rich, richer, and the poor, poorer.

We are accustomed to thinking of our times as characterized by a growing informality – in dress, in manners, in forms of address and so on. But we are also accustomed to seeing ours as the age of bureaucracy, the most formal of organizational types. This paradox may be only apparent; bureaucracies enshrine universalistic rather than particularistic values; people are treated on the basis of category rather than individuality. Universalistic values remove those distinctions which depend on the recognition of people's particular statuses. These are undisguisable in small-scale multiplex societies, but are less detectable and acceptable in large-scale societies, where the relationships between individuals tend to be one dimensional; customer–supplier, neighbour, kin, colleague, drinking companion, employer–employee, etc. Broad class distinctions remain, but within classes formality declines with increase in societal scale.

As formality between classes lessens and bureaucracy grows, social mobility increases. The kind of informality which takes its place is shallow and impersonal, replacing social distance with psychological distance – a clue to the 'privatized' society, the inward focusing of emotional ties on health and home described by Goldthorpe *et al.* (1968) in their studies of the 'affluent worker'. Both the formality of bureaucracy and the new informality are impersonal.

I have treated this at some length because it is a good illustration of how easily we may be misled into perceiving as universal a trend which is partial because it is one manifestation of something that lies beneath it. I want to remain with it for a moment because it takes us a step nearer work. Goldthorpe showed that 'privatized workers' were likely to have an instrumental orientation to their work life, obtaining their expressive satisfactions outside it. If the trend is towards greater privatization, then surely we must expect an increase in instrumental orientations. But is it? We also observe a trend towards communalism, with manifestations ranging from the hippy commune to encounter groups. Back to the surf. Both are happening at the same time to different people and possibly to the same people at different times. Perhaps then the one universal trend in social change is towards diversity, towards an increase in the number of options brought about by technology. And yet, as we say that, we simultaneously remember that technology has often reduced diversity by making standardization so much more effective.

We all possess a model of a traditional society in which fashions diffused downwards from the top. Today the picture is more confusing. The centres of diffusion, the 'early adopters', may be on the periphery, or even near the bottom. Fashions in dress and behaviour, in popular music and art diffuse upwards from the young and often from the working-class young. The middle class, middle-aged, may get there last of all or may never arrive.

All this makes the life of the prophet hard. He can aim his prophecies at a greater distance, confident that by the year 2,000 or whatever no one will remember what he said or, more likely, that something he said will come true and be remembered while his false prophecies are forgotten. But for the serious prophet who wants to help people anticipate tomorrow, so that they can plan for or against it, the search for indicators is becoming acute. What is available? We are certainly not an unmeasured society. Our political temperature is taken daily by pollsters. Our activities and possessions are all assessed and reduced, or elevated, to pounds and dollars and marks. Our prospective wants are sampled by the marketeers. These 'measures' are, however, unco-ordinated and largely unrelated; each is made for a particular purpose. And, indeed, any suggestion that they should be linked introduces the spectre of a central file containing the minutest details of our lives, our beliefs and our actions. Nevertheless, a great deal can be quarried from the data that exist. The problem is that what can be deduced are essentially short-term probabilities.

(b) *Spotting winners*

It is possible to make reasonably accurate predictions of purchasing behaviour, preferences for leisure pursuits, choice of family size and so on. Some may indeed be upset by sudden unanticipated critical events such as a large discovery of oil in a hitherto unexpected area or a deliberately engineered shortage of the same commodity. But even these events take time to produce their effects. What we have so far proved unable to predict are the revolutionary trends in society. Who predicted the various youth phenomena of the last ten to fifteen years? Or the changes in the public tolerance of obscenity? Or the emergence of 'direct action' in frustration with bureaucratic, if democratic, processes? Who can predict today how significant they will prove to have been in twenty years' time. Looking back we can now detect the early signs that such change was on the way. It is fashionable now to point to signals like the play, *Look Back in Anger*, for example, which explained the frustrations of the university-educated but culturally *déraciné* product of the working class, or to the obsession with 'ugliness' in certain forms of art, or the break-up of the formality of construction of the novel and the poem. Is there any way better than retrospective forecasting of detecting the trends which will survive? Could we have known at the time that the post-war New Look, the revolutionary reaction against functionalism in dress, would prove to be a romantic retrospect whereas the land girls' and service women's workaday trousers would become well-nigh universal feminine wear? Perhaps we could. There is a parallel in organic growth.

Gesell and Amatruda (1946) describe the 'synergized behaviour trait' of an infant picking up a tiny pellet by precise pincer prehension. They trace it back to earlier skills now superseded – radial raking which, synchronized with a new adaptive adduction of the thumb, brings about a simple scissors type of grasp. This and its successors give way to new developments which, when they pick up and combine with other nascent skills, eventually produce the final trait, to which they have all contributed essential elements but in which they are each unrecognizable.

If social processes follow a similar pattern, they are going to be exceedingly difficult to detect and unravel. And the potentialities for pathological development may be many times greater. Emery and Trist (1972) looked at the emergence of social processes in a way somewhat similar to the approach of Gesell and Amatruda. They see social processes begin as 'intrusions' unrecognized for what they are. 'We have to live for some time with the future before we recognize it.' As these intrusions command no resources – the energy they need is met parasitically – they appear to be something else. They share with other processes parts which may continue to play traditional roles, eventually emerging as a fully fledged new system. The parasitic period has weakened the traditional system on which it has fed. After symptoms of intrusion, which, however, may only represent passing observations, we next observe 'mutual invasion', but our awareness of what is happening is limited. Emery and Trist go on to point to the possibilities of content analysis of new movements, linguistic usage, etc. as signals of emerging phenomenon.

What I have said, and quoted, indicates both the enormous complexity of identifying and analysing those social traits which will enter into new combinations in the future and the variety of possible futures which may succeed one another without end. The danger of drawing on the embryological analogy is its inherent teleology – behaviour and change are future-oriented; each manifestation is a stage towards a completed development.

In social processes there are no stages, each manifestation is a complete though transitory present. Although we may comb the present for hairs pointing to the future and look, say, to artistic productions for signs, we must remember that while the strange behaviour of the sculptor who leaves holes in unexpected places, or the poet who ignores grammar and sense, or the painter who decorates his canvas with a smudge may indeed be the precursors of anarchic movements in education and elsewhere, they are intended to say something of relevance to today; they are complete in today's terms, their meaning is not what will emerge in the future.

It is equally important to recognize that there is not one today any more than there was only one yesterday. To the extent that the future is implicit in the present, so the present is implicit in the past. And no two countries have the same past.

Thus when we comb today for signs for the future we should not overread those which apparently point towards convergences. Social and technological change will not necessarily make the world a homogeneous place. Certainly production technology tends to make industrial plants in different parts of the world bear considerable similarities in their social systems. A closed-system technologically determinist viewpoint would predict total convergence of their social systems. Open-system thinking reminds us of the different experiences, beliefs, orientations and attitudes that people in different countries and in different parts of the same country bring to their work. And social systems have options in the ways in which they use apparently identical technologies. And, as we have said before, social change affects different people and different groups of people in different ways. Greater 'permissiveness' in society may stimulate children who have experienced a permissive education to welcome or demand more permissiveness in the work place, and simultaneously provoke other workers tortured by the removal of many of their cultural landmarks to seek a reassuring discipline at work.

Thus we misread if we conclude that all workers everywhere are going to demand participation or work-place democracy or any other form of increased involvement and reduced formality and discipline. Indeed, we can predict that the faster the pace of social change that has been experienced, the deeper the wedge that any change will drive between different groups in society and between different generations.

The speed of change can polarize society more than its tardiness. We can expect great resistances to fundamental change in the work place. We cannot be certain that this change will come, but we can be certain that we have the technology and the knowledge to make it possible. As we try to introduce it we may see ourselves as the bearers of the future, but it is one among many probable futures.

Because work has been the lot of most men and its products essential, the organizations which have arisen to get it done have become our leading cultural institution. The Jesuits claimed that if they could have a boy in their hands for his first seven years, he was proof against other influence thereafter. In the same vein, as industry is a sensitive indicator of cultural change, if we could make over industry to new values, we could safely leave the rest of our cultural institutions to follow.

Our work organizations embody the values of their designs, often the values of the designers of the organizations from which they are descended and the values of the designers of the technologies which shaped them. The machines of the industrial revolution required some skill and often much strength to operate; their successors, in eliminating the need for the latter largely reduced the former. Since the workers who moved into the new industries were untrained, unskilled and mostly illiterate, the more decisions that could be taken by the machine, the more reliable the product. The problem was the human error. The more the machine controlled the behaviour of its operator, the better. Thus production technology enshrined the concept of man as an unreliable machine to be controlled. And still does; the assembly line represents its apotheosis. But not all industries have assembly lines, although even the traditional craft industries such as shipbuilding and construction have adopted many of its features. Process industries have removed the man from the production line itself but have often left him as an adjunct to the machine, its nursemaid not its master. Still the first response of the designer to a source of variance is to programme the machine to eliminate it; his values, although unrecognized by himself, are those of the industrial engineers in the days of F. W. Taylor. Thus our industry embodies the values of an earlier age and in this respect acts as a conservative force.

If, however, we are alienated from our work and adopt an instrumental value towards it, then naturally it must be designed to be proof against our uncaring errors and an exploitation of the rewards it offers. The vicious circle is complete. Our attitudes to work are a product of the way in which work is organized; the way work is organized is a product of our beliefs, values and attitudes to work. And this circle lies within the larger one we have described: industry is the leading part of the social system, its values dominate those of other parts which are fashioned to serve it; our educational system labours to produce people with the right attitudes to fit its demands.

Let me draw together the threads of my last few paragraphs. We chase an illusion when we look for the impact of social change on attitudes to work. Our changing experience of work is as much a part of social change as any other. A moment's thought will reassure us of this. A powerful agent of social change is technological change; the first area of our lives affected by technological change is our place of work.

Thus the meaning of technological change and its effect on attitudes and values towards work will differ from culture to culture. We have discussed the possibilities of predicting social change and favour the view that changes manifest themselves early in artistic, literary and symbolic products. It would make a fascinating and valuable study to examine the treatment over time in different cultures of the symbols concerned with work, their different and changing meanings and associations. Supposing we examined the use of the words for 'participation' over recent years. We would find at least two quite different meanings. In the *Mitbestimmung* sense it is used to describe formal systems of representation. In the 'workplace democracy' sense it describes the delegation of responsibility and control to working groups. In between, it is used to describe a whole range of formal and informal consultative procedures. Why has the first use been dominant in West Germany and Yugoslavia, the second in Norway and the third in Britain? Is it because representative democracy is new in Yugoslavia, recently restored in Germany and vitally precious in both, while democracy is familiar in Norway, a sufficiently small and culturally homogeneous country for direct democracy to be possible? Britain has a long tradition of

339

representative democracy but has deep class divisions. And what should we expect in France where, according to Crozier (1964) in *The Bureaucratic Phenomenon*, free collaboration is easy within strata but constrained to the utmost formality between strata?

Scenario

If predicting the future of work is so difficult, what can we do? Surprisingly enough we may be more able to influence it than to prophesy about it. Action research is the new positivism. And one of its tools is the scenario, the design of a possible future.

Even if industry is bowing out as the leading institution in society, organizations remain the most persuasive aspect of communal life. And while the structure of an organization reflects to some extent its functions and purpose, as the design of a building reflects the life and activities of its occupants, the same limitations apply. Function varies more than structure. What are the possibilities, then, of major structural change? And what would be its effects? Organizational structures, like scientific management, exist to prescribe and control behaviour, to limit the range of the human activities within them. They accustom us to produce behaviour according to a particular kind of rationality. Realizing this, organizations have recourse to pathetic, patented attempts to elicit 'creativity', divergent-thinking, synectics and whatnot. But the behaviour constraints we acquire in organizations are learned too well; we use them outside organizational settings where they are less appropriate and adaptive. It is not only an affectation for the creative artists and writers of our society to shun organizational life. Changes in organizations aimed at replacing its constraining influences with liberating ones would do more than any other change to engender imaginative and original solutions to our wider social dilemmas. A few tentative models of learning organizations exist; their success could even lead us to a learning society.

Chapter 18
Work or Life

Introduction

In our introduction to the preceding chapter we discussed the meaning of work, and a similar introduction would suit this chapter. But let us think: what happens to a society when technology has eliminated the need for work as we have hitherto understood it? Work in the sense of self-discovery, self-creating, would presumably still be essential; work in the biblical sense would not, nor would man's work be the instrument of man's exploitation by man.

There are signs, though they have been much exaggerated, that the dominance of industry as the principal form of work organization is passing, at least in those countries sufficiently advanced to be labelled optimistically as 'post-industrial societies'. They have been the highly successful industrial societies and have been so successful just because their social institutions have developed to a high degree those characteristics needed for the supply and maintenance of industry. Just because they were so efficient at instilling and developing the 'work ethic', they are now in less need of it. Social and moral changes of this kind take time to develop; meanwhile the society's institutions are all predicated on an older morality, one example of the phenomenon described as culture lag. When society needs a change in such a fundamental aspect as its definition of work, upon which all its institutions have been built, it is bound to suffer an intense and prolonged crisis. This is part of the meaning of the anomie, the obliteration of the moral landmarks, which advanced societies have been experiencing; the worst symptoms appearing soonest in the most advanced of all, but quickly manifesting themselves in the rest. Alienation, in its guise of 'normlessness', the individual counterpart of the collective anomie, has followed the same pattern.

First, I should try to describe the signs of change to which I referred. For many years we have been accustomed to the steady decline in employment in agriculture and in the other 'primary' industries: mining and quarrying. From the start of the Industrial Revolution the workers who left the land entered manufacture, and the employment in manufacturing industry grew steadily. It is now declining. Between 1961 and 1971, manufacturing industry's share of the work force dropped in Britain from 39·3 to 38·3 per cent of a smaller employed population. The actual drop was from approximately 9·63 to 9·25 million (*Social Trends*, no. 3, HMSO, 1972, p. 72).

All primary and secondary industry – agriculture, extractive industry, manufacture, construction and utilities, dropped from 53·5 to 49·1 per cent – under 50 per cent for the first time in our history. And the gain was not in the tertiary sectors – transport and communication, distributive trades, catering, hotels and miscellaneous services – but in the quaternary sector – financial, professional and scientific services and public administration – up from 17·4 to 24 per cent. In the United States these trends have been in advance of ours and still more rapid. The factory, paradigm of a work organization, is now the work place of little more than one worker in three.

Sign 1 *Manufacturing industry is ceasing to be the principal type of employment*

We in Britain have also grown accustomed to the sight of coloured workers on the railways and the buses and on London's underground and we may have become uneasily aware of the extent to which certain services have become dependent upon them. We have probably also observed the reliance of hotels on foreign workers, male and female. We are probably less aware, because it is less visible, that certain kinds of factory work, usually the most arduous, are also manned extensively, if not exclusively by immigrants. On the Continent the phenomenon of the *Gastarbeiter* is even stronger; whole sectors of German and French industry keep going by employing workers from Greece, Yugoslavia, Turkey, Spain and North Africa; in the Swedish motor-car assembly plants of Volvo and Saab the assembly lines are manned by people from southern Europe, Turkey and Finland, because young Swedes will not take the jobs. Nearly 40 per cent of all workers in Swiss factories are foreigners (Castles and Kosack, 1973). In the USA there co-exist for the first time persistent unfilled vacancies alongside persistent pockets of high unemployment.

Sometimes this phenomenon takes another form which is less visible. An alternative to importing labour is exporting jobs. Some corporations are moving parts of their operations outside the United States because they cannot get people to do certain jobs 'regardless of what they are paid'. In developing countries there are still people anxious and ready to take them (US House of Representatives, 1970).

Sign 2 *Young native workers in the developed countries are refusing to take certain kinds of job*

These jobs are not just the hot, dirty, noisy ones, but those which deny personal satisfaction.

The worst working environments and conditions have improved out of all recognition over the last fifty years. The sweatshops are things of the past, work is cleaner and safer, hours of work have steadily declined, the five-day week and the three-week holiday is the norm. Unemployment benefit, severance pay, personnel and welfare services have all made the physical conditions of work manifestly easier. Yet absenteeism, high labour turnover are worse rather than better. An enlightened society which does not need everybody's contribution to work is a society where the individual can settle for not working if he will also accept the ambiguous status and comparatively low living standards of a drop-out. Without seeing signs of an alternative society all round us, we can yet see in Britain symptoms corresponding to those described in North America:

the growth in the number of communes;
numerous adolescents panhandling in such meccas as
    Georgetown, North Beach, and the Sunset Strip;
various enterprises shifting to four-day work weeks;
welfare caseloads increasing;
retirement occurring at ever earlier ages (US Senate, 1973).

Sign 3 *More young people are opting out of 'work' altogether; more older people are retiring as soon as they can*

More young people are also deferring their entry to the work force.

343

Not only are many more staying in education after the statutory school leaving age, but many of them also prefer not to seek a permanent career immediately after leaving university or college.

But if manufacturing industry needs fewer workers, what is there to fuss about? If fewer want to work in industry, so much the better; industry needs fewer workers.

We have already mentioned that it is not industry, even manufacturing industry as a whole, which cannot find workers; it is some jobs in some industries that are hard to fill. If the assembly line keeps cropping up in this connection, it is because it is the paradigm of a particular kind of work organization. And it is on the assembly line that is encountered the most absenteeism, the most persistent conflict and even deliberate sabotage. Indeed, in view of the objective evidence, the often quoted figures of workers who express satisfaction with their jobs can only be an indication of the low expectations people have of what their working lives will be like. But these same figures show the young are far less satisfied than their elders with their jobs. In the United States only one-third of white occupants of blue-collar jobs are satisfied 'most of the time' with their jobs, compared with half of those over thirty and nearly two-thirds of those over fifty-five (Quinn, Mangionie and Maldi de Mandilovitch, 1972).

Sign 4 *Dissatisfaction is higher among the young*

Now in the absence of longitudinal data, we can only conjecture whether the middle-aged worker of today was equally bolshy in his youth. We cannot know for sure and of course today's 45-year-old was entering employment in wartime and his seniors experienced the Depression. But we do know that in Japan, where social change has been far more rapid, the difference in attitude between young and older workers is even more marked (Takezawa, 1975). We know too that today's young workers are better educated than their elders, or at any rate have stayed longer at school.

Does it matter? If more and more people are employed in white collar jobs, in service industries, in scientific and professional services and in public administration, does that not mean that the problem is diminishing of its own accord? Will not automation remove all the repetitive jobs? And if all the necessary work can be done in four days a week or three, will people not be prepared, indeed quite happy, to put up with jobs they do not like for such a short time each week? And then people can retire early. And in a world that has no need for everyone to work, why worry if some

344

want to opt out of work altogether? Can we not already see 'alternative life styles' emerging to validate a life devoted to not working?

These are all pertinent questions and in the long run they may all be answered in the affirmative. They, and many more, are needed to question our assumptions about work and about life. I propose to deal only with their shorter-term implications, which is a different matter.

What are the implications of the shift from manufacturing industry and the growth of the white-collar sector? One of the attractive aspects of service as against manufacturing industry has been its comparative freedom from close supervision and the degree of control it offered over the way you did your job and the way you laid out your time. And among the attractions of a white-collar job was its higher status, its closer and more matey relationship with management. 'Us' and 'Them' divided the manual worker from the non-manual, rather than the employee (manual and non-manual) from the employer. False consciousness no doubt, but from a psychological viewpoint, it is not clear how false your consciousness is.

But disaffection is prominent among workers in the service industries and in public employment, and white-collar unionism is growing and is no less militant than among manual workers. Nor is their militancy confined to matters of pay, although pay and conditions are prominent factors in their bargaining. They are demanding a voice in the way public services are run and in their objectives.

What do these manifestations mean? There has been a vogue for 'efficiency' and 'productivity', work study and scientific management in the service sector and for the introduction of 'systems', electronic data processing and whatnot in the white-collar jobs. Independence has gone out with inefficiency and pressure has come in with productivity. Simultaneously the advancement to 'staff' status of many manual workers has removed some of the more blatant status differentials between them and the clerks. In Britain, the requirement that public services shall yield a profitable return on investment (which they very seldom do) has devalued the pride in providing a public service which motivated past generations of railwaymen and post office workers. What all this means is that parallel with the shift of employment from manufacture to tertiary industry and from manual to non-manual occupations, tertiary industry has been acquiring more of the characteristics of manufacturing industry and white-collar jobs have been getting less attractive.

And automation? There is no doubt that automation has already removed some of the heavy, hot, unpleasant jobs. But it does not of itself remove dull, uninteresting, uninvolving jobs, though it *can* be

345

designed to do so. It can also provide tedious, lonely, nerve-wracking jobs, monitoring dials in isolated clinical surroundings. Automation, like every other technological change, provides an opportunity for, and a choice of, job design; it does not necessarily provide good jobs or good working lives which is not, of course, quite the same thing.

Thus, in the development towards a post-industrial society there are no automatically operating factors which will ensure that working lives improve, or that future jobs will provide more intrinsic satisfaction or provide the worker with more control over his own work.

But perhaps work itself will become a thing of the past? After all, working lives are shorter, working hours are fewer, holidays are longer. Surely there may come a point where the investment of time in work is small enough for its discomforts to be a minor matter? There is another seductive argument. Many appear to prefer, given the choice, a 10-hour day, 4-day week to an 8-hour day, 5-day week. Once adapted to a 4-day week a majority would probably again prefer to take a further reduction in hours in the form of a three and a half day week and so on. But the pattern of absenteeism persists in the face of changes of this kind. It is highest on the first and last days of the working week *of whatever length*. And the fewer days there are in the working week, the greater is the proportion of the week represented by one day's absence. The reduction of the working week as an incentive implies and encourages an instrumental orientation to work. An instrumental orientation to work generates the pressure to reduce it still further. There is no reason to postulate a point at which this instrumental orientation would be reversed. Nor is there any reason why there should be a particular length of working week which would simultaneously satisfy the need for society's work to be done and the collective wish of people to be at leisure. We might even find that the less the work that had to be done, the harder it would be to persuade people to do it.

Discussion of shorter working weeks and working lives raises the question of leisure. I do not want to pursue that topic here. I do just want to point out that leisure, like money, is one thing when you have little of it and another altogether when you have a great deal of it. Unlike money, however, it may be less attractive in large quantities than small. And leisure 'activities' can become suspiciously like work. I am reminded of the pathetic response of the boy entrant in the Royal Air Force, who was interviewed during the hour set aside compulsorily for creative leisure activities – 'This is me 'obby and I 'ates it.'

It is true that work is a central life interest for some, not for all of

346

us, and that the proportion for whom it is may be declining. Furthermore, those for whom it is not a central life interest probably invest less of themselves in their work. They are the instrumentally oriented workers Goldthorpe (1968) encountered on the assembly lines of Luton. Faunce and Dubin (1975) have argued that if their low self-investment allows them to invest more of themselves in out-of-work activities (a 'compensatory' theory), then there is much to be said for not trying to involve them further. If, on the other hand, their low self-investment in work impairs their ability and motivation to invest themselves in other activities, there is reason to be concerned about a purely instrumental orientation to work. Faunce and Dubin on the whole incline to the compensatory view. Some studies, however, have shown that increased participation in decision-making at work has been accompanied by increased participation in local politics and community activities (Walton, 1972). While this question remains unsettled, it seems reasonable to believe that both hypotheses are correct, but for different people. For some, emotional withdrawal or dissociation from their work is deliberate and leaves them freer for whole-hearted involvement in other matters; for others this dissocation is imposed by their situation and is emotionally debilitating. Certainly the picture of accommodation presented by Goldthorpe needs careful review in the light of the subsequent protracted industrial unrest among the groups he studied.

We are therefore led to conclude that current trends do not look like removing or reducing the problem. Indeed it seems that the problem will appear to grow because (a) we are less willing to tolerate the harshness our society showed in the past which coerced people into work at the penalty of starvation or pauperism; and (b) the supply of immigrants willing to take on the disagreeable jobs is closing down and the native progeny of immigrants are not likely to want them. Even the first generation is beginning to rebel, as the Renault strike of 1973 displayed. The withdrawal of their labour would be quite catastrophic. It has been estimated that there are six million foreign workers in the expanded European Economic Community and one million in Switzerland. It has also been estimated that there are more Korean nurses in West Germany than in Korea and that whole districts of Turkey are without able-bodied males (*Industrial Relations*, Europe, no. 6, vol. 1, June, 1973).

Improving working lives

So, if a benevolent Providence is not solving our problems or washing them away, what then? Then we must set out deliberately to improve working lives, improve jobs. Do we know how to? And do we know what makes for good jobs, good working lives? We do not want nostrums. Some tell us to liberate human creativity by transferring (or 'restoring') ownership and control to the worker. No longer alienated from the product of his toil, the worker will presumably invest in it what at present he withholds or yields under duress. Unfortunately, most transfers of 'ownership' replace the owner-manager or his agents with managerial agents of a public (i.e. state) ownership. Unless accompanied by other changes, this resembles the replacement of King Stork by King Log. Others assure us that the obstacles to a good working life are the communication blocks we carry within ourselves which can be removed through the mind-blowing of an encounter group. Such experiences would be of value if they revealed the underlying causes of the alienation of man from man or at least recognized that in the work organization there are *four causes* – those arising from the social structure, those arising from the design of the organization, those arising from the nature of the task, and those arising from the participants' personalities. While the radical social critic addresses himself only to the first, the humanistic psychologist addresses only the last. In both cases the relevant arena for change lies outside and beyond the organization.

We can also and independently tackle the second and third. However, the answer to the question, 'Do we know what makes for good jobs?', remains largely a matter of inference, drawn from disparate sources and resting on the kind of psychological theory for which direct evidence is by its very nature hard to get. This kind of theory states that people have needs which can be classified in certain ways and that develop with expanding possibilities for their satisfaction, culminating in those which enable man to realize his 'true' nature, and overcome his alienation from his own self. This kind of theory (hierarchy of needs) is trans-scientific, not entirely metaphysical nor yet susceptible to confirmation by scientific evidence. Unlike most other theories, the value system supporting this kind is evident and may even be admitted by its proponents. It may lead to circular arguments. If we say that to realize his true nature in all his activities man needs to express himself in his work and we then find people who apparently do not want to express themselves in this, we retort that they are psychologically crippled by their experience and prevented from rising to their true capacity. This effectively deals with objections in the time-honoured manner perfected by gentlemen of the psychoanalytic persuasion, 'If you accept my interpretation, that shows I'm right; if you reject it, that proves that we have encountered deep resistance whose existence is evidence that I am right.'

We have, then, neither good *a priori* grounds nor the base of well grounded theory on which to base our views of what constitutes a 'good' job or a 'good' working life. Nor are the empirical data unassailable. Fortunately we can always hope to amass more and better data. But these cannot be obtained by conventional methods. You can ask people if they are happy in their work, satisfied with their jobs and so on. And you can indeed obtain consistent 'measures' of job satisfaction. You can go further and identify those aspects of their job that people find satisfying and those they find the reverse. And providing that you can find ways of altering jobs so as to include more of the one and less of the other, you can then check again to see whether people are now more satisfied. This kind of procedure is now well established and is loosely described as 'job enrichment'. This procedure takes job satisfaction as an outcome variable and seeks to maximize it, admittedly in the hope, not always realized, that more job satisfaction means more productivity. But what is really being maximized? Does more job satisfaction mean less alienation? Yes, if by alienation we mean the psychological state we refer to when we say, 'I am alienated from (or more likely 'by') my job; it is boring and dull.' No, if we mean the 'objective' condition of classical alienation theory. The difference is between using oneself as an instrument in achieving one's objectives and perceiving oneself to be the instrument of the will of others. Both constitute alienation; they have different psychological meanings. The first is related to the empirical psychological literature on work alienation; the second to the theoretical and structural.

But beyond this there are three traps. The first is that if the hierarchy of needs is a sound concept, then the enriching of jobs to satisfy needs should and would evoke the emergence of new higher needs leading to new dissatisfactions. The logic of this theory and of job enrichment is a commitment to an ever-widening horizon, a continuous process of enrichment. Self-actualization, the 'highest need' is itself limitless.

The second trap is that of adaptation or habituation. We are most familiar with this in terms of income. A handsome salary increase is very welcome; commitments rapidly grow to absorb it and render our financial position as precarious as ever. We are soon no more satisfied with our income than we were before.

The third trap is this. When you ask people about their jobs they can tell you what bugs them, what pleases them – along the dimensions of their actual experience. It is a far more risky matter when

349

we ask people to evaluate what they have not experienced or have experienced only in very small degree. When people say they would like more 'participation', for example, they know that they would like to have their views listened to and their ways of doing things adopted. They cannot be expected to be thinking about the problems of accommodating old Joe's crazy notions. But in practice participation does not mean me and my boss talking things over and coming to an agreement; it means Joe and Tom and Bill, even Mary, and me working things out together. Until we have experience of this kind of thing we cannot have valid views about whether we want more or less of it or indeed of what we would be letting ourselves in for. If, then, we want to explore the advantages and disadvantages of making changes of this kind, we can only do it by the time-honoured device of 'suck it and see'.

But surely this is the good old scientific procedure of experiment? Alas, no. In a scientific experiment you manipulate one variable and examine the effect on another. If many variables are present, you sample their different states systematically and produce from the conjuror's statistical hat an estimate of the influence of each. And in any case you try to obtain 'controls', similar phenomena with which you have not interfered and whose variables can therefore be assumed to have been subject only to random variation. In experiments with changes in the organization of work, we are denied these scientific safeguards.

To begin with we are not moving from one static situation to another; we are intervening in a process. In any situation involving groups of people not in overt conflict there are many forces at work, held in some form of dynamic equilibrium. The importation of any new element strengthens some, weakens others and introduces entirely new forces. When the experimenter enters the situation, and even before he has begun to initiate change, change has occurred, forces are regrouped, expectations and fears aroused.

This phenomenon of change in the situation, induced by the presence of the experimenter, has long been recognized as a hazard – the Hawthorne effect, as it is known. Only comparatively recently has it been seen as an advantage. Certain kinds of information essential to a full understanding of the workings of a system can only be acquired by engagement with that system. Action research, the engagement of a researcher with a system to induce change whose nature is agreed as the first outcome of the engagement, is a new, powerful and dangerous tool, as we have discussed in previous chapters.

Although we do not know scientifically what are the characteristics of a good job and we have not a scientifically validated method for producing the changes we want, we have in action research a technique for producing change into which can be built adequate safeguards, one of which is the integrity of the action researcher. And we have a body of theory and of experience which enables us provisionally to list the features of jobs which give men and women the opportunity to exercise the skills, social as well as physical, which are implicit in a human organization. We have considered such a list under principle 8 of sociotechnical design in Chapter 16.

It may be that some jobs can be improved very little in the face of existing technology, or without great expense. In the long run the technology can be changed or new ways sought of obtaining ends. The first step is to identify these jobs and to set on foot research and development towards new sociotechnical designs. Meanwhile, a variety of expedients is called for. Few technologies are so intractable as to be susceptible of no improvement; where they are, their operation should be regarded as limited-term employment and manned where possible by those who, either through their personality structure or by virtue of their family situation, feel themselves adequately recompensed for the deliberate knowing sacrifice of other satisfactions. Let them be the people who correspond to the Faunce and Dubin compensators.

The search for new sociotechnical designs will, in my view, be encouraged by new trends in product design. The process which treats the worker as an expendable replaceable part is ideally matched to the expendable replaceable product. If in the future we require cars, for example, which are safe, reliable and durable and made with the accuracy required to save fuel and minimize pollution, we shall require new processes for which semi-skilled assembly will be far too crude.

We have seen changes in industry's relationship with the community in terms of greater social responsibilities – for instance, anti-pollution laws, product standards, training acts, etc. There are, therefore, several ways in which organizations can be induced to improve jobs. Since research and development aimed towards improving the quality of working life of their members is not likely to yield organizations an obvious commercial advantage, there is good reason in the public interest for it to be subsidized or treated favourably for tax purposes. The present standards of conditions of work and safety enforced by the factory inspectorate could and should be widened to cover the factors we have been discussing.

The emphasis has been on the design of jobs and their content, but it is not only what we *do* at work that matters; we must equally consider the lives our jobs force us or allow us to lead. If we are obliged to spend long hours in uncomfortable travel at inconvenient times or to work shifts which disrupt the life of the community or oblige it to provide unprofitable services, we and the community are carrying burdens only very partially compensated by shift premiums or other premium payments. Those who argue that the secular decline in working hours may make 'what happens at work' less significant in our total life experience may be right; but even if we work only 35 hours a week and 40 weeks a year, our work largely determines where and how we live.

Sir Winston Churchill, when Britain's wartime prime minister, used to complain about the ever-growing ratio of tail to teeth in the armed services; we tend to have a similar perception of productive and extractive industry as the source, and other activities as the sink of wealth. But we must balance this with a clear perception of industry as a consumer of our lives and some of the tertiary and quaternary sectors as life producers. Our present systems of measurement are all biased one way; economists and accountants have provided us with ways of measuring the production of goods and services, but not, so far, ways of measuring the value of health and education, except in terms of their cash value in employment. Is there no way of measuring the value in our lives of an educated polity for example? If the new search for social indicators leads to the emergence of a new kind of social economy and social accounting, we may eventually be equipped with better concepts for evaluating the place of work in life. But we may have to wait a long time.

Chapter 19
The Quality of Working Life

Introduction

Let me summarize as briefly as I can the origins and development of what I shall call QWL. It owes its origins to the marriage of the structural, systems perspective of organizational behaviour with the interpersonal, human relations, supervisory-style perspective. Its basic assumptions are:

1 that organizations have a technical system which
2 sets the parameters for the operation of its social system, consisting of
3 patterns of interactions which are partly task-based and
4 partly in the service of preserving the integrity of the system itself, and
5 that the objectives of any organization allow a choice among technologies;
6 that people have their own needs, some of which they expect to have satisfied in their work and
7 others which may emerge, and require satisfying, in the work situation.

Associated with these assumptions or axioms are certain values:

autonomy is preferable to dependence;
high levels of skill are preferable to low;
learning is good;
a high degree of self-investment in work is good, provided that the work itself and the work situation offer opportunities for growth and self-realization.

That I choose to describe these as axioms and values does not

353

imply that they have no empirical content or support. They are axioms and values because they describe the parameters for the construction of an organization which will permit the empirically verifiable evidence to present itself. In this respect they are design criteria. The point is simply made: if *all* work were done in totally Taylorist organizations, there would be no way of putting the theory to the test.

Now, for any reason you please, you can reject the values; but you cannot dispute design criteria on other grounds except in so far as you can demonstrate that their application fails.

Four criticisms

Of course there are those who reject these values or reject the design enterprise on the ground that its success will endanger other values. For example:

1 The efficiency (productivity) of the enterprise must be paramount. This implies either (a) that it is more efficient to maximize the technical parameters than to attempt joint optimization of technical and social and (b) that our present methods of assessing efficiency (productivity) truly represent the enterprise's contribution to the common need.

2 Joint optimization implies a systems, structural–functional analysis of organizations and ignores or underplays their essentially conflict-based nature.

3 Allied to (2), by constructing organizations which conceal or blur the differences of essential interests between workers and management, we are hindering the class struggle (a) by distracting attention from the real issues, (b) by weakening the position of the trade unions as sole guardians of workers' interests, (c) by 'co-opting' workers on to mechanisms for attaining management goals.

4 It is wrong to manoeuvre people into investing much of themselves in their work lives because (a) without guaranteed tenure you are inviting people to put more at risk than they do already, (b) work is becoming less necessary for society and the present pattern of society already depends to a dangerous degree on make-work, (c) the worker is alienated from his work by the capitalist mode of production; increased self-investment in work leads to false consciousness or self-alienation or both.

Examination of the four criticisms

Let us turn to *objection 1, the efficiency argument.* This is essentially one that comes from management and expresses a genuine fear on increased costs, especially at a time as anxious as the present. I believe it is fallacious, not just because there is no evidence that organizations have lost efficiency as currently measured (and against this I am bound to say that there are examples of changes being abandoned), but more because I believe our current measures of efficiency to be misleading. I doubt if even the most unrepentant economist would maintain that the measures whereby we assess the productivity or efficiency of a company reflects adequately the true net balance of its contributions to the welfare of society. The fiction of the free market can no longer be sustained nor can the total neglect of non-economic inputs and outputs.

This cannot be done until our methods of measurement are far further advanced. It is often the community and not the organizations concerned which pay for the diseconomies of employment practices and ways should be sought of attributing to organizations a more realistic representation of the value of their inputs and outputs. One result of this would, in my view, have quite significant impact on the concept of 'productivity'. For years we have known that measures of job satisfaction and measures of productivity have been weakly related. Correlations in twenty studies have ranged from $+0.86$ to -0.32 with a median correlation of 0.14 (Vroom, 1964). Obviously job satisfaction as measured does not lead to increased productivity as measured. But why should it? Theory says we work better if we are happy. But we don't necessarily work better towards our employer's measured objectives. And when we look at the measures of productivity we realize what an arbitrary thing it is. It represents a ratio of arbitrarily selected outputs over arbitrarily selected inputs. From the community's point of view job satisfaction is itself a desirable output, alienation an undesirable one. Time willingly given is one kind of input; time reluctantly afforded is another. De-skilled effort is one kind of input, effortless skill is another. But 'productivity' does not discriminate any of these inputs and outputs.

There is, however, a price to be paid for not doing the job properly, for ignoring or forgetting the systemic nature of an organization. The progress of the first Norwegian experiment in industrial democracy was suspended for a year and nearly wrecked because the impact of the successful first stage in one department through pay relativities on other departments had not been foreseen. The

355

improvement of QWL through job and organization redesign, whatever the motives, is not unattended by risk but nor is any other innovation; it is however in no sense a trade off for efficiency, however measured.

Objection 2 makes a perfectly fair point in maintaining that the sociotechnical approach to *QWL adopts a structural–functional perspective*. If it ignores the fact that any organization is in some respects a battleground for the struggle of different groups for power, so much the worse for it. But these conflicts are between groups of many different kinds; functional groups, occupational groups, even age, sex and ethnic groups as well as, and often much more than, groups divided by class or by ownership. The serious objection is a programmatic one, whether the objectives of change should be the sharpening of a particular dimension of conflict or the elimination or reduction of task-based conflict. This brings objection 2 into the same category as *objection 3(a), the distraction of attention from the 'real' issues*, which is unanswerable as it depends upon what you consider the real issues are. More pressing perhaps is the relationship of QWL to those other issues of ownership and control, a question which has contemporary significance in Sweden as I shall discuss later.

Objection 3(b), the weakening of the trade unions, is a serious worry. The protections won for workers by trade union struggle are not so secure that they can be put lightly at risk. And there is no doubt whatever that, especially in America, the motivation of some companies to improve QWL has been to head off demands for union representation. Nevertheless, I think this is really a tactical question: it has been known for unions to insist that pay rises offered by management but not asked and bargained for by the union is an unconscionable liberty but not for them to argue that a pay rise was bad in itself. And if the danger of a unilateral offer by management of better QWL stimulated unions to negotiate for it, that would be a happy outcome. As is well known, the trade union movements in Norway and Sweden have given their blessing and been closely involved in the direction of the changes that have been taking place. I do not know of any evidence which suggests that workers' more favourable experience of their work situation and greater control over their day-to-day work has led to any decline in their interest in their unions where these have supported the changes. My own expectation is quite the contrary; that the real challenge to the union might come from such workers demanding more control over their unions. I have observed a certain contradiction, too, in the posture adopted by some critics. Those most strongly wedded to the virtues of 'representative democracy' in industry, rejecting job and organization redesign with the direct democracy they provide as potential distractions from representative democracy and union participation on company boards, number among themselves many who are severe critics of representative 'shamocracy' in national and local government and vociferous supporters of direct democracy in all communal affairs.

Objection 4(a) points out that *the insecurity of a job is made more tolerable by our lack of commitment to it.* So long, then, as jobs are insecure, lack of commitment is a defence. Furthermore, and here is an economic rather than a welfare argument, strong commitment to a particular job hinders modernization whether from re-equipment or the replacement of unsuccessful firms or declining industries by new ones. There are really two arguments here: one concerns self-investment in *work* and the added disruption thus produced by unemployment; the other concerns commitment to a particular job or a particular firm. The two are related but not identical. It is, of course, true that the kind of firm that mounts a programme for enhancing QWL is likely to be secure. It is true also that nationalized industry, government and local government bureaucracy and public, educational and health institutions together make up perhaps 40 per cent of all employment and that there is a great deal of scope in this sector, but even here redundancy is not unknown. But the opposite argument is untenable; would one seriously argue for increasing work alienation so as to soften the shock of unemployment? And if not, what reason is there to assume that we have the amount of alienation just right? Nevertheless, I feel worried about this; it would be at least justified to demand at least as much commitment by management to the protection of the worker's job as commitment by the worker to the organization.

Objection 4(b), which stresses *the declining need for work*, turns the last objection on its head, but it still looks formidable even in that posture. It all seems to turn on the question: Does greater self-investment in work imply less self-investment in activities outside work (the compensation hypothesis) or does it lead to greater involvement in outside activity? (the spillover hypothesis). If the first, the compensation hypothesis, is correct, then increasing people's work involvement is a disadvantage, granted that society has more need of the individual in his other capacities. There is, as it happens, no conclusive evidence either way, although there are reports which support the spillover hypothesis of increased participation in community affairs of workers who have acquired more participative roles in their work. It is probably safe to assume that there is a personality variable intervening between involvement in work and participation in outside activities; certainly neither spillover nor compensation will prove true for all. And only a complete verification of the compensatory hypothesis would constitute a serious objection to improving QWL.

Objection 4(c), false consciousness and self-alienation – this is the final confrontation between a Marxist stance and any attempt to co-opt workers within a capitalist system of enterprise. As I do not know how to measure false-consciousness, I cannot think of any way of determining whether involvement in work increases it or not. As far as self-alienation is concerned, manifestly self-involvement in work decreases our self-alienation if we seek our identity partly through our work. Our self-alienation will doubtless increase if we perceive ourselves as wage slaves on whom illegitimate demands are being made to love our chains.

My concern is less to argue the case for the sociotechnical approach to QWL, although I wish to do this, than to examine the nature and validity of the objections. These, as we have seen, are of two kinds, theoretical and ideological. Both have weight but, at least as far as the theoretical argument is concerned, I believe QWL has the edge. As I hope to suggest later, the sociotechnical approach is least effective when attempted within a context of conflict; by this I do not mean during an industrial conflict, but at a time or in a setting in which conflict analysis is more appropriate.

For the moment I want to turn to the question – *How significant is QWL?*

The evidence from surveys

For those of us who believe that there is much wrong with the way work is organized and with the quality of the experience it provides, survey evidence provides scant support. It is worth looking at the report, 'Subjective Social Indicators' in the 1973 edition of *Social Trends.* The November 1971 pilot quota sample of 593 is the larger and later of the two samples reported. Both were conducted by extended interview. Given twelve 'domains' of life, the level of satisfaction was highest in, first, marriage, second, family life, third, job, with housing, standard of living, education and democracy well down the list. In order of importance to the respondent job came only sixth, after marriage, family life, health, standard of living, and house. (Religion, democracy and education occupied the last three places in both importance and satisfaction.) Eighty-one per cent rated their satisfaction with their jobs in the three highest ranks, five and above on a seven-point scale – a figure remarkably close to the 80–85 per cent 'satisfied' and 'very satisfied' respondents reported by successive national surveys of working conditions in the United States. Furthermore, job satisfaction was particularly high among women (6·3), those over 44 years of age (6·4) and unskilled workers (6·3). Finally, 'the work is interesting', average 6·0, but the opportunity to develop one's own abilities comes low with 4·9, as low as 4·2 among socio-economic classes D and E. None of the data indicates a particularly revolutionary situation and even 4·2 is the 'right' side of the mid-point between satisfaction and dissatisfaction. This is all very exasperating; people ought to be far more dissatisfied than they are; they are deficient in divine discontent.

Of course job satisfaction must be to a considerable extent a measure of the congruence of expectation and experience; dissatisfaction is expressed when the reality fails to match anticipation or the feeling of what is due. Clearly our educational system does not arouse unrealistic anticipations, our 15 to 17-year-old workers are the most satisfied of all under 65, with the 18 to 24-year-olds the least satisfied. Maybe the contrast with school for the early leavers is strongly in favour of work. And if those dissatisfied with their jobs are thereby spurred to seek other jobs in which they are better satisfied, the 6·9 per cent of men and the 3·8 per cent of women who are rather or very dissatisfied could be those for whom the accommodation process is still incomplete. It is a pity that we have no comparable data from Blake's dark satanic mills – they would probably provide similar figures with perhaps the highest satisfaction ratings among those under five years of age! It is no part of my intention to discredit measures of job satisfaction; they have their uses in enabling organizations to compare one department with another, for example, to see whether there are special areas for concern. But I would be very cautious about their interpretation on a national or international scale. I would not, for example, expect the widespread development of QWL to push average satisfaction scores up; on the contrary, I would expect (and hope) that it would bring them down by importing a new meaning to the concept.

I wish there were some accepted mode of measurement of the degree of conflict and consensus in decision-making systems. I would like to postulate that, as I hinted earlier, a conflict context requires conflict analysis and action based on it, while a consensus context is more amenable to systems analysis. Can we say how conflicted our society is? In comparison with the favourable assessment of job satisfaction, the dissatisfaction of the same sample with democratic processes is marked. Forty-two per cent consider the voter to have no or very little influence on the way the country was run. (Means of 3·1 on the seven-point scale.) I do not want to argue from that figure anything more than it states, particularly as democracy is of low salience – tenth out of eleven in 'importance'. It would, however, be instructive to have comparative data from Sweden and Norway where QWL is most advanced. A recent EEC study reported that, within the EEC, inhabitants of small countries were more satisfied with the quality of their lives than were those of the large countries. Are people in the small countries conscious of their greater influence as voters? Is a consensus context more easily obtained within small countries with homogeneous populations of the Scandinavian type?

The international scene – culture and diffusion

I should resist the temptation to chase attractive generalizations; nevertheless, for whatever reasons, historical, demographic or situational, trade unions in the Scandinavian countries, and more generally in the smaller countries of Western Europe, have adopted a less confrontational, more co-operative approach towards employers and towards government. If we were to rank the countries of Western Europe in order of advance in QWL, we would place Sweden, Norway and Holland in the van, with perhaps Denmark next. Britain, France, Italy and Germany would bring up the rear. Belgium, the most conflicted and inhomogeneous, is the last of the small countries with perhaps the exception of Ireland.

I am hesitant to 'explain' why the pattern is the way it is. If I had forecast these developments I would be on strong ground, but I certainly did not and I don't know of anyone who did. Emery (1973) suggests that there is more room to manoeuvre at the periphery than at the centre of a system; Herbst (1974) advocates a strategy of moving into the 'empty space' between what is prescribed and what is prohibited. To what extent we should regard Norway as empty space or merely peripheral I should not like to say; what is certain is that the ideas generated in the late 1940s by the Tavistock Institute in Britain found their first real expression (an exception is the Ahmedabad experiment which survived but failed to diffuse) in the Norwegian experiments of the early 1960s under the joint auspices of the unions, employers' federations and the government. Progress was slow, but each experiment which involved a great deal of technical and social science intervention was well consolidated. What the Norwegians did not solve was the problem of obtaining rapid diffusion; the large investment of time and effort by the social scientists of the Work Research Institute at Oslo was at least one of the limiting factors. It is in Sweden and Denmark that there has been something of take-off with the social scientist's role confined for the most part to monitoring and evaluating, rather than directly participating in, the change processes. A review of the state of play in the ten countries of Western Europe (Sweden, Norway and the Nine less Luxemburg) was published by *Business International*. The following summary is reprinted:

Participation through organizational change

	Country
Interest just now beginning in unions and employer groups, but a few companies have made notable strides.	Belgium
Some notably advanced democratization projects have been put in motion by employer–union co-operation, but little activity just now, and there is no strong push in this area.	Denmark
Growing interest in recent years, and many firms have made rapid strides. Union hostility frequent.	France
A few companies have made notable progress, and government is now subsidizing experiments.	Germany
Low level of interest.	Ireland
Changes in assembly lines and work organizations brought about through labor contracts, but affecting only a few companies.	Italy
High level of sophistication and knowledge, and some companies are among the most advanced in Europe. Supported by both employers' groups and unions.	Netherlands
First country to use work-reorganization as part of a political 'industrial democracy' program. Projects supported by both employers and unions. Level of sophistication extremely high.	Norway
Most advanced European country. Company democratization aggressively promoted by employers, unions and government. Employers and unions have considerable expertise.	Sweden
Very advanced theoretical knowledge and some company projects have shown very positive results. But little organized interest among either unions or employers' groups.	United Kingdom

(*Source: Industrial Democracy in Europe, Business International* European research report, December 1974, p. 97.)

This seems to be a fair summary. If I were to try to add the United States to the list I would write that 'a large number of firms have been involved in recent years and interest is now spreading to federal and state government activity. A few unions have become positively interested, notably the Autoworkers. The Ford Foundation has shown considerable interest and has helped whenever possible; some federal government money is now available. Levels of sophistication have been variable and the social science inputs have been mainly those of individual academics on a consultancy basis. The lines between job enrichment packages, "OD" and substantial reorganization have been hazily drawn, making many projects hard to evaluate.'

But although interest has arisen as a response to pressures which differ from country to country and from enterprise to enterprise within any one country, and although developments in each country must be seen against the background provided by its pattern of industrial and company legislation, the nature and operation of its labour markets and the posture and power of its unions, these projects are, with few exceptions, linked. The linkage is provided by the diffusion of the concepts involved. There are a few exceptions, but the main body of projects have been the result either of diffusion through management channels or through the spread of ideas and experience through social scientists or both. The Norwegian experiments, which are of far greater importance for the part they played in the diffusion channels than for their own positive achievements, have been the Mecca for industrialists and social scientists alike interested in work-place reorganization. Here for once the channels of diffusion are reasonably clear. Union leaders and politicians around 1960 were pressing for industrial democracy of the representative type. Thorsrud, who worked with members of the Tavistock Institute, advocated a sociotechnical approach and the objective of autonomous work groups. Because the sponsorship of the experiments was at national level, it was possible to diffuse the knowledge of the results and the methods to other organizations. Nevertheless, the difficulty of this model is its one-off character. Industrialists prefer packaged solutions whose cost and outcomes are, if not guaranteed, at least defined and limited. Today, the interest has shifted to Sweden, partly because of the brilliant use by Volvo of the potential for advertisement (the 'buy cars made by happy workers' theme reminiscent of nothing so much as the 'buy your milk from contented cows' campaign), and partly because of the sheer weight of numbers of experimental reforms (>500), partly because their approach, though strongly influenced by the sociotechnical model, has been greatly eclectic. It is still I think possible to chart the networks of diffusion of this social innovation; from it much could be learned both of a theoretical and a practical nature. I can offer only a sketch of what I take to be the parameters involved.

Diffusion and the cultural context

The first notable point is that although. the whole sociotechnical idea and the description of the autonomous (or composite) group emerged first in the work of the Tavistock Institute in the British coal mines, reported in a series of papers in the 1950s and published as *Organizational Choice* in 1963 (Trist, *et al*.), you would be hard put to find anyone in the industry in Britain who has ever heard of it. It was a social innovation (or, as the authors described it, a 'rediscovery'), which met a particular need at a particular place at a particular time. It was a response not to a newly felt need but to a sense of recent loss. However relevant and generalizable the principles involved, the conditions for diffusion and transplantation were just not there. Where autonomous group working has spread has been where the pressure of need has been felt and articulated. Isolated instances have occurred as a result of the enthusiasm and drive of an employer or his conversion to a faith in a particular social scientist or a particular dogma. But these remain isolated, and are seen by other firms as exceptional, dependent upon some 'special' factors – a specially selected work force or a particular history, interesting but not relevant to their situation. Isolated, they persist only if they are successful in generating the ideology and commitment to support them. They are vulnerable to environmental change and to the exigencies of management succession.

The widespread need and its recognition have indeed been most marked in Sweden, where we can see the five signs of change towards a new conception of work that we pointed to in the previous chapter, but reiterate here.

1 Manufacturing industry is ceasing to be the principal form of employment.
2 Young native workers in the developed countries are returning to take certain kinds of job – those that bring them personal satisfaction.
3 More young people are opting out of 'work' altogether; more older people are retiring as soon as they can.
4 Dissatisfaction is higher among the young.
5 The increasing concern of our large industrial companies with their image, frequently articulated as their 'social

responsibility'. The decline in shareholders' influence, coupled with the growing professionalization of management have been contributing factors, but a stronger factor has been the growing criticism of industrial aims and practices, especially from students.

Now these phenomena taken together constitute the kind of pressures that motivated Volvo, for example, to move away from the traditional assembly-line working. They were acute in the country in Europe which had advanced furthest towards the post-industrial syndrome. Few young Swedes were coming to work for Volvo and none on the assembly line which was manned very largely by foreign workers. Advances in the Finnish economy, which began to attract Finns back across the border, presented Volvo with a bleak future unless young Swedes could be enticed into automobile manufacture. The Norwegian shipping industry saw the same writing on the wall.

The conditions for rapid diffusion of QWL seem to be:

(i)   the pressure of a post-industrial ethos;

(ii)   the framework of a consensus system which allows unions and employers to co-operate; if all actions of the unions have to be seen in terms of class conflict, it is very difficult to adapt the rhetoric of confrontation to the conduct of problem-solving – it can be done but the result is brittle;

(iii)   the support of other organizations, other firms, other unions;

(iv)   government willingness to assist in removing obstacles, if necessary by legislation. Swedish legislation, for example, which confers on guestworkers the right to a substantial minimum of instruction in the Swedish language does not so much remove an obstacle as to remove one of the supports of the existing accommodation. This kind of consensus is apparently very fragile. The Swedish unions have now given notice to end their collaborative arrangements with employers and to dissolve the joint 'committee on collaborative questions'. Whether QWL developments can continue in the new atmosphere remains to be seen. There is so far no evidence that unions will want to oppose these developments; they are more likely to seek to bring them within the framework of 'negotiation'. If they wish, they can use their abrogation of the clause in labour agreements, which at present allows to employers the right to determine methods of work to insist in future agreements on QWL-type work reorganization. But the going will be harder, without the umbrella of collaborative arrangements at national level.

364

The United States, pluralistic here as everywhere, can sustain pockets of advanced practice as oases in the desert. A few large companies in a particular industrial sector or in a particular geographical region can provide the necessary system of supports. We cannot expect anything as simple as diffusion on the basis of perceived merit alone. Although it is doubtful whether the conditions I have outlined are yet fulfilled in Britain, it seems to me that we are getting nearer their fulfilment. One positive sign is that the current economic setback has interfered comparatively little with companies' plans for change. The repeal of the Industrial Relations Act and the government's apparent readiness to sponsor legislation aimed at worker representation on company boards, while not removing union suspicions, at least gives more freedom of action to those unions which are comparatively favourably disposed. On the other hand, the five signs of post-industrial climate are rather less in evidence than they were two years ago and greatly less in evidence than in Sweden and the more advanced countries of Western Europe. The data I quoted earlier from *Social Trends* are equivocal but give little indication of strong pressures growing among young workers.

Perspectives of the social science disciplines

The centre of gravity of those who have contributed to the development of QWL has been in social psychology, among people to whom the satisfaction of the needs of the individual is important but who also have some sense of social structure and who see small groups as the focus for the meeting of the individual and the structural. The tradition of industrial psychology has been to accept organizational goals as unproblematic, a perspective shared by only a proportion of industrial sociologists who have thereby earned themselves the opprobrious soubriquet of plant sociologists. Yet it is they who have told us what people do in their work, a topic almost entirely neglected by the sociologists of occupations who tell us much about how workers are recruited and socialized. In so far as sociologists have been frankly normative, they have been reluctant to commit themselves to any position which would detract from their critical stance toward the capitalist mode of production. It has largely been left then to social psychologists who are less sensitized to the broader issues to engage in action research with the aim of promoting human values within the existing framework of ownership. But now these developments are sufficiently widespread to cease to rank as 'experiments'; they can no longer be contained within that perspective. For sociologists the problems are real. Even if the intense involvement of social scientists in QWL changes in organizations is no longer needed, their help is still required in evolving strategies of diffusion which avoid their encapsulation and erosion. Their aid is also needed to work out methods for bringing the quality of working life into the schema of calculation, whereby the exchanges between work organizations and the community are assessed. If he works to this end of obtaining a shift in the basis of accommodation between work organizations and society, his role becomes a part of that accommodation. If he refuses to become involved, the awkward situation arises: QWL is one of the very few constructive developments which owes a great deal to the research and activity of social scientists. What has already been done has improved the QWL of a few thousand workers directly and perhaps a few tens of thousands through the interest raised and the partial changes so inspired. These changes are fragile. The pockets where change is systemic will remain, but can become encapsulated; those where change is partial can easily be reversed and are likely to be as soon as they are exposed to other changes and pressures. The social ecology of QWL is complex; I doubt if one can even study it without affecting it, as anthropologists have discovered in a different context.

Section IV
Development

Chapter 20
Social Sciences and Development

Introduction: can social sciences help?

We are in danger of overselling ourselves and our sciences. Danger lies in the expectations that have been aroused in governments, among politicians, administrators and members of their many publics. They have been led, or have led themselves, to believe that the social sciences will solve their problems. As social scientists, then, we are under strong and increasing pressures to deliver goods of whose nature neither we nor our 'market' are clearly aware. The demands vary from society to society and from time to time. But although there may be problems of disorder in the streets here and the collapse of consensus there or the persistence of pockets of poverty in the other place, there is one demand more common, more widespread and more insistent than any other, the demand for help in the process of 'development'. There persists a widespread expectation that the social sciences, or at any rate social scientists, will be able to provide help *on a large scale* in the planning and execution of economic and social development.

Meaning of terms

If we are to face this demand honestly we have to be clear about certain fundamental issues. First, what is meant by 'development' and what the processes are whereby a society 'develops'. Secondly, what are the social sciences, what skills are possessed by social scientists and what part can and should these disciplines and these

367

skills play in the processes of devising development plans, executing them, and appraising and evaluating the outcome. The third step is to examine the base upon which any edifice we devise must be built. This base is the present state of knowledge, the educational base for providing trained people, the institutional bases for research, application, evaluation and advice, and the capabilities of societies for using knowledge and advice. Many of these areas we have already considered when thinking about social science policy in Chapter 1 and in Part I, Section V, when we looked at comparative social science policy and considered the development and use of the social sciences in selected countries. In this chapter we shall discuss the processes of development and planning for development and the relationship between research in the social sciences and the processes of development and development planning. We shall attempt to review the needs of the social sciences if they are to contribute more fully to development and to planning.

In the *International Social Science Journal*, vol. 24, no. 1, 1972, we have a set of articles viewing development from the perspectives of individual social sciences. Each contributes its own themes but some occur repeatedly – for example the problem of the distortions brought about by the use of unidimensional 'indicators' such as GNP per capita. Another such theme is the complicating effect of the 'demonstration effect'. Some contributors also comment on the limitations of the approach from a single discipline. There is agreement that the social sciences, with the exception of social anthropology, are modes of analysis and understanding of economically advanced, literate societies, developed within these same advanced, literate societies. To analyse and understand, let alone prescribe for, underdeveloped countries, they have to rid themselves of some of the models derived from advanced societies.

So in this chapter I shall try to indicate what needs to be done in the light of the conclusions of these papers and of other contributions to the theory and practice of development.

Nature of development process

Before we can discuss the needs for social science research directed towards development, we need to examine the nature of the development process, the nature of the planning process and the nature of the social sciences.

The process whereby a society transforms itself from one based on a predominantly agrarian non-market economy to a predominantly industrial market economy, with its associated paraphernalia of government and its characteristic urban base, has naturally been a matter of absorbing interest to social scientists of all descriptions. Consequently, we know a good deal about the path traversed by the societies which became industrialized in the eighteenth and nineteenth centuries. Those societies were somnambulist; they could have no idea of the terrain further along the road, nor could they read the signposts which had not been erected by previous pilgrims. One of the perplexing difficulties facing the analyst or prophet watching their twentieth-century successors set off along the path is just this difference in awareness and knowledge. The process of development is like most other processes radically affected by the state of consciousness of those guiding the process. The experiences of the developed countries has only limited value as a guide to the developing. Furthermore, the process is additionally complicated by the existence in the environment of the developed models; their route to modernity is too easily seen as the single modernizing road. After false starts and disappointments we now see the errors in this appreciation; few did twenty years ago.

This 'demonstration' effect is a recurrent theme in the set of papers we are considering. It is located theoretically by Alatas as an aspect of cultural diffusion. The diffusion channel consists partly of Western advisers whose practice had to precede theory and Asian scholars whose minds had been captivated by the West. But the most important channel of all is the United Nations and its agencies. One major consequence both for theory and for practice is that international relations have to be part of the study of development and must be taken into account in all analyses and plans for development. The demonstration effect brings with it a 'potential elimination' effect, ruling out potential use of indigenous innovations in favour of Western models. Finally, by operating on consumer expectations more rapidly than on production, it builds in an atmosphere of conflict before development even starts. This effect is moreover virtually built into the concept of development in so far as this is defined by reference to westernizing or 'modernizing'. Development need not be defined in this way.

However congruent their goals, the existing situation of the countries loosely described as the third world presents a wide diversity (see Pearson, 1969). It is not possible to summarize too succinctly without oversimplifying, but it seems fair to say that the realization has grown that there is no one process of development, that what is involved in development is not just an economic or technological change of tempo but a vast transformation of a whole society; and that the processes of change which a society can undergo are not

369

only related to the existing pattern, situation and level of attainment of that society, but also to the endemic processes whereby change takes place in that society. The processes of change in India with its 530 million people and 17 states are vastly different from those in Gabon with its 0·5 million people (Pearson, 1969). The notion that development has different meanings for different societies is, however, relatively new and still not fully learned, nor has the realization fully sunk in that there are many possible routes to broadly similar goals. *A choice of route is often a choice of value system.* Too often the values associated with development are technocratic values which are impatient of, and denigratory of, the existing social values and unappreciative of social practices and their potential importance as stabilizing agencies during a period of rapid change. Russell (1970) exposes the technocratic ideology underlying not only the selection of goals in his example – population control in East Africa – but also the means. A typical technocratic assumption is that the chosen route to the goal of economic development is obstructed by customs and practices which are irrational. By describing them as irrational the technocrat justifies his efforts to sweep them away. In this he is frequently abetted by the very social scientists – psychologists and sociologists – who are most concerned to explain the customs and practices by reference to their latent functions and role in maintaining structural stability. This technocratic approach alienates the social scientist where he does not fall into this trap. The difference in perspective of the social scientist and technocrat is described by Belshaw (1972), 'Given man, how can science and technology help him, not given science and technology, how can man be made to fit?'

But there is also the question of rationality. Apter and Mushi (1972) ask: Whose rationality? 'During the 1960s the irrationalities of the donor were neglected. In a very real sense the recipients were only too willing to be rational.' But they appear to accept that the actual behaviour was irrational. Attacking the economists' assumptions they paraphrase Wilbert Moore, 'In other words, economists tended to take for granted the existence of the "rational" economic man in every society', and imply that the psychological assumptions underlying classical theories of economic behaviour are less appropriate in developing than in advanced societies. Ignacy Sachs (1972) denies the existence of 'some suprahistorical economic rationality of universal applicability', '. . . indeed the criteria for assessing alternatives vary from one socio-cultural context to another'. There is, however, probably no need to propose a different kind of rationality. Lipton (1969) has demonstrated elegantly the essential rationality of the Indian peasant in adopting a 'survival algorithm' in conditions of uncertain rainfall and imperfect markets.

The choice of goals and the choice of means are more closely linked in a way still imperfectly understood. It is not a question of the choice of goal specifying the means. The choice of means, because it is a choice among value systems, is even more influential than choice of goal in determining the likely shape of the outcome. This is only one of the reasons why understanding of the *processes of development* is so essential.

Paul Streeten (1968), after examining and rejecting the theories of inevitable 'stages of growth' through which each society must pass, finds equally unhelpful those theories which single out one factor as a hindrance to growth whose removal would permit the society to develop. He describes the complications of the co-existence of rich, poor and poorer and concludes that 'only a systems analysis with fully and explicitly formulated value judgements can lead to an understanding of the development process and only a multi- and interdisciplinary, problem-orientated approach can form the basis of effective development planning'.

Need for interdisciplinary approach

The processes of development are unlikely to be adequately explored and understood where practitioners of one discipline alone are approaching the problem. If ever a topic cried out for the multidisciplinary approach, this is it. The authors of the papers we are considering are in general agreement on this score. Two positive proposals emerge. To avoid the distorted image of reality which results from taking the point of view of a single discipline, Sachs (1972) recommends that we 'learn how to handle, as parameters of the single-discipline model, the strategic variables of other single-discipline models'. Whether Sachs is drawing a fine distinction here between 'parameter' and 'strategic variable', I am not sure, nor am I sure whether the social scientist can hope to do more than 'abridge', in Gluckman and Devons's (1964) terms, the findings of another (social science) discipline. What all will, however, agree is that one may 'hope to see the disappearance of that highly convenient but blighting formula', the *ceteris paribus* of the economist – an example not of abridgement but of circumsumption.

Belshaw (1972) leads directly from the view that development is a matter of interdisciplinary concern to the suggestion of a 'profession of development advisers, concerned with advising governments, ministries and agencies in a completely interdisciplinary manner'. Social scientists should devise an interdisciplinary curriculum for their training.

Introducing his study of modernization in Tanzania, Peter Gould (1970) argues that 'No social scientist, no matter what disciplinary viewpoint he assumes, will feel that his work is being disparaged when I say that our knowledge of (the sequential patterns involved in modernization) in Africa is slight, while our understanding of process is non-existent.'

The difficulties surrounding an understanding of the processes of development seem to grow the more the topic is discussed. To quote Streeten (1967):

> We know very little about the impact of population policy, education, medical expenditure, nutrition, industrialization, trade union activities of private enterprise on people and the policy makers are often left without guides to their most important decisions. In order to help, we must understand. This understanding requires breaking down existing barriers between established fields of study, between analysts and practitioners and between utilizers of different nations.

Now it is not quite true to say we know very little about the impact of education, etc. upon people: of course in a sense we know a great deal. But *in the context of development* it is surprisingly true, not least because of the complex and often unforeseen interactions between each of these activities, and because we are seldom, if ever, in a position to hold the others constant while we examine the effects of one.

The complex interrelationships of social and economic factors in development create difficulties both for the development planners and for the social scientists trying to conceptualize the process in a way which can assist the planner and the administrator. The tendency has grown in industrialized societies to regard the motive power of growth of the economy in economic terms alone, with social variables treated as largely exogenous to the economic system. The contrary tendency has prevailed in the study of primitive societies. These approaches represent the virtual abandonment to the economist of the study of advanced economics and to the anthropologist of the study of primitive societies. This example from Joy (1967) illustrates the point.

> Take for example questions of land reform (or is a society no longer primitive when land reform is imposed upon it?). An economist might analyse the effects of a proposed reform in

terms of changes in the opportunities open to various people involved.

In this context, 'opportunities' is a neutral word indicating simply 'possibilities.' Predicting the economic consequences of a land reform involves predicting what people will do in the face of new opportunities. Given an understanding of their values and customs, the direction – if not the speed – of response might be predicted. But values themselves – and social institutions, too – may change in the face of new opportunities. A model of change in this situation would need to incorporate, endogenously, both economic and social variables. Economists are gradually becoming aware of the significance of this interdependence. A study of development economics reveals values and social institutions to be of unavoidable significance and models of economic development must allow for changes in social values and institutions resulting from, and affecting the process of, economic development. What is true for the economist is equally true for the anthropologist. One cannot take economic opportunities as given. They are changing and will continue to change, not only exogenously, but in response to changes in values and social institutions. A study of the mutual inter-relationships of economic and social factors seems ultimately to demand a joint approach by the two disciplines.

Most of the papers under review were both critical of existing theories of development and conscious of the need for viable theory. Theory has been discredited, not solely because of the limitations of single discipline analyses, but also because the practical exigencies of development have so narrowed the field of choice that as Apter and Mushi (1972) put it:

> . . . arrangements have little or nothing to do with imitation of any particular model; nor are they based on any particular social science theory . . . hence theories which point certain 'scientific' stages of development, through which every country must pass, have been discredited in most countries in the Third World. . . . [Gunnar Myrdal's] exploration of the causes of failure in Asia leave us with little hope that present bodies of theory provide a satisfactory solution to the crucial problem of the Third World.

Indeed, the concept of 'development' itself may be a hindrance to understanding in the same way that 'delinquency', a legal category,

373

has served ill as a concept in social science. Even when we broaden our conceptual approach to the level of 'social change' we are little better off: '. . . societies are never in equilibrium. They are constantly in the process of change. . . .' Nor can we erect, Apter and Mushi argue, a theory of change or development of man's inherent needs or capacities: '. . . individual adaptations to virtually any cultural norms are so ingenious and complex that the cultural determinism implied by the work of Hayer and others can be refuted'. Balandier is sympathetic to a reconceptualization of tradition and modernity as dialectically, rather than dichotomously, related. Other critics have pointed to the importance of the undeveloped parts of their known world as essential contributors to the process of development through which the advanced countries passed. We may perhaps extend Balandier's view to maintain the existence of a dialectical relationship between underdevelopment and advance.

If indeed, joint approaches are needed for understanding the processes of development, we are faced at once by the familiar difficulties of interdisciplinary work, difficulties which are partly intellectual, partly institutional and almost wholly intractable. Nevertheless, it is clear that the benefits from overcoming them will accrue not least to the disciplines themselves. Let us also remind ourselves that, in the words of the OECD Report (1971), '. . . economic growth is not the only objective of societies'. The report goes on to argue that no one would maintain that the sole function of education is to contribute to that end. We may need to remind ourselves that this is not the sole function of the social sciences either, and that even in developing countries, the provision for social science teaching and research must go beyond the needs for their use arising from the development process.

The planning process

Planners do not need social scientists to tell them that planning is a complex process and that planning decisions often have to be made in the light of even less, and less accurate, information than is available for other administrative decisions. Dror (1969) says:

> Political stability, strong symbols of identification, ability to
> recruit support, implementation capacities, some
> professionalization of the bureaucracy and some acceptance of
> a merit system – these illustrate the characteristics of the
> political and administrative system recognized as requirements

for accelerated socio-economic development. . . . Many development aid activities are directed at encouraging these. . . . But at least one critical aspect of the political administrative system, which constitutes one of the most important variables for shaping all facets of development, is very neglected in theory and action alike: this is the policymaking function.

Dror attributes this neglect to four factors:
(a) the study of policy-making is new, even in the most highly developed countries;
(b) improvements in policy-making involve change in political institutions, a highly sensitive area;
(c) worthwhile improvement in the process of policy-making requires a large number of separate but interrelated changes; each by itself can have little impact; and
(d) qualified people, political support, time and information are all scarce.

But these are not the only complications. Policy-making in the field of development planning can be analysed into a series of interlinked decisions, each involving the systematic collection of information, analysis and feedback. In each of these steps an input of knowledge, method and information generated by the social sciences is required. But not only are different social sciences likely to be needed at different phases of the process, different types of research are needed also.

Types of social science research

In the social sciences four types of research are discernible: basic, objective, operational and action research (see Chapter 7). Whereas objective research is likely to be the most appropriate to that phase of planning which involves clarifying options, pure basic research may play an even more fundamental part in increasing options by exposing possibilities not hitherto foreseen. When we attempt to realize the selected option, action research is likely to be the most appropriate social science input, with its flexible and sensitive response to changes as they unfold. Lastly, operational research is needed both to provide the feedback – informing us of the actual impact of our policies – and to explore the most appropriate routes and methods of reaching the goals we have set. Each of these types of research has its own characteristic channels of diffusion and each has its own most appropriate type of institutional matrix (see Chapter 7). Thus, for example, basic research tends to flourish best within universities, objective research in institutes, operational research and action research within in-house facilities. Thus the planning function requires access to a range of institutions providing research, if it is to make the optimum use of potential inputs from the social sciences.

When we turn to the developing countries we see that few possess a range of research institutions of this kind and none has a systematic technique for utilizing the facilities which do exist. We shall need to examine what possibilities are open to them to draw on social sciences from other countries, from shared regional facilities, or from international agencies. These considerations are of great importance as the provision of social science research institutions cannot conceivably be the first or even a very high priority for any developing country.

Roles of the social sciences

We have attempted to show that the social sciences are needed to contribute to a greater understanding of the processes involved in development and their interactions and to a greater knowledge of the planning and decision-making processes. In our discussion of the policy process we have already indicated some of the other roles of the social sciences, but predominantly we have been considering their contribution to understanding – their *analytical* role. But the development planner has a natural impatience with what he perceives as too great a concern with analysis: 'The problems are clear; can we not now get on with the business of solving them?' Unfortunately the problems are not all clear and, where they appear to be, their clarity may be misleading. There is a considerable interaction between what we perceive as a problem and the modes of understanding and explanation that we use; there is a further interaction between these and the 'technology' available for coping with them. For example, we now perceive in social terms problems which we were conceptually unable to perceive in that light before. Poverty, for example, is no longer seen as either the will of God, punishment for sin, or due to constitutional individual weakness, but as a feature of the way society is organized. This is because we now believe we understand the socio-economic reasons for the uneven distribution of wealth. This has two consequences: first, we tend to see *as problems* those phenomena for which we have some system of analysis and some technology for control. Secondly, the increased control that we obtain over one feature of the environment enables another to appear as a problem. In medicine, for example, our increasing control over infectious ailments helps to expose the problem of degenerative disease. There is a circular interaction of science and technology; of modes of explanation and techniques to tackle problems. Thus the analytic and synthetic roles of the social sciences are indissolubly linked; furthermore, the framework of analysis we adopt determines both the problems we shall identify and our appreciation of the possible futures among which we can select.

The indicators we choose are derived from the analytical frameworks we use. Many of those in current use are positively mischievous in their impact. The publication of economic indicators inevitably directs politicians and administrators towards action which will show an 'improvement' on economic indicators. GNP is the crudest and potentially most dangerous. Sauvy (1972) raises serious criticisms. By adding in the costs of, for example, the Civil Service and Armed Forces to GNP, wasteful administration contributes directly to 'improving' the GNP indicator. By using the dollar cost of dissimilar items the GNP cannot discriminate between items which will add to future production and those which will not. Thus:

> The statistics for many developing countries over the past twenty years show a considerable increase in the GNP per head coupled with a virtual standstill in production and food consumption. The latter result, which is perhaps more important than the former, is often ignored.

Belshaw (1972) shows how indicators used for judgement and comparison 'are derived from data about the formal system which provides for the exchange of goods and services, as recognized by economic statisticians' and proposes indicators which are more appropriate to the values of the society in which they are applied. He proposes a 'behavioural profile' and a 'potential profile' of a culture, the former being a list of those things which people in a culture actually express through behaviour, the latter consisting of their goals and aspirations. The relationship between these profiles indicates the 'state of performance'; their complexity indicates the 'state of development'. Of course we must not underestimate the difficulties of quantifying these profiles; but we must avoid the temptation to take the easy way and project social and political factors on to an economic axis. Cost-benefit analysis is, of course, an attempt to do just that: to quantify each social benefit and each social cost by which people would be prepared to pay for it or to

377

escape it. But economic costing does presuppose some freedom of market and a high degree of knowledge of the market, both of which are frequently lacking. The need remains to obtain 'a positive change in the social and economic system . . . at the least cost'. And Balandier (1972) claims that 'some sociological studies provide a body of information and elements for the answer'. Without quantification it is hard to see *how* governments are going to use this knowledge. Of course, quantification *per se* will not save governments from error or from facile optimism. Even in the use of demographic knowledge for population policy, governments in practice 'adopt such measures as they consider appropriate and feasible in terms of the financial and human resources, fixing birth-rate targets that are largely a matter of guesswork and err as a rule on the side of optimism'. As Sauvy comments, there is no law governing the relationship between a given effort and the result to be expected from it. At least one can avoid undertaking activities whose input exceeds output on some single measurable scale, if what is being measured is of overriding importance. As Sauvy suggests, 'Any work unlikely to bring in as many calories as would be needed to perform it should be ruled out.'

If GNP and similar economic indicators are seriously inadequate for comparing two successive states of a single country, they are even more grossly inadequate in drawing comparisons across countries: '. . . micro-economic indicators are comparable practically without limitation (due account being taken of technological requirements posed by natural conditions), whereas the indicators that depend on the macro-economic structure can be compared only between countries of the same size'. An interesting attempt to exploit as fully as possible all available and quantifiable material yields a 'General Development Index' which 'correlates better than does the per capita GNP, not only with individual social indicators, but also with individual economic indicators. Similarly, it predicts missing scores better. Thus in tests involving simulated ignorance of the scores on life expectation and electricity consumption of nine countries, the estimate from the general index (constructed without the missing score) gave significantly smaller average errors in both cases than did estimates based on the per capita GNP (or the logarithm of the per capital GNP)' (McGranahan, 1971).

GDI is more stable and fluctuates less than GNP per capita and where it is discrepant from GNP per capita the maldistribution of GNP appears to be responsible. Furthermore, money may buy well in some factors and poorly in others in the same economy; this of course leads to differential regional development within one country. 'Regions differ from each other not so much by what they produce but rather by how they do it, for what customers, in whose interests, etc.' (Volsky, 1972).

Thus the social sciences in their analytical roles clarify and increase our options for action and in their linked, synthetic roles they may assist in our attainment of the options we have selected. In the intermediate process of selecting among options (the policy-making process) the contribution of the social sciences is again in clarifying the processes involved and in helping to set up the machinery for more efficient performance of these processes.

The administrator and the planner most easily comprehend the role of the social sciences in providing 'data'; they are frequently less interested in the explanatory power of social science 'theory'. As a result a good deal of the collection of data for administrative purposes is at a prescientific stage in that the data are not being collected in relation to theory. As ever, nothing is as practical as a good theory; and better analytical frameworks are prerequisites to better use of the social sciences in the formulation and realization of development policy.

The infrastructure for research, training and advanced training in the social sciences

In a word, the infrastructure is education. In all countries the main part of teaching and research and advanced training in the social sciences is carried out in institutions of higher education. The particular characteristics of any one system of higher education will be prominent among the determinants of social science policy.

Among the developing countries of Africa and Asia there are two main educational heritages, that derived from the French and that from the British systems of education. It has been claimed that the 'French university system is the least suited to advancing research within the university structure' (Mitchell, 1965). Thus we shall tend to find that a country's social science research base depends upon:

(a) the state of development of its higher education;

(b) the traditions of higher education.

There is, of course, no *a priori* reason why the state or tradition of higher education should provide a satisfactory basis for social research, for development or for planning for that matter. As Hurd and Johnson (1969) say:

The expansion of higher education in 'developing' countries . . . has taken place with little reference to the demands of the planning process. In particular the universities which were implanted in British colonies and ex-colonies were not only irrelevant to their particular needs but were derived from models which had been largely irrelevant to the industrialization of Britain itself.

Higher education is, of course, not only the outcome of its history and present situation, it is also the result of pressures to adopt a particular fashionable model of education which carries, sometimes unnoticed, within itself a model of society. Thus the adoption of a particular model of education may, by affecting the stratification as well as the values of the society, precept certain social policies.

Higher education and research

We would emphasize the needs for more, not less, planning of education and educational provision in the developing than in the developed countries; and that the planning of both education and employment have to be linked. Our techniques for doing this are so far extremely limited. Furthermore, in those countries where research is closely linked with higher education, this factor has to be considered on both the demand as well as supply side of the equation. Where, as in the British and American traditions, provision for research is semi-automatically built into the provision for higher education, control over the research and the researchers is weak. This excellent academic tradition of 'free' research may, or may not be, a luxury for a society struggling to raise its standards of living; we are certainly not arguing that it should be weakened, still less abandoned. The point is that, in the way in which statistics of research expenditure are calculated, this kind of research still tends to be lumped together with other categories. At the very least, attempts to compare research provision in countries with different educational traditions rest on a very weak comparative basis (see Chapter 10).

Research agencies

Thus we shall expect to find that the part played by the educational system in a country's infrastructure of research will differ not only with the state of development of that system, but also with its tradition. Whatever the traditions, it is in any case almost the only source of highly qualified manpower in the social, as in other, sciences. It is, however, only one of the bases from which research is conducted. The other bases which we must consider are research

380

institutes associated with universities and other institutions of higher education, independent institutes, research institutes under government sponsorship or control, and in-house research agencies within government departments. All of these are to be found in one or another developing country and associated with groups of countries there are also regional research centres under international auspices, particularly UNESCO's.

Research councils

Looking at the infrastructure for research and teaching we must not neglect the instruments of science policy. Hardly a developing country now lacks a research council or national research institution for the physical sciences on the model either of the Western-style research council or the east European academy of sciences. In many cases this is also the chosen instrument for supporting research and research training in the universities. Few possess the equivalent of a social science research council, but most have provision for sponsoring research in the social sciences attached to some central organ of government – planning commission, ministry of education, and so on. But we need to know more about the function of these various bodies and their modes of financing and directing research and their degree of concern with the articulation of research and policy.

Utilization of research

We now turn to look at the problems associated with the utilization of research, the relationships between researchers and policy-makers. At one extreme we have the case of Latin America where the ideological separation of social science from government, of social scientists from administrators appears to be complete. To quote Labbens (1969):

> Latin America is passing through a crisis; the sociologist is asked not only to account for and explain it, but also to deal with it . . . knowledge is an element in the situation and increased knowledge alters the data and gives the action taken a greater chance of success. Thus the theories and assumptions of the sociologist necessarily tend to prove true. . . . The only choice he can suggest is between conservation and change; he inevitably contributes towards one or the other.

381

So we must grant that at the level of conceptualizing the existing situation, of formulating the possible options for development, the social scientist has a role. But even more, as Solari (1969) puts it, it must develop a research infrastructure with a view to:

(a) having sociology accepted as a theoretical science, empirical in nature . . .;
(b) establishing suitable institutions for the training of professional sociologists;
(c) setting up a suitable organization for the permanent task of sociological research;
(d) modernizing the teaching of sociology.

So we see that social crisis has favoured the spread but hindered the institutionalization of sociology, thereby reinforcing other tendencies which have their roots in other aspects of the social crisis. These include, besides the poor state of communications among sociologists, the discontinuities in research caused by the frequency of replacement of the top echelons – yet another development paradox. Modernizing teaching usually means copying US and European models. In sociology in particular this tends to mean studying US social phenomena and social problems. Neither the concepts nor the methods are necessarily appropriate to the study of the local scene. The same problem has been described by W. B. Reddaway (1962):

The difference between the economics of developed and under-developed countries lies not so much in the problems which confront them . . . as in the assumptions which one 'naturally' makes in considering the problem . . . and all too often fails to specify explicitly.

We can think of the example of the concept of 'unemployment'.

We see, then, that an attempt to establish a secure infrastructure for research by strengthening the institutionalization of teaching and research and by modernizing the teaching by introducing concepts and methods derived from, and found useful in, conditions in advanced countries may hinder as well as help the development of usable research. The infrastructure appropriate to a particular society, then, must be designed and developed with reference to the problems and state of development as well as the traditions of the country.

Relationship between researchers and users

Among the factors affecting the potential utility of research and its desirable location are the traditional relationships between administrators and academics. In many developing countries the academic is regarded as an ivory tower intellectual with little concern for, and less understanding of, the practical, the politically possible. This contempt is reciprocated by the academic, who views the administrator as a blunderer who, in his absolute conviction of his own superior knowledge, will not listen to wisdom – at least of the native brand – though he may to a visiting expert. At present the danger is that so far from paving the way for a more fruitful relationship between the native scientist and the native planner the expatriate expert may be helping to keep them apart. In many cases visiting scientists have been unaware of the status relationships between administrator and scientists in the country they visit, operating on the implicit assumption that it is identical with those in their own country. We may hope that the days of the naive visiting expert are over.

The future needs of social science research with a view to contribution to development

It is by now plain that the following needs are manifest if the contribution that the social sciences can make to development is to be maximized.

(i) *The social sciences themselves* have to be permitted, encouraged and enabled to develop. It is not enough that their concepts, theories and methods should develop in a few advanced countries. Far more than the natural sciences they are comparative disciplines and furthermore, where natural sciences *are* comparative, the variations for comparative purposes can be created and controlled in the laboratory; in the social sciences they cannot. Nor can forays from the advanced countries make good the lack of comparative material, if only because the visiting team needs the local help of trained auxiliaries who can be produced only if continually required for good-quality studies. For example, much research requires a small army of trained interviewers fully conversant with the language and culture of respondents. Nor is this all. There is not one economics, one political science, one sociology, one psychology. While basic concepts, basic methods are common to all variants, each of these sciences has developed out of study of the existing social arrangements and their problems in particular cultures. This argument should not be pressed too far; I do not wish to suggest that we need as separate disciplines an Indian sociology, an Argentinian sociology, a French, an American sociology, and so on, but even if the science were exportable when required, solutions to problems certainly are not. The utilization of research in problem-solving implies the processes of diffusion and these are characteristic of the social structure and social processes of the particular community concerned. These not only need expert study before the implantation of knowledge, technique or result of experiment; they are an integral element in the choice of appropriate techniques and experiment. This leads to the second need.

(ii) *The processes of diffusion and utilization* of social science knowledge and social science research requires to be studied on a considerable scale and on a fully comparative basis. This can only be done with the aid of and within the framework of international collaboration. As we have shown in Chapter 7, where diffusion has been most effective it has been because of what we describe as 'mutual learning'. The basis of mutual learning is, of course, in shared experience and shared values. But for many years we shall face the problem that most administrators, planners and politicians will not have had experience of the social sciences. The social scientist working with them cannot and should not take for granted either their understanding of the concepts he uses nor their acceptance of the legitimacy of these concepts. If he is to make headway, the social scientist must explain and justify his conceptual framework – a salutary experience in itself – thus equipping the administrator with another way of looking at reality. In turn, he needs to acquire from the administrator an understanding of the conceptual framework he brings to his problems – in other words, 'mutual learning'. But special training does not exist for social scientists in the problems of utilization of social research and in the processes of diffusion and articulation with policy. This is the case not only in the developing, but also in advanced countries.

If the essence of the dialogue is to be taught to social scientists and administrators, the appropriate institutional frameworks for this to occur must be developed. These

frameworks will differ from one society to another and may
be only incompletely present in any one country. Here, as in
other aspects, there is a notable part to be played by regional
and international organizations.

(iii) *The documentation necessary* as a base for informed
research advice from a social science standpoint must be
readily available. It is not only a question of avoiding needless
repetition of previous work. It is also a matter of speed and
cumulativeness (Isaac and Rao, 1965).

> In the context of the general acceptance of the principle of
> national planning in most countries, it has become
> necessary that decision making by the government in
> matters of vital importance to the community is directed
> and controlled on the basis of informed empirical studies
> and systematic researches. Time being an important factor
> in all decision making, it is necessary that surveys are
> completed within an assigned time schedule. . . . The role of
> documentation is to collect the currently known facts from
> the various sources, systematically digest and organize
> them, retrieve and disseminate them in a helpful way to the
> researchers in the shortest possible time.

This 'expeditious servicing' is a skilled operation and requires
a good deal of interinstitutional organizations and UNESCO
in particular has been notably active. Building up
documentation centres and encouraging the training of
appropriate staff is a task for which UNESCO is particularly
fitted. Its importance in the context of development policy is
underlined by the essentially international nature of the
process.

(iv) *Manpower in the social sciences* is a peculiarly
intractable topic. It is notoriously difficult to obtain figures of
qualified people in any one country, let alone produce valid
international comparisons. We have already discussed this
problem in Chapter 10 and will not repeat it here.

(v) *Indicators and evaluation.* No one is satisfied with
existing methods of assessing the state of development of
societies. This would be a matter of small moment were it not
for two things. First, there has developed a passion for league
tables, and woe betide the government of the country whose

385

position in the league is slipping. Secondly, we need to know whether a particular policy will result, or had resulted, in improvement: improvement has to be measured. We therefore tend to judge success by some available measure, for example, GNP per capita. What can be measured thus assumes ever-increasing importance; what cannot be measured is ignored. As Bauer (1966) argues, because economic indicators are more readily available than non-economic ones, economic growth has been sought at the expense of social goods of a non-measurable, or at least unmeasured kind: 'In many of the areas in which social critics pass judgment, and in which policies are made, there are no yardsticks by which to know if things are getting better or worse.'

It is true, Bauer says, that this need has been identified for 'post-industrial society . . . in which the satisfaction of human interests and values has at least as high a priority as the pursuit of economic goals'. I see no reason why such indicators and such concern should be any less relevant to developing countries. Perhaps they are more important in their case; measures taken to improve economic performance are especially likely to affect the quality of life in unplanned ways and to set on foot social change and disruption. For lack of measurement these changes and the disruption they cause are taken as merely a matter of opinion and anyway as inevitable and as more than compensated for by the economic growth which *is* measurable. The development of social indicators whereby a country can chart its course both with reference to its own baselines and to the course pursued by other countries if of prime importance. The task will not be easy, as shown by Robert Mitchell (1968). Again, international co-operation is essential and again UNESCO could well assume leadership.

(vi) *National policy-making for the social sciences.* Few countries possess explicitly a policy-making machinery for the social sciences – a need we have already highlighted in Chapter 10 of this book. What exists is sometimes related to educational policies, sometimes to science policies, sometimes both. Sometimes only a small part of the resources devoted to the social sciences is related to government policy; this is likely to be policy for developing planning.

International policy-making

The issues of social science policy have been under-researched. However, in 1970, under ISSC auspices, a conference was held devoted to problems and issues of social science policy. While not specifically concerned with development, the discussions led to conclusions which are relevant to social science policy-making in all countries and to the role of international bodies in particular.

One field in which it can be said international bodies have taken a policy lead is the application of social sciences to the mass of problems subsumed under the heading of 'development'. UNESCO in particular has been vigorously active in sponsoring conferences, research, and experiments in the field of development and, of course, has now a long history of efforts to promote social science capabilities in developing countries. Some of the assumptions that were made in the early stages of these efforts have now been modified as a result of experience; in fact a good deal has been learned about the problems of 'implantation'. Even more is now known about the problems of applying the social sciences to the field of economic development; the early enthusiasm, even naivety, which too readily assumed that economic development was a matter of applied economics, has been replaced by a sober estimate of the tasks facing social scientists of all varieties. To some degree this is taking the form of a concern with the social science utilizing capability of developing countries as well as with their social science capability. As usual, problem-solving capacity is least where problems are greatest – particularly when part of the problem is the lack of problem-solving capacity – a meta-problem indeed! The greatest need for social science is met by those countries whose own supply of social scientists is least, whose social scientists are least likely to want to work in 'applied' fields of low prestige, and whose social scientists are most likely to emigrate. Plugging the dyke with short-term attachments from abroad has often yielded little more than minor relief and has sometimes brought major problems of its own.

In contrast to policies for national social science policy-making – the meta-policy of the international body – this area of social science and development is one where international bodies alone can have an effective substantive policy, concerning as it does the international movement of social science and social scientists and the development of trans-national, cross-cultural knowledge and expertise. But this in turn must form one of the environmental factors to be taken into account in national social science policy-making. International bodies themselves have the resources neither of people nor of material to carry out a policy of this nature. Its effectiveness depends upon the co-operation of national bodies and implies that this co-operation is a part of the national social science policy. UNESCO, ISSC, and other international bodies which have concerned themselves with the social sciences have been in the social science policy game all along; the national bodies whose co-operation was required were, and are, often not. One of the many problems that UNESCO faces is the fact that its own policy-ratifying body consists of delegations appointed by national governments that may or may not contain social scientists and whose social science members may or may not be representative of national social science policy-making bodies. This issue in itself may prove crucial in any attempt by UNESCO to develop an international social science policy.

Chapter 21
Social Psychology and Development

As in the previous chapter, my interest here is not in development as such, but in how the social sciences, and in particular social psychology, can be relevant to an important area of concern.

It is easy to criticize the economists who have been concerned with development and to illustrate the psychological naivety of some of their assumptions. Of course, development is too serious a matter to be left to the economists, particularly if one has regard to the implicit psychological assumptions that are built into the economist's model. In these models we find what I might describe as a 'market psychology', yet in fairness I must say it is the economists who have pointed out that market economics, based upon market psychology, are inadequate and who regard all sorts of positive intervention as necessary. And who is to blame them if once again the assumptions that replace the old ones are themselves not ones that a psychologist would make? One can point to very few contributions from what I should like to term 'macro-psychology'. Among the most ambitious of these are McClelland's (1961) attempts to correlate achievement motivation with economic growth, and Lynn's (1968) attempts, also on the 'macro' scale, to correlate economic growth with levels of anxiety in the general population.

Economists are aware of the political, psychological and sociological aspects of economic planning, but their awareness is not always shared by the planners themselves (Streeten and Lipton, 1968). I give as an example the extreme economo-technocratic point of view as expressed to me by a planner. Starting with the basic problem of economic growth, he conceives his task as that of identifying the constraints and removing them; this is the process. First you imagine the future with a higher national income and to do this it is necessary to analyse the economy in dynamic terms. Many of the present parameters are unknown and even more unknown is the answer to the question: What processes are operating in the transformation from the present to the future? From this he proceeds to review the help he can get from psychologists and sociologists, dismisses them as impractical, and arrives at the following approximation. If the economic answer is good enough and it results often in rough and ready methods, nevertheless this will circumvent issues of a sociological kind and the sociological and psychological research worker is, after all, not an agent for social change. The initiative must be with the psychologists and the sociologists to show how their work can be relevant and there is not much yet of a significant character. Let them choose a sector of our planning, issue a warning as to the psychological mistakes that may be made and say what should be done or offer a simple remedy to some problem that we are faced with. When we publish a plan this is an invitation to economists to concentrate on the problems set out and, as far as the psychologists are concerned, it is an invitation to them to point out the difficulties that are likely to be encountered in achieving the results and to undertake studies to this end.

However, the statement I have just repeated is the most extreme and one knows many economic advisors and finance men who are less arrogant in their outlook and who can readily set out the psychological and sociological concomitants to planning. They know from their own experience and that of others that each step in economic development requires a step in the development of the social infrastructure and that this is a complex operation which could not always be hurried. They know that social processes of many kinds are involved, each operating with its own dynamic and characterized by its own time scale. Education, communication systems and the acquisition of appropriate motivations are among the necessary components of social infrastructure, and social habits concerning the use of surpluses, including propensity to save, invest or blue it in a *potlatch*, are not only relevant but variable from group to group and sometimes very hard to shift.

Nevertheless, the economist/technocrat, coming first into the field, tends to draw up terms of reference for the social psychologist. Naturally enough, these are likely to be couched in terms of removing obstacles to his plans; and this proves to be one great impediment to effective co-operation from psychologists.

I listed above some of the relevant components of social infrastructure and in doing so was moving towards an attempt to describe

390

the economic system in terms of the sociotechnical approach. Here, after all, the psychologist should be at home. The concept of the sociotechnical system is that of the social psychologists and the notion of an open sociotechnical system allows the relevance of community structure and community habits to be related dynamically to the behaviour of the system.

Much of the knowledge which would enable the psychologists and sociologists to participate effectively in social change and economic development already exists. *The research problem is at least as much how to render this knowledge effective as to develop new knowledge.*

I should like to move towards an area where I think our knowledge is less complete. It is clear that some family and some community structures are more amenable to urbanism than others, and this may be true also of personality structures. For example, it may be true that monogamous patrilocal groups find it easier to fit in with the Western style of industrial urbanization, as the dislocating impact of urban environment is clearly smaller in their case. Yet we have remarkably little information from psychological sources on these topics. Even on the subject of the typical personality structure of social groups, the running has been made by the cultural social anthropology of the Margaret Mead variety. One of the few attempts by psychologists to tackle this sort of problem has been made by Aronoff (1967), who discusses two very different styles of life on the Island of St Kitts: of cane-cutters on the one hand, and fishermen on the other, representing two subcultures. He claims that the choice of subculture is voluntary, i.e. anyone can become either a fisherman or a cane-cutter and the choice is determined by the psychological needs of the individual. Basing himself on Maslow's well-known hierarchy of needs, Aronoff proposes that those choosing to be cane-cutters are fixated at the level of safety needs, while those choosing to be fishermen are motivated by needs for self-actualization. The typical early experiences of the cane-cutters turn out to be of comparative emotional deprivation and loss; those of the fishermen, however, do not. The typical responses of cane-cutters and fishermen to projective tests show the same differences and the method of work organization and style of life generally support the same conclusions.

Has Dr Aronoff made his case? Certainly his data are most suggestive, but there are two weaknesses. Despite the use of statistical analysis, the fact remains that the numbers involved in the studies are very, very small – only 21 cane-cutters and 19 fishermen make up the population studied, and in many comparisons we are down to 14 and 15 of each. Some may remain sceptical of findings based on so small a number. The second weakness is that Maslow's theory is more convincing for instantaneous states of the individual and the argument for the mechanism of fixation is not well-sustained. Nevertheless, there is a great deal for thought here and we have a model of two social systems, each with its own cultural manifestations, sustained by differential recruitment on the basis of psychological need.

If we can show how the socialization of the individual relates to his choice, not just of an occupation but of a style of life, then we can contribute to the identification of appropriate life-style/occupational structures, which may mean that the kind of industrialization that is most appropriate to a particular society may be as important a matter to consider as the type of industrialization appropriate to the physical resources of the society.

Further evidence of the relevance of life styles is provided by the work in India of Durganand Sinha (1970). He selected, with the aid of the state authorities in Uttar Pradesh, the most advanced and the most retarded blocks of villages in the state. He then selected the most advanced and the most retarded villages in these blocks. His aim was then to test the hypothesis that the motivational structure of the villagers differed from the most to the least advanced. He developed a 'happy life' questionnaire instrument. A great deal of spade-work was necessary to provide the interview schedule that allowed villagers meaningful choices between alternatives put to them. Sinha proved his point and demonstrated that the inhabitants of the backward villages possessed static motivations, their greatest hopes being focused on the avoidance of catastrophe or unaccustomed change, contrasting with the dynamic motivation of the inhabitants of the more advanced villages. What would our technocrat say? His solution would be to force the change and make the villagers change their motivation, and who can say that this might not be effective, though at high costs?

But motivation is not the only area of psychological study of relevance to development; social perception is another. Here I know of very few, if any, relevant studies. My own unsystematic observation suggests that a great deal of what is legitimately done by authority is defensively seen by its recipients as evidence of corruption. The identification of corruption and conspiracy are, of course, classic responses to stimuli which are either unfamiliar or unacceptable, or both. It is anyone's guess how much damage is done to development plans by their being seen in this way but perceived corruption on a grand scale is seen as a justification for corruption on a small scale, and although it is arguable that corruption is merely grease on the wheels of progress (Nye, 1967), few can doubt that a great deal of it removes the wheels completely or puts them in reverse motion.

Where does all this lead? As regards the need for new knowledge, I think that the use of existing techniques and methods would provide it. New concepts are probably not required. Concerning the use of knowledge, both existing and new, a great deal more needs to be done. One great advantage of the economists lies in this. Happily or unhappily, we have a technology for putting economic knowledge to use. In some areas of psychology we can say the same. In the use of tests, for example, we have a technology for putting the psychological knowledge of the structure of abilities, or the structure of personality to use in the industrial or clinical contexts. We lack a technology for putting to use psychological conceptual knowledge in other fields, particularly on a macro scale.

In the rest of this paper I want to make some tentative suggestions we might take in this direction. First, let me revert to the concept of sociotechnical system analysis. One notion of major importance which has emerged from this approach has been that of organizational choice (Trist, *et al.*, 1963). Broadly speaking, this states that while the primary task of an organization, and the technology it selects to achieve it, set certain limits to the kind of organizational structure that is appropriate, they do not define this structure completely. There remains a range of choices of the shape the structure should take, in which the important parameters are the characteristics of the social groups concerned, their interrelations with other social groups in the outside community, and the philosophy and style of management or administration. This concept would seem to be wholly appropriate to the situation of the developing country.

There may be routes to economic growth via modernization and among these routes there will be some better fitted than others to the psychological, social and political characteristics of the communities involved. Thus we must find some way of presenting these characteristics in precise enough terms to be able to influence the choice of path to development. Here, studies such as those of Aronoff and Sinha, may prove to be path-breaking.

The second concept that I would like to borrow is that of the critical path. Many writers have appreciated that a particular step in economic or technological development is most appropriately taken when certain political, educational and sociological requirements have first been met. The notion of the critical path requires that our plans and time scales for political, social and educational development should be related to, and form the basis of, the time scale of our plans for technological and economic development. As many of these social processes have to be seen against comparatively long time scales, a critical path analysis would show that comparatively great efforts are needed for these fields in the earlier stages of development.

Unfortunately, our ability to quantify, or even to represent in a non-parametric form, social and political characteristics in such a way that they can be meaningfully brought into planning is very rudimentary. But after all, we have done little so far by way of conceptualizing these factors. I said above that it was not new knowledge that we required, so much as better use of the knowledge we already have. I should amend this to state that we need new knowledge less than reconceptualization of our existing knowledge within the framework of action that I have attempted to set out here.

Chapter 22
Political Science, Public Administration and the Problem of Population

The student concerned with 'population' finds great difficulty in excluding anything from his field of study. Inevitably what we choose to regard as the 'system' is bound to be arbitrary. What follows is therefore in some senses an arbitrary selection, but the selection is made on the basis of its relevance for anyone concerned with population law in its widest sense.

Why do populations grow?

Man is a species of animal and like most animals a social animal, one that cannot survive in a solitary condition. The characteristics which differentiate him from other animals are those broadly subsumed under the term culture. Other species have certain learned ways of doing things which are passed on by example from one generation to the next – among them the songs of birds and the hunting and gathering practices of apes. Man alone has the complex culture which enables him to start where the last generation left off and to develop in a desired direction – a cumulative culture. He has thus effectively replaced genetic evolution by cultural evolution, a process infinitely faster. Animals and man have in common needs which must be met for survival of the individual and for survival of the species. In animals many of the ways in which these needs are met are specified by instinct. It is, however, fallacious to infer that the same needs are met in man by instinct; culture provides an alternative solution in the form of social institutions. He can be 'programmed' by culture and can therefore be left unprogrammed by his genes, a far more flexible arrangement and one that has enabled him to adapt to the extremes of habitat and climate afforded by our planet. He can even modify his environment so heroically that for short periods at any rate he can survive in extraterrestial environments.

But our genes still carry the propensities to the behaviour that was essential for the survival of the individual and the species before institutions developed that could assume these responsibilities. We can never be quite sure just what these patterns of behaviour are. Some have argued that human aggression is an instinctive pattern shared with, and derived from, our prehuman ancestors. I personally do not share the views of the noted protagonists of this and similar theories (Lorenz, 1961; Morris, 1967, 1969; Ardrey, 1961, 1966), nor do I concur with those of their opponents who would see all behaviour as environmentally determined, culturally programmed. In matters so fundamental as survival, both the most powerful biological devices and the most firmly established cultural institutions have evolved and are at work to fulfil the first commandment – thou shalt survive.

For the species to survive, its members must procreate. And the products of procreation must be fertile. All species and races develop 'breeding systems' (Darlington, 1969) – a set of rules or practices or behaviours which maintain an adequate gene pool to avoid genetic disaster. We are familiar with the dangers that threaten in-bred populations. They are notoriously susceptible to new diseases, and also to occasional morbid mutations. Although in-breeding can be highly successful in terms of producing desired characteristics, faced with new environments or new demands, such breeds are far less adaptive than their hybrid competitors. Thus small isolated populations tend to be unadaptive and when their numbers fall below a critical level they tend to die out.

But we can hardly ever disentangle the biological, genetic, from the cultural. A population small enough to have an inadequate gene pool is a population too small to generate the institutional diversity which affords a quality of life attractive to people who have once encountered it elsewhere. Thus exposure to more developed hybrid societies not only demonstrates the inability of the small population to compete in adaptation, but also draws away its most energetic and adaptable members.

Nor can we confidently ascribe the universal human proscription of incest to a protective 'instinct' evolved through the process of the natural selection of societies which happened to acquire it genetically. The shunning of incest is equally easily attributed to its destructiveness for the most fundamental of all human institutions –

the family. Competition for sexual mates between father and son, mother and daughter is incompatible with the parent–child relationships essential for child-rearing. It is just this kind of multiple determination of human behaviour that misleads practitioners of a single discipline and simultaneously renders so unpredictable human response to deliberately engineered change.

Population dynamics, then, have as their motive power survival of the race by preserving its adaptability; one of its mechanisms is the maintenance of an adequate gene pool. This is provided for by institutional arrangements regulating mating behaviour and the up-bringing of children. With the shift from genetic to cultural evolution, the amount of learning required before an individual can become a fully fledged member of the society lengthens and the period of tutelage exceeds that required for bodily and sexual maturation. The universal human invention to cope with this is the institution of the family, which is also charged with the task of regulating sexual behaviour and, hence, is the effective population unit of all societies.

What limits population growth?

Thus far we have discussed the need for a minimum population. Defensive limitation of population is new neither for animal nor human populations. Malthus's description of the pressure of resources on population is well known. He regarded mankind's inevitable fate to be a continuous pressure of population against the limits of natural resources, which could be increased only by arithmetic progression, while population tended to increase geometrically. Minimum subsistence level was the most man could aspire to in his analysis. Faced with ecological calamity of this kind, many animal species appear to have mechanisms which reduce population size before they arrive at famine levels. One such mechanism is territoriality. By defending a territory against invaders the males of territorial species ensure an adequate source of food supply for their mates and offspring. Those adult males for whom there is no territory available must either find territory elsewhere, thus extending the species' habitat, or fail to mate. Migration of surplus population of lemmings is a well-attested event. Other species of rodents and small primates display pathological behaviour in conditions of severe overcrowding, including a total refusal to mate, discharging sexual tensions by homosexuality and masturbation (Meade and Parkes, 1965). We shall find the relevance of these phenomena in two respects relating to our theme of population dynamics and

397

population control. First, they describe a population control system with in-built 'negative feedback'. Secondly, they illustrate the kind of behaviour change we shall encounter in a more sophisticated form in human populations.

The 'demographic transition'

The long history of human development, with its very slow rate of growth of populations until modern times, suggests the operation of negative feedback. Migration, with empty spaces to fill, has been a continuous feature. And within territorial areas, the Malthusian famine-type regulator appears to have been a comparatively rare event. Populations have found ways of restricting growth; babies thought likely to grow into weaklings in ancient Sparta were exposed on hillsides; old people in many tribal societies are reported voluntarily to seek death. Birth control techniques have ranged from the obvious methods of abortion through abortificient drugs to the adoption of social norms calculated to restrict family size. Of these, late marriage, particularly of women, has been a recurrent feature. The common modern Western pattern of marriage at around 24–25 for men and 2–3 years younger for women obviously meets the requirement that the man has had the opportunity to complete his education and training and establish himself adequately in his work life to support a family, and that his wife should have as long a child-bearing period ahead of her as is compatible with the amount of education and training felt necessary for a woman. If the goal of marriage was as long a joint life as possible, men would marry younger and women, whose expectation of life is longer, would marry men younger than themselves – a pattern by no means inconceivable. But what I have described as the modern Western pattern is shifting; women are tending to marry slightly older and the age gap between husband and wife is diminishing. In human populations the process of negative feedback is not through protractory disturbance but through social norms. These, however, are influenced by many factors other than direct population pressure, making control in human populations a great deal more complex, chancy and liable to fail to act in time.

In fact, we do not know how social norms are influenced by factors as broad as those of population growth; we do know that the time scale for the processes concerned is long. This is best exemplified by describing the phenomenon known as the 'population transition'. Most populations at most times have been fairly static or have grown very slowly. Births and deaths have balanced. After war or pestilence, births have exceeded deaths until the losses have been restored. The sudden spurt of population beginning with the industrial revolution in Europe was brought about by a gradual lowering of the death rate, lengthening the expectation of life without a concomitant decline in births.

Some 50–100 years after the death rate started to decline, the birth rate began to follow. In the meanwhile several generations of children had reached maturity in greater numbers than ever before, having survived the dangerous first years of life. When birth rate finally dropped to near replacement level the population had grown, as in England and Wales, four-fold in 110 years (Marsh, 1958; Cipolla, 1962). This 'demographic transition' is currently occurring in most of the underdeveloped world. However, both birth rates and death rates start there from a far higher figure than in Europe before the transition, and the drop in the death rate has been far more precipitous. As a consequence the rate of growth is anything up to twice as fast as the most rapid experienced in Europe. Nor are there now the empty overseas lands of the colonial period to absorb the surplus population.

Two questions present themselves. Why did birth rates tend to decline with lowered death rate? And why the lag between the two? We do not know, but we can surmise intelligently. Behaviour in these as in other respects is influenced by social norm. We acquire as we grow up attitudes and expectations about the kind of life we shall lead. We learn that people have families of 3, 4, 5 or 8 children or whatever; we learn that children frequently die; that people expect to be provided for in their old age by their surviving children; that children are needed to work on the family farm, or in workshops or cottage industry. During the early days of the industrial revolution in Britain, urban families often depended upon the earnings of their small children in the mills and factories. Children are economically desirable if not essential and the costs of feeding, clothing and educating them are low.

Now the death rate begins to fall. The need for large families declines. But there is no disadvantage attached to them. Disadvantages begin to mount as living standards rise, as education becomes compulsory and extended, as children consume more than the value of what they produce, now that their labour is no longer required. Large families now stand in the way of a desired higher standard of living. Other attitudes and values change. As welfare provision extends to cover necessities for the old, not only is the need to have children to provide removed, but the responsibilities of those we do have are reduced. With rising levels of living, the economic role of the family is diminished, rising provision of formal education

399

diminishes the family's role in education and socialization. Fewer children means shorter child bearing and rearing period for women and promotes their return to the labour force. A higher proportion of families have no dependent children at home, as parents live longer as well as having fewer children. The constraints upon divorce are weakened. In Western society, as the sanctity of the family as an institution is eroded, other living patterns are experimented with and are, if not approved, at least tolerated. And, as we reach the point where ecological considerations begin to influence attitudes towards population limitation, value changes become even more marked. The single state is no longer regarded as evidence of failure or irresponsibility or faint heartedness but as a legitimate option. Nor does it any longer imply the assumption of celibacy, particularly when contraceptives are effective, widely available and socially sanctioned. Homosexuality becomes tolerated and homosexuals then demand not mere toleration but acceptance. Society has turned towards values which conduce to a low birth rate, weakening the institutions which protected it and establishing and strengthening institutions which reduce it.

Law and population

From the standpoint of the lawyer, the public administrator, the planner and the politician these are most significant features. It looks as though a general liberalization in the laws of governing personal status is likely to conduce towards a lowering of birth rates. But we cannot ignore the restraining influence of religion. 'Be fruitful and multiply' was God's injuction to Adam and many of the laws of Judaism were directed towards this end. The laws of purity, of forbidden degrees of marriage, of levirate marriage, the practice of polygamy and the prohibitions on bestiality, homosexuality and masturbation were all instrumental in maintaining fertility and ensuring that all fertile women were kept in circulation, as it were. And while polygamy and levirate marriage were abolished in Judaism and the laws of purity relaxed by Christianity, the latter religion took an even firmer stand against abortion and contraception. The religious emphasis on the sanctity of marriage and the family helped to maintain population levels in hard times. It is notable that the forms of religious expression now finding favour among the young Western societies emphasize mystical withdrawal and contemplation, a gentle monasticism not excluding or prohibiting sexual relationships but undermining the energetic impulse to engage in it, and certainly discouraging established patterns of family life.

A further question is: Will the developing countries follow this pattern of declining birth rate after a lag of two generations or so? Many, and not unduly gloomy, prophets forecast that the end must come before that. Two generations of growth at present rates would precipitate a Malthusian disaster and even an immediate decline to near replacement level would only just avert calamity. Yet we cannot confidently predict that the pattern of the advanced countries will be followed. Many of the changes we have described have been energized more by rising living standards than by the direct consequences of lower death rates and longer life expectancy. And the lower death rates in developing countries have been brought about not by generally increased living standards but by the specific importation of medical technology and sanitation and of famine relief from outside. These do not create the conditions under which the peasant in the Indian village, say, has strong reasons for having fewer children.

Indeed, it is essential to recognize that the problem of overpopulation is not the same as the problem of family planning. Much of the discussion on family planning is predicated on the assumption that access to family planning will necessarily lead to a voluntary restriction of the birth rates. Under some circumstances this is clearly correct, but not under all. Furthermore, it is assumed that even though voluntary restriction is unlikely to bring the birth rate down to replacement level in the short term, it will do so in the medium term. Unfortunately, we cannot be at all sure of that, and in any case ecological disaster could well occur before then. The arguments for family planning become confused when it is offered as the solution to the problem of overpopulation. The case for family planning rests on a conception of family planning as a human right; if population limitation is essential, family planning can only be one part of the answer.

From the political point of view it appears that the focus on family planning derives from several factors. First, politicians, planners and administrators live in a milieu dominated by middle-class values, predominantly those of the middle classes of developed countries. Development appears as a process of realization of middle-class aims and goals by the masses. As the industrial countries developed, the middle classes grew in numbers and importance; their values became dominant. As groups and individuals improved their socio-economic position, their ambitions centred largely on their children; educating them, 'giving them a good start in life', so that they should aspire to, and achieve, higher status than their parents. Family planning is seen to mean family limitation – indeed the concept of planning itself implies the acceptance of the middle-class values of concern with the future.

401

Planners and public administrators in developing countries are also essentially urban dwellers while the mass of the population is still rural (Lipton, 1968). While they seek to deal with the villagers on the basis of law, the villagers seek interaction on the basis of mutual relationship of obligation (Bailey, 1966). The combination of urban policies and urban-legal modes of transaction erects barriers of misunderstanding and mistrust. In this way reports of, for example, the number of IUDs fitted, or voluntary sterilizations carried out, can be grossly misleading. Left alone, the villagers revert to the practices appropriate to the local power situation and local custom.

Again the planner and the public administrator live in an international network; their reference groups include planners and administrators abroad. This has the positive advantage of exposing them to ideas, solutions, innovations and techniques developed elsewhere; the negative side is that these may be powerful in other more developed societies but inappropriate, ineffective and possibly even counterproductive in their own country.

Second, family planning has a democratic resonance, although recent events exemplified by the activities of Sanjay Gandhi show how hollow that resonance can be. It is something done *by* not *to* the 'target' population. The responsibility for the decision as to how many children to have rests with the parents. Help and guidance are available to them as resources, but there is no compulsion on them to use or even to seek them. Needless to say, it is most likely to work where there is some tradition of democratic decision-making, where people are accustomed to regarding public provision as resources to have recourse to rather than as forms of compulsion. And it probably works best where the position of women in the society entitles her to a voice in family decisions.

Yet another factor accounting for the emphasis on family planning is that the movement predated the widespread alarm at the prospect of a doubling of the population of the world every thirty years and was therefore already in place to be used and had already achieved some success in combating religious objections. I have said enough to show that for all its value it should not be looked to as the main hope for averting the population explosion.

The politics of population and the politics of development

Over the last decade and a half the twin question of development and population have become internationalized in a new way. Previously, the poverty of the majority of the countries of the world was seen as a set of national predicaments requiring the help of advanced countries. More recently we have come to recognize the indivisibility of the problem of development and to perceive the whole nature of development–underdevelopment as systemic (Furtado, 1964). Single country solutions are inadequate outside those large enough like China to be virtually autarchic. In a similar manner, the problems of population are international. As it becomes progressively less acceptable and indeed less practical to consume one-third of the world's energy resources in a country housing one-twentieth of its population, thus countries are obliged to be concerned with one another's population policy.[1] Unfortunately this means that population policy can be perceived or represented as a device on the part of the rich countries to keep poor ones in a state of permanent subjection. It has been pronounced (UNESCO, 1972):

> Such programmes bore a distressing and familiar message of dominance and imperialism. The political nature of current population control programmes in the developing countries was constantly reiterated . . . an economic [message] which implied that birth control in The Third World was an effective means of maintaining the developed world's economic superiority over the developing countries.

Perhaps there is another 'message' underlying this one; that some people in developing countries can perceive the threat to standards of living in the developed countries from the unlimited growth of population in poor countries. Thus we must recognize that population policy is part of the world power game, the emergence of population politics. Of course, population policy as a political weapon is not new. Nazi Germany encouraged a rising birth rate to ensure an adequate supply of soldiers and to legitimize the claim for lebensraum. France especially and Britain at the same period feared that a declining population would weaken their international position as well as face them with an ageing population, and encouraged a higher birth rate.

Serious problems arise when the numbers game is directly related to power and to the rivalries of ethnic groups or religiously divided sectors. Protestant majorities fear that they will become minorities in countries like Belgium and Northern Ireland. One of the most

---

[1] See *Man's Impact on the Global Environment*, MIT Press, 1970, Table 7.3, p. 294: the United States' proportion of world consumption of energy is estimated at 34·8 per cent.

catastrophic of all demographic clashes was the civil war in Nigeria. Under the federal constitution the number of seats in the federal parliament was allocated to regions on the basis of their populations as recorded by the census. Fear of domination by the Muslim Northern Region over other regions contributed very substantially to the outbreak of civil war. Thus we see that only the naive could approach problems of population limitation as scientific or social or economic problems without recognizing their high political sensitivity.

So much of the literature and discussion on population problems has concentrated on family planning that it is appropriate to examine its attractiveness. It avoids the suggestion of compulsion; it appears to the liberal reformist imagination as a means of liberating poor women from the continuous drudgery of child-bearing and child-rearing, and it shifts responsibility from the politician, planner and administrator. In fact, it transforms the problem for them into one of coping with the 'resistance' of the people to accept what is offered. This now becomes a problem of 'acceptability' of the various means proposed – a technical problem, and one of obtaining 'attitude' change by education and inducements, leading people to perceive where their true interests lie – a management problem. The trouble is that the true interests of the whole do not coincide. The plight of the peasant without children, particularly male children, to help in his agriculture and domestic work is serious. When he is old, no state pension protects him from his poverty, even pauperism. What sense does it make for him and his wife to incur these risks? And as in most peasant societies daughters, when they marry, move to the homes of their husbands' families and are not the guarantees of a comfortable old age, it is necessary to have a son to succeed you and prudent to have at least two, risks being what they are.

In a word, it is in everybody else's true interest that a particular couple should restrict the size of their family, not necessarily in their own. And yet on the face of it family planning has reduced population growth in some countries. Taiwan is a frequently quoted example, South Korea another. Success stories are quoted for selected areas in India: Sinjur in West Bengal is one example. Close analysis of the statistical evidence indicates that in all these cases birth rates had begun to fall *before* the family planning programme began, and that while family planning sometimes appears to have accelerated the rate of decline, in other cases it appears to have slowed it down (Mamdani, 1972). Much depends on its meaning for people in the situation and the values it carries with it. For example, in South Korea the family planning programme accompanies the official discouragement of abortions, which are illegal, with a positive emphasis on the advancement of child health and maternal care, both undisputed goods but which carry with them the values of women as home-makers rather than women in other roles.

It is, nevertheless, too pessimistic a conclusion to infer that family planning has failed; it is, however, bound to fail unless the conditions are present that make it rational for people to wish to have small families. As we have shown, these conditions apply in modern developed urban cultures; they do not necessarily exist in agrarian societies.

Creating the conditions under which it is 'rational' to want fewer children

Before we pursue this aspect, we have to make it clear that this could not be totally effective unless socially acceptable means of realizing these wishes are readily available, together with the knowledge of how to obtain and use them.

Again, social processes being what they are, draconian measures could either excite a reaction or initiate a downward spiral to national suicide. I say this only to warn that the range of policies within which the politician and planner can work are none too wide.

Nor is it easy or sensible to try to tackle the problem in isolation. The policies have to be applied along with other policies, using the machinery, structure and style of public administration that have developed to meet the society's needs and the needs of law enforcement in that society over a period of time. These have reflected and in turn influenced the underlying values and assumptions of the society. New policies must, to be effective, not be glaringly incompatible with these values and assumptions.

The role of political science

The discipline of political science has been undergoing rapid change in recent decades. There has been more concern with detailed analysis of political systems with a study of political behaviour supported by quantitative data, and with the analysis and evaluation of policies and policy-making. Some of these changes have been brought about by developments in neighbouring social sciences such as sociology and economics, some by the pervasive growth of systems-thinking, some by the availability of data on voting behaviour and voting intentions provided by sample polling. The

405

introduction of computers has made possible detailed correlational studies. And finally the unprecedented emergence of new states by the score has set a new problem, not that of the more old-fashioned constitution-making, but of the construction of political systems capable of handling the task of economic and social development.

In a way all these developments and concerns have been inherent in the nature of the discipline from its beginnings, but different aspects have achieved prominence and dominance at different times. The study of politics has been concerned with how men have been governed in the past, how they are governed contemporaneously and how men should be governed – political history, political description and political philosophy. Some have chosen to take a positivist view of politics and emphasize the effect of political institutions and state policy on society; others have emphasized the effects of political events on non-state institutions and factors such as family structure, economic and technological change, the growth and spread of religious movements and so on.

But until well into the nineteenth century all were engaged in the study of philosophy. The separating out of the social sciences into individual disciplines has been brought about more by the dynamics of specialist teaching and research within the universities than by the demands for their utilization. And although it has comparatively recently become the practice for social administrators to study sociology and for public administrators to study politics and economics, there is growing recognition that the distinction between academic disciplines does not correspond to distinct categories of problems. The topic of population can stand as an excellent illustration of just this point. Population law and its administration is already within the political field. The lawyer and the public administrator are obliged to take into account the social and economic structure of their society, and its ecological context, the cultural and educational influences upon it as well as its political structure and legal traditions. At the same time, however, as Lipset (1969) points out:

> The concern with processes of social change, which has been reactivated by interest in the development process in third world nations as well as by the increasingly conscious efforts to reduce birth right inequities in the more affluent nations, has also increased the significance of political science as the field concerned with the key set of social institutions, which constitute the legitimate mechanism for expressing society's will to attain commonly agreed upon objectives.

Because political science, unlike economics and sociology, has inherited the concern with 'ought', with how man 'should' be governed (or should govern himself), with the normative aspects of policy, it has inherited the key problem of reconciling individual freedom with the needs of society as a whole. Nowhere is this problem more acute than in the field of population law.

Policy-making

The form that policy-making will take is strongly influenced, if not determined, by the model the policy-maker has of the system he is managing and the 'problem' with which he is dealing. We have to remember that measures in regard to population law are not taken in isolation. They must compete for resources with other claims. If the system goal is 'development' then the policy-maker must have reason to believe that population policy will contribute heavily to development. Although it is frequently 'sold' on the ground, the evidence is in fact weak. There is little doubt that modernization and decline in population growth are connected but the nature of the connection is obscure. A model in which population control is the 'leading sector' of the development process is not only false to the facts but additionally misleading as the administrative infrastructure needed to mount an effective policy of control is absent in underdeveloped countries (Kirk, 1969). Nor does the 'virtuous spiral' model of increased prosperity–declining birth rate–increased prosperity carry the confidence it once did. Once it gets under way it may indeed represent a mutually enforcing sequence, but the threshold levels of prosperity and population restraint may be hard to reach. Not only must population policies compete for resources with other policies adopted, they must be consistent with them; the laws based upon them must not be in conflict and they must be compatible with the legal and administrative 'culture': the network of values and attitudes relating to law which determine when and why and where people turn to the law or government or turn away (Meagher, 1973).

Not surprisingly, then, governments show preference for 'soft' measures before 'hard' ones; unfortunately the failure of soft policies may simultaneously make hard ones more inevitable and more difficult to impose.

407

Application of political science to the policy processes

It has always been recognized that public administration is more than the application of the law. For one thing the law cannot cover every possible transaction between the citizen and the public bodies which exist to regulate behaviour, supply services, assist his endeavours in one way or another. For another thing the law needs interpretation in individual cases and to meet individual circumstances, and the courts cannot possibly be invoked to settle every case where interpretations differ. As a consequence government departments, statutory bodies, local authorities and other public institutions operate under 'directives' laying down broad lines of policy. Within these broad policies, myriads of daily decisions are taken at all levels, from counter clerk to chief executive or minister. Complex bureaucracies are interposed between high policy and the final transaction with the citizen. The behaviour of bureaucracies is a fit subject for study by social scientists of many persuasions – sociologists, social psychologists, students of management, as well as political scientists. The disciple of 'public administration' has to encompass all these viewpoints. But he also seeks answers to such questions as who makes 'policy' and how? What is the nature of the policy process? And how is it transformed into those thousands of daily decisions? How is the success of a policy in meeting its objectives assessed? What is done to adjust the policy if it appears to fail to attain these objectives? This set of questions makes up the new field of policy analysis. In principle, of course, the politician determines the policy, the public administrator carries it out. But in practice it is impossible for the politician to scan all possible alternatives, to be aware of the possible consequences of each and every option. To quote Bergram Gross (1971):

> It would be ridiculous to assume that public administrators by themselves can make decisions on . . . major problems of 'meta-policy'. But it would be just as ridiculous to assume that political leaders can make any decisions in these areas without being helped or impeded by public administrators who feed them basic information, control many channels of policy implementation and help to formulate specific alternatives from which political leaders can make choices.

The 'meta-policies' which Gross is considering here are ideological – to plan or not to plan, to follow materialist or humanist values and such-like. But the same is true of another kind of meta-policy – to

408

employ particular kinds of information systems or management systems for their own policy-making and evaluation. The choice of information system largely determines the kind of information you will take into account. This is effectively a decision as to the boundaries of the system you are going to concern yourself with and that in turn preselects the range of policy alternatives you will consider. Because narrowly defined systems seem manageable, we tend to circumscribe problems and try to deal with them in isolation (Gross, 1971, p. 353). But it is no help simply to come full circle to the first sentence of this paper. Nevertheless, it is clear, as Berelson (1969) has stated, that any policy for limiting population growth must satisfy at least the following six criteria:

(i)   scientific, medical and technological readiness
(ii)   political viability
(iii) administrative feasibility
(iv)   economic capability
(v)   moral, ethical and philosophical acceptability
(vi)   preferred effectiveness.

He illustrates the use of these criteria on eight proposals (see Table 8). This table represents an assessment of how the selected proposals would be evaluated in one society; in others the evaluations would differ. Nor does it examine the interactions among policies which is likely to make the outcome matrix still more complex for the policy-maker. However, in principle this illustration helps to show how alternative policies can be assessed in advance. A totally different problem arises once the decisions are taken. They may be contingent decisions, that is to say, a policy may be selected for a trial run. In the latter case it is very likely that an evaluation of its results will be called for. Again, in principle, that looks straightforward enough. You select two areas which are similar on relevant criteria, apply the policy in one, using the other as a 'control'. After an appropriate period of trial you compare the results. Alas, it sounds simple, but is not. To begin with it is very difficult to find areas which are similar on even a small number of different criteria if these include income distribution, racial mixture, religious mixture, degree of urbanization, traditions of female employment, degree of political mobilization, political coloration, to mention only a few. Second, it is difficult to be certain what criteria represent relevant and significant variables. Third, it is difficult to avoid 'contamination' – the effect on area 2 of the knowledge that the policy has been applied in area 1. Fourth, it is difficult to know for how long measures have to be taken before you are reasonably

TABLE 8 *Illustrative appraisal of proposals, by criteria*

Proposal	Scientific readiness	Political viability	Administrative feasibility	Economic capability	Ethical acceptability	Presumed effectiveness
A Extension of voluntary fertility control	High	High on maternal care, moderate-to-low on abortion	Uncertain in near future	Maternal care too costly for local budget, abortion feasible	High for maternal care low for abortion	Moderately high
B Establishment of involuntary fertility control	Low	Low	Low	High	Low	High
C Intensified educational campaigns	High	Moderate-to-high	High	Probably high	Generally high	Moderate
D Incentive programs	High	Moderately low	Low	Low-to-moderate	Low-to-high	Uncertain

E Tax and welfare benefits and penalties	High	Moderately low	Low	Low-to-moderate	Low-to-moderate	Uncertain
F Shifts in social and economic institutions	High	Generally high, but low on some specifics	Low	Generally low	Generally high, but uneven	High, over long run
G Political channels and organizations	High	Low	Low	Moderate	Moderately low	Uncertain
H Augmented research efforts	Moderate	High	Moderate-to-high	High	High	Uncertain
Family-planning programs	Generally high, but could use improved technology	Moderate-to-high	Moderate-to-high	High	Generally high, but uneven on religious grounds	Moderately high

Source: Berelson, B., *Global Ecology*, p. 255, edited by J. P. Holdren and Paul R. Erlich.

certain that (a) the changes observed result from the policy[1] and (b) that the changes, if resulting from the policy, are not evanescent. Many innovations have beneficial short-term effects but prove disappointing over the longer run. And finally the true comparison is not between applying the policy and refraining from doing so, but between the costs and benefits of applying the policy and applying each of the alternative ones. And what changes should you be looking for? If your policy is, for example, the free issue of IUDs, is the number fitted an acceptable criterion? The people who accept it may simply be using it in place of other methods of birth control. Should it be the birth rate over the next year or so? But your population may simply be using it to space births more widely rather than reduce total family size. Can you wait until families can be supposed to be completed before assessing the outcome? Or should you be looking for changes in attitudes and values known to be so associated?

I mentioned earlier in this paper that even where we know a good deal about social processes we find it very difficult to predict their time scales. This creates a major problem for us in evaluating the outcomes of policies. We can be helped, however, by knowing what are the early signs that changes are on the way. The political scientist thus shares with other social scientists concern with the search for social indicators, especially early warning indicators of social change. The difficulty is with the very nature of change which does not pursue a linear path and whose emergence is therefore hard to detect (Emery, 1968). The first symptoms of emergent processes will be felt in the use of symbols. Man's symbolic representation of the world may change to represent changes in that world without his being conscious that there has been any change at all; the social symbols, myths, beliefs, values, language, fads and fashions change without any necessary awareness of what the change means or to what it corresponds. We can therefore explore future changes by the use of symbol analysis, value analysis and analysis of linguistic usage. McLuhan sees his own method of detecting the

---

[1] A well-known example of the traps in identifying results with a particular policy is given by the decline in the death rate in Ceylon between 1944 and 1959. The drop from 19·7 to 9·1 per 1,000 was attributed to the elimination of malaria by DDT spraying. It now appears that this decline is more closely associated with other changes, notably indicators of levels of nutrition. That this is not simply a relationship between nutrition and resistance to the disease is shown by the fact that deaths from malaria are now increasing without change in nutrition (see: *Thinking about the Future*, Cole *et al.*, Chatto and Windus, 1973, p. 49).

future as essentially an application of the analytical techniques of modern art criticism: 'At the social level the analysis of linguistic usage has been applied in the content analysis of films, women's magazines, etc., and to tracing out the subtle shifts in the meanings of key concepts like "work", "leisure", and "justice".' We can take these only as suggestions. If they can be developed to the extent that planners, politicians and administrators acquire confidence in them as early warning indicators, they will serve not only for early evaluation of policies but more importantly as advance indicators of emergent problems or as signals that problems are changing. Typically our political actions are directed at problems which are already in the process of changing into some other problem.

However, a word of practical caution is needed (Cole, 1973, p. 196):

> In social systems, when policy makers elaborate policies, they may fail to achieve the results intended not because they have misperceived the situation, not because their analysis was correct – and certainly not because they used their intuition only to find that the system is counter-intuitive – but rather because of the very nature of the political process. Politics is the art of compromise, and every politician knows that half-hearted, watered-down policies often are the necessary result of going through that process.

It is reasonable, though, to insist that in the field of population law measures which fail to obtain changes in social values among the target population are most unlikely to be effective. It makes practical sense, therefore, to tease out first the pattern of values that will be necessary for the desired goal, next to evaluate possible policies in the light of the desired value change, and then to find means of detecting changes in the values concerned. Early indicators of such value changes should be sought where possible.

This is not made any easier by the fact that value changes do not necessarily affect the whole population; indeed values can be changing in one direction within one sector of the population and simultaneously changing in the very opposite direction within other sectors. Attitudes and practices with regard to having children tend to diffuse downwards through the class structure. Thus an increase followed by a decrease could result in an upper class or middle class decreasing birth rate at the same time as a lower class was still increasing it. Really good early warning indicators would show us the future downturn even during the upturn. Second order differentials represent rate of change. When these turn negative the rate of

413

change will continue positive for some time before dropping to zero and then becoming negative. More and more planners will be brought to recognize the importance of second order differentials as indicators of longer-term change. Unlike the planner, the public administrator is obliged to cope with short-term problems; the measures which commend themselves to him very easily conflict with the longer-term perspectives of the planner. Increasingly the political system is under strain as it has to control and accept responsibility for both.

Governments in parliamentary democracies are often restrained from taking measures which will lead to gains in the long term if they have uncomfortable or undesirable short-term consequences. A government which does not have to submit itself to a test of popular approval every four or five years can afford to absorb the unpopularity of measures over the short term; few popularly elected governments are able to show the altruism which would be needed in their case. What too often happens is that a government adopts a plan and simultaneously adopts measures which are in conflict with it. The legal enactments supporting the plan tend to be comparatively weak and the settlement of disputes arising from the laws concerned tends to be protracted. This is particularly obvious in measures which reinforce, or provide the backing for, policies more obviously aimed at reducing population growth. Housing policy, educational policy, nutrition policy, policy with regard to sex discrimination, taxation policy, development policy, industrialization policy, agricultural policy, land policy, all effect people's needs for children, desires for children and capacity to afford them. A housing policy which subsidized well-appointed houses for small families; an extension of the period of compulsory schooling with the remission of fees for the first and second children only of each family; income tax which allowed the tax payer to claim dependant's relief on two children only; family allowances for first and second children only; all amount to an expensive fine on those whose religious beliefs, personal wishes or inadvertence were strong enough to have more than two children. A policy for land inheritance which prohibited the division of landed property into more than two or prohibited its division at all might simultaneously prevent uneconomic division of landholdings and the production of children. It might, however, merely increase the number of landless agricultural labourers and the flow of dispossessed peasants to the cities. It is not our task here to parade all the possible policies which might in a particular society diminish the birth rate; what we are concerned to do is to indicate the extent to which such policies are likely to be seen as unacceptable to the people concerned. The hardships that they would inflict on those unfortunate enough to be born into larger families would outrage the humanitarian impulses of most societies. Before such measures and laws could have much effect on people's attitudes and behaviour, they would tend to engage sympathy for those penalized by them; and laws which are not seen as just by the majority, or even by large minorities, can be quickly reduced to impotence and become unenforceable. No sensible government pursues unenforceable legislation not only because it is self-defeating, but also because such laws bring the machinery of law enforcement into disrepute; the courts and the police bear the main impact through being obliged to act against offenders in breach of those laws.

From the standpoint of the political scientist and public administrator, laws have to meet a number of obvious criteria, only some of which we have touched upon. Besides being enforceable and acceptable, not overloading the machinery of law enforcement and public administration, they must be mutually reinforcing and not in conflict with other laws. And they should be desirable from some political or administrative philosophy. The difficulty is that no broad statement of philosophy or human rights can solve the basic dilemma of human government. The rights of one individual are limited by the rights of other individuals. That is obvious. What is perhaps less obvious is the fact that the point of balance is continually changing. In regard to population, for example, in the individualist conditions of the frontier days in America, it would have appeared unthinkable to challenge a couple's right to have as many children as they chose. When communities accept the responsibility of protecting the poor from the extremes of poverty, they acquire some right to challenge the right to the unrestricted production of children whom their parents cannot afford to maintain, and the community has an understandable and justifiable concern with the production of children carrying dangerous inheritable genes. Communities have long asserted the right to interfere with the individual's claim to the 'right' to terminate his own life or to terminate the life of an unborn foetus or even embryo. With increasing mutual interdependence the claims of the community to restrict the rights of individuals increases. Paradoxically the acceptance of the rights of the community to concern with, and influence or control over, growing areas of the life of the individual is combined with the simultaneous claim for, and acceptance of, more rights for the individual in areas where those rights had traditionally been restricted – abortion, homosexuality and the use of drugs for example. As we remarked earlier, certain values are conducive to population limitation, others hostile to it. We are seeing the gradual promotion of the former over the latter.

Lee (1972) raises the two questions of how individual and collective rights can be harmonized, and how individual rights can be kept from conflicting with one another. To some extent the answers to both are located in the emergence of a hierarchy of values. Widely held values may be in conflict with one another but there is a tendency for some to achieve dominance while others decline, in accordance with superordinate values in a more of less fluid hierarchy and influenced by deep-rooted social processes which seldom penetrate the level of consciousness. This makes the listing of 'rights' an oversimplification unless accompanied by some organizing principle. Thus the list provided by Lee of fourteen such rights as preconditions 'without which the family planning right would prove illusory', already includes some which are contradictory and others which are plainly illusory unless heavily qualified:

1 The right to adequate education and information on family planning.
2 The right of access to the means of practising family planning.
3 The right to the equality of men and women.
4 The right of children, whether born in or out of wedlock, to equal status under the law and to adequate support from natural parents.
5 The right to work.
6 The right to an adequate social security system, including health and old age insurance.
7 The right to freedom from hunger.
8 The right to an adequate standard of living.
9 The right to freedom from environmental pollution.
10 The right to liberty of movement.
11 The right of privacy.
12 The right of conscience.
13 The right to separation of Church from State, law from dogma.
14 The right to social, economic and legal reforms to conform with the above rights.

Problems of administration

A rational policy must be administratively feasible and legally enforceable – everybody will assent to that. Yet many schemes are put forward which do not meet either of these requirements in the setting for which they are proposed.

416

What are the criteria for administrative feasibility?

(i) the rules must be clear to those whose job it is to administer them and to those at the receiving end;

(ii) there must be effective communication to the administrators and the recipients of the rules and the way they are to be administered;

(iii) there must be enough adequately trained staff to implement the rules;

(iv) the data needed to make a determination under the rules must be available or collectable;

(v) the feedback data required to evaluate the degree of implementation and its outcomes must be available or collectable;

(vi) the administrator must be adequately motivated to administer the rules fairly.

It is not unfair to say that most or all of these criteria are not met by policies adopted or suggested for adoption in most developing countries. Even the most elementary data about vital statistics are unreliable and politically suspect when available. Officers in central government are unable to assess the outcome at village level of the measures for which they are responsible because the staff required to collect such data have not been allocated to them, and it takes time to find out, which competes with other demands upon them.

Many proposals which look attractive are simply beyond the capacity of most developing countries to implement. Much the same is true of legal enforceability.

Measures which require discriminatory taxation or licensing or discriminatory allocation of resources such as housing are, even if politically possible and technically feasible, legally unenforceable because, first, the proof required of infraction is unlikely to be forthcoming. If you raise the legal age of marriage for women, for example, you can only enforce it if you can prove the age of the bride; where births are not registered such proof is unavailable. Taxation in most countries is far too inexact in its incidence to be effectively enforced with the refinements required to penalize large families. Furthermore, divergences between law and practice tend to favour one group in society against others, thus compounding the political difficulties of adoption of the law. Many policies proposed would be unacceptable to the people affected, who would bring strong pressure to bear on enforcing agencies to ignore or to avoid proceeding against violations.

While discussing the criteria for feasibility of a policy, we should not ignore the question of when a policy is a policy, or more specifically, when does a measure or set of measures add up to a

417

policy for population? A true population policy is one that takes into account present and potential demographic facts in all areas of planning. But there are many partial policies as Lyons points out (1973).

Related problems

While the immediate problem of seeking to restrain population growth naturally holds the centre of the stage in discussions of population law and policy, scientific developments in the field of genetics are already threatening to pose legal problems and problems for national policies and administration.

Biogenetic engineering is possible in principle, that is to say, for example, the deliberate choice by parents of sex of a child. AID (artificial insemination by donor) raises questions of paternity; techniques of implantation of fertilized ova in the uterus of a 'host' potentially raises the question of who is the 'mother' and indeed, the legal meaning of the word. Advances in biogenetic engineering offer prospects of developing 'clones', large numbers of genetically identical individuals. Techniques of prolonging life by organ transplants raise demographic problems; brain transplants would raise additional questions of legal identity and responsibility. Medical methods already maintain severely handicapped people in life, the responsibility for whom raises legal and administrative problems.

Screening techniques are available for the elimination of embryos carrying the genes of hereditary diseases such as sickle-cell anaemia. It is, of course, wholly desirable that prophylactic measures should be available to diminish the risk of severe handicap, but they carry with them grave problems. Should screening be compulsory? To whom should the information obtained belong, be available? If screening signals a high probability of handicap, whose responsibility is it to decide whether the couple concerned should marry, or the child conceived be aborted? And how foolproof must the screening be before the action taken should be legally protected or legally prescribed? What rules should there be to protect society from the carrier of a truly lethal gene?

Apart from such questions as the cost benefit of prophylactic and counselling services, each of these issues involves questions of rights to privacy, ownership of, and right of, access to information, the rights of the individual to decide whom to marry, whether to have children, whether to bring a foetus to full term. They arise in far more acute form than in the case of compulsory vaccination, which was not accompanied by tests which might reveal damaging or disturbing information.

The lawyer, rightly anxious that the law should be determinable, and, together with the politician and public administrator, concerned that it should be enforceable, would probably prefer that legislation in this area should be postponed until the diagnostic methods are perfect, the prophylactic measures reliable, and foolproof techniques for protecting the security of computer-banked information available. But the pressures for action at the present state of the art are bound to grow. Indeed in any plural society containing people of different races or different religions or even, if you like, more and less devout people of the same faith, the legal and ethical and administrative problems are compounded by their intergroup sensitivity. For instance, the frequency of the genes for sickle cell makes screening in the United States sensible only among the black minority. The questions cannot be resolved by scientific and technological progress and inventiveness, however 'value free'. The very choice of which scientific problem to tackle is political as well as scientific: it is irresponsible to assign funds for 'research' into a problem, claiming that research is value free and therefore its support is value free and non-political likewise, while making no preparation to utilize the results. I am not arguing for the suppression of scientific research on the grounds that it may produce unpalatable results; on the contrary, I am arguing that the sponsorship of research is a political act and has political and administrative consequences which must be foreseen and faced; the institutional framework for handling the outcomes must be prepared. This involves research and development of a different kind, involving lawyers, political scientists and other social scientists at a far earlier stage than is customary at present.

To conclude, we have often been told that politics is the art of the possible. The most arcane element of the art is to recognize what *is* possible. In the field of population law this requires an understanding of the dynamics of population and of the associated value systems. In this paper we have tried to show how these are related and how the existence and changes of values can be recognized. We have sought to show that the planner, the politician and the public administrator rely on conflicting, confusing and inadequate indicators. Even 'neutral' matters such as census returns are pregnant with political significance.

Our analysis and argument has led us to suggest that some order can be discerned in the shape of a value-ordering principle, a system of meta-values producing a dynamic value hierarchy, although these may be different for different sectors of a country's population.

419

Chapter 23
Traditional Values and Modern Organizations in Developing Countries – The Prospects of Technology

Introduction

What is the 'appropriate' technology for a developing country? The broad answer usually offered is technology which can be operated and maintained by native skill, which will generate needed employment and put modest demands upon the limited capital available. This I take for granted, but wish to add that an appropriate technology is also one which can be managed by forms of work organization whose values are compatible with those of the society in which it is incorporated.

Traditional values and the value of tradition

Whether we start from a Marxist viewpoint or not, we are all prepared to agree that the values of a society or community are consonant with its technology. Marxists would say that this was because value systems are part of the superstructure erected upon the econotechnical infrastructure; from the structural–functional point of view a technological innovation will either be acceptable because it fits the social values, or will be rejected because people's values are opposed to it, or it may be acceptable in a modified form for at any rate long enough for values to change. As we have suggested several times already in this book and in particular in Chapter 16, what is often overlooked is that there is more than one way of utilizing any given technology, both in regard to the purposes to which it is put and the organizational arrangements for operating it. This view is in direct opposition to the technological determinism which perceives technology as developing according to its own inherent logic and which sees the technology of an organization as the determinant of organizational roles and relationships. But we do not imply that a given technology is compatible either with any set of values or with any set of organizational roles and relationships. Nor do we imply that we have in any society an unfettered choice of technology. We do mean to suggest that the degree of compatibility of values and technology may be greater than is often thought and that in any society we have a wider choice of technology than is usually believed. As a complication, we should add that 'traditional' values are not all as traditional as they look.

One of the troubles with tradition derives from our tendency towards binary conceptualization. As psychologists we are aware of this tendency and of its neurological and linguistic bases. But we do not adequately guard against it, especially when as social psychologists we tramp the field of the sociologist and the anthropologist whose affinity for dichotomies approaches addiction. In our approach to tradition we tend to conceive a dichotomy between 'traditional' and 'modern', and to focus our attention on the 'transition' from the former to the latter. But this is an arbitrary procedure. It suggests that there was a time before change, whereas a moment's thought reminds us that time is change. Tradition is not timeless. If any society evolved an unchanging tradition, it would condemn itself to death. Thus there are no traditional values, only the values which inform the selections from the past which we take to explain ourselves to ourselves or to others. It is necessary to make this point because unless we treat values as continuously changing, unevenly distributed in society and often more symbolic than expressive, we shall be misled into seeking ways of obtaining value change or of designing organization to 'fit' traditional values.

Nor does it help to speak of pre-industrial values or the values of a pre-industrial society, which is frequently synonymous in the Western mind with traditional values and traditional society. What is referred to is the nineteenth-century European conception of what eighteenth-century society looked like and the values which it ought to have had. Mingled with this is often a confusion between the values of a late feudal and those of a post-feudal society. Again, what is referred to is either the values ascribed to an agrarian society of the (dichotomous, again) sets of rural and urban values seen as existing separately and in conflict where they interacted. They stress the extended family, the family as an economic unit, the acceptance backed by religious authority of a system of stratification and

421

deference based on the ownership of land, the nobility of birth and the possession of wealth, the importance of locality.

To people not brought up in this Western 'tradition', or to the anthropologically minded, traditional values are less convergent. They are more aware of the marked differences between the values of nomadic pastoral and of settled agricultural people and, among agricultural people, between those whose principal crops conduce to a plantation system and those which do not. They are aware of the immense variation in the values expressed in the myths which different people use to explain themselves and the beliefs and practices which they adopt to manage their transactions with the unknown and their navigation of the ineluctable life crises of birth and bereavement, of status transition in general.

But if the values of pre-industrial societies, whether past or present, are so variable and liable to change, can we nevertheless detect any firm relationships between economy and technology on the one hand and value system on the other? If not, we would be obliged to conclude that it is likely that any technology would be compatible with any value system. The most systematic attempt to plot such relationships in the context of society's mode of organizing its work is that of Udy (1970). He extracted data from ethnographic material of 125 pre-industrial societies, not all of which was fully usable. His analysis indicated:

(a) that the predominant form of work organization always represented a compromise between the work objectives and other social objectives imposed by the society;

(b) that the normal course of pre-industrial social development culminating in a settled agriculture rendered a society less, rather than more, capable of evolving forms appropriate to industrial development.

Clearly, then, there is a considerable gap between the values of a settled agricultural society and those of industrial work organizations. If societies in different stages of pre-industrial development are differentially penetrable by the values which make industrialization comparatively easy, can we envisage different forms of industrial work organization, which will be differentially acceptable by different societies? Can we match the industry to the society?

Rationality

We are bound to discuss the factors which affect the acceptance of particular forms of change, especially those concerned with technological innovation. This is important not only in considering

422

whether people will be found willing to accept the discipline of work in an industrial-type organization, but also in assessing whether the products of such work will prove acceptable and will be demanded in the society.

The rationality of advanced technology is frequently contrasted with the 'irrational' beliefs and behaviour of 'primitive people' or of poor peasants whose life is seen to be dominated by religious or magical beliefs, by ritual demands and by the inflexible bonds of custom. All this adds up to a 'resistance to change' rooted in emotional attachment to custom against their own true interests. When viewed in this light the major problem is conceived to be how to overcome resistance to change with, for the social psychologist at least, the attendant technology of attitude change, the two-step strategy of obtaining adoption of innovations and so on. We are getting enough disappointing experience to suggest that something is wrong with this approach. Even with such apparently successful innovations as 'the green revolution', the benefits, such as they are, do not appear to be shared by the poor peasants or the landless. Maybe their reluctance derives from a more rational assessment of their own situation than that reached by the outside expert. They know from long experience that the ways in which the economic and political systems distribute rewards make innovation rebound to their disadvantage. Once people were taught that the Luddites were backward-looking, unrealistic opponents of progress; today young people learn that they were oppressed, threatened with the loss of their livelihood and reacted in a revolutionary way, by taking what is nowadays described as 'direct action'. That the means they chose for protest were doomed is clear and perhaps should have been clear; and maybe was clear, to them, but it is also clear that their understanding of their own interests was rational enough.

A similar analysis indicates that the Indian peasant who resists adopting new crops, seeds, fertilizers or methods is aware of the personal benefits to be obtained from them, but is also only too painfully aware of the consequences of failure. Existing on the borderline of destitution, for him even the smallest real risk of failure is unacceptable. This has been convincingly demonstrated by Lipton in his theory of the 'optimizing peasant' (Lipton, 1969). Concerned with a 'survival algorithm', he rationally takes whatever steps are needed to ensure that he does not expose himself to a risk that could ruin him. The crops he grows and the methods he uses never yield much surplus, but even in the worst conditions they guarantee his survival. Better crops would give him a larger surplus, but if there is any possibility of complete failure with a succession of bad seasons, he dare not accept the risk, even if its statistical

423

probability is low – low enough indeed to be abundantly acceptable to anyone who risks less than extinction. Investigators like McClelland and Winter (1969) and Atkinson and Feather (1966) have stressed the importance of the motive of avoiding failure, MAF, which they have contrasted with nAch, achievement motivation. In accounting for the varied distribution of these motivations, they point to differences in child-rearing practices, particularly maternal behaviour.

With this we need have no quarrel; doubtless the recipe for survival is learnt where so much else is learnt – at the mother's knee. But we need to emphasize what may be inadequately stressed by these authors, that maternal example and exhortation are often the guidance required by the situation, not just the consequence of their own upbringing. To put it another way, there is a fit between the personality type developed and the pressures of the economic environment. Whether there is a maladaptive 'irrational' element or consequence of this survival motivation remains to be seen; if *all* objective possibility of failure were removed, would the situation become too stressful for rational response to be tolerable? The question is unfortunately academic. If the 'traditional' value that has been learnt is 'Cut your costs, reduce your risks', will it persist when circumstances change so as to remove its reinforcement by experience? It is possible that the adherence to the learned behaviour may prevent any other outcome's being experienced. In that event the deliberate attempt to intervene in the cycle of child-rearing practices → behaviour → child-rearing practices would be justified. On the other hand, there would be little justification if changed opportunities allowed the learning of new contingencies of reinforcement. As a matter of parsimony I would argue that we should prefer to assume the rationality of behaviour and at least should avoid the possibility of intervening in the additional and motivational spheres unless we are assured that the consequence could not be self-exposure to potential catastrophe, however low its statistical probability. It is at all events wise to seek first for the rationality in behaviour. And purely psychological methods can assist in this as well as, but not in place of, study of the economic and political background.

I am referring to methods such as those developed in personal construct theory, whose use could well be extended to identify and analyse the structure of rationality of situations as experienced by the people in their grip.

Rationality and change

If we start by assuming that people's behaviour is rational, having regard to the way in which their knowledge allows them to control their environment and having regard to the range of experience available to them, need we look only to exogenous change as the source of value change? Of course this depends to some extent upon what we mean by exogenous, which is not by any means necessarily the same as what is *experienced* as exogenous. Spontaneous genetic mutations and chance concatenations of events apart, all change, whether experienced as endogenous or exogenous, is influenced by external events from climatic variations to Armageddon. But of those changes *experienced* as endogenous, the most profound may well be the demographic. Wide-ranging and deep value changes are consequential upon what we have come to describe as the demographic transition. This process has been discussed at some length in the previous chapter and so we will not repeat it here.

However, we should note that in all developing countries the demographic transition is incomplete, and we have no warrant for supposing that it will be completed in any particular way, although we tend to assume that there will eventually be a balance between births and deaths, ensuring for a time at least a virtually static population. The implication of this is that social values in developing countries are changing, particularly the values concerning the significance of the individual as against the collectivity, the values of personal growth and development, values about individual freedoms. In so far as these changes have at present gone far less far than in some developed countries, social values in developing countries may be more consonant with what has become the 'traditional' pattern of industrial organization than are values that develop when *work organizations incorporate the values of the era in which their technologies first developed and that these values lag well behind the changes in society.*

These arguments are reinforced by the behaviour of multinational corporations who tend to seek to expand their operations in countries where 'traditional' values are still strong – not just because wages are lower but because strikes and 'unreasonable' demands by workers and by organized labour are less likely. The rationality of workers' behaviour, on which they rest their assumptions, is that of their overriding need to work if they are to eat, a constraining motive thought to be no longer effective in advanced industrial societies. I am far from suggesting that they are mistaken or that their calculations about motivation are incorrect, and that

425

the reasons for workers being less independent lie only in the fact that the social values do not stress independence. But employers are also aware that they show behaviour which is apparently economically non-rational; they are inclined not to work with the same regularity when their basic requirements have been met; they may neglect work for family and other social obligations; they may indeed find that more pay brings more obligations, making its economic rationality doubtful. Thus there may be value and behaviour change well before change in economic circumstances would apparently warrant. Indeed, it appears that this may occur in advanced and developed countries; Britain, for instance, may have acquired in advanced form the values and attitudes appropriate to an affluent society, while her economic problems clearly show she isn't one. In developing countries the progress of the demographic transition may produce value changes ahead of their degree of adaptiveness to their stage of industrialization.

The complications are endless when we remember that work organizations themselves promote value change in at least four ways: first, by providing work roles which put a premium on certain values in their occupants; second, by increasing the amount of work and pay packets and the consequent general level of affluence; third, by their tendency to increase urbanization; and fourth through the changes in life style brought about by the availability of their products. As we shall discuss later, the potential for social engineering through the design of work organizations is considerable and may offer a route to development which avoids some of the painful aspects of that traversed by existing industrialized societies. The Chinese have certainly perceived this possibility, although whether they have been able to realize it is arguable, as we shall see. But whatever other impact modern organizations have on developing countries, they almost invariably promote the discontinuities both in time and in space. Because of the technical, economic, social and educational infrastructure that they require, they promote regional disparities, emphasizing those that exist between port and hinterland, between town and country, between the metropolis and the provinces. Understandably keen to locate themselves within easy reach of sea communications, which in underdeveloped countries are quicker, cheaper and more reliable than overland, near the seat of government from which licences and other permits and favours are to be obtained, in areas where reasonably sophisticated labour is available, organizations acquire, if they can, sites near other organizations. Thus are created the oases of modernity in the wastes of traditionalism. Some conclude from this that the next step is the gradual diffusion of the modern through the traditional. At least as likely and probably more commonly occurring is a growing polarization, the 'dual economy', with divergence rather than convergence of attitudes and values.

I have said that organizations incorporate the values of the era in which their technologies emerged. That statement requires both qualification and explication. By way of qualification I should perhaps point to the bureaucratic values of all large organizations. In so far as notions about the economy of scale, or of safety in numbers, or of the values of bigness for its own sake, or for the sake of the importance and prestige conferred by it, have encouraged a preference for growth in organizations, organizations tend to enshrine the values of bureaucracy as well as whatever values are implicit in its technology. That is to say, it has two technologies, its production of work technology and its technology of internal control (bureaucratic method). That the objectives served by these tend to conflict is a matter of everyday observation and complaint. The tradition of design, inspired by the work of F. W. Taylor (see Chapters 4 and 5), has persisted well into a period when labour is more sophisticated, better educated and less tolerant of rigid constraint. Paradoxically, the principles of 'scientific management' also spread to technologies which had predated it and which had been based on a craft tradition. Some of our present-day dissatisfactions are due to this development. It follows that we can assume neither that the values incorporated in the design of an organization are appropriate to its work force nor that it is appropriate to its technology. This apparently discouraging conclusion is from our point of view full of hope. It implies that we have some choice of the values we can design into organizations; that modern organizations are not necessarily antithetical to traditional values and can indeed, within reason, be designed around them. 'Within reason' may represent quite considerable limitations however. For one thing, organizations must be free to evolve and, on the other hand, they must be able to take their place in whatever organizational network they belong to. If, for example, that is the network provided by membership of a multinational corporation, the constraint applies that the differences between one member and another cannot be such as to make movement from one to another at managerial level too difficult.

Furthermore, there is no need for organizations to be designed simply to be compatible with some existing set of values. Values, as we have said, change and must be free to change; we do not want to repeat the Taylorist error of embalming them in the organization. So, if we cannot design a set of values into the organization, what then? Perhaps the clue lies in the concept of 'meta-values' – values

427

about the ways in which decisions about values should be made, and values about the worthiness of values. I do not suggest that consensus could or should be obtained in any society abo⁴t meta-values. But values about the way things should be done are more pervasive and long lasting than values about what should be done. *The quality of life in a society is characterized more by the means that society adopts to achieve its ends than in the nature of the ends themselves*; indeed, societies differ much more in regard to the former than the latter. If we design organizations, or rather help organizations, to design themselves so as to enhance the responsiveness of their decision-making capacity, we simultaneously improve their capability of coping with environmental change and incorporate humanistic values into its design. We are designing 'learning organizations', in which the organization and its members are simultaneously acquiring increased capacity. The bureaucratic or hierarchical functional design of organizations inhibits learning. As we all know, individuals and groups within the organization learn, but their learning is not shared and its benefits not widely diffused through the organization; because what the individual learns is how to make the organization work despite itself, how to achieve the objectives in the face of rules and methods which make it impossible. The appropriateness of the concept of a learning organization to the situation of the developing country should need little underlining. One of the major benefits an organization can confer on a developing country is the upgrading of the knowledge, skills and capacities for decision-making of its people. If in the first part of the chapter I cast doubt upon the concept of 'traditional values' used in such a way as to imply their homogeneity, I have now in the second part sought to cast equal doubt on the concept of the 'modern organization' used in such a way as to imply a similar homogeneity, and to claim that we have adequate choice of methods of organizational design to enable it to adapt itself to societal values and to incorporate values about the ways in which change in these should come about. It all sounds idealistic and one may well ask where in the developing countries has this been done or even attempted.

Before answering this, I should point to the slipperiness of the evidence. We are accustomed to regard Japan as a country which successfully adapted modern technology to the traditional culture, evolving the giant enterprise with its paternalistic and family-oriented personnel policies, carrying over into industry the traditionally feudal relationship between peasant and proprietor. As Okochi (1973) somewhat acidly comments in this context, 'Like other peoples, the Japanese are not averse to inventing "traditions".' We have to be careful not to assume that unusual problems are the product of previous firm and idiosyncratic traditions. Thus when we examine the Chinese evidence we need to exercise care.

Richard Baum (1975) has discussed the deliberate selection by the Chinese of technologies which permit, indeed require, worker participation, the best known of which was the abortive 'backyard steel-making' project. Deliberately selecting a technology which would lead to community development, the Chinese authorities aimed to meet simultaneously the need for more steel production and the social goals of community development. In the case of steel, the sophistication of the technology was beyond the scope of a do-it-yourself approach. But in other less basic industry, the manufacture of agricultural implements for example, the method has been more successful. The technology selected has been appropriate to operation and decision-making by working groups. The decision to set up a particular manufacturing facility has been in the hands of community representatives or even open meetings. Without support from higher echelons, doubtless such decisions would remain empty but there appears to be no reason to doubt genuine community involvement. Operating the industrial process has meant the development of new skills, both of a craft nature and social and political ones. Communities have graduated from the simpler and more agriculturally oriented industries to more sophisticated consumer products – bottling and canning factories and the like.

Nevertheless, it appears that when it comes to more advanced technologies, any attempt to incorporate systems of direct participation or autonomous work grouping has failed. In its place, representative democracy of the familiar works council type has been preferred. This is, of course, disappointing but may represent an intermediate step, imposed by the lack of experience and skill of Chinese industrial workers and the consequent danger of enthusiastic anarchy. It may be, and probably is, the inevitable consequence of the importation of foreign technology with built-in scientific management principles of behaviour control. Indeed it may well be a combination of both. The lesson is not necessarily a tragic one. For other developing countries the most appropriate conclusion to draw is the advantage of devising appropriate schemes which combine the potential for industrial production with that for community development. The participative skills acquired by the workers should find their outlet in participation in community decisions. The learning of the appropriate industrial skills can be also a learning how to learn.

Cultures, like individuals, have characteristic learning styles. It cannot be taken for granted that the style appropriate to one culture

429

is equally appropriate to another. Values about learning, what should be learned in what way, are deeply culturally rooted. Yet they are little explored. If modern organizations are to be learning systems, they must embody values about learning appropriate to the culture in which they are located. I would suggest that it may often be more fruitful to study learning styles and cognitive maps than to explore the more popular areas of motivation. Not that they are unconnected. However, I do not need to dwell upon this point here.

Modern organizations of a highly efficient but idiosyncratic kind have been developed in Japan (Sumiyo, 1973). The value systems on which they are built are different in several respects from their European and American counterparts. The psychological contracts, between worker and organization differ notably in terms of the expectations they raise and satisfy with regard to career and continuity of employment and responsibility for the health and welfare of the employee and his family. These values have apparently been perfectly compatible with efficiency and productivity and have also seemingly encouraged the continued acquisition of industrial skills by employees. These organizations have been seen as the cultural successors of the Japanese feudal organization of agriculture. It would appear, however, that the Japanese, like other natives, are not beyond inventing traditions. And this particular one may yet not survive another generation. Already the young generation of workers in Japan express less satisfaction with the slow advancement, paternalism and other aspects of life in the giant Japanese corporations, which will have to be redesigned on new lines if they are to attract and hold the young workers they need (Shin-Ichi Takezawa, 1975). The values of Japanese society have rendered the corporation far more pervasive of the life space of the people than the more familiar Western models. If we look back to the early days of industrialization and the comparative continuity of life and work, we realize that the immense change brought about by industrialization represents a discontinuity in tradition which is by no means inevitable. It was assisted by the large-scale migration of workers from the land to the new urban areas, which in any case created a discontinuity in their lives and those of their families. But the organization of industry today does not need to tear up families from their roots.

Summary

So we see that we have the chance of designing organizations to be compatible with traditional values or to ease the learning of new values which do not represent an abrupt discontinuity in tradition – which is what I conceive to have occurred in Japan. We can put more emphasis on the development of communities constructed around values which fit the evolving aspirations of people. Best of all we can aim to provide localities with emerging sense of community with the additional resources of knowledge and skill to design organizations for themselves. What we should avoid above all is to regard traditional values as hostile to the development of modern organizations and to seek to eliminate them.

Chapter 24
Social Development and the Assessment of Technology

In the previous chapter we looked at the relationship between values and organizations in the context of the use of technology in developed and developing countries. I want to continue this theme but with more emphasis on how we assess the appropriateness of a technology for a society.

We can see development today as a dialectical process but the dialogues are of many kinds and between different participants. The first to come to mind is that between the developed and the developing; we recognize that development is to some extent a relationship, that developed and developing countries do not descend from two separate evolutionary trees, but represent differentiation within a world order. Another dialogue occurs within a developing country itself, between the planner and the planned; it appears a little one-sided maybe for a true dialogue, but that is because we hear the planner but only note the seemingly obstructive behaviour of the planned. In many developed countries today, this dialogue is cast into procedural forms and debated in public. Yet another dialogue is between technology and society. Apparently an exercise in balancing the benefits of modernization against its social and human costs, it is in fact a struggle for the initiative: Shall developments in technology oblige society to respond or shall society set objectives for technology to seek the means to attain? What I have to say is I hope relevant to all three dialogues; if to me the third is the most crucial, it is because I believe it is a key to the other two.

Every schoolboy knows, and even some schoolgirls have been let into the secret, that the marvels of our civilization are the products of technological mastery. It is, of course, equally true that they are the products of our social organization. Emphasis on the first rather than the second encourages a view of technological determinism.

Because we are nowadays aware of the hardships and the disruptions which technology has wrought, we are evolving means of enquiring in advance what effects a new technology will have. Under the name of technology assessment, government agencies are seeking more effective and more sophisticated approaches to measuring environmental impacts, the direct and the indirect consequences of proposed technologies. If this is shutting the stable door after the horse has bolted, we can hardly expect to roll back the technologies of the past; doing so would in fact have quite as much disruptive potential as the acquisition of new ones.

But essentially the techniques which have been developed for assessing technology are reactive, responsive, leaving the initiative with the technology. The input is a specific technology; assessment consists of examining its indirect consequences and its possible side effects, by no means all of which are likely to be considered negative. Nor is this an easy task, and a considerable arsenal of methods has been displayed at least in simulation. Delphi projections, cross impact-matrices, input–output analyses and other intricacies are available as instruments, albeit of low precision. Their application, backed by political and economic function in the past, could have averted, for example, some of the disastrous consequences to cities of the internal combustion engine. What application of this technology would have been adopted is, of course, incalculable. Today the candidates for assessment are such technologies as are proposed for wider scale development, such as the supersonic transport or nuclear power, or new products such as drugs recognized to have potentially dangerous side effects. It is doubtful whether, although the methodology is available, the potential impact of a new drug on the doctor's relationship with his patient is likely to be given much consideration. But, with all its sophistication, this form of technological assessment is only the first of three types discerned by Hetman (1973). These are:

(i) Examining recent technologies and exploring their potential impacts and side effects.
(ii) 'Environmental' technological assessment:
    (a) Preparing an inventory of the existing 'insults' to the environment;
    (b) tracking the insults to their technological origins, identifying the processes which led to the undesirable effects; and
    (c) searching for remedies.
(iii) Assessment of new desirable technology. This constitutes

a considerable shift in perspective to one which regards technology not as an initiating force, an independent variable – but as contingent, depending upon social goals, values and choices. It also requires different forms of organization, technological task forces with missions derived from designated social objectives.

As I have already indicated, almost all the work that has been done so far is concerned with (i). This need occasion no surprise: not only do (ii) and (iii) obviously encounter greater difficulties, they involve greater conceptual and philosophical difficulties as well. Indeed, it is probably likely to lead to less confusion and corresponding disappointment if we, partly following Hetman, go further and distinguish three different activities: technological assessment, environmental analysis, and sociotechnical assessment. The first two correspond exactly with Hetman's first two types, the third requires more than a shift in emphasis.

Selecting social goals and searching for new (or partly adapted) technologies to attain them, i.e. regarding society as the independent and technology as the dependent variable is an improvement on the reverse. But it commits us in part to the same error. Both observe the fact that technology is a social process and that to attain any objective, society employs a technology even if the objective we are discussing is the taking of a decision. In other words, there is a technology of decision-making which is anything but value-neutral in its assumptions and consequences. We cannot separate decisions or choices from the way they are made, or technological systems from the social processes whereby they are developed.

It may now be clear how the mode of conceptualizing sociotechnical assessment – the third dialogue, that between society and technology – affects the second, the dialogue between the planner and the planned.

To begin with, I will revert to the first type of assessment, which examines technology in relation to its impact. Even this has two meanings. Our purpose may be (a) to adapt a given technology to our existing social system; (b) to minimize the social disruption of adopting a given technology: while (a) implies our acceptance of the goals served by the existing system, of its pattern of operation and of its distribution of power, rewards and life chances – essentially a conservationist posture – (b) implies accepting some new goal superior to those served by the existing system and using the means provided by the latter for achieving the supersession of its goals with a minimum of disturbance – essentially a technocratic posture. Since the concepts and methods of technological assessment can be equally well directed towards either social conservation or technocratic control, it is potent ammunition in the battle of the 'people' versus the 'planners'. Knowledge about the effects of technology, like knowledge about technology and like technology itself, affects the location and balance of power in the social system. Environmental assessment begins with acceptance of the values of the dominant groups in society about what constitutes an 'insult' to the environment or at least about what an environment free of insults would be like. I am not suggesting that the objective of environmental conservation is the protecting of the environment of the 'rich and powerful' from the consequences of the poor having more. That is not the point I am making at all. What I am saying is that the technology of technology assessment embodies, as does every other technology, certain social assumptions and that these are seldom recognized.

Sociotechnical assessment explicitly recognizes this issue; herein lies its importance for the first of our dialogues, that between the developed and the developing. It recognizes that the technologies of the developed world embody the social assumptions and values of that world. This is true, not only of the products and their uses, but also of the processes by which they are designed and made and the process by which the decision whether to develop or not is arrived at. Inevitably, then, sociotechnical assessment opens up a new set of questions for the dialogue between the provider of technological expertise and the recipient, the developed and the developing. To the questions about the appropriateness of technology to the market situation, resources of skills, environmental impacts and infrastructure, it adds questions about the social assumptions underlying the type of organization needed to operate and maintain it, about the technology of decision-making implied by it.

To be more specific, let us consider the type of question that may arise. The advocates of appropriate technology rightly concern themselves with such issues as the need to provide jobs, the need to develop industrial skills and so on. They have not yet brought into their ambit the need to develop social skills and the capacity to participate in decision-making – all those concerns which define the sociotechnical approach to the quality of working life. We see here the choice between the vicious circle and the virtuous spiral. On the one hand, the choice of an admittedly labour intensive technology may yet provide jobs which require little, and encourage less, participation in decision-making, which emphasize individual tasks rather than group co-operation and which, therefore, serve in no way to spread the capacity to make informed judgements about future technological developments nor to nourish the aspiration and self-confidence to wish to do so. On the other hand, the choice may be a technology which trains people in these social skills, enhances their feelings of competence and widens their horizons. If we prefer the latter, can we be sure that the consequences of such a choice can be successfully handled by the fragile social institutions that characterize many developing countries? For them, there is a real and vital question of where to start. We shall return to this question, which does not mean that we can give a satisfactory answer. From what I have said already, it should be clear that my version of sociotechnical assessment is more easily attainable where:

(a) power is already widely dispersed;

(b) the goals of the system are, if not already well known, at least readily determinable by enquiry;

(c) the means for modifying or changing the goals are understood and are in good repair.

A good example of such a system would be the kibbutz. The social skills of participation are widely distributed; the goals are well known and voluntarily accepted; the democratic process is highly developed. That these are necessary but not sufficient conditions for wise choice of technology is clear from the kibbutz movement's experience with industry. It is well known that the kibbutzim adopted the industrial mode of production both to diversify their own economic base and to provide jobs for their own members. Also well known is the fact that, following the apparent logic of industrial expansion and specialization, many found themselves, contrary to their cherished system of values, employing non-members in their factories. It is perhaps less widely known that it is not always easy for kibbutzim to get their own members to work in their factories and that, despite their recognition that they are working for the good of their own community, many kibbutz factory workers express symptoms of what is surprisingly like what in other circles would be called alienation. The kibbutz movements now recognize that their choice of technology has not always been appropriate. So little has the technology been modified to suit the social system that in some instances you may walk into a kibbutz factory and imagine yourself in Germany, where the plant was designed.

The remedy is in the hands of the kibbutzim; they possess or can acquire the skill and expertise required to redesign their plants. How they will handle the problem of employed labour is another question. What is certain is that continuance of a practice which conflicts with an institutional ideology must eventually weaken either the ideology or the institution. It may already be necessary for the self-understanding of the kibbutz to derive its concept of its own philosophy from the way in which it is expressed in practice.

For the first step in the development of an appropriate sociotechnology in any institution is the articulation of a philosophy of management. This is needed whether the institution is industrial, commercial, educational, custodial, governmental or whatever. A philosophy of management or an administrative philosophy or however it is called is a statement about ends and means.

It is against that statement of philosophy that the choices posed by technology are to be assessed. And the wider the participation in the evolution of the statement, the more understanding will be its interpretation in practice. It is time now to return to an earlier point – that technology is a social process. A technology, however 'hard', however 'soft', is an organizational and institutional product. The values, the philosophy of the organization in which it is developed are expressed in the technology. The need for the match between the philosophies of provider and user of technology is clear. Perhaps to the question as to where the developing country can begin, we can give half an answer – it can begin in its technological institutions. And I fear that it is in just these institutions that the philosophy and values of 'scientific management' take root most easily. Once this has occurred, the developing country has imported within its own system the most alien of products, and right into its bloodstream. The dialogue between planners and planned is frustrating indeed, if the former speak in an alien tongue. A constructive dialogue between planner and planned is one from which the planned learns to plan for himself. Sociotechnological assessment, then, should and can be a learning process. Learning is often best by doing, but always by doing with immediate knowledge of the outcome of doing; and a learning organization or institution is one in which people at all levels learn. Thus our ideal choice of organization with which to begin in a developing country is the local community. It is the community we wish to see acquire the capacities to determine its own needs and to assess the available ways of meeting them. The harnessing of simple technology to a limited social goal can be relatively quick with immediate feedback, enabling the community's capacity for goal-setting to keep pace with its capacity to attain goals and to foresee consequences. Such a community would need to be able to provide, or at least develop and modify, its own technology at the level of its basic needs. For the choice of technology to meet its evolving and more sophisticated needs, it would then be able to engage in informed dialogue with technical institutions or with commercial providers. The kibbutz offers itself once again as the ideal model of such a community. And this model provides us

437

with a further clue. Kibbutzim are capable of providing themselves with any specialized help they need in the form of advisers and experts who share their basic values through their membership of a movement. By sharing their resources in a network mode – the 'movements' are there to provide services not to control their membership – they enormously strengthen their capacity to cope with their environments. Communities in developing countries, and in developed ones too, can utilize these properties of networks if they can exert themselves to oppose tendencies to convert networks into instruments of domination. Here as elsewhere the price of freedom is eternal vigilance. Whether this approach can be generalized to developed countries depends upon their capacity, and will, to encourage people's sense of community. Sociotechnical assessment at the level of the community implies a much broader but shallower concept of planning and administration than complex societies have become accustomed to. It involves network relationships across functions at a low level, rather than functional planning and administration at high level. At present, the willingness of centralized governments and bureaucracies to lose control to decentralized, relatively small community organizations is very low indeed, despite growing evidence of their inability to cope adequately with environmental turbulence.

Thus 'dialogue', as I have interpreted it, represents a timely insight. And since real dialogue can only take place where there is reasonable equality of power and knowledge, the concept of sociotechnical assessment as outlined here can contribute to strengthening the prospects of dialogue between developed and developing, between planner and planned and between technology and society.

Section V
Science and Technology Policy

Chapter 25
The Sociology of Scientific and Technological Policy

Introduction – contemporary reminders

Since 1973 one of the most discussed topics at all levels and in all countries has been the 'Energy Crisis'. It has united or disunited international existing or ad hoc bodies; it has emphasized in dramatic manner the interdependence of countries and of people. Most importantly from our point of view, it has exposed the basic and total inadequacy of scientific and technological policy-making at the national and international level.

Now we are all asking: Where have our technological policies been? We have made our investments in fuel-using, particularly oil-using, technologies; scientific research has at best been neutral with regard to fuel. Yet the dwindling of reserves of fossil fuels has been predicted, perhaps too often to carry conviction. But in the technological and industrial rat race it was unthinkable for an advanced country or an industry to 'opt for a policy of fuel economy' or the development of alternative sources of energy. Even now it is not the potential exhaustion but the cost of oil that has precipitated talk of crisis and new behaviours. So long as the cost to the consumer of oil was based on the marginal cost of its retrieval from the ground, rather than its value as a diminishing resource, the state of development of a country or industry could be measured by its use rather than its conservation (not that the present cost of oil is based on such rational considerations). So the energy crisis exemplifies some of the most serious problems of, and gaps in, scientific and technological policies.

439

The dimensions of scientific and technological policy

1 The international dimension involves:
   (a) problems of global resource exploitation and utilization;
   (b) the political relationships between states or between blocks or groups of states;
   (c) the economic relationships between resource owners and resource users, between developed and underdeveloped;
   (d) moral beliefs about obligations, justice, fairness and the like;
   (e) the fragile legal institution of international bodies.
2 The national dimensions include:
   (a) commitment to economic growth and development;
   (b) the distribution or redistribution of wealth and income in their political, social, economic and moral aspects;
   (c) the political and economic relationships between producers and consumers, between regions, between industries, between industry and the community.
3 The industrial dimension includes:
   the relationships between large and small, advanced and backward firms, between firms and their suppliers, firms and their customers and between the firm and its local community. These relationships also have social, economic, political and moral aspects.

We could continue to cite elements in these dimensions of policy, but the point we wish to make is that each is complex. And of course all these dimensions are quite closely related. In a capitalist or mixed economy much of a government's technological policy is concerned with encouraging industrialists to make certain kinds of technological decisions rather than others. If, as has been the case over recent decades, that has usually meant investing in more advanced technology, this has been done in several ways: by fiscal and financial inducements to invest; by financial inducement to undertake R & D, including the giving of government R & D contracts; by conducting R & D in government establishments; and by measures to facilitate the supply of scientific and technological information to firms.

On the international level the role of the multinational corporation has demonstrated the difficulties facing a country in pursuing an independent technological policy; and the virtual helplessness of developing countries in selecting, let alone generating, the technology that would most suit their circumstances has been a knotty feature of development policy.

Is scientific and technological policy a separate field of policy?

One complicating feature is immediately apparent. We have been talking about matters that can be seen as coming under the headings of economic policy, industrial policy, development policy, energy policy, conservation policy and doubtless others as well. How realistic is it to identify an area of policy-making as 'scientific' or 'technological'? Is the decision by a firm to invest in developing a new process to make use of a new source of raw material a technological decision or a financial decision or a commercial decision? It is clearly a decision which has technological, financial and commercial components or aspects.

Is the decision by a government to invest in research and development of nuclear sources of power, a scientific decision, or a technological decision, or an economic decision, or a strategic decision? Again it is a decision with all these aspects. And inevitably, as it has identifiable and predictable social consequences, it must be regarded as entailing social decisions as well. At this level there are no specifically scientific or technological decisions; a scientific or technological policy at this level must, then, be a policy about how technological and scientific aspects are to be brought into consideration, about how scientists and technologists are to be used in the decision process.

Another kind of scientific and technological policy concerns the global amount of R & D a country should aim to have. This area of policy is not only about the percentage of GNP (or whatever measure is adopted) that should be devoted to R & D but also, in a mixed economy, about how this level should be reached or maintained. Subsidiary questions arise as to what is included under the R & D rubric, how it should be measured and classified and so on. These are not primarily scientific or technological questions, but political and economic questions to which scientists and technologists bring expert opinion and advice. Questions concerning the allocation of resources among different lines of scientific enquiry and technological development, on the other hand, are often left within the political and administrative process to determination by scientific or technological experts.

What we have, therefore, is a range of policies with a graduation of scientific and technological components; at each level scientific and technological knowledge are used, but in different ways. At each level different roles are performed by scientists and technologists.

What is the content of scientific and technological policy?

A comprehensive view of scientific and technological policy-making would then require us to consider:

(a) policy-making about resources to be allocated to science and technology;

(b) policy-making about the allocation of resources as between:

(i)   indigenous R & D and purchase of R & D from abroad;

(ii)   different forms of R & D;

(iii)   different sciences and their associated techniques;

(iv)   different projects within particular categories of R & D;

(v)   teaching, research and research training within each scientific and technological specialism.

(c) The roles of scientists and technologists in policy-making;

(d) the use of scientific and technological knowledge in policy.

And, since we are talking about policy-making,

(e) in whose interests are the decisions made and how are the interests of other groups affected?

Category (d) opens up the question of the distribution and diffusion of scientific and technological knowledge in society. Category (c) raises the issues of the status and prestige of science and scientists and of the technologies and technologists. Nor can we proceed far without making far greater distinctions than so far in this analysis between science and technology and among the sciences and the technologies themselves.

In economically advanced, English-speaking countries one group of technologists has very high prestige and a virtual monopoly of decision-making in all matters affecting their technology, except its global allocation of resources. I refer, of course, to medical practitioners. The prestige and influence on policy exerted by mechanical engineers or architects is far lower. The position in non-English-speaking countries is different and even within English-speaking countries the prestige of engineers, for example, is probably lowest of all in Britain; a factor frequently adduced in Britain as conducing to its poor technological record in the twentieth century.

If scientific and technological policy-making has culturally specific aspects, influenced by social and political structure as well as by the needs as perceived by different actors in the political process of each country, we may ask to what extent there are consequential differences in what people labelled 'physicists' or 'civil engineers' actually do in different countries when they are 'doing physics' or 'doing civil engineering', or 'doing research'. What differences do political and social structures make to the content of scientific research? Or are differences only manifest at the level of manager or director of scientific research? Apart from the purely intellectual curiosity aroused by such questions and their political overtones, the question is highly practical when we come to examine the content of international policies for science and technology, in whose making only aggregate data is considered and global concepts employed whose verbal expression may be the same but whose referent may be quite different in the different countries concerned. Any profitable study on an international or comparative level of scientific and technological policy will require far greater analysis of the roles of scientists and technologists and the content of their jobs than is available at the level of statistical data.

Who can have a scientific or technological policy?

To a limited extent, industrial companies, universities and research establishments make decisions which affect all the issues of policy we have mentioned, but they are closely constrained by the policies of larger entities, especially government.

But what possibility is there for, say, a small undeveloped country to have such a thing as a scientific and technological policy? It probably possesses few highly trained scientists and technologists, and virtually no centres of scientific or technological research. In any field of science or technology, its R & D is dwarfed by that of developed countries, possibly by that of any one developed country. If, as a consequence, it decides to import its technology, what freedom of choice has it in determining the kind of technology it will import? And the people who have to take the decisions at the level of the enterprise probably have no or very little technological or scientific knowledge, or recourse to advice from indigenous scientists or technologists with an intimate knowledge of the processes and products concerned.

Can the country at least have a policy about the use of the scientists and technologists it possesses? If it adopts as its first priority the teaching and training of more scientists and technologists, thus directing its stock of existing scientists and technologists to teaching, this means not only that it must import its technology but also virtually ensures that the training its scientists and technologists receive will be in the technologies of the same kind as it is importing – technology developed and selected for and by a country at a totally

443

different level of development and with totally different factor proportions and totally different needs. If it decides to import teachers, using its own scientists and technologists to develop indigenous lines of research, the result is the same until the research is far enough advanced to provide a new teaching curriculum. And by then all the scientists and technologists graduated in the meantime are accustomed to the imported technology on which they have been trained and are likely to be unfamiliar with, mistrustful and even contemptuous of, indigenous technology.

Essentially, then, the concentration of science and technology in a handful of advanced countries dominates decisions about the use of science and technology on the part of less developed countries. And science and technology, especially the latter, are themselves both the products of and the agents of the social and political structures of their countries of origin. This statement requires further analysis.

Scientific culture and scientific policy

Science is conducted according to special sets of rules in defined organizational settings. The scientist then is socialized into scientific and organizational values. So that these two sets of values should not be contradictory, special types of organization have emerged, and the values of science have become to a large extent the values of the scientific organization. This has many important consequences. One consequence is for the nature of science itself. Some exceptional cases to the contrary, science is becoming more and more an organized social activity involving 'teamwork' – the loose interlocking of roles in which at different stages of the activity or process different mutual dependencies occur. Simultaneously the scientist's perception of reality has shifted from an emphasis on the behaviour of the individual particle – the atomistic approach, to emphasis on their interactions, on the 'field of forces', the gestalt – the holistic approach. This same shift of forces or emphasis has occurred across a broad spectrum of science.

And now for technology the ecological aspects are beginning to dominate research and policy – I do not refer merely to fashionable concern with the environment. We are perceiving the shift of attention from specific modes of locomotion to transport systems, from fuel technology to energy systems, towards an ecological perspective on industrial conversion processes and so on.

Another consequence is for the shape of organizations. The need to construct organizations consistent with the requirements for teamwork and the scientists' values of self-fulfilment in work has resulted in innovative designs of organization of a less hierarchical, more matrix type than is typical of work organizations. This leads to misunderstanding and conflict. Their non-hierarchical nature creates difficulties for the policy-making bodies to which they are accountable. The latter, accustomed to relating to more traditional forms of organization, find scientific organizations hard to direct or to evaluate and perceive them as behaving as 'laws unto themselves' and irresponsibly. When R & D units exist alongside production units within the same enterprise, a conflict of styles and values frequently occurs. The outcome is not infrequently a virtual severance of relations to the detriment of the utility of the R & D. Thus in order to operate successfully in the field of science policy, government planning organizations have to acquire an openness of operational style which may be alien to them. The response is often to hive off science policy-making to scientists who understand science and scientists but whose position in the general policy machinery of government is so peripheral that science policy hardly enters into policy-making in other fields at all.

This opposition between the scientific culture and the culture and ethos of policy and planning in society with its consequent isolation of scientific and technological policy-making means that a real and effective policy for the use of science and technology is contingent upon the society's ability to evolve a special kind of policy culture, which when evolved would impact upon other kinds of organization in society.

One further consequence of the isolation of science and technology and of scientific and technological policy-making is reflected in the kind of science and technology which results. If science is pursued as an activity isolated from the social pressures which impinge upon other forms of activity, the dynamic for development comes from within the science itself – a kind of scientific determinism which, on the whole, has served science well. But it leads to concern with the leading edges of science and a lack of concern with the less glamorous, but more socially valuable areas. This is exemplified by the powerful scientific attack on the aetiology of cancer and on the immunological problems of organ transplants compared with the low-key efforts devoted to the aetiology of rheumatism or the hazards of the communication of disease by the methods of delivery of health care.

And the technological culture

If this is true of science, it is as true of technology, and far more consequential. Technological determinism is far more dangerous and pervasive than the kind of scientific determinism we have just described. It takes two forms: (a) that any technology that is possible must be developed, and (b) that the technology determines the nature of the social system that can exploit it. Together these become a theory of the inevitable convergence of social systems. If technology develops according to its own laws and under an inner dynamic, and if technology determines social and economic arrangements, then as societies develop technologically, they will become more like one another. This misreading is possible only for people who do not understand technology. Unfortunately that class includes most policy-makers and many technologists. Only since the products of technology have begun to frighten us have we begun to perceive that there is always a choice of technology and that the technologists who persuaded us that the direction of its advance was predetermined and only the pace under our control, that therefore we must make haste if we were not to be beaten in the race, were motivated by a competitive impulse which was built into our society's arrangements for technological education training, research and development. These were the motives which had enabled technology to obtain such a firm base in our society. Change will not be easy. In the two previous sections of this book we have discussed the implications of technological choice and its relation to the quality of working life. Chapters 23 and 24 look at this question with particular reference to developing countries, where we suggest that sociotechnical assessment of needs will be effective within a community framework.

Social indicators and technological policy

We now live in an invented society where organizations, jobs, and technology are all the inventions of man. It may be mind-boggling but this means that there are choices in every instance and that careful decisions based on an assessment of their implications have to be made in relation to each invention. The mounting difficulties arising, as between many aspects of human welfare and productivity, have caught advanced societies unprepared. Few employing organizations foresaw that their employees would demand more from their work than more money, better physical working condi-

446

tions, better fringe benefits etc. Nor did social scientists warn them of what was to come. Those who did could offer no more than the plausible but unsupported prediction that better education would render workers less willing to accept authoritarian supervision or monotonous jobs. Where was the evidence that values were changing? The evidence of change in the dominant social values in these societies has been around for a decade and for much longer if we include the convulsions of the world of art. But one would expect to have little influence with the heads of firms if they were to be advised to initiate radical changes in their organizations on these grounds.

Unfortunately, we can do only somewhat better than that. We know a fair amount about the interrelationships of value systems and about the processes of diffusion in society but we do not know enough to make more than very vague predictions and we honestly know next to nothing about the time scales involved. Little surprise then that there is a strong movement to develop reliable and consistent systems of social indicators which we hope will include indicators of attitudes and values as well as their tangible consequences.

With an appreciation of changing values buttressed by social indicators, society will still be dependent on how technology is developed and applied, i.e., on how competent are engineers, technologists, and architects in the newly recognized social environment. The path ahead is quite clear. It has two forks: engineers and technologists as broad based and deeply competent sociotechnical professionals or as technique-specific technicians kept from the main arena of societal decision-making. The consequences for societies of each path are also quite predictable.

Science policies for development

The Sussex Group (Freeman, 1971) has, among others, pointed to the low proportion of scientific research that is conducted in the developing countries, and to the low proportion of research in the developing countries which is oriented towards the problems of the developing countries. The group proposes that more money be allocated specifically for such research. On a more radical view research conducted in advanced countries would be too saturated with the scientific culture of advanced societies to render the service needed to developing countries. China, pursuing its own path of development, appears to take such a radical view of science, requiring that, like other cadres, scientists should spend periods of time working in the fields or in workshops. There is considerable argument as to whether this makes any difference to scientific method and approach to scientific questions. Certainly it is intended to have effect upon the kind of problem that is tackled by scientists. We can certainly predict that it would have an effect upon technologists. Our technologists are accustomed to hierarchical, Taylorist principles of work organization and habitually design technology appropriate to this social concept. Experience of our industrial organizations confines them in this conceptual orientation. Experience in other forms of social organization, combined with appropriate training in technology, would set up a different cycle of design–experience–design. We learn however (Baum 1975), that while in China low-technology industry is organized around the concept of semi-autonomous work groups or 'group technology', in high-technology industry workers' participation takes the 'representative' mode – the works' council and works' committees. This is disappointing. It may be a consequence of the importation of advanced technologies designed for traditional organizations, while the Chinese low and intermediate technology is indigenous and designed for the work group. If the outcome is a growing pressure on the advanced technology to follow even more recent Western trends towards democratization of the work place (delegated decision-making to work groups), then selection of technology to achieve human values will appear to predominate. If the reverse trend becomes apparent, the subordination of human values to a materialist technology, we shall have to wait for other demonstrations of a humanist technological policy. Meanwhile the apparent discrepancy between policy in the advanced sector and that in the lower technology sector may be related to differences in the decision making processes that are inevitably associated with them. The acquisition and direction of the large resources needed to instal plants in an advanced technology require specialist knowledge and expertise and the direction and co-ordination of trained people. There is little room for naive initiative. Hence the importance attached to ensuring that the experience of scientists and technologists includes work among the peasants and to promoting cadre participation in labour. Whether this experience will be reflected in technological design, it may be too soon to say. There is, Baum (1975) argues, certainly a tendency towards 'flatter' organizations in industry:

> The putative motivational effects of cadre participation in labor have been the subject of numerous articles and monographs, and need not be reiterated here. In the context of recent developments in Chinese industrial management,

448

however, two points require elaboration. First is the fact that the reduction of middle-level management personnel in many Chinese industrial enterprises has placed an added burden of supervision and verification upon leading cadres, who are no longer free to delegate such responsibility to underlings. This may well serve to 'close the information gap' between higher and lower levels while at the same time insuring that leading cadres will become directly involved in implementing their own decision, thus facilitating the establishment of more direct and accurate feedback mechanisms. Second, as leading cadres are forced into closer functional contact with the basic-levels, hierarchical relationships may tend to be redefined in terms of the cadres' ability to secure cooperation among workers rather than in terms of their greater authority, 'expertise', salary benefits, or perquisites of office. Similarly, as vertical communications become more personal and informal, rather than mechanical and bureaucratic, the 'social distance' between mental and manual workers may be significantly reduced.

Some observers have expressed the view that it is in the area of technological innovation and design that rank-and-file workers have attained their greatest sense of participation in China's industrial development. Three-in-one innovation teams, which include workers, technical personnel, and cadres, are ubiquitous in Chinese industry. The vast majority of technical innovations in which workers participate are the product of such team efforts, usually organized at the workshop level. Yet, such data as do exist suggest that only a small minority of workers in any given enterprise actively participate in such innovation teams.

This excursus into the micro-level in Chinese industry will serve to illustrate the intricate relationship between technological and social policies. It is not just a question of using science and technology to secure social purposes; the choice of technology imports social consequences because it is itself based on social assumptions. But how much attention need be paid to this? Is it a minor side issue? Does it matter how a particular enterprise is organized, provided the output serves a social purpose? And after all, advanced technology employs a very small minority of the people.

Advanced technology is the 'leading part'

The answers to these questions turn on two issues. What is the 'leading part' of the system? And what is the relationship between work life and non-work life?

The leading part of a system is that part whose goals tend to be subserved by the goals of the other parts and whose degree of success in achieving its goals now tends to determine the degree of success of all the other parts in achieving their goals tomorrow. The values expressed in the design of the leading part will tend to predominate the values of the other parts. We have seen over the last two centuries the dominance of industry as the leading part of industrial society – the very term 'industrial society' makes this point quite dramatically. Developing countries have embraced industrialization as their route to 'modernization'; thus the values expressed in the design of their industrial technology are likely to express themselves very strongly in the society as a whole.

The relation between work life and non-work life is controversial. It has been strongly represented that people will accept willingly an unsatisfying work experience for the sake of the satisfactions they can obtain with the money so earned. This instrumental approach to work provides them with the basis for non-instrumental choices in their non-work lives. Against this there are two kinds of evidence. The first is that it appears that greater intrinsic satisfaction in work is associated with more rather than less participation in non-work activities. This in itself is indeed an oversimplification. Not all combinations of satisfactions have been available in the past; many choices were forced. Now that more choices of life styles are genuinely available the true relationships between work life and non-work life can emerge. The second kind of evidence is that increased bureaucratization of work was followed by a tendency towards increased bureaucratization of leisure and non-work generally. A progressive debureaucratization of society will have to start with its leading part.

The principal issues of scientific and technological policy have been how to attract more bright young people into science and technology; how to attract them more into technology than into science; how to allocate resources so as to direct science and technology towards modernization or towards the amelioration of social conditions; how to obtain the benefits of other countries' science and technology without distortion of the domestic economy or at the cost of political and economic status. Without derogating any of these important features of policy, we would claim that a vitally

450

important area of policy is the nature of the inner logic of the technology itself.

Two conclusions are inescapable. A coherent policy for science and technology is impossible unless scientists and technologists can perceive their activities in the light of an understanding of the policy dimensions we tentatively sketched at the beginning of this chapter. Nor can it be achieved without an understanding on the part of policy-makers of the values and logical and social assumptions inherent in the enterprise of science and the pursuit of technology.

Section VI
The Armed Services

Chapter 26
Services Organization and Manpower: A Study in Contradiction

The great poet–prophet Parkinson once observed that when an organization grows to about 1,000 strong it no longer requires any external output or goal. Enough administrative need is generated to keep them all fully occupied in paying, documenting one another, sending one another on leave and on internal training courses, controlling and exercising discipline to maintain internal cohesion. The joke is, of course, that he need not have been joking.

Looked at another way, if an organization has no task other than internal control, its structure will accommodate itself to providing full-time jobs for all, directed towards the maintenance of internal control. A substantial number of levels of authority may be required to achieve this. Let me give an example of what I mean. In an RAF training school, whose size justified its command by an air commodore, every rank below his was established to correspond with some subunit organization. Thus levels of authority existed without any reference to the actual number of levels of responsibility that could be discerned. In such a situation the struggle for something to do between officers of successive rank levels is pitiful to observe. In this situation it is only if an officer in one of these levels, preferably a high one, is sufficiently detached to be able to sit back and leave things to his subordinates, that anything resembling a true match of authority and responsibility emerges at the lower levels.

But to look at military organization in a more general way, we find it useful to regard the organization as an open sociotechnical system (see Chapters 15 and 16). Let me first introduce the definition of the operation of an organization as seen by Perrow (1967):

Organizations are seen primarily as systems for getting work done, for applying techniques to the problem of altering raw materials – whether the materials be people, symbols or things. This is in contrast to other perspectives which see organizations as, for example, co-operative systems, institutions, or decision-making systems. . . . this perspective treats *technology* as an *independent* variable, and *structure* – the arrangements among people for getting work done – as a dependent variable,

And

By technology is meant the action that an individual performs upon an object, with or without the aid of tools or mechanical devices, in order to make some change in that object. The object or 'raw material' may be a living being, human or otherwise, a symbol of an inanimate object. People are raw materials in people-changing or people-processing organizations; symbols are materials in banks, advertising agencies and some research organizations; the interactions of people are raw materials to be manipulated by administrators in organizations.

In the course of changing this material in an organizational setting, the individual must interact with others. The form that this interaction takes we will call the structure of the organization. It involves the arrangements or relationships that permit the co-ordination and control of work. Some work is actually concerned with changing or maintaining the structure of an organization.

Arising from the fact that any enterprise is an open system, management is concerned with managing both an internal system and an external environment. In peacetime the management of the external environment becomes, for services, both difficult and delicate, exposing the people in these 'boundary roles' to grave suspicion, both from within and without the organization. But the main impact of attention from the managers falls upon the maintenance of, and control of, the internal environment and the attempt to maintain internal equilibrium. For this to be done effectively the technology of control is concerned with the avoidance of exceptional and unprogrammed situations and, traditionally, flexibility of a kind is obtained by acquiring a large number of interchangeable parts, rather than a large variety of programmes. In order to make the 'parts', i.e. the servicemen, interchangeable, they have to be de-individualized; the technology becomes the technology of internal control.

Organizational choice

Does this give the services a choice of organizational structures? As I have said, the maximum control of internal environment is obtained when the parts are de-individualized and interchangeable and the decision-making procedures specified. Such control can be provided by a hierarchical structure of almost arbitrary shape with high role specificity and low task definition, i.e., the powers and responsibilities of each management position are laid down, but the task content is low. This enables a position to be filled by virtually anyone of the appropriate rank. The shape is arbitrary because the number of levels of authority is set by the book of rules for the exercise of authority, rather than by the emergent levels of responsibility deriving from the demands of the technology. Now, if your book of rules allocates certain types of decisions to certain hierarchical levels, it follows that if all these decisions are to be taken – and taken in the specified way – you must provide that number of authority levels, virtually independent of the size of the organization and its other characteristics. So we see that the ranks in, say, the Royal Air Force, are one-to-one transformations from Army ranks and that the Army ranks had remained unchanged since they emerged from their origins through the technological requirements of warfare in the seventeenth and eighteenth centuries. Obviously there would be resistance to changing them, but one wonders how they had been successful in resisting the scrutiny of suspicious-minded establishment review teams.

What influence has all this on flexibility (by 'flexibility' I mean the capacity to cope with a wide range of environmental conditions)? An organization of the kind we have described confers considerable flexibility in the choice of primary task, providing it is of comparable technology. Thus a well-trained Army unit can guard a camp, garrison a town, repair roads (using simple technology), replace striking dock workers (again using simple technology), among other functions, but a change in technology becomes very hard to achieve. As soon as military units approach an operating role exercising a distinctive technology, the inappropriateness of the organizational structures becomes clear. Observation shows that whenever operational tasks become uppermost, the organization behaves much more like the organismic structures of Burns and Stalker (1961), than the mechanistic picture I have just described and 'task forces' of highly unorthodox structures take their place.

Tasks in the organization

Why do we get this dominant organizational pattern? What kind of response is demanded from it? It must be predictable – a superior commander must be able to rely on a subordinate formation's being able to carry out the task he assigns to it in a standard manner. This is important because one unit may be withdrawn and replaced by another for all sorts of reasons and the change should have no adverse effects beyond a mild military hiccough. Not only must the unit's response be predictable, it must be predictable over a wide range of tasks – it must have a multiple capability – in defence, in attack, in occupation, in aid to the civil power, in support to other arms, or supported by other arms. Of course there is a danger that what is predictable to a commander will also be predictable to his opponent. As the art of war consists of avoiding engagements, it may be even more important for your opponent to believe that your unit's performances will be what would be predicted of such units. The more highly technical the unit, the fewer the responses that can be demanded of it, but the insistence that it have a secondary combat role enforces serious organizational requirements.

Difficulties therefore arise as primary tasks become further differentiated, while still having to be combined with a secondary task which carries the distinctive military flavour of the whole. Sadler (1962) described the effects on the military status system:

Changes in the military system of social stratification over the past twenty years have been considerable. In many instances, these changes have become social facts before they have been officially recognized or sanctioned. The role of technological development in producing these changes has been an important one which has exercised its effect in various ways.

First, the increasing complexity of weapons and equipment has necessitated increased recruiting of other ranks of high ability and of good education, who are very much in demand in the civilian labour market. There has been a marked tendency for such people to feel considerable dissatisfaction with the social status traditionally accorded to 'other ranks', and in order to attract them into the Services, adjustments to the status system have been made. These adjustments have been effected mainly in regard to the symbols of status, – pay,

455

uniform, accommodation and the like, and in such measures as ceasing to refer to 'other ranks' because of the low status associations of the term.

Such formal and deliberate adjustments to the status system are, however, insignificant in comparison with adjustments that have occurred informally, spontaneously, or as indirect results of measures aimed at resolving quite different problems.

For example, the increasing differentiation of military roles has disrupted the traditional cohesion and homogeneity of military groups and has resulted in the development of a system of social differences based on occupation, of the kind to be found in civilian society. Whereas previously a soldier's status was determined almost entirely by his rank (and in particular by whether or not he was commissioned) today his status depends very much on what particular job he does – and it is significant that technical roles generally carry high status.

To state that this system of occupational status exists does not, of course, mean that its development has been encouraged or even recognized by military authorities. In many aspects of personnel administration status differences of this kind are ignored and all 'other ranks' treated as one status group. While this may give satisfaction to those exercising low status roles, it obviously gives rise to dissatisfaction among those who feel that their particular skills and abilities warrant differential treatment. Occupational differentiation is, of course, deplored and discouraged by many military commanders, who fear that it will tend to disrupt unit cohesion and will restrict their ability to deploy their men at will.

In the British forces, official recognition of the existence of informal social status differences within the 'other ranks' group, based on occupation, has not been completely withheld. Pay differentials have, of course, been developed to a considerable extent as a means of compensating for low status. More important have been other measures – for example, the introduction, in the Royal Air Force, of a 'technician ladder' parallel with the traditional 'command ladder'. This device enables the technical expert to advance in status irrespective of vacancies in the establishment for command NCOs and irrespective of the technicians' qualities of leadership and command. Unfortunately, this system creates problems in the area of authority at the same time as it eases the status problem.

Furthermore, military units have ceremonial as well as efficient functions, latent as well as manifest functions; they must be capable of inspiring confidence at home as well as terror abroad, and of evoking patriotic pride and sentiment.

All these requirements impose rigorous standardization and although units can be permitted their own special traditions and the display of a certain panache, there are real operational reasons for keeping differences within strict bounds. The need for units to be able to replace one another is matched by the need for individuals and subunits to be able to replace one another; there is always the possibility of sudden decimation or worse. Within units, therefore, roles have to be standardized as do training procedures, which can therefore allow little latitude for individual variations in aptitude.

Again, because units have to be able to work closely alongside one another in mutual support with interlocking command structures, they must be able to have complete confidence in one another. This puts a premium on the sharing of experiences, of knowledge and of values – all most easily born of similarity and interchangeability of training and people.

People in the organization

But organizational structures tell us about people as well as about tasks. If you look at the structure of an organization, you ought to be able to tell both what the organization is for and what sort of people it contains – or to put it in more pretentious terms, on what theory about human nature it is constructed.

The model of military man implied by the structure of military organization is of man as an interchangeable element. But the model does not imply that all men are interchangeable with all others; on the contrary, men are both 'types' and occupy differentially marked strata. There are technical types and flying types, brown jobs and blue ones (of two shades), armoured types and sappers, infantry types and gunners 'A' types and 'Q' types, no interchangeability here. And strata – besides the caste distinction of officers – there are levels of responsibility such that only a few have the capacity to become admirals, generals or air marshals, while many have the capacity to attain the lowest levels of 'field rank'.

The organization structure, then, implies an essentially two-class model of society and a model of man with hierarchically distinguished levels of capacity but essentially interchangeable within each level. There is, however, no necessary correspondence between the model underlying the organization design and the perspectives and experiences of the recruit who may perceive a more complex system of stratification. And although capacity may be channelled in different ways, making you a born sapper or a born gunner, and although there are, of course, temperamental differences between a born guardsman and a born fighter pilot, the fact that each arm requires exactly the same number of different rank levels with their corresponding organizational units and subunits implies strongly that these differences are independent of the most important difference – capacity.

A structure may also imply a model of motivation and of human nature more generally. The military organization structure designed for exercising internal control implies that man needs to be controlled. He will do what he has to do because the consequences of not doing so are unpleasant. The codes of Queen's Regulations and manuals of naval, military and air force law, so inseparably bound up with the shape of the organizational structure, reinforce this model. In Etzioni's terms the 'involvement' of the lower ranks implied by this is 'alienative', as it must truly have been in the days of the press gang or more recently in the days of conscription. The fact that the structure and the laws supporting it needed no change to deal with the advent of conscription or its end again emphasizes the extent to which it is designed to ensure internal control. Among the higher ranks the emphasis in the structure on the exercise of authority and responsibility within precisely defined limits implies a highly bureaucratic form of motivation which in Etzioni's (1961) terms requires at least some degree of 'moral' involvement. In the face of all the dangers of oversimplifying, we may say that the theory of motivation implied by the organization structure is that of alienative man at the lower and moral man at the higher levels.

Of course, the public image must not suggest this too strongly. Ceremonial is designed to express the moral involvement of all and public behaviour must stress self-discipline rather than discipline externally imposed.

Manpower policies

It is time now to turn to the manpower policies of the services because my purpose is to show that the policies adopted to deal with social realities and under the influence of management theories of various kinds are at variance with the organization structure, being based on different models of society, of human nature and resting on different assumptions about motivation.

The objectives of service manpower policy are clear though complex. They must try to combine the filling of present slots, the preparation of people to occupy future slots left vacant by retirement, promotion and attrition or worse, together with preparedness for a variety of contingencies as inexpensively as possible and without recourse to conscription and without the creation of a military caste. This last requirement especially renders military manpower policies permeable to the influence of manpower policies in civilian organizations in particular, and to external social pressures in general.

Under the convenient heading of manpower policies, I want to lump together a wide variety of practices, including:

Models of recruitment
Methods of selection and allocation
Methods of training and trade testing
Methods of evaluation of performance
Methods of promotion, including time promotion, promotion
exams
Methods of demotion ('busting')
Rotation of postings
Retirement policies
Policy for resignation – buying out
Preparation for post-retirement
Systems of payment – the new military salary
Provision of facilities – marriage patches – welfare
Rewards and punishments
Policy about unionization

Recruitment

Recruitment advertising does not say to the prospective entrant, come and be alienated or come and be a good bureaucrat. It never has. But over the post-war years it has undergone considerable change. At different times emphasis has been placed on different inducements – adventure, sport, travel, manliness, comradeship, learning a trade, handling sophisticated equipment, security of employment, a progressive job, responsibility, and even pay. The theme of patriotism has been muted. I doubt if anybody would try to make the case that these shifts have been reflections of the services' changing needs. They are in fact reflections of what the services believe they have to offer which will attract. Because the services are competing in the same labour market with other employers, they cannot allow themselves to be consistently outbidden. But the more they maintain their competitiveness by emphasizing the

459

returns to the individual in pay, prospects, security, the more they encourage an instrumental or calculative involvement in their recruits. I am not disputing that this may be necessary in order to bring them in; I am simply identifying the consequences. Nor are these consequences purely theoretical. When the RAF invited boys to join the RAF and learn a trade, the result was that two-thirds of boy entrants at induction gave as their principal reason for wanting to join – to learn a trade. Fine. But they meant it and the service didn't – or rather, the service had other aims for the boys which they didn't share – general service training and further schooling among them. The consequences were a high wastage rate among boys who had the capacity to acquire the technical skills, which produced a manning shortfall which produced more advertising which . . .

Selection

The systems of selection and allocation have varied from a rigid view of aptitudes and job requirements to an 'anyone can do anything' approach. Obviously, the former was stronger when conscription was relied upon almost exclusively, the latter gained ground when the hunt was on for regulars. And as conscripts were not assumed to have much particular job motivation while volunteers were, the underlying theory had to change from an emphasis on aptitude to one on motivation. Lack of aptitude could be compensated by length of training. Apart from this, training policy made little concession to aptitude; courses are of a given length rather than to a given standard. You can't 'pass out' early because you are a quick learner, though you can take longer if you are backward. Of course this is mostly true of universities as well, with the difference that there it matters what class you get and there is also an argument that you need 3 years' exposure to the civilizing influences of the university's equivalent of the barrack-room. However, the impact is to emphasize the interchangeability of one WP Mech 2 (AR) with another WP Mech 2 (AR) (this trade classification exists, so far as I know, only in my imagination).

Methods of evaluation of performance are highly standardized and bureaucratized. Their principal aim is fairness. As thousands of people are writing reports on their subordinates and having reports written upon them by their superiors, a whole industry exists within the Ministry of Defence to make sure everyone gets a fair deal. The evaluators are evaluated and corrections applied to their scores. The values underlying this are the good old bureaucratic values of universalism, legality, rationality and impersonality. Bureaucracy calls for a nicely balanced mixture of moral and calculative involvement on the part of the bureaucrats, and induces alienative involvement among those in power positions who are more bureau-crated than bureaucrating.

Promotion

Promotion systems are a compromise of meritocratic principles and bureaucratic rewards, the former represented by promotion exami-nations and the latter by time-promotion. Experience alone can carry you over the jump in responsibilities from platoon to company or troop to squadron or battery, but special selection is required for the next big jump. Among the NCO ranks, time and a clear crime sheet can take you a long way. Promotion as a reward for long service and good conduct is either a way of paying you more and giving you greater privileges without demanding a great deal more capacity, or a recognition that experience and not capacity deter-mines the difference between the responses required at different ranks – either of which principles is at odds with the organization structure which in the Army for example allows you to move from second lieutenant to lieutenant without changing your level of responsibility and authority, but gives you time promotion to major *and* requires a change of job level.

Demotion, interestingly enough, is within intermediate ranks hardly ever a consequence of poor performance, although the naval tradition of court-martialling the unfortunate gives another twist! It is far commoner among NCOs than officers, partly because of the palaver involved at commissioned level, and is nearly always the consequence of bad behaviour. This sends yet another message about the meaning of rank and responsibility among NCOs, indicat-ing that moral involvement is expected.

Postings policy

We have already referred to the postings system and the effects of rotation upon organization design. Together with promotion policy postings make up career planning and development. A postings policy which is based on frequent job rotation is hostile to special-ization – indeed where specialization is inevitable, it doesn't work; you can meet officers in middle high ranks in the smaller branches of the RAF, for example, who have twelve years to serve and only two or at most three jobs they can be given. However, a series of jobs

461

with somewhat different responsibilities at the same level is held to be an essential requirement for promotion to the next level and you can time nicely when you have entered the zone for promotion. The thrill of anticipation may turn to serious anxiety before the half-yearly list, which finally carries you to safety or dooms you to celebrating the feast of the passover. However, the system is regarded as fair if not just – justice is not done, but is seen to be done.

This mode of career planning always seems to be less concerned with filling present jobs with the most suitable people than with ensuring the right age distribution among ranks – avoiding bottle-necks and vacua, and with the future occupation of jobs higher up the pyramid. It emphasizes calculative and even alienative rather than moral values of commitment to the present job.

Retirement

Retirement policy and policies for post retirement which end most service careers at relatively early ages, with pensions which make further careers highly desirable if not essential, oblige the services to emphasize the relevance of service experience to civilian occupations. Some of the recent stressing of officers as managers derives from this; if civilian firms are to employ ex-service officers as managers, they must be persuaded that managing is what officers do. And while it is difficult to persuade employers outside the ranks of Securicor and the angry brigade that experience with personal fire-arms is relevant to their trade, the mass of soldiers and airmen, even of matelots, acquire saleable technical skills many of which trade unions, though banned from organizing in the services, have been brought to recognize. These manpower policies pull on the side of calculative involvement as do developments in military concepts of pay.

Pay

The King's Shilling could have been the deciding factor in entering military service for very few. In the compensation package of those days, what we now call fringe benefits were of far greater value than the cash remuneration, which was virtually pocket money. Housing, rations, 'all found', wife's and dependants' allowances all served to make the soldier a dependent being encouraging now moral, now alienative involvement, but surely seldom a calculative one. You weren't in it for the money though you might be here for the beer. Progressively this has changed until, with the concept of the military salary, a calculative involvement is stressed simultaneously with an equation of military and civilian employments as alternative outlets for the same motives.

The logical extension of this development would be to encourage the serviceman to seek his sport, his entertainment and his welfare from the community in which he lives. That however is a quaint heresy. A 'good' camp or station or ship with a 'good spirit' is one where the serviceman stays aboard willingly; the general exodus at weekends is lamented, and steps are taken to tempt them to stay where they cannot be coerced. Going away at weekends, off camp in the evenings, etc. are symptoms of a calculative involvement which is to be discouraged; participation in station sports or camp theatre is evidence of moral involvement and is to be welcomed.

Reward and punishment

Rewards – gongs and 'mentions', commendations and the like – are clearly normative, emphasizing moral commitment; punishments are coercive and emphasize alienative commitment.

Finally, the policy of non-unionization is compatible with a demand for moral or for alienative commitment but is incompatible with a calculative one.

We can summarize the relationship of manpower policy to values in the following way:

Policy	Value expressed	Value denied
Recruitment	Calculative	Moral
Selection and allocation	Bureaucratic	
Training and testing	Bureaucratic	
Promotion	Bureaucratic confused	
Demotion	Moral	
Postings policy	Calculative, alienative	Moral
Retirement ⎫ Post-retirement ⎭	Calculative	
Resignation, buying out	Alienative	
Payment	Calculative	
Facilities	Moral	
Rewards	Moral	
Punishments	Alienative	
Unionization	Moral, alienative	Calculative

463

The management ethos

A joint outcome of the general-purpose organization structure and the postings policy, which is highly congruent with it, is the susceptibility of military organization to modern management techniques. The only thing that looks common to all the posts at the same level which an officer may hold in succession is 'management'. Officers are 'managers' and like managers need 'management services' to make up for the fact that they have no specialist managerial skills, though they may have specialist technical skills. So we have management information systems, systems analysis, work study, OR, OD, management accounting, MBO, PPBS. They all owe their development to the dominant model of civilian organization; and they all centralize information, power and control. At the same time, military action requires more and more decentralization.

The impact of all these techniques tends to be a proliferation of specialist departments at high but not at intermediate or low levels of command. The tasks of grappling with complex and changing social, economic and technological environments are located centrally at high levels; the learning that takes place at the bottom, where soldiers and airmen are in daily contact with civilians, is left as isolated individual experiences; the organization as a whole is equipped to learn only at the top. The gap between the response of the organization and his own experience is mystifying and alienating for the individual.

So what we see is a mixture of motives: alienative behaviour with regard to ceremonial; calculative behaviour with regard to military postings; and bureaucratic behaviour with regard to promotion. These inconsistencies and contradictions are encouraged by the system, in that manpower policies appear to be adopted without examination of the social and psychological theories or models they embody, without indeed recognition that they do embody theories. If more attention were given to this, less frequent changes, of course, might occur with less confusion and mystery.

464

Chapter 27
Task and Organization

This chapter reports on a study undertaken within Training Command of the RAF, where it was hoped to follow up some of the ideas expressed in the previous chapter on applying a task analysis approach to the design of a service organization. Training Command was chosen because training is one of the activities which are performed both by civilian organizations and military ones, and in both cases in special purpose institutions. Training, furthermore, is one of the activities for which the military developed a specialized organization in advance of similar civilian models. Although we did not set out to draw specific comparisons between service and civilian organizational frameworks for training, the differences, as well as the similarities, were in our minds.

Despite greater use of modern management theory and practice, the military training establishments adhere more closely to traditional military patterns of organization structure than do their civilian counterparts. We advanced the hypothesis in the previous chapter that the secondary task of internal control was a dominating factor in the organizational design of military establishments and that this was one reason why military units, seeing vastly different functions, nevertheless possessed strikingly similar structures.

The function of internal control is of major importance, both because of the necessity for instant preparedness and because of the 'total' nature of military institutions. The latter is, of course, partly a consequence of the former. Military values emphasize separateness from civilians because local community ties would hinder mobility and readiness for action. The inculcation of distinct military values means that the military unit itself must serve as its own community;

i.e. as a 'total' institution. Because of the less obvious nature of the organizational requirements deriving from the total nature of the institution as compared with those imposed by the primary task these are in danger of being squeezed by attempts to apply to them techniques of cost effectiveness.

One further attraction of the training establishment as the focus for this study is just that it comes into Perrow's category of 'people-processing' organizations (as discussed in the previous chapter). The ambiguities both of Perrow's approach and of other task analysis approaches are emphasized when the 'raw material' is people and when the basic unit of raw material is sometimes the individual, sometimes the group.

In consultation with the service we selected for our field sites (the fieldwork upon which much of this section is based, was carried out by my colleague, Mr Stephen Parrott, whose help we gratefully acknowledge) three RAF training stations, one concerned with recruit training, one with trade training, one with flying training. The basis for this selection was as follows. First, these three functions represent as wide a range of tasks as could be found in training. Second, the stations selected were, as far as possible, typical, but uncomplicated examples; i.e. they did not house other activities. The organization of all three was basically similar, the differences being small compared with the differences in tasks. And this, of course, is the nub. We were interested to see why this was so and what were the consequences.

In our research we were able to test for ourselves the value both of the approach derived from task analysis and of the concept of sentient group boundaries (Miller and Rice, 1967). It is, of course, true that the value of an approach depends upon the objectives of the study. And in this particular study we had multiple objectives. First we aimed at understanding, explaining to ourselves, the behaviour of men under training and the people responsible for their training in the RAF. Here our perspective was limited by an interest in organization; we were more likely to be interested in, to observe and to draw conclusions from people's behaviour in relation to the service's objectives than their behaviour in relation to private objectives of their own, unless these were in direct conflict. Our second aim was description, the development of concepts (and the language in which to express these concepts), which would enable us to generalize from the behaviour we observed. Here again our perspective was limited by our concern that these concepts should enable us to generalize in a way that would be recognized by people whose aims were the official service objectives. Our third aim was communication – communication of our description to the service. Once again our perspective was limited by our understanding that the service's interest would be in prescription, however much we insisted that prescription was not our purpose. We expressed our own intentions as to develop with the service a language which would enable us to express our descriptive concepts in terms which could be handled in their action frame of reference.

Two consequences flow from these terms of reference. First, for our own understanding we would tend to use a grounded theory approach, but one in which sociological rather than psychological categories would predominate. Second, for description we would isolate categories on which we could compare and contrast the field situations we had chosen to observe. Third, for communication we would enter the frame of reference of the service training organization and evaluate the behaviour we observed and described in terms of official goals.

It seemed to us that the insights derived from task analysis were of greatest value in relation to communication, while those derived from the consideration of sentient group boundaries were of most use in relation to description. Neither helped us to any great extent in understanding.

The field sites

1 Recruit training station

Our first field site was a recruit training station. This station is the basic organization concerned with 'people processing', the process by which the civilian becomes an airman. During his six weeks' training, the recruit receives an induction into service life and procedures and a basic military training: in the modern service this is viewed as essential but still only a very small part of the journey towards a man being fully trained. Recruit training with its associations of drill and 'bull' is the traditional form of military training from the viewpoint of a wider public and is usually carried out against the potentially traumatic break from civilian life, home, family and 'outside' values. The station is organized to 'process' efficiently the throughput of recruits. Its organizational chart shows an adaptation of basic RAF pattern with a straightforward 'two-prong' system of two wings, a training wing and an administrative wing. Within the two squadrons of training wing, the basic training unit is the flight, comprising flight commander (flying officer/flight lieutenant), a senior NCO, and two junior NCOs – each flight being responsible for up to sixty-five recruits during the period of training.

The behaviour of recruits at their training school can be described in terms of their adaptation to the formal demands of the organization and is largely evaluated in such terms. It is, however, unlikely that this description would have meaning for the recruit as an account of his experience. For him recruit training is a *rite de passage*, a transition from one status to another. His new status as fully-fledged airman is given him by the service, but its personal validity is warranted by his peer's acceptance of him in that status. His experience is better described as a continuous re-evaluation of self and identity in response to his ability to meet the expectations of his fellow recruits. The NCO, the principal immediate representative of organizational demands, is experienced more as the vehicle for the constraints within which this experience has to be played out than as the role model for the recruit, or we can say that the sentient group for the recruit excludes the NCO; but the task group sometimes includes him, as when the squad and NCO are together on trial on parade. We observe that the variances the squad generates are of three kinds – intra-individual, inter-individual and intergroup – and that only the last is within the control of the NCO. The first requires self-control, the second controls generated within the group itself. The organizational response to this is to provide some sort of informal authority figure, a senior recruit without formal power but hopefully with charismatic influence. This appointment is one which is liable to create considerable misunderstanding. He is appointed, not elected, yet the sanctions he has at his command are informal rather than formal. He is therefore an appointed leader expected to behave as would an emergent one.

When we talk of 'exceptions' as in Perrow's use of this term (see Chapter 13), we imply that there is a norm to which exceptions occur, that this norm is defined by the person controlling that particular situation and that this norm is shared by others in similar controlling situations. But when we substitute the concept of 'variance' as used by Emery (1959) we have less obvious rules for deciding what aspects or elements are to be taken as variable. As Perrow and Emery use these terms, exceptions appear to have objective status, whereas the concept of variance implies an experiential element. Thus what is experienced as varying will depend upon where the control is located. As it is also used to indicate the most appropriate location for such control, there is an inherent circularity which does not, of course, necessarily invalidate but does complicate its usage. The problem is most acute in the context of 'people-processing'. Here, as we go on to show, the control may be placed at several levels. When located as low in the hierarchy as possible, i.e., at the level of the *individual under train-*

ing, what is experienced as variance may differ profoundly from the overt differences among individual behaviours which would constitute variance for the superior officer or which would throw up 'exceptions' for him.

There are some variances relevant to task performance, whose very nature differs from one individual to another. It is true that from the organization's point of view the task to be performed can be specified without consideration of the special characteristics of the individual, but the meaning of these tasks differ for different individuals and their salience for the individual's own goals differ too. The significance of this in the service situation is that the recruit is the raw material as well as the operator. The traditional choice of 'technology' is based on assumptions about the nature of the 'raw material'. The assumptions that are made then determine both the nature of the control to be applied and the interpretation of the response of the individual – the raw material. Because the task and the technology are defined in this way, in attempting to understand the world of the recruit, formal organizational categories, task analysis, are barely relevant. For descriptive purposes the concept of sentient boundaries takes on value. The recruit is a member of one smaller and one larger sentient group: the barrack room and the flight. The principal group tasks are based likewise on these units. The boundaries here are clearly drawn in the right place. At a higher level of organization, however, questions do arise. The change in legal status of the recruit occurs at attestation, i.e. before he enters the recruit training station. The change in his perceived status takes place on graduation from recruit training. The service's organization design links recruit training with subsequent trade training, allocating recruiting and attestation to a separate organization. This means that there is a contrived contradiction between the perceptions of the staff and those of the recruit or trainee. Does this matter? It may mean that certain objectives are harder to achieve than they might be. But on the whole it is doubtful whether the contradiction is a significant hindrance to services' immediate goals of socializing the recruit. For the recruit the experience of self-development may be less satisfactory but both his short- and long-term performance is unlikely to be significantly affected.

The simple skills and behaviours that are taught at recruit school, all within the compass of virtually all recruits, together with the acquisition by the recruit of certain habits of punctuality, turn-out, and so on, lend themselves to face-to-face leadership and control without the mediation of machine or specialism. The line system of command is perfectly suited to this purpose. Furthermore, the interchangeability of one squad, section or flight of recruits with another presents no difficulty for the system of postings, which moves officers and NCOs in and out of the organization. A station whose concern is solely recruit training performs what we should describe as a 'pure' task.

2 Technical training station

Having considered the initial 'socialization process', our next choice of site was a station where the airman's technical training begins for trades in the field of ground radar and ground communications. The organizational picture is complicated. Like a large technical college, the station copes with a range of students at different stages in technical training. As well as recent recruits, apprentices receive training in a combined recruit and trade training course. The station also provides 'further education', i.e. for airmen improving their skill and knowledge within a trade group, and also 'conversion' and 'assimilation' training to allow for changing demands within the trade structure.

The organization is somewhat more complex than that of the recruit training station: a basic studies wing, a trade training wing and an apprentice wing take the place of the single training wing of the recruit station. A senior wing commander has the role of senior training officer, providing an intermediary level of authority between the group captain (station commander or commandant and the other wing commanders). The senior training officer controls a wide range of training activity, from general education in basic studies wing through to very specific instruction on equipment and techniques in trade training wing. Within the training function are two basic types of trainers: the first we might describe as the 'professional educators' and the second, technically trained personnel involved in the instructional function. However, within the second category will be a number of officers with training experience within their particular field. Also, there exists a tradition of engineer officers returning to the station on an instructional tour of duty.

Unlike other trainees, apprentices have a mixed course, i.e. it involves the military socialization process as well as technical training. In their case responsibility is split between the basic studies and training wings and the trainers within apprentice wing who are responsible for the apprentice as a person, and for his general and basic military training. Another feature of this 'mixed' training programme for apprentices is the separation in all general respects of apprentices from airmen, though in practice they may be similar

470

in age if not status. For them the service has responsibilities different from those applying to airmen.

In technical, trade training the station's task is immeasurably more complex. Not only are there many trades, many levels of training, many equipments on which men have to be trained, but the differences among the capacities of different trainees is highly important. Competence is less easily acquired than in recruit training; few fail the latter, containing wastage in the former is a continuous problem and effort. The 'task' of the station and of its subunits can be expressed in terms of numbers of men to be trained in various skills. For convenience men must be assigned to classes but the class as such cannot be said to have a task. The class members are only to a very small extent dependent upon each other's performance for the success of their own. But the shared experience, the shared work situation and stress makes the class a sentient group. In so far as this results in the stronger helping the weaker, in equitable sharing of facilities, task performance is thereby aided. But treating the class as if it were a task group obscures certain realities of the task. The individual trainee, the equipment he is trying to master, and his instructor constitute the immediate task group. The variances set by the differential capacities of individuals can only be partially controlled by the instructor in the class situation. He can control the pace of instruction and allocate his time and that of the equipment to fit the capacities of the broad middle section of his class. The price of this is that few proceed at their ideal pace; almost automatically some are irretrievably behind the rest and a few fail. The ideal of self-paced instruction, whereby the control of variance is delegated to the individual himself, is consonant with an organization structure and style in which the instructor is a resource to, not commander of, the trainee.

One can very quickly become engulfed in complexities here; there are many different kinds of training at different career levels, all conducted within one technical training station. Some courses are provided at advanced level for NCOs and men senior enough to live off the station while under training if their homes are near. At the other extreme are wings for apprentices who are receiving their basic service training and undergoing socialization as well as trade training. Because of the apprentices' prestige their socialization is of an elite character; the apprentice is taught to regard his future as a cut above that of the adult airman trainee. Apprentices are organized primarily into flights based on their 'domestic' wing organization. The wing is divided into squadrons, each containing elements of each 'entry' and each trade. Squadrons, in turn, are divided into flights. Traditionally the sentient group is the 'entry'. But the entry has no organizational counterpart. Its existence is recognized by its number so that an apprentice will be identified as of no. 'X' entry and by its graduation as an entry. For all other activities, however, it is divided among flights and squadrons in which it is mixed with other entries. Educational instruction classes will be made up of members of the same entry who are learning the same trade; but trade is not the basis of the flight and squadron structure. Sentient and task boundaries do not coincide for apprentices and this is recognized by everybody concerned with apprentice training.

The elite aspect of the apprentice training demands a different structure of organization from that required by their technical training. Special esprit needs to be fostered. Identification of the apprentice with an appropriate role model is also needed, and the senior technical NCO, preferably ex-apprentice who would symbolize the apprentice's future role, would ideally provide this. But an organizational design which made this possible, i.e. one in which the apprentice's immediate commander for all purposes was a senior technical man in his own trade, is one which conflicts with the service's solution of segregating service and technical training. It would also make combining the technical training of apprentices and airmen on the same station extremely difficult, the alternative being a costly duplication of expensive equipment. The nature, too, of such a relationship of apprentice with role model combines with difficulty with postings policy. A rapid cycle of postings conflicts both with the establishment of organizational subunits according to a special design and with the establishment of close ties of sentiment between a group and its commander.

The task of a technical trade training station is mixed in more than one sense. First, it has several groups of trainees which differ substantially from one another. Second, the goals of training also differ and in the case of the apprentice an elite socialization has to be combined with trade training. The more mixed the task in this way, the more the station organization tends towards the exercise of management functions – managing the facilities with the main training tasks delegated to separate subunits – units which do not differ from one another. Yet a design ideally suited to providing familiarization with advanced technical equipment is very different from that tailored to elite socialization. Further, the location of the managerial and caretaker functions at the highest, most prestigious level endows them with an undesired priority over the separate training functions. Here, again, our understanding of the experience of apprentice and adult trainee, which alerts us to the points of strain in the system, is derived from fieldwork far removed from consideration of variances. For purposes of description the sentient group analysis evokes immediate recognition by the service; the task analysis of variances enables the organizational design problems to be communicated.

3 *Flying training station*

The third station selected was a station where the straight flying training task is performed. The training organization here is an epitome of basic RAF organization. In terms of its organizational chart, the station shows the three-prong organizational structure with the flying wing of the operational station replaced here by the flying training wing. Flying stations tend to be geographically isolated and to have a day and night commitment in terms of flying training, and of 24-hour Master Diversion Airfield facilities at all times. This necessitates the provision of amenities for officers (instructors and trainees) and airmen.

The flying training school in RAF Training Command has on the face of it a pure task. In the main, one homogeneous population undergoes training as pilots. In fact, flying training is also part of the officer-training process; the student is being evaluated all the time in terms of personal and officer qualities, as well as on his ability to fly an aircraft. Thus flying training is not simply the inculcation of a technical skill. We shall see, however, why this does not raise the same complications as in the case of apprentice training.

The experience of the trainee is one which approximates most closely to the popular stereotype of service life in the RAF. It includes the constant sight and sound of aircraft, the presence of instructors and students in flying gear, and the camaraderie of the crew room and the mess with its distinctive language and technology. The dangerous aspect of flying is a constant theme in the background and conduces to the students seeking support from one another, their instructors and commanders, who are all flying men. This supportive community has its intense side, and the student experiences strain from the constant surveillance under which he feels placed as part of his training as an officer. He is able, however, to identify with his instructor who represents for him a true role model – flyer and officer and with whom he shares a series of potentially dangerous experiences whose successful outcome depends on their mutual trust. Against them both, and against the organization as a whole, is a constant enemy, the weather, whose vagaries call for periods of maximum effort and stretching of resources. The shared experience of a successful all-out effort to

473

make good time lost through adverse weather conditions is expressed in a state of high morale in which mutual respect permits, without danger to discipline, a relaxation of normal rules and constraints.

We can abstract from this lightly sketched picture an analysis of the sentient groupings. The members of one entry or intake share the same battle with the weather, the same dangers and hazards, are under surveillance together. In their officer training exercises they are allocated from time to time group tasks, but for the most part the task interdependencies are low. From the point of view of the instructors, each has a handful of pupils for whom he is responsible and the task group is always the pair, instructor–pupil. In the battle with the weather and with the aircraft state of readiness he is allied with other instructors, technical staff, his squadron commander, and so on. His principal sentient group is the group of instructors in his flight and squadron, responsible jointly for taking an intake through training. Less salient is the group which includes the technical and support staff responsible for the state of readiness of the aircraft and equipment with which the task must be performed. In all these cases the sentient group and task group coincide reasonably well. For example, for the student pilot the peer group is in a sense a task group where the task is mutual support under conditions of stress. But we are all the time conscious of the many nuances with which we are using terms like task, task group, sentient group. A constant difficulty is introduced by the dual role of participant and raw material for processing, which we have to attribute to our trainees, students, recruits.

In considering this analysis we see that the variances among individual students and the exigencies of flying together promote the need for a close student–instructor relationship, in which the student is teamed with one instructor. The requirements of elite socialization equally argue for a close association of student with role model. Thus, in this case, the components of the task mix have the same implications for organizational design.

Implications for organizational design

One special characteristic of the service situation which has a bearing on organizational design is the postings cycle. In civilian industry organization structures are not only frameworks representing communication, reporting, task allocation, but they are also career ladders. But it is in the military and in the Civil Service that we are confronted most acutely with the implications of careers for organization design. In the first place the regular and frequent posting of officers means that there are few jobs of the kind which have edges of responsibility blurred by the comfortable chafing of the incumbent in the chair, the jobs which are 'made' by an individual and are unlikely to be filled in the same way again. Second, as roles must be learned quickly, positions at the same rank level cannot differ more widely than the differences in the tasks make inevitable. The incoming officer must be able to learn his way about the structure without difficulty. Third, the equation of position with rank provides a further constraint. All three constraints exert pressure to make all service structures look alike.

What might be the most effective organization design for the particular tasks a station is performing may cut across these other important considerations. Again, there is always a secondary role which service units must be prepared to perform – its emergency role, aid to the civil power. Too task-specific an organization structure could be a hindrance here. And yet again each station has the functions of providing a military presence, of maintaining the military and civilian boundary. Finally, and perhaps most important of all, the station's organization has to cater for the whole-life needs of the airman. A whole underground of secondary tasks have to be performable within the structure adopted for the primary tasks. Activities which a civilian discharges in his own time must be programmed into service time; the organization takes the strain which falls on the individual civilian. This is not to say that approaches to organizational analysis and design appropriate to civilian organizations cannot be appropriate to military units, it is to say that factors which can safely be ignored in the one situation must be taken into account in the other.

In the course of our study we were impressed time and time again by the mixed nature of the task that stations are required to perform. Tasks which look homogeneous from an administrative point of view – e.g. a single source of intake of standard size and duration may contain mixtures which have conflicting requirements for organizational design. Woodward (1965) showed the consequences for industrial organizations of the attempts to combine different technologies within one unit. There is not necessarily an easy solution to problems of this kind. One avoidable danger, however, is that they may not be recognized. RAF training establishments require developed airfields and their associated buildings as well as the other buildings needed to house training and administrative staff and their families, trainees and complex equipment. They are thus relatively permanent compared with changes in the training task brought about by changes in equipment and manning requirements which are, in turn, dependent upon changes in defence policy or changes in the role of the RAF dictated by developments in the technology of warfare. The service has always to be prepared to redeploy existing training or accommodate new training requirements and this implies that mixed tasks are likely to increase rather than decrease. Under these circumstances there is a need for knowledge of which kinds of training are organizationally compatible and which less so. Faced with accommodating a mix of tasks the services sometimes resort to the 'lodger unit' device. This is effective in protecting the special task of the lodger. As the number of such units grows new danger appears. The task of the dependent station organization becomes that of administration and the presentation of internal order. These essentially secondary tasks now have greater weight in terms of rank and authority and the administrator's tail begins to wag the functional dog.

Increasing specialization has as its aim the induction of mixed to pure tasks. But the costs of specialization are, as we know, loss of flexibility. In turbulent environments more and more civilian organizations seek the flexibility that comes from diversification. They, too, are faced with the organization consequences of task mixes. This would justify a good deal more study than it has hitherto received.

Conclusion

In our study of the problems of applying a task analysis approach to the design of service organization we found ourselves confronting from a different standpoint some of the issues which Rice and his colleagues (Miller and Rice, 1967; Rice, 1970) had been facing during his latter years. The task analysis approach which owed its origins to the study of manufacturing and extracting industries has acquired a great deal of sophistication as its practitioners have tackled other organizations, commercial, service and educational. The concept of the sentient group became more prominent in these latter organizations when their boundaries could not be made to coincide with task boundaries and had to be organized differentially. We have seen the kind of problem this raises for apprentice training. And Miller and Rice described the problems this raised for airline organizations: 'An effective sentient system relates the members of an enterprise to each other and to the enterprise in ways that are relevant to the skills and experience required for task performance.' The sentient groups of airline pilots and aircraft apprentices relate them together all right, but *against* rather than *to* the enterprise. The problems set by the need to relate organization to task *and* to sentient groups increase as we move away from production organizations. Does this *reduce* the relevance of task analysis?

Let us look at Rice's study of university government. 'A central concept used in the analysis is that of the *primary task*. . . . universities are multiple-task institutions; and each task, though interdependent with other tasks, requires its own characteristic organization which differs from the organization required for other tasks and for the whole.' What then? Rice analyses separately the main functions of the university and traces out the appropriate 'operating systems' for each. Thus he describes a model 'first-order managing system' for undergraduate education. This has to contain 'task-oriented sentient groups for both faculty and students'. 'Each member of the faculty and each student should have more than one role, and more than one route, through which he can make his voice heard.' Rice admits that all this could result in 'a Babel of "voices" ', but looks to mechanisms for simplifying procedures for making views known. When to all this is added managing systems for postgraduate education, professional training and for research, the result is formidable. A 'model' organization which accommodates task groups and sentient groups but whose probable result would be that hard decisions about priorities would be even less easy to make than they are now.

So we are thrown back on a dual organization which exemplifies the point that each task requires its own characteristic organization, which differs from that required for other tasks. In plain facts, the tasks of internal control and of cultural transmission require one kind of organization which differs from that required, say, for the acquisition of technical and administrative skills.

In a word, the task analysis approach emphasizes the linkage task → role and the subsequent building of organization structure to relate these roles in an integrative fashion. Different analysts, the sociotechnical school of Rice, Trist, Emery, Miller *et al.*; Perrow, Woodward; have grounded their systems on different aspects or dimensions of task and technology and each has contributed valuable perspectives. Each, as we have found, has something to offer to the description and communication of organizational problems to managements. The concept of sentient group has added another dimension, allowing us to explore the relevance of the shared values of professional and skill groups and their divergence from those of other groups within the enterprise. But this again does more to describe the differences which have to be organized for than the qualities they represent. When the business to be organized is as mixed as the preservation of internal order (as an overriding goal) combined with the transmission of values and a culture, as well as technical skills, the weaknesses of these approaches become apparent. Again Rice was thinking along these lines: '. . . the [supervisory] system will not achieve an integrative function merely by putting it into the organizational model. It will work effectively only . . . if the culture of the school is congruent with the definition and method of performance of its primary task'; and, 'Each specific task requires specific skills, an appropriate organization, and a congruent culture.' The concept of culture which belongs to a different domain of discourse from task, technology and sentient groups can become the joker in the pack.

An organization whose overriding value is that of internal control has to hold to a minimum transaction across the system's boundaries. Modernization of weapon systems and their associated skills requires constant and increasing transactions across the boundaries or the continuous enlargement of the system. The more that transactions across the system boundary grow in number and in salience for the organization's goals and the more that these transactions consist of intake and output of people, the more permeable becomes the organization to the society to which it belongs. What goes on inside the organization can less and less be described in terms of the organization's own characteristics. The more the description of the organization is couched in terms and concepts which would offer prescriptive advice to management, the more it leaves out. The more the study of organizational behaviour becomes another of the management sciences, the less valuable it will become to management. But if it is to be a social science, then social scientists, especially sociologists, will have to make it so.

Bibliography

Alatas, S. H. (1972), 'The Captive Mind in Development Studies', *International Social Science Journal*, vol. 24, no. 1.

Apter, D. E. and Mushi, S. S. (1972), 'Contribution of Political Science to Development', *International Social Science Journal*, vol. 24, no. 1.

Ardrey, R. (1961), *African Genesis*, Allen & Unwin, London.

Ardrey, R. (1966), *The Territorial Imperative*, Allen & Unwin, London.

Arensberg, C. M. and Niehoff, A. (1966), *Introducing Social Changes*, Aldine, Chicago.

Aristotle (1969), *Politics*, Penguin edn, Harmondsworth, trans. T. A. Sinclair.

Aronoff, J. (1967), *Psychological Needs and Cultural Systems: A Case Study*, Van Nostrand, London and New York.

Atkinson, John W. and Feather, Norman T. (eds) (1966), *A Theory of Achievement Motivation*, Wiley, New York.

Bacon, Francis (1938), *The Advancement of Learning and The New Atlantis*, Oxford University Press, London.

Bailey, F. G. (1966), 'The Peasant's View of the Bad Life', *The Advancement of Science*, December.

Balandier, G. (1972), 'Contribution of Sociology to Development', *International Social Science Journal*, vol. 24, no. 1.

Bauer, R. A. (ed.) (1966), *Social Indicators*, MIT Press, Cambridge.

Baum, R. (1975), 'Technology, Economic Organization and Social Change: Maoism and the Chinese Industrial Revolution' in Otto Harrassowitz, *China in the Seventies*, Wiesbaden.

Belshaw, C. S. (1972), 'Contribution of Anthropology to Development', *International Social Science Journal*, vol. 24, no. 1.

Ben David, J. (1971), *The Scientist's Role in Society*, Prentice-Hall, Englewood Cliffs, N.J.

Bennis, W., Benne, K. D. and Chin, R. (1961), *The Planning of Change*, Holt, Rinehart & Winston, New York.

479

Berelson, B. (1969), 'Beyond Family Planning', *Science*, vol. 163, February.

Berelson, B. (1971), in J. P. Holdren and Paul R. Erlich (eds), *Global Ecology*, Harcourt Brace, New York.

Bernstein, B. (1970a), 'Elaborated and Restricted Codes: Their Social Origins and Some Consequences' in K. Danziger, *Readings in Child Socialization*, Pergamon, Oxford.

Bernstein, B. (1970b), 'A Critique of the Concepts of Compensatory Education' in Rubenstein and Stoneman (eds), *Education and Democracy*, Penguin, Harmondsworth.

Bott, E. (1957), *Family and Social Network*, Tavistock, London.

British Academy (1961), *Research in the Humanities and Social Sciences*, Oxford University Press, London.

Buckley, W. (1967), *Sociology and Modern Systems Theory*, Prentice-Hall, Englewood Cliffs, N.J.

Burns, T. and Stalker, G. (1961), *The Management of Innovation*, Tavistock, London.

Cairncross, A. (1969–70), 'The Managed Economy', *The Advancement of Science*, no. 26, pp. 64–74.

Carter, C. F. and Williams, B. R. (1967), *Industry and Technical Progress*, Oxford University Press, London.

Castles, S. and Kosack, G. (1973), *Immigrant Workers and Class Structure in Western Europe*, Oxford University Press, London.

Chomsky, L. (1972), *Language and Mind*, enlarged edn, Harcourt Brace, New York.

Churchman, C. W. and Emery, F. E. (1966), in J. R. Lawrence (ed.), *Operational Research and the Social Sciences*, Tavistock, London.

Cipolla, C. (1962), *The Economic History of World Population*, Penguin, Harmondsworth.

Clapham Committee Report (1946), *Provision for Social and Economic Research*, Cmnd 6868, HMSO, London.

Clark, P. A. (1972), *Action Research and Organization Theory*, Harper & Row, New York.

Cole, *et al.* (1973), *Thinking about the Future*, Chatto & Windus, London.

Crawford, E. and Perry, N. (1976), *Demands for Social Knowledge*, Sage Publications, London and Beverly Hills.

Crozier, M. (1964), *The Bureaucratic Phenomenon*, Tavistock, London.

Darlington, C. D. (1969), *The Evaluation of Man and Society*, Allen & Unwin, London.

Dennis, N. *et al.* (1956), *Coal is Our Life*, Tavistock, London.

Douglas, J. (1964), *The Home and the School*, MacGibbon & Kee, London.

Dror, Y. (1969), 'Accelerated Development and Policy Making Improvement', *Civilizations*, vol. 19, no. 2, pp. 209–15.

Dror, Y. (1972), 'Social Science Meta Policy: Some Concepts and Applications' in Cherns, Sinclair, Jenkins (eds), *Social Science and Government*, Tavistock, London.

Durkheim, E. (1960), *The Division of Labour in Society*, Free Press, Chicago.

Eisenstadt, S. N. (1954), *Absorption of Immigrants*, Routledge & Kegan Paul, London.

Eisenstadt, S. N. (1967), *Israeli Society*, Weidenfeld & Nicolson, London.

Eisenstadt, S. N. (1973), *Tradition, Change and Modernity*, Wiley, New York.

Emery, F. E. (1959), *Characteristics of Sociotechnical Systems*, Tavistock Institute Paper TIHR 527, London.

Emery, F. E. (1968) in M. Young (ed.), *Forecasting and the Social Sciences*, Heinemann, London.

Emery, F. E. and Trist, E. L. (1972), *Towards a Social Ecology*, Plenum Press, London.

Emery, F. E. *et al.* (1973), *The Futures We're In*, Australian National University, Canberra.

Engelstad, P. H. (1972), 'Sociotechnical Approach to Problems of Process Control' in L. E. Davis and J. C. Taylor, *Design of Jobs*, Penguin, Harmondsworth, pp. 328–56.

Etzioni, A. (1961), *A Comparative Analysis of Complex Organizations*, Free Press, New York.

Fairweather, G. (1976), *Methods of Experimental Social Innovation*, Wiley, New York.

Faunce, W. and Dubin, R. (1975), 'Individual Investment in Working and Living' in L. E. Davis and A. B. Cherns (eds), *The Quality of Working Life: Problems, Prospects and the State of the Art*, vol. 1, The Free Press, New York.

Finer, S. E. (1962), *The Man on Horseback*, Pall Mall, London.

Ford, J. (1969), *Social Class and the Comprehensive School*, Routledge & Kegan Paul, London.

Freeman, C. *et al.* (1971), 'The Goals of R and D in the 1970s', *Science Studies*, vol. 1, pp. 355–456.

Fromm, E. (1947), *Man for Himself*, Holt, Rinehart & Winston, New York, p. 88.

Fulton Committee (1963), *Report of the Committee on Higher Education*, Cmnd 2154, HMSO, London.

Furtado, C. (1964), *Development and Underdevelopment*, University of California Press, Berkeley.

Gesell, A. and Amatruda, G. (1946), *The Embryology of Behaviour*, Hamish Hamilton, London.

Gluckman, M. (ed.) (1964), *Used Systems and Open Minds*, Oliver & Boyd, Edinburgh.

Goethe, J. (1959), *Faust Part Two*, p. 269 (Frankelin), trans. Philip Wayne, Penguin, Harmondsworth.

Goffman, E. (1961), *Asylums*, Anchor-Doubleday, New York.

Goldthorpe, J. (1960), 'The Treatment of Conflict in Human Relations Training: A Case Study from the British Coal Mining Industry', Leicester University Mimeo.

Goldthorpe, J. H. (1971), 'Theories of Industrial Society', *Archives Européenes de Sociologie*, vol. 12.

481

Goldthorpe, J. H. *et al.* (1968), *The Affluent Worker: Industrial Attitudes and Behaviour*, Cambridge University Press.

Gould, P. R. (1970), 'Tanzania 1920–63: The Spatial Impress of the Modernization Process', *World Politics*, vol. XXVII, no. 2, January.

Gross, B. (1971), 'Strategy for Economic and Social Development', *Policy Sciences*, vol. 2, no. 4, December.

Haldane Committee (1917), *Machinery of Government*, Cmd 9230, HMSO, London.

Harris, H. (1949), *The Group Approach to Leadership Testing*, Routledge & Kegan Paul, London.

Hauser, P. M. (1967) in M. Leeds (ed.), *Washington Colloquium on Science and Society*, Mono Book Corporation, Baltimore.

Herbst, P. G. (1974), *Sociotechnical Design*, Tavistock, London.

Hetman, F. (1973), *Society and Assessment of Technology*, OECD, Paris.

Heyworth Report (1965), *Report of the Committee on Social Studies*, Cmnd 2660, HMSO, London.

Hill, P. (1971), *Towards a New Philosophy of Management*, Tavistock, London.

Hirschman, A. O. and Lindblom, C. E. (1962), 'Economic Development, Research and Development, Policy Making: Some Converging Views', *Behavioural Science*, vol. 7, pp. 211–22.

HMSO (1972), *Social Trends*, no. 3.

Hofstadter, R. (1955), *Social Darwinism in American Thought*, Beacon Press, Boston, Mass.

Hornig, G. (1967), in Mackie and Christensen, *Translation and Application of Scientific Research*, Human Factors Research Inc., California, January, TR 716–1.

Horowitz, I. L. (1967), *The Rise and Fall of Project Camelot*, MIT Press, Cambridge.

Hurd, G. E. and Johnson, T. J. (1969), 'Sociology in the Third World Situation', *International Social Sciences Journal*, vol. 21, no. 3.

Isaac, A. M. and Rao, K. R. (1965), 'The Role of Documentation in Social Science Research', *Indian Journal of Social Work*, vol. 25, no. 4, January.

Jackson, B. and Marsden, D. (1961), *Education and the Working Class*, Routledge & Kegan Paul, London.

Jenkins, W. I. and Velody, I. (1965), *Behavioural Science Models for the Growth of Interdisciplinary Fields*, OECD Background Paper, Paris.

Jones, G. N. (1969), *Planned Organizational Change*, Routledge & Kegan Paul, London.

Joy, L. (1967), 'One Economist's View of the Relationship between Economics and Anthropology', *ASA Monograph no. 6*, Tavistock, London, pp. 31–2.

Kaldor, N. (1972), 'Capital Accumulation and Economic Growth', ch. 10, p. 177 in *The Theory of Capital* F. A. Lutz and D. C. Hague (eds), quoted in *The Frontiers of Development Studies*, Macmillan, London.

Kerr, M. (1958), *The People of Ship Street*, Routledge & Kegan Paul, London.

Kirk, D. (1969), 'Natality in Developing Countries' in Freedman and Carsa (eds), *Fertility and Family Planning*, University of Michigan Press.

Labbens, J. (1969), 'The Role of the Sociologist and the Growth of Sociology in Latin America', *International Social Science Journal*, vol. 21, no. 3, pp. 428–44.

Lawrence, P. R. and Lorsch, J. W. (1967), *Organization and Environment: Managing Differentiation and Integration*, Harvard University Press, Cambridge.

Lazarsfeld, Sewell and Wilensky (eds) (1968), *Uses of Sociology*, Weidenfeld & Nicolson, London.

Lee, L. T. (1972), 'Law, Human Rights and Population', *Virginia Journal of International Law*, vol. 12, no. 3.

Lenin, V. I. (1917), *The Immediate Tasks of the Soviet Government*, prepared for the Central Committee of the Communist Party of the Soviet Union.

Lippitt, R. (1965), 'The Use of Social Research to Improve Social Practice', *American Journal of Orthopsychiatry*, July, pp. 663–9.

Lipset, S. M. (1969), *Politics and the Social Sciences*, Oxford University Press, London.

Lipton, M. (1969), 'The Theory of the Optimizing Peasant', *Journal of Development Studies*, vol. 5, no. 3, April.

Little, A. (1963), 'Sociology in Britain since 1945', *Social Science Information*, vol. 2, no. 2, July, pp. 64–92.

Lorenz, K. (1961), *On Aggression*, Harcourt Brace, New York.

Lupton, T. (1963), *On the Shop Floor*, Pergamon, Oxford.

Lynn, R., Zahraee, R. and Rim, Y. (1968), 'Psychological Factors in Economic Growth', *Manpower and Applied Psychology*, vol. 21, no. 1, pp. 76–83.

Lyons, G. (1969), *The Uneasy Partnership: Social Science and the Federal Government in the Twentieth Century*, Russell Sage Foundation, New York.

Lyons, T. C. (1973), 'Population and Policies and Politics', lecture given at Seminar on Law and Population, Fletcher School of Law and Diplomacy, February 1973.

Mackenzie, N. (ed.) (1966), *A Guide to the Social Sciences*, Weidenfeld & Nicolson, London.

McClelland, D. (1961), *The Achieving Society*, Van Nostrand, Princeton, N.J.

McClelland, D. E. and Winter, D. G. (1969), *Motivating Economic Achievement*, Free Press, New York.

McGranahan, D. V. (1971), 'Analysis of Socio-Economic Development through a System of Indicators', *The Annals of the American Academy of Political and Social Science*, January.

McGregor, D. G. (1960), *The Human Side of Enterprise*, McGraw-Hill, New York.

Mackie, and Christensen (1967), *Translation and Application of Scientific Research*, TR. 716–1, January, Human Factors Research Inc., California.

McLuhan, M. (1964), *Understanding Media*, Routledge & Kegan Paul, London.

Maheu, R. (1970), in *Main Trends of Research in the Social and Human Sciences*, Part I, Mouton/UNESCO, Paris.

Maine, H. S. (1905), *Ancient Law*, Routledge & Kegan Paul, London.

Mamdani, M. (1972), 'The Myth of Population Control', *Monthly Review Press*, New York.

Marsh, D. C. (1958), *The Changing Social Structure of England and Wales*, Routledge & Kegan Paul, London.

Marx, K. (1972), *Capital*, vols. 1 and 2 (Everyman edn), Dent, London.

Maslow, A. H. (1954), *Motivation and Personality*, Harper, New York.

Meade, J. E. and Parkes, A. S. (eds) (1965), *Biological Aspects of Social Problems*, Oliver & Boyd, Edinburgh.

Meagher, R. (1973), 'Law and Development', lecture at Seminar on Law and Population, Fletcher School of Law and Diplomacy, March.

Merton, R. K. (1949), 'The Role of Applied Social Science in the Formation of Policy', *Philosophy of Science*, vol. 16, no. 3, pp. 161–81.

Merton, R. K. (1968), *Social Theory and Social Structure*, Free Press, New York.

Miller, E. J. (1959), 'Technology, Territory and Time: The Internal Differentiation of Complex Production Systems', *Human Relations*, no. 12, pp. 243–72.

Miller, E. J. and Rice, A. K. (1967), *Systems of Organization: The Control of Task and Sentient Boundaries*, Tavistock, London.

Mitchell, R. E. (1965), 'Barriers to Survey Research in Asia and Latin America', *American Behavioral Scientist*, vol. 9, no. 3, November.

Mitchell, R. E. (1968), 'Survey Materials Collected in the Developing Countries: Obstacles to Comparisons', ch. 13 in *Comparative Research across Cultures and Nations*, Mouton, Paris.

Morris, D. (1967), *The Naked Ape*, Cape, London and McGraw-Hill, New York.

Morris, D. (1969), *The Human Zoo*, Cape, London and McGraw-Hill, New York.

Myrdal, G. (1968), *Asian Drama*, vol. 3, Panther, New York.

National Academy of Sciences/National Research Council (1957), *Foreign Area Research: A Conference Report*, Washington DC, January.

National Academy of Sciences/National Research Council (1968), *The Behavioral Sciences and the Federal Government*, no. 1680, Washington DC.

National Science Foundation (1969), *Knowledge into Action: Improving the Nation's Use of the Social Sciences*, Washington DC.

Niehoff, A. H. (ed.) (1966), *A Casebook of Social Change*, Aldine, Chicago.

Nye, J. S. (1967), 'Corruption and Political Development: A Cost Benefit Review', *American Political Science Review*, no. 61, pp. 417–27.

OECD (1966), *The Social Sciences and the Policies of Governments*, OECD, Paris, p. 46.

OECD (1971), *Science, Growth and Society: A New Perspective*, OECD, Paris.

Oeser, C. A. and Emery, F. E. (1956), *Information, Decision and Action*, Melbourne University Press, Melbourne.

Okochi, K., Karsh, B. and Levine, S. B. (1973), *Workers and Employers in Japan*, University of Tokyo Press, Tokyo.

Parsons, T. (1951), *The Social System*, Routledge & Kegan Paul, London.

Parsons, T. (1968), *The Structure of Social Action*, Free Press, New York.

Paterson, T. T. (1955), *Morale in War and Work*, Max Parrish, London.

Pearson Report (1969), *Partners in Development*, report of the Commission on International Development, Pall Mall Press, London.

La Père, R. T. (1934), 'Attitudes versus Actions', *Social Forces*, no. 13, pp. 230–7.

Perrow, C. (1967), 'A Framework for the Comparative Analysis of Organizations', *American Sociological Review*, pp. 104–208.

Perrow, C. (1970), *Organizational Analysis: A Sociological View*, Tavistock, London.

Pugh, D. S. (1969), 'Organizational Behaviour: An Approach from Psychology', *Human Relations*, vol. 22, no. 4, August, pp. 345–54.

Quinn, R. P., Mangione, T. W. and Maldi de Mandilovitch, M. S. (1973), 'Evaluating Working Conditions in America', *Monthly Labor Review*, November.

Rainwater, C. and Yancey, W. L. (1967), *The Moynihan Report and the Politics of Controversy*, MIT Press, Cambridge.

Rapoport, R. (1960), *Community as Doctor*, Tavistock, London.

Rapoport, R. (1968), *The Therapeutic Community Revisited*, Tavistock Institute of Human Relations, TIHR 144, London.

Reddaway, W. B. (1962), 'The Economics of Under-Developed Countries', *Advancement of Science*, vol. 19.

Revans, R. (1967), *Studies in Institutional Learning*, European Association of Management Training Centres, Brussels.

Rezsohazy, R. (1972), 'The Concept of Social Time: Its Role in Development', *International Social Science Journal*, vol. 24, no. 1.

Rice, A. K. (1970), *The Modern University: A Model Organization*, Tavistock, London.

Riesman, P. (1955), *The Lonely Crowd*, Yale University Press, New Haven.

Rose, R. (ed.) (1969), *Policy Making in Britain*, Macmillan, London.

Rostow, W. W. (1960), *The Stages of Economic Growth*, Cambridge University Press, Cambridge.

Russell, M. (1970), *Values and Ideologies in Population Planning*, University of Sussex Institute of Development Studies, Brighton.

Sachs, I. (1972), 'The Logic of Development', *International Social Science Journal*, vol. 24, no. 1.

Sadler, P. J. (1962), 'Technical Change and Military Social Structure' in F. E. Geldard (ed.), *Defense Psychology*, NATO Conference Series, vol. 1, Pergamon Press, Oxford.

485

Sauvy, A. (1972), 'Contribution of Demography to Development', *International Social Science Journal*, vol. 24, no. 1.

Shils, E. (1967), 'The Ways of Sociology', *Encounter*, no. 28, June.

Sinha, D. (1969), *Motivation of Rural Population in a Developing Country*, Allied Publishers, Bombay.

Sinha, D. (1970), *Indian Villages in Transition*, Allied Publishers, Bombay.

Smelser, N. (1959), *Social Change in the Industrial Revolution*, Routledge & Kegan Paul, London.

Snyder, R. C. and Paige, G. D. (1958), 'The US Decision to Resist Aggression in Korea: the Application of an Analytical Scheme', *Admin. Science Quarterly*, no. 3, pp. 341–78.

Solari, A. E. (1969), 'Social Crisis as an Obstacle to the Institutionalization of Sociology in Latin America', *International Social Science Journal*, vol. 21, no. 3, pp. 445–56.

SSRC (1968a), *Research in Political Science*, Heinemann Educational Books, London.

SSRC (1968b), *Research in Social Anthropology*, Heinemann Educational Books, London.

SSRC (1969), *Research in Economic and Social History*, Heinemann Educational Books, London.

SSRC (1970), *Research in Human Geography*, Heinemann Educational Books, London.

SSRC (1974), *Newsletter*, no. 22, February.

Stouffer, S. A. (ed.) (1949), *The American Soldier*, Princeton University Press.

Streeten, P. (1967), 'Development and the Institute of Development Studies', *Journal of Administration Overseas*, vol. 6, no. 4, October.

Streeten, P. (1968), 'European Development Policy and Development Concepts', *Rivista Internazionale di Scienze Economiche e Commerciali*, Anno 15, no. 5, p. 432.

Streeten, P. and Lipton, M. (eds) (1968), *The Crisis of Indian Planning*, Royal Institute of International Affairs, Oxford University Press, London.

Streeten, P. (1972), *The Frontiers of Development Studies*, Macmillan, London.

Sumiyo, M. (1973), 'The Emergence of Modern Japan', in *Workers and Employers in Japan*, University of Tokyo Press, Tokyo.

Takezawa, S. (1975), 'Changing Worker Attitudes and Implications in Policy in Japan' in L. E. Davis and A. B. Cherns (eds), *The Quality of Working Life: Problems, Prospects and the State of the Art*, vol. 1, The Free Press, New York, pp. 327–46.

Tavistock (1964), *Social Research and a National Policy for Science*, Occasional Paper no. 7, Tavistock Institute of Human Relations, London.

Thorsrud, E. (1972), 'Policy-making as a Learning Process' in A. B. Cherns, R. Sinclair and W. I. Jenkins (eds), *Social Science and Government: Policies and Problems*, Tavistock, London.

Tönnies, F. (1955), *Community and Association*, Routledge & Kegan Paul, London.

Trist, E. L., Higgin, G., Murray, H. and Pollock, A. B. (1963), *Organizational Choice*, Tavistock Publications, London.

Trist, E. L. (1968), 'The Professional Facilitation of Planned Change', paper given at the International Congress of Applied Psychology, Amsterdam.

Trist, E. (1970), 'Social Research Institutions: Types, Structures and Scale', *International Social Science Journal*, vol. 22, no. 2, pp. 301–26.

Tully, J. (1964), 'Towards a Theory of Agricultural Extension', *Human Relations*, no. 19, pp. 391–403.

Twain, M. (1943), *The Adventures of Tom Sawyer*, Dent, London.

Udy, S. H. (1970), *Work in Traditional and Modern Society*, Prentice-Hall, Englewood Cliffs, N.J.

Ullman, L. P. (1967), *Institution and Outcome*, Pergamon, Oxford.

UNESCO (1970), *Main Trends of Research in the Social and Human Sciences*, Mouton/UNESCO, Paris.

UNESCO (1972), Young Scientists Conference: Population and the Environment, Paris.

UNESCO (1974), *Social Science Organization and Policy*, Mouton, Paris.

US House of Representatives (1967), Senate Sub-Committee on Government Operations: *The Use of Social Sciences in Federal Domestic Programs*, Washington DC.

US House of Representatives (1970), Committee on Finance, 91st Congress on HR 16211 Family Assistance Act: *The Use of Social Research in Federal Domestic Programs*, US Govt Printing Office, Washington DC.

US Senate (1973), *Work in America*. Report of a special Task Force to the Secretary of Health, Education and Welfare: Sub-committee on Employment, Manpower and Poverty of the Committee on Labor and Public Welfare, US Govt Printing Office, Washington DC.

Volsky, V. (1972), 'Contribution of Economic Geography to Development', *International Social Science Journal*, vol. 24, no. 1.

Vroom, V. (1964), *Work and Motivation*, Wiley, New York.

Walton, R. E. (1972), *Work Place Alienation and the Need for Major Innovation*, paper prepared for the US Department of Health, Education and Welfare, May.

Webb, E. J., Campbell, D. T., Schwartz, R. D. and Sechrest, L. (1966), *Unobtrusive Measures*, Rand McNally, Chicago.

Weber, M. (1930), *The Protestant Ethic and the Spirit of Capitalism*, Allen & Unwin, London.

Weber, M. (1950), *On Methodology of Social Science*, Collier-Macmillan, London.

Wieland, G. (1967), *Evaluating Action Research: Some Psychological Problems*, paper presented to 21st Congress by International Institute of Psychology, Madrid, October.

Williamson, D. T. N. (1972), 'The Anachronistic Factory', proceedings of the Royal Society, A331, pp. 139–60.

Wirth, L. (1951), 'Urbanism as a Way of Life' in Reiss and Hart (eds), *Cities and Society*, Free Press, Chicago.

487

Woodward, J. (1965), *Industrial Organization: Theories and Practice*, Oxford University Press, London.

Wootton, B. (1959), *Social Science and Social Pathology*, Allen & Unwin, London.

Young, M. and Willmott, P. (1957), *Family and Kinship in East London*, Routledge & Kegan Paul, London.

Zuckerman Committee (1961), *The Management and Control of Research and Development*, HMSO, London.

Index